Writing Systems

Blackwell Textbooks in Linguistics

The books included in this series provide comprehensive accounts of some of the most central and most rapidly developing areas of research in linguistics. Intended primarily for introductory and post-introductory students, they include exercises, discussion points and suggestions for further reading.

1	Liliane Haegeman	*Introduction to Government and Binding Theory* (Second Edition)
2	Andrew Spencer	*Morphological Theory*
3	Helen Goodluck	*Language Acquisition*
4	Ronald Wardhaugh	*Introduction to Sociolinguistics* (Fourth Edition)
5	Martin Atkinson	*Children's Syntax*
6	Diane Blakemore	*Understanding Utterances*
7	Michael Kenstowicz	*Phonology in Generative Grammar*
8	Deborah Schiffrin	*Approaches to Discourse*
9	John Clark and Colin Yallop	*An Introduction to Phonetics and Phonology* (Second Edition)
10	Natsuko Tsujimura	*An Introduction to Japanese Linguistics*
11	Robert D. Borsley	*Modern Phrase Structure Grammar*
12	Nigel Fabb	*Linguistics and Literature*
13	Irene Heim and Angelika Kratzer	*Semantics in Generative Grammar*
14	Liliane Haegeman and Jacqueline Guéron	*English Grammar: A Generative Perspective*
15	Stephen Crain and Diane Lillo-Martin	*An Introduction to Linguistic Theory and Language Acquisition*
16	Joan Bresnan	*Lexical-Functional Syntax*
17	Barbara A. Fennell	*A History of English: A Sociolinguistic Approach*
18	Henry Rogers	*Writing Systems: A Linguistic Approach*
19	Benjamin W. Fortson IV	*Indo-European Language and Culture: An Introduction*

Writing Systems

A Linguistic Approach

Henry Rogers

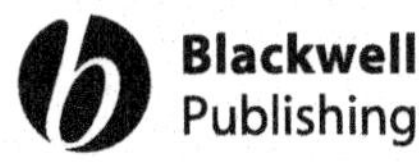

BLACKWELL PUBLISHING
350 Main Street, Malden, MA 02148-5020, USA
9600 Garsington Road, Oxford OX4 2DQ, UK
550 Swanston Street, Carlton, Victoria 3053, Australia

First published 2005 by Blackwell Publishing Ltd

7 2011

Library of Congress Cataloging-in-Publication Data

Rogers, Henry, 1940–
Writing systems: a linguistic approach / Henry Rogers.
p. cm. — (Blackwell textbooks in linguistics; 18)
ISBN: 978-0-6312-3464-7 (paperback : alk. paper)
1. Writing. 2. Writing—History. 3. Graphemics. I. Title. II. Series.

P211.R638 2005
411—dc22

2003026165

A catalogue record for this title is available from the British Library.

Set in 10/12pt Sabon
by Graphicraft Limited, Hong Kong

For further information on
Blackwell Publishing, visit our website:
http://www.blackwellpublishing.com

Gu mo mhic
Daibhidh 's Iain

Contents

Acknowledgments

Toronto is blessed with a multicultural diversity which is ideal for learning about languages and writing. I am very much indebted to the many friends, colleagues, students, and innocent people who wandered into my office for all the help, information, and support that they have given me over the years. I would especially like to mention Abdel-Khalig Ali, Cheryl Caballero, Vera Chau, Vincent DeCaen, Elan Dresher, Karl-Jürgen Feuerherm, Elaine Gold, Daniel Currie Hall, Timothy Gianotti, Dennis Helm, Kaoru Hashimoto, Jennifer Hellum, Manami Hirayama, Mary Hsu, Bridget Jankowski, Liú Crystal Jīng, Alan Kaye, Cynthia Lee, Ron Leprohon, Ted Lutz, Mary MacKeracher, Paul Mercier, Laura Miller, Keir Moulton, Kenji Oda, David Olson, Joe Partington, Hoa Pham, Táo Yuánkē, Insup Taylor, Ann Wehmeyer, Zhou Joy Hong, and four anonymous reviewers. I am grateful to Tami Kaplan for her initial encouragement, to Margaret Aherne for her excellent and enthusiastic editing, and to Sarah Coleman and the staff at Blackwell for their fine work on a difficult book.

The author and publisher gratefully acknowledge the permission granted to reproduce the copyright material in this book:

Figures

Figure 3.3 from Wayne Senner (ed.), *The Origins of Writing*, figure 6, p. 181. Lincoln, NE: University of Nebraska Press, 1989. © 1989 by University of Nebraska Press. Reprinted with permission.

Figure 3.8 from Fang-yü Wang, *Introduction to Chinese Cursive Script*, p. ii. New Haven, CT: Far Eastern Publications, Yale University Press, 1958. © 1958 by Yale University Press. Reproduced with permission.

Figure 5.10 from Hans J. Nissen et al., *Archaic Bookkeeping*, figure 34, p. 38. Chicago: University of Chicago Press, 1993. © 1986 by University of Chicago Press. Reproduced with permission.

Figure 5.11 from Edward Chiera, *They Wrote in Clay*, p. 63. Chicago: University of Chicago Press, 1966. © 1966 by University of Chicago Press. Reproduced with permission.

Figure 6.2 from Sir Alan Gardiner, *Egyptian Grammar*, plate 2. Oxford: Griffith Institute, Oxford University Press, 1950. © 1950 by Griffith Institute. Reproduced with permission.

Figure 6.4 from Anthony Loprieno, *Ancient Egyptian: A Linguistic Introduction*, chart, p. 16. Cambridge: Cambridge University Press, 1995. © 1995 by Cambridge University Press. Reprinted with the permission of Cambridge University Press.

Figure 8.2 from Fred Woudhuizen, *The Language of the Sea Peoples*, p. 70. Amsterdam: Najade Press, 1993. © 1993 Jan Best. Reproduced with permission.

Figure 8.3 from John Chadwick, *The Decipherment of Linear B*, 'Ventris grid, 28 September 1951', figure 13, p. 59. Cambridge: Cambridge University Press, 1967. © 1967 by Cambridge University Press. Reprinted with the permission of Cambridge University Press.

Figure 8.4 from Jan Best and Fred Woudhuizen (eds.), *Lost Languages from the Mediterranean*, figure 1, p. 2. Leiden: E. J. Brill, 1989. © 1993 by Jan Best. Reproduced with permission.

Figures 8.5 and 8.6 from Jan Best and Fred Woudhuizen (eds.), *Ancient Scripts from Crete and Cyprus*, pp. 32–3, 106. Leiden: E. J. Brill, 1988. © 1993 by Jan Best. Reproduced with permission.

Figure 8.8 from John Boardman and N. G. L. Hammond (eds.), *The Cambridge Ancient History, 3.3*, figure 16, p. 100. Cambridge: Cambridge University Press, 1970. © 1970 by Cambridge University Press. Reprinted with the permission of Cambridge University Press.

Figure 9.1 from Giuliano Bonfante and Larissa Bonfante, *The Etruscan Language: An Introduction*, no. 12, p. 132. Manchester: Manchester University Press, 1983. © 1983 by Manchester University Press. Reproduced with permission.

Figures 12.7, 12.8, 12.9, 12.10 from Dr. Merle Greene Robertson, *The Sculpture of Palenque*, vol. IV, S13/17 (including R14–R17). Princeton: Princeton University Press, 1991. © 1976 by Merle Greene Robertson. Reproduced with permission.

Figure B.1 from International Phonetic Association. © 1993 by the International Phonetic Association. Reproduced with permission. http://www.arts.gla.ac.uk/IPA/ipa.html.

Plates

Plate 1 from Buddhist text written in Japan in the Chinese language. Reproduced with permission from Freer Gallery of Art, Smithsonian Institution, Washington, DC.

Plate 2 from portion of Dead Sea Scrolls. Reproduced courtesy of the Israeli Antiquities Authority.

Plate 3 from Ottoman *tughra*. Reproduced with permission from Freer Gallery of Art, Smithsonian Institution, Washington, DC.

Plate 4 from Trajan column cast. Reproduced courtesy of R. R. Donnelley & Company.

Plate 5 from Indus seal. Reproduced with permission from Harappa.com.

Plate 6 from *Presentation of Captives to a Maya Ruler, ca.* 785. Reproduced courtesy of the Kimbell Art Museum, Fort Worth, Texas.

Every effort has been made to trace copyright holders and to obtain their permission for the use of copyright material. The publisher apologizes for any errors or omissions in the above list and would be grateful if notified of any corrections that should be incorporated in future reprints or editions of this book.

A Note on Dates

The traditional abbreviations in English for eras are AD (Latin *Anno Domini* 'in the year of the Lord') and BC (Before Christ). To avoid the Christian bias in the traditional terms, some scholars have used CE (Common Era) for AD and BCE (Before the Common Era) for BC. In my view, this is well intentioned, but in fact substitutes a Judæo-Christian bias for a Christian one and could be inadvertently insulting to other religions. (For a Muslim, 200 CE is not common to anything.) To avoid these problems, I have used the terms OLD and NEW as substitutes. These are unconventional, but clear and neutral.

The year 1 OLD was followed immediately by the year 1 NEW. There was no year 0. Sometimes, however, I have referred to a time 0 as a convenient fiction, as in 'by the time 0, the old writing system was no longer in use'.

1 Introduction

1.1 The Importance of Writing

Writing is one of the most significant cultural accomplishments of human beings. It allows us to record and convey information and stories beyond the immediate moment. When we speak, we can only inform those in our immediate vicinity. Writing allows us to communicate at a distance, either at a distant place or at a distant time. Nowadays, we can record and send a spoken message with audio or video recordings, but these require special equipment at both ends. For writing, we need only a piece of paper and a pencil.

With writing, we can supplement our own memory. We can record much longer texts than we could ever hope to memorize. The written text is also less fallible than human memory. Many of us have made a great deal of effort to memorize even a fairly short poem. Just think of trying to memorize an entire book! or several!

With written records and manuals, we can create a much more complex society than would otherwise be possible. By keeping records of weather observations, meteorologists are able to discern patterns, allowing them to predict the coming weather. A manual allows an appliance to be repaired. A map allows us to navigate unfamiliar areas. An encyclopædia allows students to learn the history of distant places, peoples, and events.

Writing creates not only a more complicated society, but as some have argued, a more just society. We frequently hear that 'the control of information is power'. When information can be readily written down, printed, and distributed, there is less chance for it to be manipulated by a few people. During the 1930s, the Canadian government distributed *Hansard*, the record of parliamentary proceedings, free to those requesting a subscription. Many a politician regretted being met in a small rural community with a farmer pulling out a copy and saying, 'But it says here that on the thirteenth of May you stood up in Parliament and said . . .'. However, writing itself is not pure; it allows us to publish lies, to mislead, to libel, to cover up, to put a spin on the truth.

We must also be careful not to equate a 'literate society' with a 'good society'. For most of human history, most people have been illiterate. Even today, illiterate people around the world lead productive and satisfying lives. Who in the western world has not at some time identified with Paul Gauguin, who left literate France for Tahiti, where literacy was of less importance? For many people today, even though they are literate, reading and writing play only a small role in their day-to-day lives.

Before we go on, we should also point out that spoken language is clearly primary for humans and written language is secondary. All languages are spoken; only some are written. All people learn to speak as children. Some later learn to write; others do not. The acquisition of language and speech is normal for children and happens automatically, like learning to walk. Writing must always be consciously learned.

1.2 Definition of Writing

In English, the term *writing* is used in various senses. It can mean 'penmanship': *Mary's writing is much better now that she is in Grade Two*. Writing can refer to the content or literary style: *Mary's writing is much better after her year in journalism school*. Finally, writing can refer to writing systems: *Arabic writing goes from right to left*. In this book, we will normally use writing in the last sense.

We can define **writing** as the use of graphic marks to represent specific linguistic utterances. The purpose of a definition is to distinguish a term from other things. To understand what writing is, it is helpful to investigate some similar things which are not writing according to our definition.

Writing is not language. **Language** is a complex system residing in our brain which allows us to produce and interpret utterances. Writing involves making an utterance visible. Our cultural tradition does not make this distinction clearly. We sometimes hear statements such as *Hebrew has no vowels*; this statement is roughly true for the Hebrew writing system, but it is definitely not true for the Hebrew language. Readers should constantly check that they are not confusing language and writing.

Although writing is not language, writing does represent language, and in our definition, only language. Humans engage in many non-linguistic types of communication. These other types of communication may at times be visual, but they are not writing. For example, a painting may represent Noah entering the ark with various animals. Such a painting may communicate many things, such as memory of the story, emotions, æsthetic feelings, information about the ark or the animals, or about Noah, but we would not consider the picture to be writing because it does not represent a specific utterance. The picture might evoke various utterances: e.g., *Noah entered the ark*, *Noah brought the animals on board*, or *The animals accompanied the old man as he set sail*, or even German *Noah betrat die Arche mit den Tieren*. We cannot say that any one of these utterances is specifically the one communicated by the picture. On the other hand, if we see the written sentence *Noah entered the ark*, we recognize it as writing since it is the visible manifestation of a specific linguistic utterance, one which I would pronounce as /ˌnowə ˌɛntəɹd ði ˈɑɹk/. (See Appendix C for an explanation of phonetic symbols.) From this discussion, we can see that writing is related to language, not to ideas in general.

An example somewhat closer to writing is known as the Cheyenne Indian Letter (figure 1.1). Cheyenne is an Algonquian language spoken in the United States. Mallery (1893) cites a nineteenth-century document which purports to be a message from a man, Turtle-Following-His-Wife, to his son, Little Man, telling his son to return home and enclosing $53 for the cost of the trip. According to Mallery, the message

Figure 1.1 The Cheyenne Indian letter

was understood. Our initial reaction is likely skeptical, as we think that we ourselves would probably not have been successful at deciphering the message. Possibly it was sent with some prior arrangements. Crucially, a semantic interpretation does not seem to proceed systematically from the picture according to any definable system. We would not know how to interpret it reliably, and there is no system which would allow us to formulate a reply or other message. Even if our skepticism about the ease of interpretation is unfounded, the document still does not qualify as writing under our definition since it does not correspond to a specific linguistic utterance; rather, we expect that several different Cheyenne utterances could be accepted as correct 'readings' of the message, as with our picture of Noah.

A crucial element missing in the Cheyenne Indian Letter is a systematic structure. The primary focus of this book is expressed in its title *Writing Systems*. Writing is systematic in two ways: it has a systematic relationship to language, and it has a systematic internal organization of its own. The Cheyenne letter is not systematic in either sense: there is no set of conventions linking the elements in the drawing to the Cheyenne language, nor are there conventions which structure the elements of the drawing with each other. We can refer to non-linguistic graphic communication, such as the Cheyenne Indian Letter, by the term **picture writing**.

Now let's look at the history of the word *writing*. Knowing about the etymology of a word does not really help us understand its meaning better, but the history is often interesting. The word *write* comes from an Indo-European root **wrīd-* 'tear, scratch', perhaps related to Greek *rhīnē* 'file, rasp'; presumably, early Indo-European writing was seen as scratching marks on a surface. From this Indo-European form, a Proto-Germanic form **wrītanan* 'tear, scratch' developed, producing forms such as Swedish *rita* 'draw, scratch', German *reißen* 'tear' and *ritzen* 'scratch'. The oldest English form *wrītan*, attested in *Beowulf*, originally meant 'score, draw', and somewhat later 'write'.

Other related words include *scribe* and *script*, which are borrowed respectively from Latin *scrība* 'secretary, scribe' and *scrīptum* 'something written', both derived from the Latin verb *scrībere* 'write'. At first *script* meant a piece of writing; its use for a system of written marks is quite late, probably first occurring in the late nineteenth century. *Letter* is borrowed from the French *lettre* from Latin *lītera* 'letter of the alphabet'. In the plural, Latin *līterae* meant 'a piece of writing, epistle, literature'. *Graph* is from Greek *gráphein* 'scratch, write'.

1.3 Aspects of Writing

This book examines four important aspects of writing:

- the creation and history of writing
- the relationship of writing and language
- the internal structure of writing systems
- the sociolinguistics of writing

1.3.1 Creation and history of writing

Writing can be created in three basic ways. It can be invented as a completely new phenomenon. More frequently, writing is borrowed from one language and applied to a new language. Finally, a new script can be developed, not as a completely new phenomenon, but as a new form of writing.

Rarely has writing been invented from scratch, that is, without knowledge of any other existing writing; but it has happened on at least three occasions. We know that the earliest **invention of writing** was about 5000 years ago by the Sumerians in Mesopotamia. Some 1500 years later, the Chinese again invented writing. The last certain invention of writing was over 2000 years ago by the Maya in Meso-America. Some scholars have claimed that the Egyptians and the people of the Indus Valley also invented writing, but these claims are controversial.

Although the invention of writing is rare, the **borrowing of a writing system** from one culture to another has been extremely common. Almost all the writing systems in use today, except Chinese, involve some sort of borrowing. In Asia, several neighboring countries borrowed writing from China. Early Mesopotamian writing likely inspired the Egyptians to develop a writing system for their language. The Semitic writing system arose under the influence of Egyptian. The Greeks borrowed the Semitic system. The Greek alphabet was borrowed by the Etruscans in Italy, and their alphabet was in turn borrowed by the Romans for writing Latin. The Roman alphabet has spread widely and has been used to write hundreds of languages around the world. Almost all writing systems in use today stem ultimately from either the Chinese or the Semitic writing systems.

Rather rarely, we have the **creation of a new writing system**. This type of creation involves an anthropological notion known as **stimulus diffusion**; with stimulus diffusion, something is borrowed from one culture into another, but only the general idea, not all the details. In the case of a new writing system, the creator is aware of the notion of writing and creates a new type of writing. What is new is the particular writing system, not the notion of writing itself; the Cherokee, Cree, Pahawh Hmong, and Bliss writing systems are examples of this sort of development. These situations are different from that of the Sumerians, the Chinese, and the Maya, who invented writing with no prior model.

In connection with his novels and stories, J. R. R. Tolkien invented a number of scripts, attributing them to various of the peoples in his stories. Tolkien was a Celtic and Old Norse scholar, and the shapes of the symbols have much in common with the mediæval scripts of Ireland and Scandinavia.

1.3.2 Relationship of writing to language

An extremely interesting question is how writing and language are related. In Finnish, for example, there is an almost perfect one-to-one **relationship** between written symbols (letters of the Roman alphabet) and the phonemes of Finnish. In Chinese, by contrast, there is a fairly consistent relationship between written symbols (characters) and the morphemes of Chinese. (Note: for an explanation of linguistic terms such as *morpheme* or *phoneme*, see Appendix A.)

Russian and Belorusian are closely related Slavic languages, both written with the Cyrillic alphabet. Russian writing corresponds to the morphophonemic level of the language, overlooking certain predictable phonological variation, whereas Belorusian writing corresponds to the phonemic level of the language, overtly specifying the type of variation that Russian writing overlooks.

In Hebrew, only consonants are generally written; the reader is expected to know the language well enough to supply the missing vowels. Special symbols do exist to indicate vowels, but they are used mostly in materials for children and learners of Hebrew.

Some languages are written with a mixture of systems. Japanese, for example, has different kinds of writing; it uses characters borrowed from Chinese, as well as two further types of writing known as *kana*, in which each symbol represents a mora (i.e. a consonant–vowel sequence or a consonant at the end of a syllable). Japanese writing is normally a mixture of these systems. Some words are normally written with characters, some with *kana*, and many with a mixture of characters and *kana*. The writer must know which type of symbol is appropriate for a given word.

In English, we use the Roman alphabet, but its relationship to the phonemes of English is not simple. For example, the vowel /i/ is written variously <ee, ea, ie, ei, y, i> as in *meet*, *meat*, *siege*, *conceive*, *city*, *spaghetti*. By the same token, the written sequence <ough> can be pronounced quite differently as in the words *tough*, *cough*, *though*, and *through*. Clearly English spelling is related to phonology, but the relationship is complex and strongly shaped by lexical and morphemic considerations.

From these examples, we can see that the relationship between language and writing is not necessarily simple nor consistent. The relationship of the language and writing system of Finnish is unusually simple, but the corresponding relationship for Japanese is extremely complex. Although Finnish and English both use the same Roman alphabet, they do so in different ways; the spelling rules of Finnish and English are quite different. Similarly, Japanese and Chinese both use Chinese characters in their writing, but the rules for using characters to write the two languages are quite different.

In our study of writing systems, we might assume that there is a simple, one-to-one relationship between written symbols and language: for example, that a writing system has a distinct symbol for each phoneme, and that these symbols are used to write utterances. In such a situation, an automatic conversion would, in principle, be possible between writing and language. Anyone who has learned to write English, however, is more than aware that this situation does not hold for English. We need only consider such pairs as *one* and *won* with exactly the same pronunciation and very different spellings to confirm this. There are, to be sure, some writing systems which are fairly regular, but none is perfect. Varying degrees of complexity are the norm. In the course of this book, we will investigate many types of complex relationships between writing and language. In the next chapter, we will develop some terminology which will help us to describe some of this complexity. In the final chapter, we will examine this issue generally and develop a taxonomic scheme for writing systems which takes varying kinds of complexity into account.

1.3.3 Internal structure of writing

Writing systems have an **internal structure** independent of the language being written. From English, we are used to writing starting at the top left corner of the page, proceeding from left to right, with each row placed under the previous row. But this arrangement is by no means universal; for example, the Arabic script is written in rows like English, but each line is written right to left, starting at the top right corner of the page. Arabic is also written cursively, so that most letters within a word are connected to each other; as a result, letters have different shapes depending on how they are attached to other letters. This internal structure of the Arabic script has been maintained even when it has been used to write other languages, such as Persian or Urdu.

In English, a very short public sign is sometimes written vertically with each letter under the preceding one. This type of writing is typically done in upper-case letters, rarely in lower-case.

Chinese writing has a different internal structure. Traditionally, it has been written in columns, from top to bottom, starting at the top right corner of the page; nowadays it is more often written in rows from left to right like English. Chinese characters may consist of only one stroke or of a large number; no matter how many strokes it has, each character is written so as to fill out an imaginary square with a fixed size; thus, each character on a page appears to be about the same size.

In Korean *hankul*, the individual letters are combined in various predictable ways into syllable-sized blocks. These blocks have the same size so that Korean writing is visually rather like Chinese with a set of evenly spaced symbols.

Clay cuneiform tablets used in ancient Mesopotamia were shaped with one side flat and the other slightly convex. Writing began on the flat side; thus the reader could easily determine which side to read first.

Apart from the general internal structure of a writing system, different types of texts sometimes have specific rules of their own. For example, on the title page of a book, the writing in the largest size of type is usually the title of the book. Writing in a smaller size of type typically indicates the author or editor. Writing at the bottom of the title page is related to the publication of the book, typically the publisher, city, and often date of publication. These matters are not without exceptions, but it would be odd to find the publisher's name in the middle of the page and the title at the bottom.

The rules relating language and writing tell us which symbols must be written to express a given utterance, but the rules of the internal structure of the writing system tell us how these symbols are actually to be written down.

1.3.4 Sociolinguistics of writing

Writing is done in a social context. For example, Scots Gaelic is a Celtic language spoken in northwestern Scotland; the language has been written for many centuries. Today, Scots Gaelic speakers may on occasion write something in Gaelic, but for most speakers of the language, writing is ordinarily done in the English language. Virtually all Scots Gaelic speakers today are fluent in English; because of the social history of the highland and island areas of Scotland, where Scots Gaelic is spoken, writing is usually associated with English.

Various spoken dialects are found throughout the Arabic-speaking area, but writing is done in a different dialect known as Standard Arabic. Standard Arabic must be learned in school and generally is not mutually intelligible with spoken dialects. Although it is quite possible to write down a text in a spoken Arabic dialect, this is rarely done. By the same token, although Standard Arabic may be read aloud, it is rare to speak the written dialect extemporaneously for any length of time.

Literacy, or the ability to read and write, varies a great deal in different societies. In technological societies, writing is so much a part of life that being illiterate is considered a serious handicap. In many parts of the world, however, literacy plays little part in everyday life.

At times, literacy has had a special significance. For example, mediæval England had special ecclesiastical courts for clergy. In the early Middle Ages, literacy was almost entirely limited to priests and monks, and thus reading was a simple test to distinguish those to be tried in the ecclesiastical courts from those to be tried in the civil courts. In time, any literate person was legally deemed to be a cleric and could claim this so-called 'benefit of clergy' to be tried in the ecclesiastical courts. This distinction had significant consequences for the offender as the ecclesiastical courts tended to be more lenient; for example, they had no capital punishment. Thus, by being literate one could avoid execution – a clear sociolinguistic benefit.

1.4 Further Reading

At the end of each chapter, there is a section labelled 'Further reading' giving some advice on exploring the subject matter of that chapter more fully. In this introductory chapter, this section mentions several general sources on writing systems. Coulmas (1989), DeFrancis (1989), Hooker (1990), all provide introductions to the material; Hooker is the easiest, Coulmas has the best coverage, DeFrancis is somewhat uneven, but excellent on Chinese. Diringer (1962), Gaur (1984), Jensen (1970), Fischer (2001) focus on the history of writing. Senner (1989) is an excellent collection of articles on the origins of many scripts. Daniels and Bright (1996) is an outstanding reference tool with chapters on most writing systems; Coulmas (1996) is also very reliable, and organized by topic. Sampson (1985) has a linguistic approach, but discusses only a limited number of writing systems. For many years, Gelb (1963) was the only book on the structure of writing systems; his data are still good, but many of Gelb's theories are now considered untenable.

1.5 Terms

At the end of each chapter, there is a section listing technical terms used in the chapter. Readers may want to use these lists for review purposes. All the terms in the book are gathered and defined in Appendix D.

borrowing of a writing system
creation of a writing system
internal structure of writing
invention of writing
language
literacy
picture writing
relationship of language and writing
stimulus diffusion
writing

1.6 Exercises

1 Can you find signs in English that are not written horizontally? What is the likelihood that the letters in a vertical sign are upper-case? How long a text would you like to read in vertical writing?
2 Do you know anyone with dyslexia? What problems do they have in reading? How do they cope with this?

2 Theoretical Preliminaries

This chapter introduces a certain amount of theoretical terminology about writing which is necessary to get us started. As we discuss each writing system in detail, we will add further terms as they become relevant.

Linguists traditionally use different conventions to indicate different kinds of linguistic transcriptions. For example, we might mention the word *toque* /tuk/ 'a knit hat, especially in Canada'. The use of italics shows that we are talking about the word as such; in this situation, we use the ordinary spelling of a word. **Phonemic** transcriptions are traditionally enclosed in slant lines: /tuk/. A gloss, or short definition, is put in single quotation marks. We use angled brackets to talk specifically about **graphemes**: e.g., 'in English, the sound /k/ is sometimes written as <que> in words borrowed from French', or 'in *toque*, the vowel /u/ has an unusual spelling of <o>'. Although we do not have much occasion to use **phonetic** transcriptions showing allophones in this book, they are placed in square brackets: [t^huk].

2.1 Internal Structure

2.1.1 Arrangement of symbols

All writing has an underlying **linear organization**: that is, symbols follow each other in some sort of predictable order. English is written in horizontal lines of symbols from left to right with the lines ordered from top to bottom. We are so accustomed to this arrangement that we may think that it is universal. In the course of this book, however, we will see several other arrangements. Hebrew and Arabic are written in horizontal lines from right to left. Chinese was traditionally written vertically in columns starting at the upper right. Mongolian is written vertically in columns starting at the upper left.

Even though all writing systems have an overall linear organization, we often encounter **non-linear elements** in writing. In Arabic, for example, writing is written in horizontal lines from right to left; however, this description applies only to consonants and long vowels. Short vowels are normally not written in Arabic; if they are written, they are written as symbols above or below the phonologically preceding consonant. In the Arabic example in table 2.1, the writing on the left shows the word /malik/ 'king' written without vowels. Vertical lines are used here to divide the

Table 2.1 Non-linear elements of Arabic writing; the example is /malik/ 'king'. Consonant division is shown on the left. On the right, the short vowels are written as diacritics: <a> above, and <i> below the consonants

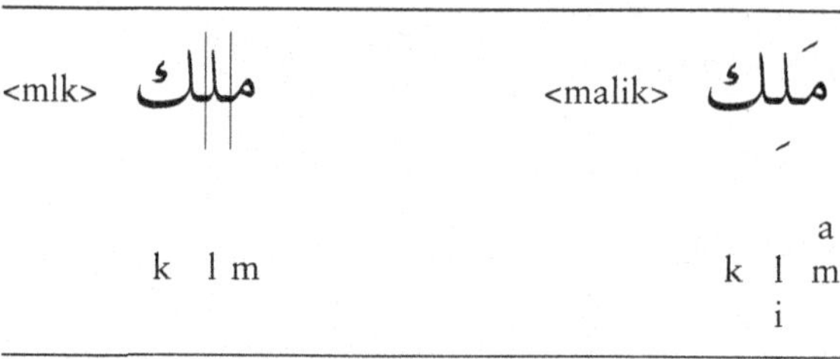

consonants from each other. The writing is right-to-left. In the example on the right, the short vowels are indicated: <a> by an angled line above the <m>, and <i> by an angled line below the <l>.

2.1.2 *Graphemes and allographs*

Since the mid-twentieth century, linguistics has had theoretical terms such as **phoneme, phonetic, allophone, morphemic, allomorph**, etc. In general, linguists posit an **-emic** level of more abstract, contrastive units (e.g., *phoneme, morpheme*) which are realized as contextually determined variants on a more concrete **-etic** level; e.g., *allophone, allomorph*. (Appendix A has a discussion of these basic linguistic terms.)

We define grapheme as a contrastive unit in a writing system, parallel to phoneme or morpheme. For example, there is a grapheme <b> in English which contrasts with other graphemes such as <p t a l r x>. The collection of graphemes for segmental units in English, i.e., for consonants and vowels, is traditionally known as the English alphabet. Non-segmental graphemes for punctuation, numbers, wordspace, etc. are not usually considered part of an alphabet. Linguists have emphasized that the crucial nature of a phoneme lies in the fact that it is different from the other phonemes. In the same way, each grapheme in a language is different from the others; each grapheme contrasts with the other graphemes. For example, the graphemic unit in Chinese is the character; each Chinese character contrasts with the other characters just as the letters of an alphabet contrast with each other. Note that this definition of grapheme refers to writing, and not overtly to language. We will want to explore the relationship of graphemes to language, but that is a separate task. I will reserve the term **symbol** as a general term for a graphic mark used in writing, which makes no statement about the structural significance of the mark. In the same way, I will use the term **script** as a general term for a writing system without any further comment about its structural nature.

Phonemes are classes of allophones, which are non-contrastive variants occurring in complementary distribution or in free variation. In much the same fashion, graphemes are classes of **allographs**. The nature of allographic variation and its conditioning factors is more complicated for graphemes than for phonemes.

Figure 2.1 Allographic variation in Roman handwriting

A grapheme often has a good deal of allographic variation related to style of handwriting or printing. We can often speak of **classes of allographs**. For example, we can distinguish cursive and printed letters as classes of allographs. We also distinguish upper-case and lower-case letters. In printed English, we distinguish different typefaces, such as Palatino, Times, Helvetica, etc., as well as certain style variations such as roman, italic, and bold. These classes often overlap so that, for example, we can speak of an italic, upper-case Helvetica <q> – *Q*. The allograph categories mentioned here do not exhaust the possibilities; for examples, in figure 2.1, two common allographs of lower-case handwritten <r> are given, as well as two allographs of lower-case handwritten <t>.

In some cases the use of an allographic category is determined by the internal rules of the writing system. In English, we capitalize the first letter of the first word of a sentence and the first letter of a proper name. To some degree, upper-case and lower-case letters are in **complementary distribution**: we have, for example, *Toronto* and not **toronTo*; the two allographs of <t> are in complementary distribution here. On further examination, however, the situation is not quite so straightforward, since we occasionally write using only upper-case letters – *TORONTO*. Note that the use of upper-case letters is not without communicative significance itself; in e-mail communications, writing everything in upper-case letters has been compared to shouting. Proper names are sometimes spelled with unusual capitalization: *MacDonald, deForest, k. d. lang, PostScript, ffrench*.

Because writing is much more varied in its structure than speech, and also because it is a more conscious process, Daniels (1991, 1994; see also Herrick 1994a, 1994b) has argued that a graphemic analysis of writing is impossible. His objections are essentially that the term 'grapheme' has not been defined carefully, and that writing, being a conscious phenomenon, is fundamentally different from language, which is unconscious. However, I believe that we can define and use our terms carefully. Further, the fact that the data of language and writing are different in nature does not preclude our using a similar theoretical framework. We use the same mathematics for counting oranges and for calculating taxes, and oranges and taxes are certainly as different from each other as are writing and language.

2.1.3 *Free and bound graphemes*

A **free grapheme** is one which occurs independently. In English *cat*, for example, each of the graphemes <c>, <a>, and <t> is a free grapheme since each occurs freely in other contexts. **Diacritics** are **bound graphemes** which occur only in combination with other graphemes. In French, for example, there are diacritics such as <`> which occur only with other graphemes, specifically with the vowels <a> and <e>: <à è>. Such a combination of a free grapheme and a bound grapheme, as <à>, can be considered a **complex symbol**.

Table 2.2 The position of diacritics to write different vowels in Sanskrit. They occur after, before, below, and above the consonant symbol

<k>	क	<kā>	का	<ki>	कि
		<ku>	कु	<ke>	के

Table 2.3 The non-ligatured and ligatured forms of <fi> and <fl> in Times typeface

Non-ligatured	*Ligatured*
fi	ﬁ
fl	ﬂ

In the Indian scripts, consonants are written from left to right. Some vowels are written after the consonant in this horizontal order as we might expect. Others, however, are written before, below, or above the consonant that they follow in pronunciation.

In the Sanskrit examples in table 2.2, the consonant <k> क is a free grapheme since it occurs by itself. The vowels <ā i u e> ा ि ु े are diacritics (bound allographs) since they occur only with a consonant symbol (a different allograph is used when the vowel occurs alone). The forms का कि कु के are complex symbols.

2.1.4 *Ligatures*

Ligatures are symbols where two graphemes are joined and written as one unit. For æsthetic reasons, in printing the Roman alphabet, the sequences <ﬁ> and <ﬂ> are frequently printed as the ligatures shown in table 2.3. This type of combination has no structural significance for the writing system. English readers are generally unaware of this printing convention, and consider the ligature <ﬁ> simply to represent <f> followed by <i>. We will call this type of ligature a **non-structural ligature.**

Danish, on the other hand, has a ligature <æ> which is clearly formed by joining <a> and <e>. In Danish, <æ> is considered to be a separate grapheme and is alphabetized after <z>. We will call this type of ligature a **structural ligature.** Structural ligatures are treated by the writing system as a single grapheme whereas non-structural ligatures are treated as a sequence of two graphemes. The treatment as a single grapheme often shows up in the alphabetic ordering.

In older Danish, <aa>, representing the vowel /ɔ/, formed a **quasi-ligature**; that is, the sequence acted like a ligature even though the individual letters were not physically joined. Like <æ>, <aa> was alphabetized as a unit and placed after <z> (but before <æ>). In modern Danish, <aa> has been replaced by a complex symbol <å> although the spelling <aa> is still found in many Danish proper names, such as

Kierkegaard. Spanish has traditionally considered <ch> and <ll> as quasi-ligatures, alphabetizing them as though they were individual letters; in the 1990s there was an official decision to consider <ch> and <ll> in Spanish as simple sequences of single letters to facilitate their use in computers. As a result, the alphabetic ordering in older Spanish dictionaries will differ from that in future ones.

Notice that a quasi-ligature is different from a sequence of letters in that it is treated as a single grapheme. The sequence <ea> in English is a common way to write the vowel /i/ (e.g., *heat, league*), but it is merely a sequence of letters, not a quasi-ligature, since structurally it is simply the letter <e> followed by the letter <a>. There is nothing in the writing system, such as alphabetic ordering, that treats /ea/ as a single unit. In traditional Spanish, <ll> is a quasi-ligature since it is considered a separate grapheme as evidenced by its alphabetic ordering; for example, the sequence <lla> would be ordered after <lu>.

2.2 Relationship to Language

A primary consideration for us is to determine what linguistic level graphemes represent. In the Roman alphabet, the letters are related to some level of the phonology; however, the numerals <1, 2, 3> etc. are all related to morphemes. All writing systems seem to have some variation as to the linguistic level involved, but we can often usefully speak of the level of language which is primarily related to the graphemes of a writing system.

2.2.1 Phonographic writing systems

In a **phonemic** writing system, that is, one in which the symbols of the writing system are primarily related to the phonemes of a language, we might expect that there would be a regular one-to-one relationship between grapheme and phoneme. Interestingly, there do not seem to be any such systems in the strict sense. In some languages, such as Spanish, the relationship of the graphemes and phonemes approaches a one-to-one relationship. In Spanish, for example, /sombrero/ 'hat' is written <sombrero> with a one-to-one relationship between phonemes and graphemes. However, this simple relationship in Spanish breaks down: some words are spelled with <h>, but this letter corresponds to no sound in the language: e.g., *hora* /ora/ 'hour'. Also, the sound /b/ is written both as <b> and as <v>: e.g., *vivir, beber* /bibir, beber/ 'live, drink'. To write these words in Spanish, we must know which morpheme we are writing; the phonological information alone is not enough. The amount of morphological information required to write Spanish is not great, but it does exist.

English writing, on the other hand, requires a great deal of morphological information. Very frequently in English, words which sound alike are written differently: *you, ewe, yew, U-turn*. The sequence <oo> is commonly used to write two different vowels: e.g., /u/ *food, booth, boot, smooch, bloom, noose, drool, loop* – /ʊ/ *look, good, soot, wool*. To write English, we need quite a lot of morphological information.

From these two examples, we see that there is no such thing as a pure phonemic writing system. Indeed, there is considerable variation within phonemic writing systems as to the amount of morphological information required. We can think of phonemic writing systems arranged along a continuum, with Spanish near one end, requiring rather little morphological information, and English near the other end, requiring quite a lot. The writing system for German might be near the middle; most German spelling is predictable from the phonology, but a certain amount of morphological information is required.

The segmental (consonant and vowel) symbols of a phonemic writing system are traditionally called **letters**, and the inventory of these letters is called an **alphabet**. We will continue to use these terms, but readers should keep two things in mind. One, in using the term *alphabet*, we are likely to forget the non-segmental graphemes, such as punctuation marks, numerals, word boundary space. Second, our cultural heritage in having learned to write with the Roman alphabet tends to mislead us into underestimating the role of morphological information, especially in writing English.

Alphabets are the most common type of writing system in use in the world today. Widely used alphabets today are Roman, Greek, and Cyrillic, as well as Georgian, Armenian, Ethiopic, Mongolian, and others which will be mentioned later in the book. The Arabic, Hebrew, and Indian writing systems are similar to alphabets, but they are structurally somewhat different and will be discussed later.

In **moraic writing systems**, graphemes are basically related to moræ. A mora is a phonological unit intermediate between a phoneme and a syllable. We can think of a syllable consisting of an onset, nucleus, and coda, while a mora consists either of an onset–nucleus sequence or the coda. Thus, *cut* consists of two moræ: /kʌ/ and /t/. Japanese *kana*, Cherokee, and Cree-Inuktitut are examples of moraic writing systems. In moraic systems, a symbol representing an onset–nucleus combination would be a polyphone. In books on writing systems, we frequently see the term '**syllabic** writing system' where graphemes are said to relate to syllables. As Poser (1992) has pointed out, these systems seem to relate not to syllables, but to moræ. In general, you can translate the term 'syllabic' of other books on writing to 'moraic' as it is used here. The only clear example, known to me, of a syllabic writing system is the one for the Yi language spoken in China (chapter 14). Note that, in an alphabetic system, *cut* would be written with three graphemes; in a moraic system, with two; and in a syllabic system, with one grapheme.

Phonemic, moraic, and syllabic writing systems are all termed **phonographic**, and their symbols are **phonograms**.

2.2.2 *Morphographic writing systems*

When we get to Chinese in chapter 3, we will meet a writing system where the primary relationship of graphemes is to morphemes. Such a system can be called **morphographic**, and those graphemes can be termed **morphograms**. Other authors on writing describe graphemes as related to words, rather than to morphemes, often using the term *logogram*. I am unaware of systems where the primary relationship of graphemes is to words, as opposed to morphemes. Accordingly, I will use the terms *morphogram* and *morphographic* here.

We have a few morphograms in English; for example, the dollar sign <$> represents the morpheme *dollar*. Similarly the numerals <1 2 3> represent the morphemes *one, two, three*.

Sampson (1985) described the *hankul* writing system of Korean as an example of featural writing. He argues that symbols in *hankul* relate to phonological features in Korean such as [velar], [aspirated], etc. We will evaluate this notion more closely when we look at Korean writing in chapter 4, and again in chapter 14. For now, just note that Korean *hankul* seems to be the only candidate for such a relationship and that Sampson's claim is tenuous.

2.2.3 Non-segmental graphemic elements

Apart from segmental (consonants and vowels) or morphological information, writing often indicates certain things which are not necessarily present in speech. In language, many boundaries are phonologically unmarked, e.g., word or phrase boundaries; in writing, however, boundaries are commonly marked by special punctuation graphemes. The use of punctuation graphemes varies widely from language to language. Even for a language such as English, the use of punctuation is not nearly so standardized as spelling. Further, punctuation graphemes are often used in more than one way, such as the period to mark an abbreviation or to mark the end of a sentence.

In most alphabetic writing, we have a short blank space, the word boundary grapheme, inserted between all words. This is such a strong rule with us that we are usually astounded to see an early written text of Latin or Greek where word boundaries were regularly unmarked, with words written next to each other without breaks.

In Tibetan, syllable boundaries are indicated with a raised dot placed between all syllables. The dot here is a punctuation grapheme. In Chinese, syllable boundaries are marked by character separation. Korean *hankul* is arranged in syllable-sized units.

Phrases in English are sometimes separated by a comma, but other phrases are unmarked. Sentences in English are doubly marked: the first letter of the first word is capitalized, and a period, question mark, or exclamation mark is placed at the end. Spanish uses inverted question marks and exclamation marks at the beginning of a sentence in addition to the regular ones at the end. Traditionally, Chinese did not mark phrase or sentence boundaries, but in recent times, it has borrowed some European punctuation graphemes.

Paragraphs are usually marked in English either by indenting the first word of the paragraph a bit to the right or by inserting extra space between the paragraphs. In languages written from right to left, the indentation is to the left.

The structure of a page communicates much of how we understand a text (Mountford 1990). Material at the top written in larger type, often centred, is usually a title. A number in the upper or lower (occasionally the outer) margin is a page number (note how odd it would be to have the page number in the middle of the inside margin). A small raised number in the text is a footnote reference. At the beginning of a book, a list of terms followed by numbers is likely a table of contents; at the end of a book, a list of terms followed by numbers is likely an index.

The table of contents and the index are sometimes labeled as such, but even without the labels, we recognize them by their position in the book. Correspondence has a fairly fixed format: date, salutation, text, closing signature. Letters in French used to start halfway down the page. In German letters, the salutation ends in an exclamation mark; in English, a comma or colon is used, with a sociolinguistic difference of formality.

Different styles of type often signal how the text is to be understood; for example, italics normally indicate something special about the text: a title, a cited form, a special term, etc. In newspaper headlines, however, italics are often used simply to help distinguish one article from others on the same page.

2.2.4 *Unit discrepancies*

A **unit discrepancy** involves a difference in the number of units in a specific linguistic–graphemic relationship – more phonemes than graphemes, or vice versa. A **polygraph** is a sequence of graphemes which represents a linguistic unit normally represented by a single symbol; typically, in an alphabet, a polygraph consists of two letters which represent a single phoneme. In English, the sequence <sh> is a polygraph since it represents the single phoneme /ʃ/; we might also call it a **digraph,** a special case of polygraphy, consisting of only two graphemes. In French *chaque* 'each', <ch> and <que> are both polygraphs since they each represent a single phoneme: /ʃ/ and /k/, respectively.

In English, the polygraph <sh> is not a quasi-ligature since it is not considered to be the equivalent of a single letter; <sh> is alphabetized between <sg> and <si> as we would expect for a sequence of <s> followed by <h>. In traditional Spanish, however, <ch> is a quasi-ligature and not a digraph since it is considered to be the equivalent of a single grapheme and not a sequence of graphemes, as shown by its alphabetic ordering.

A **polyphone** is a single grapheme used to represent a sequence of two (or more) phonemes. In English, the grapheme <x> is a polyphone when it is used to represent the two phonemes /ks/. In alphabetic writing, polyphones are relatively uncommon; in moraic systems, polyphones are the norm.

2.2.5 *Contrastive discrepancies*

With contrastive discrepancies, distinctive contrasts which exist in language are not represented in writing, or the contrasts of writing do not exist in language, i.e., phonological distinctions are neutralized graphemically – **homography**, or graphemic distinctions are neutralized phonemically – **homophony**.

English provides abundant examples of both of these situations. There are cases of (**heterographic**) **homophony** (different written form – same sound) as in *seem, seam*, *cede*, *siege* where <ee, ea, e–e, ie> are all ways of spelling the single phoneme /i/. Conversely, there are cases of (**heterophonic**) **homography** (different sound – same written form) as in *read* which can be pronounced either as /ɹid/ or as /ɹɛd/; similarly, the graphemic sequence <ough> has a variety of pronunciations as shown by the examples *tough*, *though*, *through*.

Sometimes the relationship between phonemes and graphemes can be quite complex. Consider the English sequence <th>. Usually it is a digraph; however, this digraph regularly represents different phonemes: /θ/, /ð/ or /t/, as in *ether*, *either*, or *thyme*. Thus, <th> is a homographic digraph which heterophonically represents /θ/, /ð/, or /t/. In *foothills*, however, the spelling <th> is not a digraph, but simply a sequence of graphemes each representing different phonemes, /t/ and /h/. In these cases, the relationship of <th> and the phonology are lexically conditioned. Although English is often cited as having a particularly complex spelling system, some contrastive discrepancy from a one-to-one phonemic–graphemic situation is normal and is found in all writing systems.

2.3 Diglossia

Diglossia is a sociolinguistic situation in which two very different varieties of a language are both used in a society, but in different situations. Typically, one is used in more formal or literary situations such as formal writing, university lectures, and news broadcasts, and is learned and encouraged in school. The other is used in conversation, informal television situations, folk literature, etc., and is preferred at home.

In the German-speaking areas of Switzerland, both Standard German and local varieties of German known as Swiss German are used; they are different enough from each other not to be mutually intelligible. Writing is almost always done in Standard German. Standard German is also used for formal speaking situations. Ordinary conversation, however, is normally in Swiss German. For example, a university course uses a textbook in Standard German, and lectures are given in Standard German; discussion after class between the professor and students, however, would be in Swiss German.

Arabic is another example of a language with diglossia. We have mentioned in the previous chapter that an Arabic speaker normally uses one dialect for speaking and another for writing. Modern Greek and the Dravidian languages also show diglossia.

The term 'diglossia' is usually reserved for quite distinct versions of the same language. However, other related variations occur. In English, there is not a sharp division between written and spoken English. *I forgot to put on my watch this morning* seems to be appropriate in any style of discourse, written or spoken. However, words such as *lest*, *pursuant*, or *vouchsafe* are much more likely to be found in written English, or in English read aloud from a written text. Forms such as *isn't, aren't, would've* are normal, almost required, in spoken English. In written English, they are regularly written as two words.

In many situations, diglossia involves different languages. We have already mentioned the Scots Gaelic situation where native speakers of Scots Gaelic are likely to write in English rather than in Gaelic. In mediæval western Europe, it was normal to write in Latin, no matter what language the writer normally spoke. In many areas of the world today, the colonial history is such that writing is normally done in French, Spanish, or English, rather than in the native language. We can refer to such situations as **bilingual diglossia.** Note that diglossia, bilingual or not, does not necessarily involve writing, although it commonly does.

2.4 Further Reading

Much of the terminology presented in this chapter has not yet been standardized, and the reader should expect a certain amount of variation. Coulmas (1989, 1996), Daniels and Bright (1996), and DeFrancis (1989) all discuss these notions to various degrees. Mountford (1990) is a particularly interesting discussion from a non-typical perspective.

2.5 Terms

allograph
allomorph
allophone
alphabet
bilingual diglossia
bound grapheme
classes of allographs
complementary distribution
complex symbol
diacritic
diglossia
digraph
-emic
-etic
free grapheme
grapheme
heterography
heterophony
homography
homophone
homophony
letter
ligature
linear organization
moraic system
morpheme
morphogram
morphographic system
non-linear element
non-structural ligature
phoneme
phonemic
phonetic
phonogram
phonographic
polygraph
polyphone
quasi-ligature
script
structural ligature
syllabic
symbol
unit discrepancy

2.6 Exercises

1 Supply the correct bracketing for each symbol or sequence of symbols given in boldface:

(a) The phoneme **x** is pronounced as **h** initially, and as **x** medially. Both variations are written as **x** .
(b) The phonemic sequence **tʃ** is written as **c** before the vowels **i** and **e** , and as **ci** otherwise.
(c) In English, the letter **c** represents two different sounds: **k** or **s** .
(d) Greek has two forms of the lower-case sigma: **σ** is used word-initially and medially; **ς** is used word-finally.

2 In the following examples, gloss each word you give as an answer, that is, define it briefly – not an elaborate definition, just enough for someone else to be sure which word you mean: e.g., *stand* 'be upright'. Use single quotation marks for glosses.

Not using the examples in the chapter,

(a) find another example of homographic homophony.
(b) find another example of heterographic homophony.
(c) find another example of heterographic heterophony.

3 How many different vowel sounds are represented by the following words? *come, cut, dome, oven, over, pull, put, putt.*
4 Find four words exemplifying different ways that the vowel sound in the word *put* is spelled in English. (*Meat* and *meet* would be examples for a different vowel sound.)
5 Suppose that in English writing each sound were always spelled the same way (no examples like *cite–site*). Would this make it easier for the reader? for the writer?

Suppose that in English writing each morpheme had a distinct spelling (no examples like *well* 'not sick'–*well* 'hole for getting water'). Would this make it easier for the reader? for the writer?
6 What is the status of the ligature <æ> in the English word *æsthetic*?
7 French writes the vowel /ø/ with the symbol <œ>. This symbol is alphabetized after <od> and before <of>. Describe its nature.
8 In Canadian English, the cost of an item worth 412 pennies is written as $4.12; in Canadian French, the same item in the same currency is valued at 4.12$ or 4,12$. Compare the relationship of the symbol <$> to the linguistic term *dollar* of each language. Is there a structural difference between <,> and <.>?
9 Can you think of an English word that you can pronounce, but which does not have a standard spelling? (Hint: think of exclamations.)
10 In comic strips, the word *says* is occasionally spelled <sez>. Does this spelling represent a pronunciation different from that of Standard English? What sociolinguistic information does this spelling give to the reader?

3 Chinese

3.1 Background, History, and Sociolinguistics

Chinese is spoken by over a billion people in the People's Republic of China (PRC), Táiwān, Singapore, and other communities around the world. Ethnic Chinese people are known as Hàn 漢, after the Hàn dynasty. Within China, there are some fifty-five other ethnic groups, most of whom speak other languages.

The Chinese language belongs to the Sino-Tibetan family, which has two major sub-families: Chinese and Tibeto-Burman. Note particularly that Chinese is not genetically related to Japanese or Korean although these languages have borrowed Chinese characters as part of their writing systems. The combining form *sino-*, from the Greek *Sînai*, occurs in a few learned words relating to China: *sinology*, *sinologist*, *sinophile*, *sinitic*, *Sino-Korean*, *Sino-Japanese*, *Sino-Vietnamese*, *Sino-Canadian*.

Today, there are seven major dialect groups in China (figure 3.1): Northern or **Mandarin** 北方方言 (a large area of the north and west including Běijīng), Wú 吳 (Shànghǎi and Zhèjiāng), Mǐn 閩 (Fújiàn and Táiwān), Hakka or Kèjiā 客家 (various communities in the south), Yuè 粵 or **Cantonese** (Guǎngdōng and Hong Kong), Xiāng 湘 (Húnán), and Gàn 贛 (Jiāngxī). Although native Taiwanese is a Mǐn dialect, the majority of people in Táiwān speak Mandarin as their native language. There is generally more dialect variation in the south of China than in the north. Cantonese, in particular, is spoken by many people of Chinese ancestry living abroad.

Spoken dialects in China are often quite different from each other. For example, Cantonese and Mandarin are not mutually intelligible; but, as we will see, all Chinese is written the same way, essentially using a Mandarin dialect, regardless of which dialect the writer speaks. Movies in Chinese often have subtitles in Chinese characters to assist viewers who speak dialects other than the one used in the film.

Some debate exists as to whether Chinese is one language with several dialects, or several closely related languages. Linguists generally consider it to be several languages. The Chinese themselves generally consider it to be one language with several dialects. The latter view agrees with the fact that the Chinese people generally feel that they share the same culture and written language even though there are considerable differences in speech. In this book, I will take the one-language view, not really to disagree with my linguistic colleagues, but because it corresponds straightforwardly with the unified writing of Chinese.

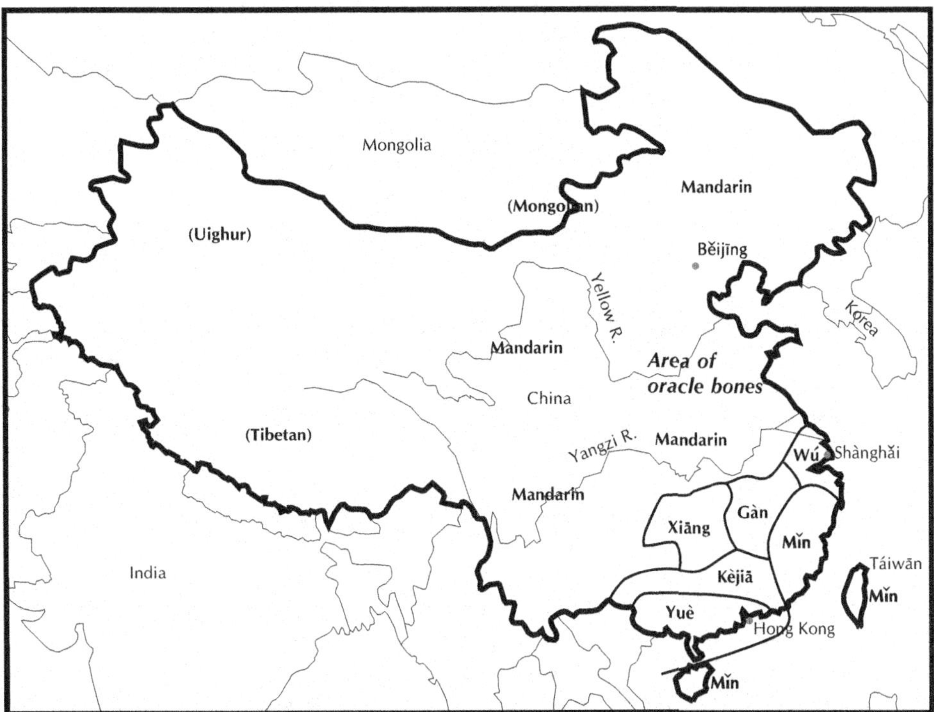

Figure 3.1 Map of China showing major dialect areas of Chinese. The Kèjiā (Hakka) people do not form a contiguous group but are scattered among the neighbouring dialect groups. Non-Chinese languages are shown in parentheses

In this chapter, Chinese words are transcribed in *pīnyīn*, the standard romanization of Chinese based on the Mandarin pronunciation. Occasionally IPA transcriptions are used where phonetic detail is needed. *Pīnyīn* and Mandarin are explained in more detail below. Further, the traditional forms of characters have been used except where simplified characters are specifically mentioned; this difference is explained in §3.7.

3.1.1 The language of written Chinese

Sinologists commonly divide the Chinese language into three periods: Old Chinese 1100 to 100 OLD, Middle Chinese 100 OLD to 600 NEW, and Mandarin 600 NEW to present. Although the spoken Chinese language has always been changing, as all languages do, the written form of the late Old Chinese period became accepted as the standard written dialect and changed very little until the beginning of the twentieth century. This written dialect of the language is known as *wényán* 文言 'literary language', generally referred to as **Classical Chinese** in English, and it was used as the normal dialect for writing until the twentieth century. Thus, in the nineteenth century, Chinese speakers spoke a nineteenth-century local dialect, but when writing, they used Classical Chinese. By this time, the spoken and written forms had diverged widely, and written Chinese was not understandable without considerable education. Besides Classical Chinese, there was a much smaller and less respected tradition of vernacular written Chinese, dating to the Táng and Sòng dynasties, known as **báihuà** 白話 'plain speech', often used in popular stories.

Early in the twentieth century, a movement gained force to use modern spoken Chinese as the written form. *Báihuà* formed the basis for this new form of written Chinese. Today, writing is done in **Modern Standard Chinese**, a dialect close to the Mandarin dialect spoken in Běijīng. This standard form of Chinese is used for all written Chinese, no matter what dialect is spoken. In the PRC, this standard form is known as *pǔtōnghuà* 普通話 'common speech', and in Táiwān, it is referred to as *guóyǔ* 國語 'national language'. The term *hànyǔ* 漢語 'Chinese language' is also sometimes used for Modern Standard Chinese, particularly in academic writing.

Until the twentieth century, to be literate was to be able to read Classical Chinese. Thus, a literate person had access to almost all of Chinese literature spanning many centuries. Modern written Chinese, however, is quite different from Classical Chinese. Literate people today cannot read Classical Chinese without special education. As a result, they are typically cut off from immediate access to traditional Chinese literature, indeed to most material written before the twentieth century.

When writing was done in Classical Chinese, the situation was diglossic for all literate Chinese speakers. Writing was in Classical Chinese, but speaking was in the local dialect. Today, for Mandarin speakers, the written form of the language is quite similar to the one they use in speaking, and thus no longer diglossic. For non-Mandarin speakers, however, the difference between the spoken and written language remains diglossic. People living in Canton, for example, use Cantonese for speaking, but for writing, they have to learn a different dialect. Note that the diglossic situation of traditional Chinese is somewhat different from that of Arabic or Greek in that the standard forms of Arabic and Greek are the normal spoken forms in certain contexts, but Classical Chinese was not normally spoken, except in reading a classical text aloud. Diglossia in China was between writing and speaking, not between two forms of the spoken language. Literacy in China was relatively widespread, but undoubtedly much more common in the wealthier classes, and very rare among peasants.

To illustrate these differences, consider the written sentence 'His home is not in America' in table 3.1 (Voegelin and Voegelin 1964). A Mandarin speaker, reading this sentence aloud from the written text, would pronounce this as /tāde jiā bú zài měiguó/. This same Mandarin speaker, talking to a friend later in the day without the paper, would say the same thing. By contrast, a Cantonese speaker from Hong Kong would read this sentence aloud from the paper as /tàdīk gà bàt joi méigwok/; this is a conventional character-by-character pronunciation in Cantonese of the written sentence. On the other hand, the same Cantonese speaker would render this sentence quite differently in ordinary speech, something like /kéuih ŋūkkei hai méigwok/.

From the Cantonese perspective, spoken Cantonese is not usually written down, at least in formal contexts, although it may appear in advertising, cartoons, or situations where the intention is to emphasize a Cantonese wording. Sometimes there is a character traditionally used to show a Cantonese morpheme, but often

Table 3.1 The written and spoken forms of 'His home is not in America'. The Mandarin is transcribed in *pīnyīn*, and the Cantonese in the Yale Cantonese romanization

他	的	家	不	在	美	國
he	poss	home	not	at	beautiful	country
					= America	

Mandarin – reading pronunciation	/tāde jiā bú zài měiguó/
Mandarin – ordinary spoken	/tāde jiā bú zài měiguó/
Cantonese – reading pronunciation	/tàdīk gà bàt joi méigwok/
Cantonese – ordinary spoken	/kéuih ŋūkkei hai méigwok/

there is not (cf. §3.4.9). Even for colloquial Mandarin, there is occasionally a word for which no standard character exists. By the same token, written Chinese, when read aloud in the conventional Cantonese reading pronunciation, may not be intelligible to a Cantonese speaker who is not well acquainted with the Cantonese conventions of reading written Chinese aloud.

Note that there is no social distinction involved here. In the Cantonese-speaking area, Cantonese is not regarded as socially inferior to Mandarin. In Hong Kong, university lectures in Chinese literature or history, for example, are typically given in Cantonese, but essays and examinations are written in Modern Standard Chinese.

Within the PRC, spoken *pǔtōnghuà* (i.e., Mandarin) has been introduced in the school curriculum throughout the country. Possibly over a period of time it may replace other dialects. But so far, this has not been the case. For most people, local dialects are valued, and *pǔtōnghuà* is most commonly used for official purposes, in schools, and in speaking to outsiders. Even native speakers of *pǔtōnghuà* who move to another dialect area often find it useful to learn at least some of that dialect.

3.1.2 Civil service examinations

Writing has been standardized throughout China for some 2000 years. For such a large and diverse country, this is quite remarkable. Lǐ Sī 李斯, a prime minister in the Qín dynasty (221–207 OLD), attempted to unify the script; his efforts were eventually adopted, but not until some time after his death. Much of the explanation lies in the history of China's civil service system. Around 600 NEW, during the Suí dynasty, the emperor introduced a system of examinations to enter the civil service. There were three levels: local, provincial, and imperial. Examinations were rigorous and focused entirely on the Confucian classics. The standardization in writing that we just mentioned arose from the requirement that the examinations be written in Classical Chinese as well as in a particular style of calligraphy.

Favourable results in the examinations ensured a successful, and often lucrative, career in the civil service. A candidate who failed could try again, and again. One reason for instituting the system was to weaken the power of the nobility by eliminating a hereditary administration. Any male subject was eligible to write the examinations; the identity of the author was kept secret so that the examinations could be marked without favoritism. Nevertheless, despite the apparent democracy, at least for men, only wealthy families generally had the money to provide the necessary education for their sons to pass the examinations. The civil service system was a fixture of Chinese society and lasted until 1904.

The civil service was important not only for the formal establishment of classical writing, but also for the informal establishment of a spoken quasi-standard dialect which civil servants used among themselves. They came from all over the country and were not permitted to work in their home area; this common dialect of Chinese allowed them to speak comfortably with each other. The capital of China moved in different dynasties; in each period the dialect of the current capital contributed to this quasi-standard dialect of the civil service. In later times, with the capital at Běijīng, the Mandarin dialect emerged most strongly as a common spoken form of Chinese within the civil service.

In Chinese an official is *guān* 官, and *guānhuà* 官話 'official speech' was the term for the form of spoken Chinese used by the civil service. The English term for *guān* is *mandarin* (from Sanskrit *mantrin* 'counsellor' via Portuguese and Malay). *Mandarin* was used as a term for these officials and by extension to the language they spoke. *Mandarin*, in addition to referring to the language, is still used in English today to refer to senior government officials, as in 'The mandarins of Ottawa recently decided that . . .'.

Norman (1988) has a helpful analogy for the traditional Chinese language situation. It is as if the people of Portugal, Spain, France, Italy, and Romania all spoke local dialects but wrote in Latin, and government officials spoke the Parisian French dialect amongst themselves.

3.2 Phonology of Modern Standard Chinese

In traditional Chinese linguistics, the syllable in Chinese has been divided into three parts: **initial, final**, and **tone**. The initial consists of the initial consonant, and the final consists of everything else, except the tone. The final can be further divided into medial, vowel, and final consonant. All parts of the syllable are optional except the vowel and tone. In a simple syllable such as /náŋ/ 'bag', /n/ is the initial, /aŋ/ is the final, and /2/ is the tone (there are four tones in Modern Standard Chinese, each represented by a number); here, the initial is the same as the onset, and the final is the same as the rhyme. In more complicated syllables, the Chinese divisions of the syllable do not always correspond exactly to the usual linguistic units for the syllable, of onset, rhyme, nucleus, and coda.

Table 3.2 shows the possible Mandarin initials and finals; the phonetic pronunciation is given after the *pīnyīn* transcription where it would not otherwise be obvious. For further details, see Stimson (1975).

Chinese has lexical tones which vary from dialect to dialect; that is, different pitch patterns distinguish different words. With stressed syllables in Mandarin, there are four tones whose shapes are shown in figure 3.2. Including tone, there are some 1840 possible syllable shapes in Mandarin; of these, only about 1359 actually

Table 3.2 The Mandarin initials and finals. Transcription is *pīnyīn*, with IPA used in brackets to show the phonetic detail more clearly

Initials					
p b	t d	c z [ts dz]	ch zh [tʂ dʐ̥]	q j [tɕ dʑ]	k g
f		s	sh [ʂ]	x [ɕ]	h [x]
	l		r [ɹ]		
m	n				
w				y [j]	

Finals											
	e	a	ei	ai	ou	ao	en	an	eng	ang	er
i	ie	ia			iu	iao	in	ian	ing	iang	
u	(u)o	ua	ui	uai			un	uan	ong	uang	
ü	üe						ün	üan	iong		

Table 3.3 Examples of the four Mandarin tones

Tone 1	(high level)	mā	媽	'mother'
Tone 2	(rising)	má	麻	'hemp'
Tone 3	(falling-rising)	mǎ	馬	'horse'
Tone 4	(falling)	mà	罵	'scold'

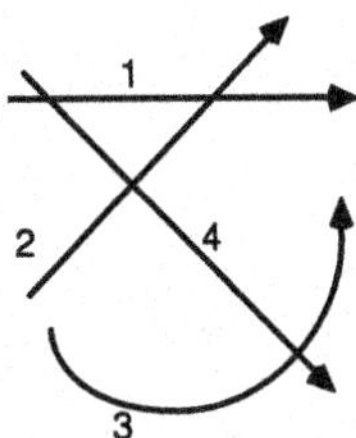

Figure 3.2 The four Mandarin tone contours

occur (Taylor and Taylor 1995). In some unaccented syllables in polysyllabic words, the tone is predictable from the context and is left unmarked.

Examples of words with four different tones are shown in table 3.3 with their *pīnyīn* tone markings.

3.2.1 *Romanization*

As Chinese is written in characters, outsiders find it extremely helpful to have a way to indicate the pronunciation of Chinese words in the Roman alphabet. A scheme to represent utterances of other alphabets or writing systems is known as a romanization. Various romanizations for Chinese have been invented (table 3.4). For many years, the **Wade–Giles** system was commonplace. A different romanization known as *gwóyǔ*

Table 3.4 A comparison of different romanizations. IPA shows the phonetic pronunciation; the tone in the IPA column is indicated as with *pīnyīn* tone marks

IPA	Pīnyīn	*Yale*	*Wade–Giles*	Gwóyǔ luómàzì
pā	bā	bā	pa^1	ba
p^{h}ā	pā	pā	p'a^1	pa
tsuɔ́	zuó	dzó	tso^2	tzwo
ts^{h}uɔ́	cuó	tsó	ts'o^2	tswo
ɕī	xī	sī	hsi^1	shi
ɕí	xí	sí	hsi^2	shyi
ɕǐ	xǐ	sǐ	hsi^3	shii
ɕì	xì	sì	hsi^4	shih

luómàzì never achieved widespread use, but it was interesting in representing the tone with letters: thus /mā má mǎ mà/ were written <mha, ma, maa, mah>. Today, *pīnyīn* has become the official romanization of the PRC and is widely used. The Yale system was similar to *pīnyīn* and was used in a good deal of teaching material prior to the introduction of *pīnyīn*. Unfortunately, at present, the advanced student in Chinese is likely to have to become familiar with Wade–Giles as well as *pīnyīn* because of the large amount of material which uses both romanizations. Note that the Yale romanizations for Mandarin and Cantonese are not the same thing.

3.3 Relationship of Language and Writing in Chinese

The relationship between the Chinese language and the writing system is relatively simple. There are many characters to learn, but the structural relationship between characters and language is not complex. The Chinese character *zì* 字 is a grapheme; i.e., a character is the fundamental contrastive unit of writing in Chinese. In an utterance, each syllable is represented by a character, and different morphemes are written with different characters.

Writing an utterance in Chinese is quite straightforward. First, we divide the utterance into syllables. In the great majority of cases, each morpheme corresponds to one syllable. For each syllable, we write the character which corresponds to the morpheme of that syllable. We need morphemic information since most syllable shapes represent more than one morpheme. The uncommon bisyllabic morphemes have two characters. Thus, in our written text, there will be one character for each syllable.

Homophony is very common in Chinese with most syllable shapes corresponding to more than one morpheme, but different morphemes are generally represented in writing by different characters. For example, the syllable /tī/ is the sound of several different morphemes, each written with a different character: /tī/ 'ladder' 梯, /tī/ 'scrape' 剔, /tī/ 'kick' 踢. This situation sometimes leads to the writing of an incorrect, but homophonous, character. Writing the wrong one of these characters is similar to writing *their* for *there* in English. If we want to write something for which we have forgotten a character and do not have a dictionary or other help handy, we would have to rephrase the utterance to avoid this morpheme.

Reading Chinese is perhaps a bit more difficult than writing. From each character, we know what morpheme is intended. The difficulty arises in that word divisions are not marked in Chinese. Reading requires that we parse the text into words and syntactic structures correctly. We must recognize the occasional bisyllabic morpheme and sort out the relatively few characters which represent more than one morpheme, such as 行 /xíng/ 'walk' and 行 /háng/ 'line, row'.

3.3.1 *What linguistic units do characters represent?*

In reading about the Chinese writing system, one frequently gets confusing information about what unit in the language a character represents. Does a character (*zì* 字) represent a word (*cí* 詞), a morpheme (*cí sù* 詞素), or a syllable (*yīn jié* 音節)? To sort this out, let's look first at the language, leaving writing aside for the moment. Although Chinese has almost no suffixes or prefixes, compounding is extremely common, and words frequently consist of more than one morpheme. Taylor and Taylor (1995) say that approximately two-thirds of all Chinese words are polymorphemic. The most common pattern is for a morpheme to consist of one syllable, but this is not necessarily so. A small proportion of morphemes in Chinese have two syllables; disyllabic morphemes are particularly common in the names for animals and plants. Thus, looking only at the language, we find that in Chinese, morphemes are generally monosyllabic but that words are commonly polymorphemic.

What then does a character represent? In table 3.5, we have examples of the typical situation. One-syllable morphemes are illustrated by *wǒ* 'I' and *hǎo* 'good'. Two examples of the less common pattern of two-syllable morphemes are *shānhú* 'coral' and *húdié* 'butterfly'. Many of the words of this type are borrowings from other languages. Words with the common two-morpheme compound pattern are illustrated by *tiělù* 'railway' (= *tiě* 'iron' + *lù* 'road') and *zìdiǎn* 'dictionary' (= *zì* 'character' + *diǎn* 'standard'). We can now easily see that there is no regular relation in the number of syllables, morphemes, or words. But if we now look at how these forms are written, we can see that the number of characters corresponds to the

Table 3.5 Different types of lexical items showing the different number of characters, syllables, morphemes, and words in each. Note that the only consistent agreement is between the number of characters in an utterance and the number of syllables

			Characters 字	*Syllables* 音節	*Morphemes* 詞素	*Words* 詞
wǒ	'I'	我	1	1	1	1
hǎo	'good'	好	1	1	1	1
shānhú	'coral'	珊瑚	2	2	1	1
húdié	'butterfly'	蝴蝶	2	2	1	1
tiělù	'railway'	鐵路	2	2	2	1
zìdiǎn	'dictionary'	字典	2	2	2	1

number of syllables, but not to the number of morphemes or words. In summary, there is a general rule in Chinese that every syllable in the language corresponds to one character in writing.

A small exception to the rule that each syllable is written with one character involves nominal forms ending in the suffix /-r/. This /-r/ is a diminutive suffix, particularly typical of colloquial speech of the Běijīng dialect. This suffix does not increase the number of syllables, but it is written as a separate character 兒, which originally meant 'child'. Thus, /huār/, the colloquial form of 'flower', has only one syllable, but is written with two characters. In the terminology developed in chapter 2, 花兒 is a polygraph since the two graphemes represent a single syllable, a unit normally represented by one character in Chinese. In this usage, 兒 is a bound character forming part of the polygraph.

A second exception is the number '20' in Chinese. This number is /èr shí/ '(literally) two tens' and is normally written with two characters 二十. There is, however, a single character 廿 which is sometimes used for '20'. This character is a polyphone since it is one grapheme used to represent two syllables.

Many Chinese morphemes have very limited distribution. The word /péngyǒu/ 朋友 'friend' is a compound. The second element /yǒu/ is somewhat restricted in that it does not occur as a word by itself, but it does occur in other compounds with other morphemes, such as /yǒuhǎo/ 'friendly'. The first syllable /péng/ is even more restricted: it does not occur in any other context, either as a word by itself or in a compound with other morphemes. The morpheme /péng/ is what is known as a **cranberry morpheme** (occurring in only one context, like the *cran-* of English *cranberry*). As for writing, the general Chinese rule still applies. Every syllable is written with one character. Accordingly if we ask a Chinese speaker to write /péngyǒu/, we get 朋友 without hesitation. If we then ask what the individual parts mean, the answer for /yǒu/ is likely to be 'friend', but /péng/ is harder. There is a reading pronunciation for /péng/ which allows us to talk about the character, but the meaning is hard to describe clearly since it never occurs by itself. We can call such a grapheme a **cranberry grapheme**. English speakers have a similar difficulty if asked what the *cran-* of *cranberry* means. Many characters are like this in Chinese; they do not form words by themselves, and they may occur in only one context.

3.3.2 *Homophony*

Homophony (two or more different morphemes with the same sound) is a prominent feature of modern Chinese. Old Chinese had less homophony, but historical changes in the phonology of Chinese have neutralized the pronunciation of many syllables which were different in earlier Chinese. The result today of the historic changes in the language is that although Chinese has a great number of homophonic morphemes, different morphemes are written differently, thus facilitating reading.

To give one example, the seven morphemes in table 3.6 are all pronounced /sù/ in modern Chinese, but they are all written with different characters. In Old Chinese, however, six of these were pronounced differently; only the morphemes for 'stay' and 'dawn' were homophonous – /*sjuk/. The Old Chinese pronunciations follow Baxter's (1992) reconstruction.

Table 3.6 Words written differently, but pronounced the same in Modern Standard Chinese

Character	*Meaning*	*Modern Chinese*	*Old Chinese*
粟	'millet'	sù	*sjok
肅	'solemn'	sù	*sjiwk
宿	'stay'	sù	*sjuk
夙	'dawn'	sù	*sjuk
素	'white'	sù	*saks
愬	'tell'	sù	*sŋaks
摵	'inform'	sù	*sok

Taylor and Taylor (1995) note that in modern Chinese, of the 1359 occurring syllable shapes (including tone), each syllable shape is written by an average of 11 characters. They note that 199 syllable shapes (14.6 per cent) have no homophony; i.e., they are written by only one character: e.g., the syllable shape /bái/ represents only one morpheme, namely the one meaning 'white', which is written 白. Thus, 白 is the only character with the pronunciation /bái/. On the other hand, a few characters have over 100 homophones: e.g. /yì/, written by 149 characters. Such figures stem from very large dictionaries, but even a small dictionary for learners (*Xuéxí Hànyīng Cídiǎn* 1998) lists 31 characters for /yì/, each for a different morpheme.

Because of the considerable homophony in Chinese, it is possible to compose entire sentences, or even stories, using the same syllable shape. The following story (table 3.7) using only the Mandarin syllable shape /shi/ is an example. Note that differences of tone are ignored. (This story is given in Taylor and Taylor (1995), but it may have come from Chao Yuenren who used it in a lecture in Toronto in the early 1970s.)

3.4 Origin and Structure of Chinese Characters

3.4.1 Early Chinese writing

Aside from some early pottery marks which are difficult to interpret, the earliest material which shows clear evidence of writing is **oracle-bone writing** (Chin. jiǎgǔwén 甲骨文), also known as shell-and-bone writing. Oracle-bone writing has been dated to 1200–1050 OLD during the late Shāng dynasty in the central east area of China. Early inscriptions have been found on bones, usually the shoulder-blade of cattle, or the plastron (undershell) of turtles. These were used in making predictions about the future. The bone or shell was subjected to heat, and the resulting cracks were interpreted. The question and prophecy, and sometimes the outcome, were scratched into the bone. Note that the character 卜 for /bǔ/ 'divination' was originally a pictograph for two cracks.

Table 3.7 A story in which each syllable is pronounced /shi/

石室詩士施氏，嗜獅，
誓食十獅。
施氏時時適市視獅，十時，
適十獅適市。
是時，適施氏適市。
施氏視是十獅，恃矢勢，
使是十獅逝世。
施氏拾是十獅屍，適石室。
石室溼，施氏使侍拭石室，
石室拭，施氏始試食是十獅屍。
食時，始識是十獅屍是十石獅屍。
試釋是事。

shí shì shī shì shī shì, shì shī,
shì shí shí shī.
shī shì shí shí shì shì shì shī, shí shí,
shì shí shī shì shì.
shì shí, shì shī shì shì shì.
shī shì shì shì shí shī, shì shī shì,
shǐ shì shí shī shì shī.
shī shì shí shì shí shī shī, shì shí shì.
shí shì shī, shī shì shǐ shì shì shí shì,
shí shì shì, shī shì shǐ shì shí shì shí shī shī.
shí shí, shǐ shí shì shí shī shī shì shí shí shī shī.
shì shì shì shì.

Translation
A poet named Shī lived in a stone house and liked to eat lion flesh, and he vowed to eat ten of them. He used to go to the market in search of lions, and one day at ten o'clock, he chanced to see ten of them there. Shī killed the lions with arrows and picked up their bodies, carrying them back to his stone house. His house was dripping with water so he requested that his servants proceed to dry it. Then he began to try to eat the bodies of the ten lions. It was only then he realised that these were in fact ten lions made of stone. Try to explain the riddle.

Figure 3.3 shows an inscribed tortoise plastron dated *ca.* 1200–1180 OLD. The text is actually written twice in similar terms. Keightley (1989) translates the right-hand portion as: 'Crack-making on *chia-shen* (day 21), Ch'ueh divined – "Fu Hao's childbearing will be good". The King, reading the cracks said: "If it be a *ting* day childbearing, it will be good. If it be *keng* day childbearing, it will be extremely auspicious." On the thirty-first day, *chia-yin* (day 51), she gave birth. It was not good. It was a girl.' The ancient Chinese had a ten-day week, including *ting*, *keng*, and *chia* as days. Since the king did not specifically mention a *chia* day, his prediction is technically correct. This text also tells us something about the appreciation of women in Shāng society.

Some 4500 different characters have been identified in the oracle-bone texts; only about 1500 have been connected with characters of later writing. For those which

Figure 3.3 An oracle-bone inscription (from Wayne Senner (ed.), *The Origins of Writing*, figure 6, p. 181. Lincoln, NE: University of Nebraska Press, 1989. © 1989 by University of Nebraska Press. Reprinted with permission)

later fell out of use, it is difficult to determine their meaning. Undoubtedly, some of the characters that disappeared represented proper names of people that dropped out of use or place-names that changed over time.

The structure of the Chinese writing system has not really changed since the oracle-bone texts although the shapes of characters changed over time. This change in shape is a calligraphic evolution rather than a structural change.

3.4.2 *Reconstructing the early pronunciation of Chinese*

An obvious question is how do we know how Chinese was pronounced in the past. If we examine the historical documents of English, we find that modern /haws/ 'house' was written <hus> in Old English times. From this, we can make a reasonable guess that it would have sounded something like [hus]. For Chinese, the situation is much more difficult. We know that the character 馬 'horse' is pronounced /mǎ/ in Mandarin today, but if we look at Old Chinese documents, we still get 馬 (or an older calligraphic variant) with no additional phonetic evidence. To reconstruct older spoken forms of Chinese, scholars look at a variety of evidence. The modern dialect forms can be used to help in reconstruction. Further, the pronunciation of the large number of Chinese words borrowed into Japanese, Korean, and Vietnamese often gives us help. Sometimes, we have early Chinese texts transcribed phonetically in other scripts from central Asia such as Brāhmī, Uighur, and 'Phags-pa (see chapter 11).

Considerable help in reconstructing the pronunciation of Chinese comes from certain Chinese texts themselves. Composed around 1000 OLD in Old Chinese times, the *Shījīng* was a collection of rhyming poems. By examining the rhymes in the *Shījīng*, we can determine that two morphemes were pronounced the same (or at least similarly). In the fifth century NEW, dictionaries of characters were written which indicated the pronunciation at that time. The pronunciation was indicated by showing that the initial of the syllable was pronounced the same as the initial of another well-known character and the final was pronounced the same as the final of another. We might similarly show the pronunciation of the English word *tongue* by saying that it has the initial of *tie* and the final of *sung*. Obviously this system requires knowing what the reference characters sounded like, but with a bit of a starting point, scholars find this information enormously helpful.

During the Sòng dynasty (960–1127 NEW), rhyme tables were constructed showing the pronunciation of characters at that time. Each page was a grid with the initials listed at the top, the finals at the left, and characters were entered in the appropriate cell according to their pronunciation. Characters with different tones were assigned to different volumes of the dictionary.

3.4.3 How characters were formed

Very generally, Chinese used four methods in constructing characters: **pictography, phonetic extension, semantic extension,** and **differentiation. Pictograms** were likely the earliest types of characters. Some of these have survived into modern times (although with substantially changed shapes). Figure 3.4 gives some examples, showing their early and modern forms.

Figure 3.5 shows some **abstract pictograms.** These are similar to the basic pictogram, but they are graphic representations of abstract notions rather than of concrete objects.

Any new writing system has the task of providing ways of writing any lexical item. In Chinese, sometimes, rather than creating an entirely new character, an existing character was used for a different morpheme which happened to have a similar sound. For example, the character for /mǎ/ 'horse' was a pictogram 𢒠 (the modern form of the character is 馬). Another similar-sounding word is /mā/ 'mother'. Rather than developing an entirely new character for /mā/ 'mother', the Chinese extended the use of the character for /mǎ/ 'horse' to write /mā/ 'mother' as well (figure 3.6). This is a process of **phonetic extension** (sometimes referred to as rebus writing). Later on, a separate character for 'mother' developed.

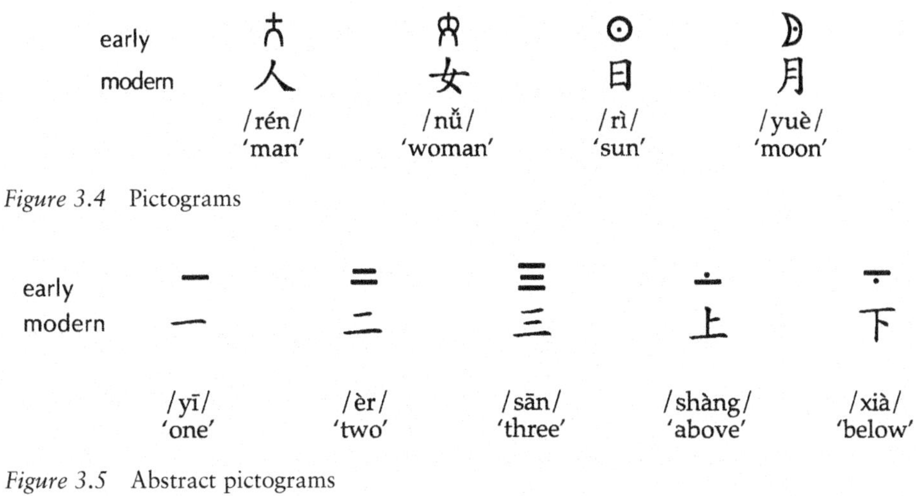

Figure 3.4 Pictograms

Figure 3.5 Abstract pictograms

馬 /mǎ/ 'horse' → 馬 /mā/ 'mother'

Figure 3.6 Phonetic extension. The arrow here shows that the character for one word was extended to write a different (but similar-sounding) word as well

Table 3.8 Semantic extension

mò	磨	'a mill'	mó	磨	'to grind'
zuàn	鑽	'a drill'	zuǎn	鑽	'to drill'
wǎ	瓦	'a tile'	wà	瓦	'to tile'
ní	泥	'mud'	nì	泥	'to daub on mud'

In some cases, characters were extended to different morphemes by **semantic extension**, a process whereby a character used for one morpheme is extended to another morpheme with a similar meaning. Most of the instances of this process have since been disguised by having additional elements added to distinguish the two characters, but in modern Chinese, examples do exist where the morphemes have the same pronunciation or differ only by tone (table 3.8).

The fourth process of **differentiation** was very common. We have seen just above that, originally, the character 馬 was a pictogram for the morpheme /mǎ/ 'horse'. By phonetic extension, it was also used for /mā/ 'mother'. Presumably, the ambiguous use of 馬 for both 'horse' and 'mother' was bothersome, so the Chinese eventually created a separate character for 'mother' by differentiation. The character for /nǚ/ 'woman' is 女. The new character for 'mother' was created by combining the character for 'woman' with the character for 'horse', giving 媽, an unambiguous character used only for the morpheme /mā/ 'mother'; thereafter, 馬 was used only for /mǎ/ 'horse'. The logic for this compounding is clear: the meaning of 'mother' was similar to 'woman', and the sound of /mā/ was similar to /mǎ/ 'horse'.

Table 3.9 Traditional categories of character formation

A. pictograms	xiàngxíng	象形
B. abstract pictograms	zhǐshì	指事
C. semantic-phonetic compounds	xíngshēng	形聲
D. semantic-semantic compounds	huìyì	會意

This differentiation has created a **semantic-phonetic compound**: one part 女 was used for its semantic value and the other 馬 was used for its phonetic value. Note that the phonetic value of 女 /nǚ/, and the semantic value of 馬 'horse' are irrelevant. I have used modern Mandarin pronunciations to illustrate this phenomenon; in early Chinese, the pronunciations of 'horse' and 'mother' would have been different from what they are today, but we can assume that they were fairly similar to each other then. As we will see, in later years the semantic-phonetic compound became the most common way to form a character in Chinese.

3.4.4 Traditional analysis of characters

Around 100 OLD, the scholar Xǔ Shèn 許慎 analyzed the structure of characters into six groups. His grouping has been widely used in discussing this subject. We must not forget, however, that Xǔ Shèn lived some 1500 years after Chinese characters were first formed, and he had no direct knowledge of the original processes.

Two of Xǔ Shèn's categories refer to their use, not to their structure. The remaining four categories are given in table 3.9.

We have already seen examples of the first three of these categories. Semantic-phonetic compounds are so important that we will look at them in more detail and then examine the semantic-semantic compounds.

3.4.5 Semantic-phonetic compounds

The **semantic-phonetic compound** is by far the most common type of character in Chinese. Its structure is relatively transparent: one part of the character is related to the meaning, and another part is related to the sound. We have already seen how the character 媽 /mā/ 'mother' is composed of a semantic element 女 'woman', and a phonetic element 馬 /mǎ/.

The semantic-phonetic compounds in table 3.10 show further cases where 馬 is used for its phonetic value. The meaning of the semantic component is given at the right. Note that the pronunciation of the semantic element is irrelevant. Note as well that a semantic-phonetic compound character is a single character and represents a single syllable, as discussed in §3.3.1.

A further example involves 勿, which originally was a pictogram for /wù/ 'creature'. By phonetic extension, this character came to be used also for /wù/ 'do not'. In time, the character for 'creature' was modified to 物 by adding a semantic element for 'ox', and 勿 was used thereafter only for 'do not'. Note that with 'horse' and 'mother', the original meaning 'horse' was kept with the original character

Table 3.10 Semantic-phonetic compounds with the phonetic 馬. The semantic element is shown as a separate character at the right

Semantic-phonetic compound			*Semantic element*		
瑪	/mǎ/	'agate'	玉	'gem'	/yù/
碼	/mǎ/	'weights'	石	'stone'	/shí/
螞	/mà/	'grasshopper'	虫	'insect, reptile'	/chóng/
罵	/mà/	'scold'	口	'mouth' (written twice)	/kǒu/

Table 3.11 Semantic-phonetic compounds with the phonetic 堯. The semantic element in its allograph as a separate character is shown at the right

	Pronunciation	*Meaning of character*	*Semantic component*	*Meaning of semantic component*
堯	/yáo/	'legendary chief'		—
澆	/jiāo/	'water (verb)'	水	'water'
僥	/jiǎo/	'lucky'	人	'man, human'
蹺	/qiāo/	'lift foot'	足	'foot'
翹	/qiáo/	'lift up'	羽	'quill
驍	/xiāo/	'good horse, valiant'	馬	'horse'
曉	/xiǎo/	'dawn'	日	'sun'
燒	/shāo/	'burn'	火	'fire'
譊	/náo/	'shout, quarrel'	言	'word, speech'
橈	/náo/	'oar'	木	'tree, wood'
鐃	/náo/	'bell, cymbal'	金	'metal'
撓	/náo/	'disturb'	手	'hand'
嬈	/ráo/	'graceful'	女	'woman'
蕘	/ráo/	'brushwood'	艸	'grass, plant'
蟯	/ráo; náo/	'roundworm'	虫	'insect, reptile'
饒	/ráo/	'abundant'	食	'eat, food'
繞	/rào/	'coil'	糸	'silk, thread'

shape, and the derived use 'mother' was associated with the new character. With 'creature' and 'do not', the derived use 'do not' was associated with the original character, and the original use 'creature' was associated with the new character.

Table 3.11 gives a large number of semantic-phonetic compounds having the phonetic element 堯 /yáo/. Notice that the phonetic similarity here is not so tight as with 'horse'. The meaning of the semantic element is given at the right of the table. It is not always clear why a certain semantic element has been chosen. Some of the items in table 3.11 are no longer used in modern Chinese.

Historically, the semantic-phonetic characters were formed in two stages. First, a character with a certain meaning and sound was extended to represent a different morpheme with the same or similar sound as the first character. This process is phonetic extension: a symbol is used for another morpheme with the same or similar sound. At this point, the character is ambiguous; it could be read in two different

Table 3.12 Examples of bound allographs. The free allograph is given at the left, then the bound form alone, and at the right the bound form is shown as part of a character, with the bound form indicated by an arrow

human, man	人	亻	↓他
hand	手	扌	↓拈
heart	心	忄	↓忖
water	水	氵	↓漢
fire	火	火	↓炒
(note different bound allographs)		灬	→ 焦
bamboo	竹	⺮	→ 箸

ways. In time, this ambiguity was resolved by altering the shape of the character for one of the meanings by adding a semantic element, thus forming a new character, but keeping the original shape for the other meaning. This process is **differentiation** in the form of adding a semantic determinative. In an historical sense, the phonetic element is 'primary', and the semantic element is 'secondary'.

In many cases, the semantic element has a slightly different shape when it occurs as a bound allograph in a character, often simplified, and generally written more narrowly. Some of these are given in table 3.12. For example, the bound allograph for 'human' is written more narrowly with the first stroke clearly above the second. With 'hand', the bound allograph is simplified by omitting the top stroke. The bound allograph for 'heart' is quite different from the free allograph. The four-stroke free form of 'water' is written as three strokes arranged vertically. 'Fire' has two bound allographs: one is simply a narrower version of the free form, but the other is four dots written at the bottom of the phonetic element. The bound form of 'bamboo' is a pair of three-stroke units written above the phonetic element.

3.4.6 Semantic-semantic compounds

Semantic-semantic compounds are the fourth category in Xǔ Shèn's analysis (table 3.13). He described them as created by the combination of two independent characters on the basis of their meaning. For example, the traditional explanation for the character 安 /ān/ 'peace' is that it is constructed of two characters which together form a woman under a roof, a peaceful notion. A woman and a child together are 'good'; the sun and the moon together are 'bright'; a man leaning against a tree is 'resting'; two trees form a 'grove'; the strength for work in the field is 'masculine'; and a 'home' is a pig under a roof.

Table 3.13 Semantic-semantic compounds

/ān/	安	'peace'	=	/mián/	宀	'roof'	+	/nǚ/	女	'woman'
/hǎo/	好	'good'	=	/nǚ/	女	'woman'	+	/zǐ/	子	'son'
/míng/	明	'bright'	=	/rì/	日	'sun'	+	/yuè/	月	'moon'
/xiū/	休	'rest'	=	/rén/	人	'man'	+	/mù/	木	'tree'
/lín/	林	'grove'	=	/mù/	木	'tree'	+	/mù/	木	'tree'
/nán/	男	'male'	=	/lì/	力	'strength'	+	/tián/	田	'field'
/jiā/	家	'home'	=	/mián/	宀	'roof'	+	/shǐ/	豕	'pig'

Modern scholars, looking more closely at the early history of this category of characters, have become doubtful of these traditional explanations. Rather than being formed purely on semantic grounds, it seems that many, if not most, of these characters were formed as semantic-phonetic compounds, but because of phonological change, the phonetic element is no longer apparent. Boltz (1996, p. 197) says: 'In origin actual characters are never formed this way; this is an artificial, retrospective category.' Quite possibly, the explanation as semantic-semantic compounds arose from pedogogical needs; that is, a teacher would make up an interesting story to help children remember the characters better. The geminate (same graphic element written twice) example of /lín/ 'grove' may, however, be a legitimate semantic-semantic compound.

3.4.7 Some examples of characters with a complex history

To illustrate the complexity that may be involved in the history of characters, consider the examples in table 3.14. All of these characters contain the element 口. By itself, 口 is used to write /kǒu/ 'mouth'. We might assume that the second and third characters are semantic-phonetic compounds with 口 as the phonetic element since they are all pronounced similarly to /kǒu/ 'mouth'. In fact, this seems to be the historic situation, but the fourth and fifth characters also seem to be semantic-phonetic compounds with 口 as the phonetic element, but in this case, it would be pronounced /míng/. Since the character by itself is pronounced /kǒu/, we can understand characters two and three, but the rationale for characters four and five is not immediately clear. However, some historic digging may clear things up (table 3.15). Note that 名 and 鳴 both have a somewhat similar meaning involving using the mouth to make a noise. What seems to have happened is that by a process of semantic extension 口 'mouth' came also to be used to write the character for /míng/ 'call, name'. With

Table 3.14 Characters with the element 口

口	/kǒu/	'mouth'
叩	/kòu/	'knock'
扣	/kòu/	'hook, fasten'
名	/míng/	'call, name'
鳴	/míng/	'cry of bird'

Table 3.15 Development of characters with the element 口 by the processes of phonetic extension, semantic extension, and differentiation

口	'mouth' pictogram			
口	/kǒu/ 'mouth'			
	– by phonetic extension	口	/kòu/	'knock'
	– by differentiation	叩	/kòu/	'knock'
	(卩 means 'kneel'; the image is 'kowtowing' – kneeling and touching one's head to the floor as a sign of subservience)			
口	/kǒu/ 'mouth'			
	– by phonetic extension	口	/kòu/	'hook, fasten'
	– by differentiation	扣	/kòu/	'hook, fasten'
	(with allograph of 手 'hand' as radical)			
口	/kǒu/ 'mouth'			
	– by semantic extension	口	/míng/	'call, name'
	– by differentiation	名	/míng/	'call, name'
	(note that later, 名 was itself used as a phonetic element and combined with the character for 'gold, metal' to form a new character 銘 for /míng/ 'engrave')			
口	/kǒu/ 'mouth'			
	– by phonetic/semantic extension	口	/míng/	'cry of bird'
	– by differentiation	鳴	/míng/	'cry of bird'

this new sound and meaning, 口 was further extended to the morpheme /míng/ 'cry of bird'; this latter use seems to be a joint case of phonetic extension and semantic extension. In time, the shapes of these characters were all differentiated from 口 by adding additional elements, namely 夕 /xī/ 'evening' and 鳥 /niǎo/ 'bird' (Boltz 1994). By itself, 口 is now used only with the pronunciation /kǒu/.

3.4.8 *Writing borrowed words*

The writing of borrowed words presents an obvious problem for any morphographic script since there are no symbols for foreign morphemes. To deal with this problem, Chinese writes the pronunciation using characters for their phonetic value only (phonetic extension).

For example, when the former US president Ronald Reagan became commonly mentioned in newspapers, it was necessary to devise a way of writing his name. In the PRC, his name was pronounced /lǐ gēn/ and written 里根. By themselves, 里 means 'inside' and 根 means 'root', together forming a meaningless phrase; the characters were chosen only because they represent the sound of the name *Reagan*. In this particular case it is interesting to note that Táiwān adopted different characters to represent Reagan's name 雷根 with a slightly different pronunciation /léi gēn/.

Canada is written 加拿大 /jiā ná dà/. Again, the meaning of the characters (加 /jiā/ 'add to'; 拿 /ná/ 'take'; 大 /dà/ 'large') is irrelevant. The pronunciation of the last two characters is obvious, but the choice of /jiā/ seems odd. Here we must realize that the first Chinese in Canada were from Hong Kong and spoke Cantonese. In Cantonese, the character 加 is pronounced /gà/, sounding like [kà]. The Chinese name for Canada was first created by Cantonese speakers as /gà nàh daaih/ 加拿大; this was then adopted by speakers of Mandarin in which the characters were pronounced as /jiā ná dà/. (The English form *Peking* is similarly from the Cantonese pronunciation of Běijīng.)

Less commonly, foreign words are translated into Chinese and then written with the semantically appropriate Chinese characters. For example, after the Watergate Hotel gained notoriety during the Nixon years in the United States, it was written as 水門, which is a simple translation of the two morphemes: *water* and *gate*.

3.4.9 Dialect characters

We mentioned above that although all speakers of Chinese use the same dialect for writing, occasionally they may want to write a dialect expression. Some dialects, Cantonese in particular, have developed **dialect characters** for many dialect words which are not used in standard Chinese writing, such as 唔 /m̀h/ 'not' and 劏 /tōng/ 'slaughter'. See D. Li (2000) for further information about current writing in Cantonese and Tiu^{n} (1998) for a discussion of writing in Taiwanese.

3.5 Structure of Chinese Characters

Simply looking at characters, we find a wide variety of shapes; nevertheless, each character, no matter how simple or complex, is written so as to fill an imaginary square. Books for children to practise their brushmanship consist of blank pages with a grid of equal-sized squares.

3.5.1 The shapes of characters

Some characters consist of only one part, which may be simple or complex: 一 工 木 戈 龠. Some characters consist of two (or three) parts placed next to each other horizontally. Although the term is not usually used in Chinese studies, we might call these characters ligatures: 林 明 媽 漢 謝. Some characters consist of two parts placed vertically, one on top of the other: 戔 字 李 焦 出. Some characters consist of a part written inside a border; such a border may be a complete or partial enclosure, or it may consist of two balanced parts: 回 國 店 門 鬧. Some characters have more complex arrangements. Generally they are formed by iterative applications of the structures given above. For example, 您 is a polite way of saying 'you'; it consists first of two parts, 你 above and 心 below. The lower part is a single unit, but the upper part consists of two units arranged horizontally, 亻 and 尔. Other types of complex structures are shown in the following: 轡 樂 騷 羅 森 蠶 鑿 韶 靡.

3.5.2 Complex numerals

One interesting kind of character is the **complex numeral**. The ordinary form of the number 'one' /yī/ is a single stroke, as shown in table 3.16. It would obviously

Table 3.16 Ordinary and complex characters for numerals

		Ordinary	*Complex*
'one'	/yī/	一	壹
'two'	/èr/	二	貳
'three'	/sān/	三	叄
'four'	/sì/	四	肆
'five'	/wǔ/	五	伍
'six'	/liù/	六	陸
'seven'	/qī/	七	柒
'eight'	/bā/	八	捌
'nine'	/jiǔ/	九	玖
'ten'	/shī/	十	拾
'hundred'	/bǎi/	百	佰
'thousand'	/chiān/	千	仟

be quite easy to alter this to a 'two, three, ten' or some other number. Because the characters for numbers generally have rather simple forms, more complex variants exist for use in contracts and other documents to avoid possible fraud.

3.5.3 *How characters are written*

The order in which the strokes of a character are written is important. The advantage of a fixed **stroke order** is that when a character is written quickly, it will still be legible. The general guidelines for the order of writing strokes are shown in table 3.17.

These are only general guidelines; there are many special rules for stroke ordering. Note especially that a box-like shape consists of three strokes; the top and right sides are made with one stroke. Figure 3.7 gives some examples. In the element 口 of character A, the left side is written first, then the top and right side as one stroke, finally the bottom stroke (guidelines 1 and 6). Character B 三 goes from top to bottom (guideline 1). Character C 心 is written from left to right (guideline 4). In character D, 十, the horizontal stroke is written before the vertical (guideline 2). In character E, 水, the middle stroke is written before the sides, following guideline 5. In both characters F and G, 中 and 閑, the outer parts are completed before the inner parts (guideline 3). In character H 固, the top and sides of the enclosure are written first, then the interior, and finally the bottom stroke (guidelines 3 and 6). Character I 跟 violates the guidelines twice: stroke 4 precedes stroke 6 to its left, and strokes 8–10 precede stroke 11, in both cases violating guideline 4. Both of

Table 3.17 General guidelines for stroke order

1. top to bottom	4. left to right
2. horizontal before vertical	5. middle before sides
3. outer before inner finished	6. close bottom last

Figure 3.7 Examples of stroke order

these structures recur in many other characters and are always written in the order described. Although stroke order is generally fixed, it is not rigidly uniform; there is a slight bit of both individual and dialectal variation.

3.5.4 Writing direction and punctuation

Traditionally, characters have been written in columns starting at the top right side of the page with the second column to the left of the first. The front of a book is what an English reader thinks of as the back; that is, when a book is lying before the reader with its front cover facing up, the binding is at the right, and pages are turned lifting the left edge.

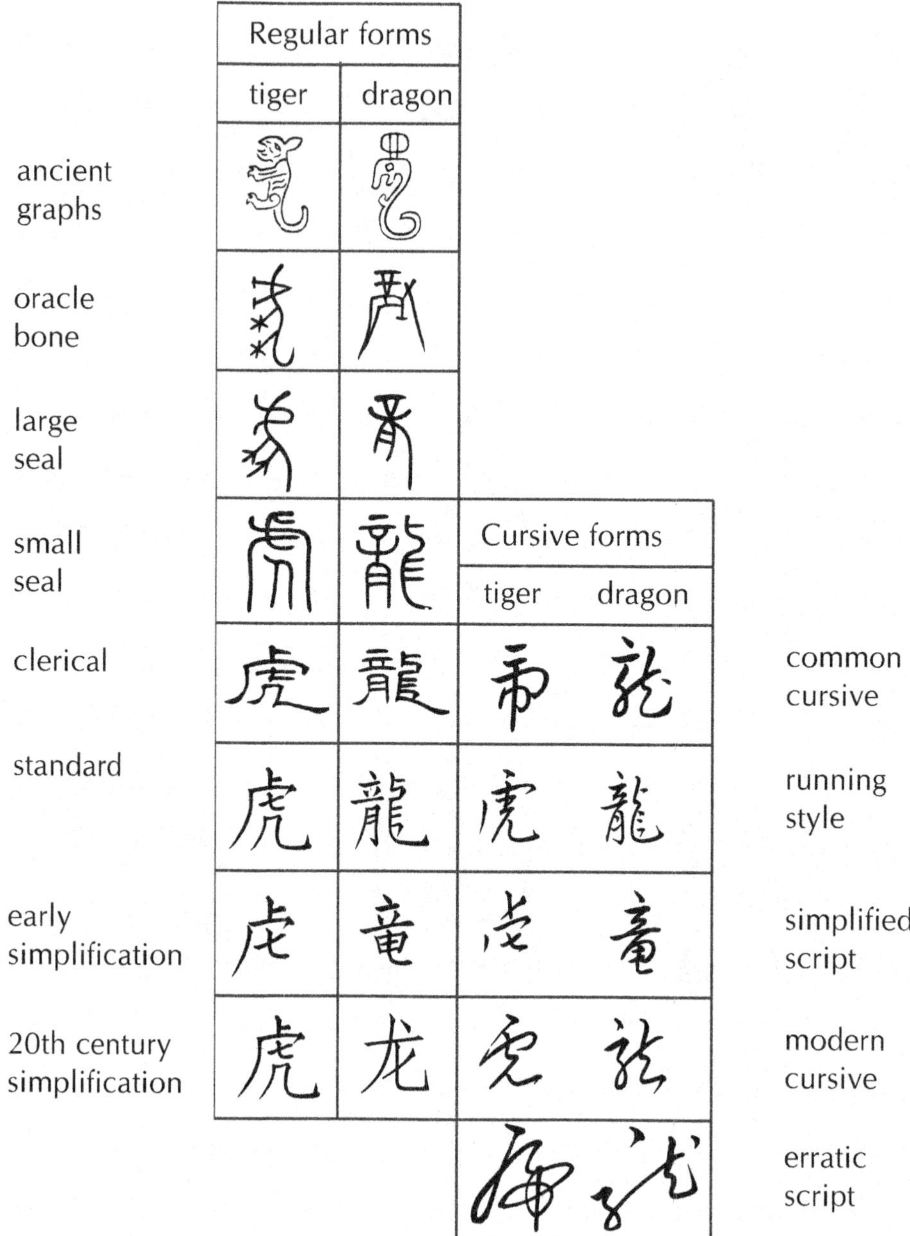

Figure 3.8 Different styles for tiger and dragon (from Fang-yü Wang, *Introduction to Chinese Cursive Script*, p. ii. New Haven, CT: Far Eastern Publications, Yale University Press, 1958. © 1958 by Yale University Press. Reproduced with permission)

In the 1950s, the PRC decreed that Chinese would be written horizontally from left to right as in English writing. Outside the PRC, some variation exists. Newspapers often use horizontal writing for the headlines and vertical writing for the main text. Occasionally, one sees a sign written horizontally from right to left.

Chinese texts have traditionally been written with no punctuation. Neither word nor sentence boundaries were indicated. Beginning in the nineteenth century, European-style punctuation has been introduced although its usage is not completely stabilized.

3.5.5 *Calligraphy*

Chinese writing has traditionally been done with the writing brush *máo bǐ* 毛筆; however, most writing today is done with a pen or pencil. **Calligraphy**, or writing beautifully, is a strong cultural feature of China with a long history. Traditionally, good scholarship and good calligraphy were thought to go hand in hand.

As we have noted earlier, the structure of Chinese writing has not changed radically from the early oracle-bone writing. The calligraphic shapes of characters, however, has altered quite a lot over the centuries. Figure 3.8 shows various forms of the characters for two words: *hǔ* 'tiger' and *lóng* 'dragon'. The earliest forms are at the top, and the later ones below. The ancient graphs are found sporadically as identifying marks on pottery sherds from around 2000 OLD. The oracle-bone characters are pictographs. The later large seal characters were found on bronze objects around 1100–300 OLD. By the third century OLD, writing had spread throughout China, and many local variants of characters had developed. The Qǐn dynasty at this time standardized the characters adopting the form known as small seal characters; these are occasionally used today for decorative purposes and on the small stone seals that are used like a signature elsewhere to indicate someone's identity on a piece of paper or a painting; they are usually in red ink. The clerical style emerged from this during the Qǐn period as a more easily written flowing style. The official style has been the normal style for characters from about 100 NEW to the present. Plate 1 (chapter 4) is an example of the standard style; this example was written in Japan in the twelfth century NEW, but the calligraphic traditions were the same for China, Japan, and Korea. The twentieth-century simplification forms are discussed further in §3.7.

In order to write more quickly, cursive forms have been in use for centuries. Generally they involve not lifting the brush and simplifying certain structures. Cursive is the normal kind of handwriting for informal purposes. Cursive styles, however, have been cultivated for their own sake. These calligraphic cursive styles are often difficult to read and have names like 'erratic style', 'grass writing', or even 'drunken style'.

3.5.6 *Ordering characters*

An obvious problem for a dictionary is how to order the characters so that users can find the one they are interested in. Quite early, scholars exploited the structure of the semantic-phonetic compound for this purpose. The semantic portion in this context is called the **radical**, the rest being the **phonetic**. In the seventeenth century NEW, a standard list of 214 radicals was developed (reduced from an earlier list of 540 radicals which the lexicographer Xǔ Shèn drew up in 121 NEW). Radicals are given an order based on their stroke number, and all characters with the same radical are grouped together. Within each group of characters with the same radical, the characters are ordered according to the number of strokes in the phonetic, the remaining part of the character. Soothill (1889) drew up a numbered list of phonetic elements, referred to in some dictionaries.

For many characters, this is quite straightforward. If we were searching, for example, for the character 李 /lǐ/ 'plum', we would look under radical 木, the radical for trees. We would count the strokes remaining in the rest of the character 子 – three, and then look for our character under those with three additional strokes. This can take a bit of patient ploughing through lists of characters, but it is generally quite workable.

3.6 How Many Characters Does Chinese Have?

Before we can answer the question of how many characters there are in Chinese, we need first to distinguish two different questions: how many characters are there in the Chinese writing system? and how many characters do people use? Think about answering these questions about words in English. A large dictionary has hundreds of thousands of words; we would consider it impossible for any individual to know, much less use, all of these words. The same is true for Chinese.

Estimates suggest that knowledge of 1500 characters is required for basic literacy; 2500–3000 for functional literacy. People with university educations tend to know around 4000 characters, although students of Chinese literature or history will know more. Figures of about 6000 characters are given for scholars. Máo Zédōng's *Collected Works* contained only 2981 different characters, and Máo had a strong traditional education.

If we look at running text, we find that 1000 characters account for 90 per cent of those found in ordinary reading; 2400 account for 99 per cent, and 3800 account for 99.9 per cent. The characters that one learns early in life are the most frequently used, and those learned later will turn up less often (Taylor and Taylor 1995).

If we look at very large dictionaries, we get figures something like 50,000. If a highly educated person knows 6000 characters, what are the other 44,000? Quite simply, they just are not commonly used. Many are archaic. Many are graphic alternatives to standard characters. Many are local: that is, they are used for local dialect morphemes or for local names and places. Some are quite specialized – names for different fish or mushrooms or parts of a harness. This of course is similar to the English situation: do you know terms such as milch, drouth, thole, bolete, or crupper?

In the end, we have two types of figures: a knowledge of about 3000 characters means that you can read most anything that comes your way that is not highly specialized. A figure of 50,000 is appropriate for a list of every single form of every character that anyone has ever used for anything, anywhere, at any time in Chinese.

Table 3.18 Different types of characters shown as percentages of the total character inventory over time. (The percentages do not add up to 100%, because certain minor categories have not been included.) (Source: Taylor and Taylor 1995)

	Period	*Pictogram* %	*Abstract pictogram* %	*Semantic-semantic compound* %	*Semantic-phonetic compound* %	*Number of characters*
oracle-bone	12–11th OLD	23.9	1.7	34.3	28.9	1,155
Shuōwénjiězì	2nd NEW	3.8	1.3	12.3	81.2	9,475
Tóngyīn	8th NEW	2.5	0.5	3.1	90.0	24,235

3.6.1 *Frequency of types of characters*

Over the centuries the proportion of the types of characters has changed. Table 3.18 shows three different periods in Chinese history; the *Shuōwénjiězì* 說文解字 (second century NEW) and the *Tóngyīn* 同音 (eighth century NEW) are dictionaries. We see that the percentage of pictograms has dropped significantly, from almost a quarter of all characters to a very small percentage. Pictograms, however, tend to be characters that are very frequently used. Abstract pictograms have always been few in number, although they also are commonly used characters. The number of semantic-semantic compounds has dropped significantly over the years. On the other hand, the semantic-phonetic compound category has increased dramatically. Obviously, this has been the most common way of creating new characters once the early period of character formation was past.

3.7 Recent Reforms

The last half of the nineteenth and the twentieth centuries witnessed many attempts to reform the Chinese language and writing system. Exposure to western alternatives inspired some of these reforms. The dominant rationales for reform, however, were that traditional education was very time-consuming and available to only a few, and that the lack of a larger literate population was holding China back internationally.

Reform of the written language did take place in the early twentieth century, as we have already learned. The ancient classical language was abandoned, and the Běijīng dialect as spoken by officials came to be used as the official written dialect, now called *pǔtōnghuà*.

The second kind of reform has been the introduction of **simplified characters.** In 1956 and 1964, the government of the PRC issued lists of new simplified forms of characters. These were required in government and schools. At present, people educated in the new system are able to recognize the **traditional characters** but are often uncertain about writing them.

Table 3.19 Simplified and traditional characters

		Traditional	*Simplified*
/luó/	'net for catching birds'	羅	罗
/mén/	'door, gate'	門	门
/mǎ/	'horse'	馬	马
/guó/	'country'	國	国
/diàn/	'lightning'	電	电
/yún/	'cloud'	雲	云
/miè/	'extinguish' (fire with line above)	滅	灭
/shuāng/	'pair' (two birds 隹 in a hand (archaic) 又 → two hands)	雙	双
/shā/	'kill'	殺	杀

The introduction of simplified characters has taken on a curious political aspect. Táiwān has been strongly opposed to the PRC for political reasons. As a result, the simplified characters have been regarded in Táiwān as 'communist' and are studiously avoided. Two totally different computer encoding systems have emerged as a result of this political split.

In Hong Kong, there has been less political tension with the PRC than found in Táiwān, and, as a result, traditional forms of characters continued to be used, out of both inertia and a loyalty to tradition. After the handover in 1997, it is expected that the simplified characters will be used in the government and schools and will gradually become used for private purposes. People of Chinese ancestry living abroad have mostly continued to use the traditional characters.

Singapore, where Chinese is an official language, has instituted some simplifications of its own, but these are not necessarily the same as those of the PRC. With Hong Kong becoming part of the PRC, it is likely that Singapore will gradually tend towards the PRC simplifications.

Simplified characters were created by various strategies: some cursive forms were used, or sometimes older, simpler forms of a character; sometimes new simpler forms were created. Examples are given in table 3.19. In some cases, two different traditional characters are written with the same simplified character. Thus it is possible to translate automatically from the traditional characters to the simplified ones (e.g., by a computer program), but it is not possible to go automatically in the opposite direction.

The simplification was based primarily on stroke count. It also eliminated alternative forms which previously existed. Psychologists have been more restrained in their enthusiasm for the simplified characters than the politicians. Fewer strokes clearly helps the writer. For the reader, however, the evidence in favour of simplification is less persuasive. In terms of complex versus simple characters, Taylor and Taylor (1995) point out that a character is recognized as a whole pattern, not as a combination of individual strokes. Thus, for readers, there is no advantage to the simpler characters, and in fact, simpler characters may present a less easily identified visual pattern. Taylor and Taylor (1995) suggest that for writing, an upper figure of 21 strokes would be appropriate and that more complex characters should be simplified for easier writing. They also point out that with greater use of computerized word processing, the advantage for simplified characters in writing can disappear. Their overall feeling is that there is insufficient evidence to make a reliable assessment of the value of simplified versus complex characters.

A third type of reform has been a proposal for abandoning characters altogether in favour of some type of alphabetic transcription. The current official romanization is *pīnyīn*. In the 1950s, it appeared that the government was moving towards replacing characters with *pīnyīn*. Later, it seemed to abandon any such scheme. Many people, both Chinese and others, feel that learning the large number of characters required for even basic reading is a useless burden and waste of time in a child's education (Hannas 1997). Critics of reform point to the large number of homophonous morphemes in Chinese. Since these are written with different characters, reading is easier than it would be using a phonographic system. However, spoken Chinese gets along fine with all this homophony, and I am somewhat at a loss to understand how writing could not cope. Having said this, I must admit that I have never met a Chinese person who could comfortably read a long text written in *pīnyīn*; this difficulty may of course be simply a lack of experience.

My own feeling about the reason that the Chinese want to keep characters is that they have a symbolic value of enormous importance. Many people would feel that giving up characters would be tantamount to giving up 3500 years of Chinese culture. Although using a computer to write Chinese is not quite so easy as writing with an alphabet, it is certainly workable.

One proposal for writing reform succeeded modestly, but in an unusual way. The *Zhùyīn zìmǔ* ('phonetic alphabet', also known as *Bōpōmōfō*) was introduced in 1913. It has special symbols for representing the initial, final, and tone of a syllable. The symbols look like very simple characters. *Zhùyīn zìmǔ* did not succeed as a way of normal writing, but it has been used extensively to indicate pronunciations in dictionaries, particularly in Táiwān.

3.8 Further Reading

Chen (1999), DeFrancis (1984), Kratochvil (1968), Norman (1988), and Ramsey (1987) all provide good background to the language in general. Boltz (1996) and Mair (1996) are good short introductions to early and modern Chinese writing respectively; Taylor and Taylor (1995) and Yǐn and Rohsenow (1994) are longer treatments. Moore (2000), Keightley (1989), Hsu (1996), and Boltz (1994) focus on historical matters. Simon (1959) is useful for the serious student despite his use of the *gwóyǔ luómàzì* romanization. There are many English–Chinese and Chinese–English dictionaries, each with its own personality and with slightly differing ways of locating specific characters. Sanfaçon (1997) and Harbaugh (1998) are both interesting specialized dictionaries whose primary aim is to explain the origin and structure of characters rather than to define Chinese words.

3.9 Terms

abstract pictogram
báihuà
calligraphy
Cantonese
Classical Chinese
complex numeral
cranberry grapheme
cranberry morpheme
dialect character
differentiation
final
hànzì
initial
Mandarin
Modern Standard Chinese
oracle-bone writing
phonetic
phonetic extension
pictogram
pictography
pīnyīn
pŭtōnghuà
radical
semantic extension
semantic-phonetic compound
semantic-semantic compound
simplified character
stroke order
tone
traditional character
Wade–Giles romanization
wényán

3.10 Exercises

1 The following is a list of possible dishes in a Chinese restaurant.

(a) 雞 丁 炒 白 菜 jì dìng chǎo bái cài
cubed chicken stir-fried with Chinese cabbage

(b) 魚 片 炒 芹 菜 yú piàn chǎo qín cài
sliced fish stir-fried with celery

(c) 肉 丁 炒 花 生 ròu dìng chǎo huā shēng
pork cubes stir-fried with peanuts

(d) 牛 肉 絲 炒 菜 花 niú rōu sì chǎo cài hua
beef shreds stir-fried with cauliflower

Glossary

肉	ròu	'meat', used to mean 'pork' if no other animal is specified
牛	niú	'cow'
片	piàn	'slice'
絲	sì	'silk, shred, julienne' (the shape of a matchstick)
白 菜	bái cài	'Chinese cabbage' (literally: 'white vegetable')
花 生	huā shēng	'peanut'
豆 腐	dòu fu	'bean curd'

(a) What is the meaning and pronunciation of the following characters?

雞 魚 炒

(b) Write the characters and the pronunciation for the following dish:

shredded chicken stir-fried with bean curd

(c) Write the characters and the pronunciation for the following dish:

fish slices stir-fried with Chinese cabbage

2 How many strokes are written in the following characters? Give the number at the right of the character.

míng 'bright' 明
chàng 'sing' 唱
qíu 'seek' 求

3 Show the correct stroke order for the following characters. Indicate the order by writing a number inside the circle next to (or overlapping) each stroke.

(a) 賣 /mài/ 'sell'

(b) 佯 /yáng/ 'pretend'

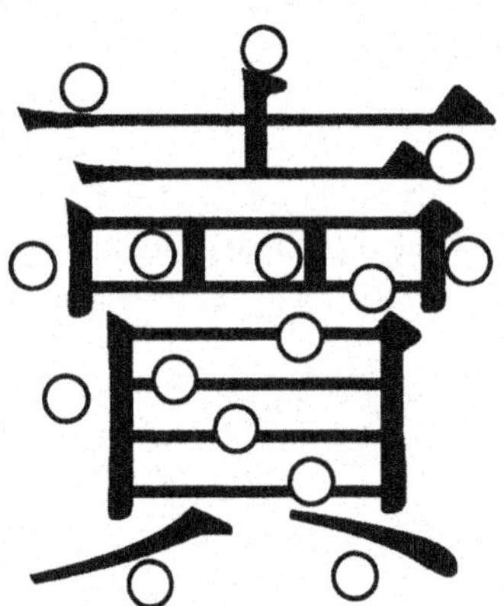

4 Japanese, Korean, Vietnamese

The cultural importance of China has been enormous throughout Asia since ancient times. The neighbouring countries borrowed Chinese writing, first writing in Chinese and then gradually adapting the Chinese writing system for writing their own language. We will examine Japanese first, because of its many special details, and then look at Korean and Vietnamese.

4.1 Japanese

4.1.1 Background and history

Japanese is spoken by essentially the entire population of Japan, about 125 million people. The standard dialect is based on educated Tokyo speech. The dialects of Japanese, although quite diverse, are generally mutually intelligible; the Ryukyuan dialect spoken on Okinawa at the southern end of Japan is different enough to be sometimes considered a separate language.

The genetic relationship of Japanese is a matter of debate. Possibly it is related to Korean, and more distantly to the Altaic languages (Manchu, Mongolian, Turkic). The connection between Japanese and these languages, however, is not so close as to be uncontroversial.

Japan was in early contact with China. Objects made in China dated to about the time 0 and inscribed with Chinese characters have been found in Japan, as well as objects made in Japan shortly afterwards with Chinese characters. Writing, as such, was introduced from China via Korea in the third century NEW. Koreans had already acquired Chinese writing, and Korean tutors came to Japan to teach the Chinese language and writing system to Japanese students. Note that the writing of this time, in both Japan and Korea, was completely in Chinese, both language and script. The practice of writing in Classical Chinese, known as ***kanbun*** 漢文 (= Ch. *hànwén*), continued in Japan for centuries. Chinese characters are known in Japanese as ***kanji*** 漢字 (= Ch. *hànzì*). Many Chinese words were borrowed into Japanese along with their characters. Plate 1 shows a Buddhist text written in Japan in the Chinese language in the late twelfth century; Japan and Korean shared the calligraphic traditions of China.

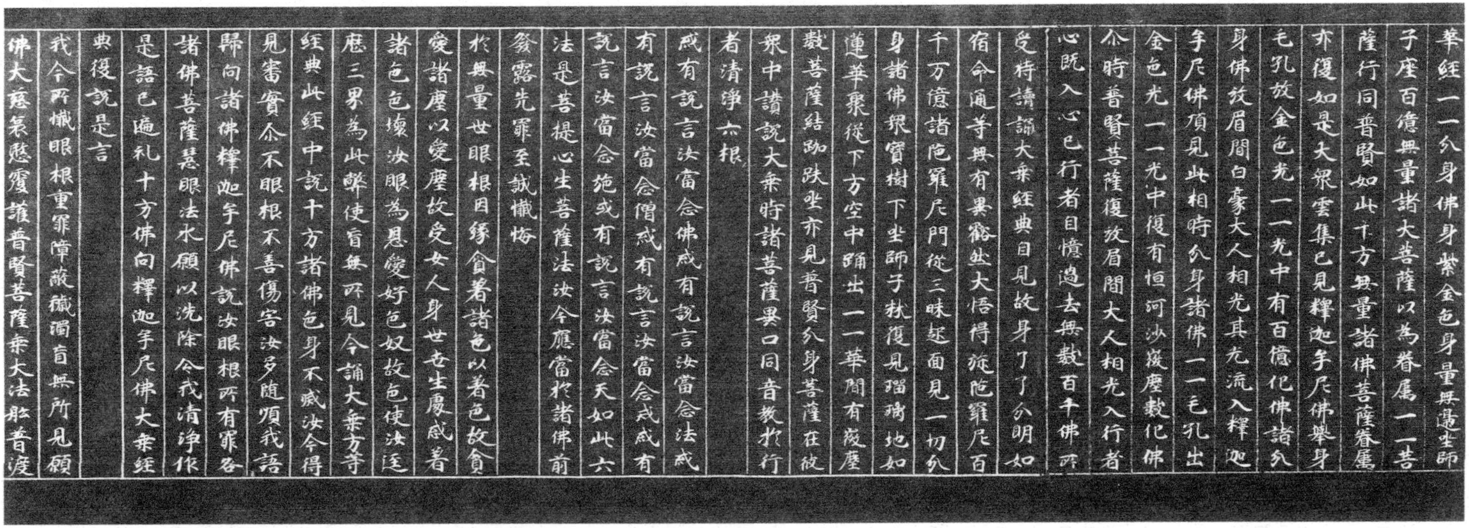

Plate 1 Handscroll. Buddhist *sutra*, written in Japan in the late twelfth century NEW in the Chinese language. Reproduced with permission from Freer Gallery of Art, Smithsonian Institution

Over time, however, writing was adapted to the Japanese language, and characters came to be associated with native Japanese words as well. For example, the Chinese word /shān/ 'mountain' was borrowed into Japanese and pronounced /san/. The Chinese character for /shān/ 山 was also borrowed and used to write the newly borrowed Japanese morpheme /san/. However, Japanese had always had a word /yama/ meaning 'mountain'. In time, the character 山 was also used to write the native word /yama/. Present-day Japanese has kept both terms for 'mountain', but uses them in different contexts: for example, by itself, a mountain is usually referred to as /yama/, but the well-known Japanese Mt. Fuji is /fujisan/. In speech this presents no problem, but in reading, both /yama/ and /san/ are written as 山, and the reader must decide at each occasion whether the character is to be read as /san/ or /yama/, depending on the context.

In looking at an early text from Japan, it is difficult to know if the author was writing in the Chinese or Japanese language, and even if we can determine that the language was Japanese, it is still often uncertain whether the author was pronouncing a specific word as a Chinese borrowing (e.g., /san/) or as a native Japanese word (e.g., /yama/). Gradually, however, scribes wrote increasingly in Japanese.

The Japanese and Chinese languages are completely unrelated to each other. The structural differences between the two languages presented certain difficulties in borrowing Chinese writing for Japanese. For example, Chinese word order is SVO (subject–verb–object), whereas Japanese word order is SOV (subject–object–verb). The Japanese could, of course, have simply written a text in Japanese word order; the prestige of Chinese, however, was so great that they continued to write the text using Chinese word order, but they sometimes added marks to indicate the order in which the characters were to be read to achieve a correct Japanese word order. Gradually, Japanese word order was adopted.

A further problem is that Chinese has almost no inflectional processes, whereas Japanese has a considerable amount of inflection, particularly verbal suffixes. There were no obvious Chinese characters to use for indicating the Japanese verbal suffixes. For these morphemes, characters were added to text, usually written smaller and between the main characters of the text. These characters were chosen from existing Chinese characters because of their sound with no reference to their meaning; this is an example of the process of phonetic extension.

We saw in chapter 3 that in China the civil service played a strong role in setting standards for writing. In Japan, instead, it was the leisured nobility which played the leading role. In earlier times, literacy was fairly restricted to the upper echelons of Japanese society; they often used writing as means of displaying their erudition and cleverness. At the more fundamental level, they preserved and encouraged character variants and many unusual or obscure spellings. At a more refined level, the nobles took positive delight in writings which presented whimsical problems for the reader. An example is the writing of the number '99' as 白. Ordinarily 白 means 'white', but if we think of the characters for '100' 百 and for '1' 一, we see that 白 is 百 '100' minus the top stroke '1', or '99'. Clearly, this type of writing is done as a learned form of amusement for the writer and reader, not for ready communication.

From time to time, reports have arisen of an early indigenous Japanese writing system called *jindai moji* 'god-age script' which purports to predate the borrowing of Chinese characters. So far, all of these reports have proved to be fraudulent. The best-known example is clearly modelled on the Korean *hankul*, a script invented some thousand years after the introduction of Chinese writing into Japan (Seeley 1991).

4.1.2 *Relevant structure of Japanese*

Japanese verbs (table 4.1) are agglutinative in that the root is accompanied by a number of suffixes.

Word order in Japanese is SOV; note that Chinese word order is SVO. Noun phrases are regularly followed by postpositions indicating case.

The phonemes of Japanese are given in table 4.2. I have transcribed the long vowels as geminates /ii ee/ etc.; some romanization schemes transcribe these with a macron /ī ē/ etc.; /u uu/ are phonetically unrounded [ɯ ɯː]. Certain palatalized consonants exist which are represented as /Cy/.

The basic syllable shape can be summarized with the following formula: (C(y))V(V)(C). A second vowel is always the same as the first, i.e., together they form a phonetically long vowel. Most syllables are open: V, VV, CV, CyV, CVV, CyVV. The only consonants occurring in the coda are /Q/ and /N/.

/N/ is a homorganic nasal when word-medial, and [n] or nasalization on the preceding vowel at the end of a word. In ordinary transcription it is written as <m> before labials, otherwise as <n>: /teNpura/ [tɛmpura] 'tempura (kind of food)', /hoN/ [hon, hõ] 'book'. /Q/ only occurs in word-medial position before a stop or /s/ and is homorganic with the following consonant; i.e., the two are geminate: /yaQta/ [yatta] 'gave', /maQsuguna/ [massɯgɯna] 'straight'.

Table 4.1 Japanese verb forms

kir 'to cut'			
kir-e	imperative	kir-are-ru	passive
kir-u	present	kir-ase-ru	causative
kit-ta	past	kir-ana-i	negative
kit-te	participial	kir-imas-u	polite
kir-eba	provisional	kir-u	infinite

Table 4.2 The phonemes of Japanese

Consonants			*Vowels*	
p b	t d	k g	i ii	u uu
m	n		e ee	o oo
	s z	h		a aa
	r			
w	y			
(/N/ and /Q/ see main text)				

Table 4.3 Japanese romanization differences

Kunreisiki	*Hepburn*	*Phonetic*
si	shi	ʃi
zi	ji	dʒi
ti	chi	tʃi
tu	tsu	tsɯ
di	ji	dʒi
zi	ji	ʒi
du	zu	dzɯ
hu	fu	ɸɯ
syV (sya, syu)	shV (sha, shu)	ʃV (e.g., ʃa, ʃɯ)
zyV	jV	dʒV
tyV	chV	tʃV
dyV	jV	dʒV

There are two common romanizations for Japanese: the *Kunreisiki* (Cabinet Ordinance System) is used in this book since it corresponds more closely with the writing system. The Hepburn system is widely used and corresponds more closely with the pronunciation. For the most part, these two romanizations agree; table 4.3 shows the points at which the two systems differ.

More than the syllable, the **mora** is an important unit in Japanese phonology; poetry, for example, is measured in moræ. A mora in Japanese is a C(y)V sequence within a syllable, or /N/, or /Q/. For example, the word /niQ.poN/ [nip.pon] 'Japan' has two syllables, but four moræ /ni-Q-po-N/ [ni-p-po-n] (with periods showing syllable boundaries, and hyphens showing moraic boundaries). Roughly, each mora takes about the same amount of time to pronounce. Long vowels constitute separate moræ; thus, /taroo/ has three moræ /ta-ro-o/, although only two syllables /ta.roo/.

Japanese has a pitch accent structure which is totally different from the Chinese tonal system. Every word in Japanese has one of two pitch patterns: i.e., with pitch accent or without pitch accent. In words with pitch accent, one mora is marked to indicate the position of the pitch accent, which can fall on any mora in the word. Pitch accent is not marked in Japanese writing although it is indicated in some dictionaries. In borrowing words from Chinese, Japanese paid little attention to Chinese tones.

4.1.3 Borrowing a writing system

Before we examine the problems that had to be solved in adapting Chinese writing to Japanese, let's see how we might adapt Chinese writing to English. To imitate the early Japanese situation, let's imagine that we don't have any way to write English at the moment, and we have no knowledge of writing except Chinese – i.e., no alphabet, etc. The first stage might be that we would simply translate our thoughts into Chinese and write them as a Chinese speaker would. For example, if we wanted

Table 4.4 Chinese sentence

Chinese	xué sheng	shì	yǐn	mài jiu
	學 生	是	飲	麥 酒
	student	be	drink	beer
English	'The students are drinking beer.'			

Table 4.5 Neo-English writing of sentence in table 4.4

Neo-English:	的	學 生	汜	是	兒	飲	迎	麥 酒
	de	*XUÉ SHENG*	sì	SHÌ	er	YǏN	yíng	MÀI JIU
	The	/ʃwejʃʌŋ/	s	are		drink-	ing	beer

to write a sentence such as 'The students are drinking beer', the Chinese translation would be /xuésheng shì yǐn màijiu/ as shown in table 4.4 (example from Inouye 1987). Each syllable is written with one character. Note that two of the Chinese words consist of two syllables and are thus each written with two characters: *xuésheng* and *màijiu*. A word-by-word translation into English is written below the Chinese.

Table 4.5 shows a possible writing of the equivalent sentence in English using Chinese characters. Unlike Japanese, English basic word order is similar to that of Chinese so we do not have a major difference here. We might try reading this sentence aloud as best we can by just substituting English morphemes where possible giving 'Student be drink beer' or 'Student are drink beer'. Although this is definitely not English, we might do it often enough that we got somewhat used to it.

We might borrow certain Chinese words into English; e.g., we might start saying *xuésheng* for 'student' (pronouncing it perhaps as /ˈʃwejˌʃʌŋ/) ending up with a sentence like *The xuéshengs are drinking beer*, which we could write as in table 4.5.

Three distinct types of borrowing are involved in this example. With /ˈʃwejˌʃʌŋ/, the Chinese word is borrowed into English as well as the Chinese characters used for writing this word. This is a semantic borrowing with the characters read as a Chinese word; we could refer to such a word as belonging to the Sino-English vocabulary. (Recall that *Sino-* is a bound form meaning 'Chinese'.) This first type of borrowing is written here in upper-case italics.

The second type of borrowing is shown in the writing for the English word *beer*. Here the characters appropriate for writing the Chinese term for *beer* are borrowed, but not the Chinese term *màijiu*. This is also a semantic borrowing, but with the characters read as an English word. This type of borrowing is indicated by upper-case roman type.

The third type of borrowing is illustrated by <de> and <sì>. These are phonetic borrowings; these characters are chosen because of the word they represent in Chinese. The Chinese word /de/ ([də]) sounds similar to the English word *the*. The meaning of 的 is irrelevant (/de/ is, in fact, a subordinating particle in Chinese). Similarly, the character 汜 represents /sì/ the name of a river in Honan; it is chosen purely for its sound value.

For *are*, we have adopted a more complicated solution. This word is written with two characters: the first is a semantic borrowing, meaning 'be'. The second is a phonetic determinative used to show which of the possible forms of the verb 'be' is intended; since the character 兒 'son, child' is pronounced /èr/ and sounds a bit like *are*, it is used to indicate a reading 'are' rather than 'is', 'am', 'was', or any other form of the verb 'be'. To show the participle ending /-ɪŋ/ of *drinking*, the character 迎 'go to meet' is used. This is used for its phonetic value; in Chinese it is pronounced /yíng/, something like the English suffix /-ɪŋ/. For *drink* and *beer*, the Chinese writing is retained, but they are pronounced as in English.

As you can see, the variety of strategies that we have used to write English has resulted in a system considerably more complex than that of the original Chinese. The complexity of the Japanese writing system arose for similar reasons. You should also be aware that Chinese readers would probably not make sense of our English sentence written in Chinese characters. This is similar for Japanese and Chinese readers reading the other language; sometimes they can identify the topic of the text, but they often go wildly astray. For an amusing presentation of the problem of script adaptation, see 'The Singlish affair' in DeFrancis (1984).

4.1.4 *Japanese writing*

The Japanese borrowed the Chinese writing system some 1700 years ago. At first, they simply wrote in the Chinese language with the Chinese script. Gradually, however, they adapted the Chinese writing system to write Japanese. The adaptation process, together with other changes in the system, has resulted in what is widely regarded as the most complicated writing system in use today (Sproat 2000). Chinese characters continue to be widely used, but usually representing more than one Japanese morpheme (as opposed to Chinese writing where they generally represent only one morpheme). In addition to characters, two moraic systems, known collectively as *kana*, are used as well.

We should state again that characters do not refer to ideas, rather they are ways of writing specific lexical units. Writers choose the appropriate symbols to write the word using the orthographic rules of Japanese. The reader has the task of deciding which sequences of symbols go together and of determining how to interpret the symbols linguistically, relying on the context.

4.1.4.1 *KANJI* 漢字

Chinese characters are known as ***kanji*** (Chin. *hànzì*) in Japanese. Chinese words and the characters for them were borrowed into Japanese at three different periods in time. The Go borrowings were early, before the sixth century NEW, from the southern Wú dialect of Chinese. The sixth to ninth centuries saw the Kan borrowings, primarily from Chang An, the capital of the Tang dynasty. In the fourteenth century, during the Tang and Song dynasties, a few terms, particularly associated with Zen Buddhism, are known as Too-Soo borrowings. The character 行 has three different pronunciations, /gyoo/, /koo/, and /an/, which are the result of independent borrowings from different time periods.

Table 4.6 Imaginary example of borrowing a Chinese character to write English

	Source		*Target*		
	Meaning	*Pronunciation*	*Meaning*	*Pronunciation*	*Example*
a. semantic *on*	L1	L1	'law'	/fɑ/	<She studies 法.> /ʃi stʌdiz fɑ/
b. semantic *kun*	L1	L2	'law'	/lɑ/	<She studies 法.> /ʃi stʌdiz lɑ/
c. phonetic *on*	—	L1	—	/fɑ/	<My 法 ther is ill.> /maj fɑðəɹ ɪz ɪl/
d. phonetic *kun*	—	L2	—	/lɑ/	<法 ma> /lɑmə/ (Buddhist monk)

4.1.4.1.1 KUN- *AND* ON-*READINGS*

In the example above in §4.1.3, we had two types of semantic borrowings. With the word for 'students', the Chinese term was borrowed, and thus 學生 was pronounced as a Sino-English word borrowed from Chinese /ˈʃwejˌʃʌŋ/. In this situation, the characters can be said to be given an ***on*-reading**. In the second type of semantic borrowing, illustrated by 'beer', the Chinese characters are borrowed, but they are pronounced as a native English word. In this situation, the characters can be said to be given a ***kun*-reading.**

The distinction of *kun-* and *on*-readings is an important one in Japanese. To introduce these notions fully, we will give a further imaginary example from our Neo-English writing (table 4.6). We will call the borrowing language L2 (Neo-English), and the language borrowed from L1 (Chinese).

Suppose that Neo-English (L2) borrowed the Chinese (L1) word /fǎ/ meaning 'law' along with its Chinese character 法. We have four possibilities depending on the details of the borrowing. (In the dialect of English used here, *law* is pronounced /lɑ/.)

In the first case (a), the character is said to have a **semantic *on*-reading.** The borrowing is semantic with the Chinese term borrowed into English as /fɑ/ with the meaning 'law' (like /ˈʃwejˌʃʌŋ/ above). In the second case (b), the character is said to have a **semantic *kun*-reading**; here the character is borrowed, but used for the native English semantically equivalent term *law* (like *beer* above).

In Japanese, the terms *kun* and *on* normally refer only to semantic borrowings; however, they could also be applied in a parallel fashion to phonetic borrowings. To continue our example with /fɑ/, examine situation (c). Here the Chinese character for /fǎ/ 'law' was borrowed into English, only for its sound, without regard to its meaning. We might then use it to write any occurrence of /fɑ/ in English, such as in the first syllable of *father*. This would be an example of a phonetic *on*-reading: phonetic because it is used for its sound value only, and *on* because it is based on its pronunciation in L1.

A **phonetic** ***kun*** is similar to a **phonetic** ***on***, but based on the L2 word. First, the character is borrowed into L2 and given a *kun*-reading – in our example /lɑ/ 'law'. Then, this use of the character undergoes **phonetic extension**, so that it is used for the same sound in other words. In example (d), we see that the character's use for writing /lɑ/ 'law' has been extended to other words with the sound /lɑ/, in this case, the first syllable of *lama*.

This fourfold typology of borrowing is complex, but understanding it thoroughly will repay the effort.

4.1.4.1.2 READING CHARACTERS IN JAPANESE

Turning now to Japanese, a *kun*-reading is a character used with the pronunciation of a native Japanese word (NJ), and an *on*-reading is a character used for a word borrowed from Chinese into Japanese (SJ [for Sino-Japanese]) retaining an approximation of its Chinese pronunciation. In our first two examples, *kimono* and *tyakusyu*, the character 着 has both a *kun-* and an *on*-reading. In *kimono*, the first part *ki-* is written with a semantic *kun*; the Chinese character for /jáu/ 'put' was borrowed and used for the native Japanese word /ki/ with approximately the same meaning, 'wear'. The second part *-mono* is written with a character which is also a semantic *kun*; here the Chinese character for /wù/ 'thing' was borrowed and used for the semantically corresponding native Japanese word /mono/. Note that the fact that /mono/ in Japanese has two syllables, but is written with only one character, is not considered significant. In the process of borrowing Chinese writing into Japanese, the one-to-one relationship between character and syllable in Chinese was undone.

/kimono/ 'clothing' 着物

	着	物
	/ki/ 'wear' NJ	/mono/ 'thing' NJ
Ch.	/jáu/ 'put'	/wù/ 'thing, creature'
	semantic kun	*semantic kun*

In *tyakusyu* 'start' [tʃakɯʃɯ] (literally 'put hand'), the first part *tyaku-* 'put' is written with the same character as we found above for *ki-*. Here, this character has a semantic *on*-reading; the Chinese word /jáu/ 'put' was borrowed into Japanese with the pronunciation /tyaku/ (remember that these borrowings took place centuries ago when both Chinese and Japanese were pronounced differently). The second character is also a semantic *on* since the Chinese word /shǒu/ was borrowed into Japanese with the pronunciation /syu/ [ʃɯ]. (Note that 手 also has a *kun*-reading as /te/, the native Japanese word for 'hand'.)

/tyakusyu/ 'start' 着手

	着	手	
	/tyaku/ 'put' SJ	/syu/ 'hand' SJ	(also NJ /te/ 'hand')
Ch.	/jáu/ 'put'	/shǒu/ 'hand'	
	semantic on	*semantic on*	(*semantic kun*)

Table 4.7 Four characters and their *kun-* and *on-*readings

着				
kun	/ki/	'wear'	NJ	
on	/tyaku/	'put'	SJ	Ch. /jáu/
物				
kun	/mono/	'thing'	NJ	
on	/butu/	'thing'	SJ	Ch. /wù/
手				
kun	/te/	'hand'	NJ	
on	/syu/	'hand'	SJ	Ch. /shǒu/
動				
kun	/ugo/	'move'	NJ	
on	/doo/	'move'	SJ	Ch. /dù/

In *doobutu* 'animal' [doːbɯtsɯ] (literally 'moving thing'), the first character is a semantic *on* since it represents the Sino-Japanese word /doo/ 'move'. (Note that 動 also has a *kun*-reading as /ugo/ 'move'.) The second character in *doobutu* is the same one that we met earlier as the second character in *kimono*, but this time with a *on*-reading *butu*.

/doobutu/ 'animal' 動物

	動		物
	/doo/ 'move' SJ	(also NJ /ugo/)	/butu/ 'thing' SJ
Ch.	/dù/ 'move'		/wù/ 'thing'
	semantic on	(*semantic kun*)	*semantic on*

Table 4.7 shows the *kun-* and *on*-readings of the four characters that we have used in these examples. As we said earlier, understanding *kun-* and *on*-readings takes a bit of work. Remember that characters in Japanese can usually be read in more than one way. There are native Japanese words, and words borrowed from Chinese called Sino-Japanese. *Kun*-readings are native Japanese words, and *on*-readings are Sino-Japanese words. Semantic borrowings are based on meaning, and phonetic borrowings are based on sound.

Up to now, we have primarily looked at semantic borrowings in Japanese; these are the only ones with which the terms *kun* and *on* are used in traditional Japanese studies, and phonetic borrowings are less common than semantic borrowings. A **phonetic *on*** is the use of a character with its Chinese pronunciation for a similar-sounding morpheme in Japanese. An example of this is the use of the Chinese character 天 'sky' /tiān/ as part of the word for 'oven' 天火 /teNpi/ because of its sound.

A **phonetic *kun*** is the phonetic extension of a Japanese-based pronunciation of a character to a different, but similar-sounding, morpheme. In early Japanese, the word for 'crane' and a perfective verbal morpheme had the same sound /turu/ [tsɯrɯ]. The Chinese character 鶴 'crane' (Ch. /hè/) was first borrowed as a *kun* reading for the Japanese morpheme /turu/ 'crane' in early Japanese, and then extended to the homophonous perfective morpheme /turu/ (Seeley 1991). This writing for the perfective marker has been lost, and it is written with *hiragana* today.

When Japanese readers encounter a character, they must decide whether the *kun-* or *on*-reading is appropriate given the context; further, there are often more than one *kun-* or *on*-readings. Taylor and Taylor (1995) state that altogether the character 生 has some twelve readings officially sanctioned by the government guidelines, plus seven unofficial but commonly used readings, as well as some eighty further rare and unusual readings.

Consider how the symbol <2> is pronounced in English. We would normally say *two*. However, read the following examples aloud, and consider the importance of context: *12*, *21*, $\frac{1}{2}$, *2nd*, x^2. This kind of contextually determined variation exists in English, but it is limited to only a few symbols. Japanese is an entire writing system of such variation (thanks to J. J. Chew for this analogy).

4.1.4.1.3 OTHER TYPES OF WRITING

Words of more than one syllable written with phonetic extension are known as ***ateji*** (table 4.8); these are written with characters which were chosen for their phonetic value only. In the past, *ateji* were commonly found in foreign names; most of these were removed in the reforms after the Second World War (see §4.1.5), and foreign words are now written in *katakana* (see below). In the example, the characters of /sewa/ were chosen for their pronunciation, not for their meaning.

Native Japanese words written with more than one character which are chosen for their semantic value only (semantic extension) are known as ***jukujikun*** (table 4.9). In the example, /otona/ 'adult' is written with the characters meaning 'big person'.

Some characters have been invented in Japan and did not exist in Chinese; they are known as ***kokuji*** (table 4.10).

Table 4.8 Ateji

世話	/sewa/	'care'
世	/se/	'world'
話	/wa/	'talk'

Table 4.9 Jukujikun

大人	/otona/	'adult'
大	/dai, oo/	'big'
人	/zin, hito/	'person' [dʒin, çi̥to]

Table 4.10 Kokuji

働	/hataraki/	'work, effect'
峠	/tooge/	'mountain pass'
躾	/situke/ [ʃitsɯke]	'upbringing'

Table 4.11 Different simplifications in Japan and China

	Chinese traditional	*Japanese*	*Chinese simplified*
'Buddha'	佛	仏	佛
'door'	門	門	门
'country'	國	国	国
'price'	價	価	价

Table 4.12 How /nippon/ 'Japan' can be written in three different ways (/Q/ is realized as gemination of the following consonant)

kanji	/niQpoN/	日本
hiragana	<ni-Q-po-N>	にっぽん
katakana	<ni-Q-po-N>	ニッポン

Some characters have been simplified in Japan. These simplifications may or may not be the same as the simplified characters of China. Thus, the character for 'Buddha' has been simplified in Japanese, but not in Chinese; 'door' has been simplified in Chinese, but not in Japanese. 'Country' has the same simplification in Japanese and Chinese, but 'price' has different simplifications in Japanese and Chinese (table 4.11).

4.1.4.2 *KANA* 仮名

The word for 'Japan' can be written in three ways in Japanese (table 4.12). The first way is with *kanji*, and the other two are with one of the two additional scripts used in Japanese: either ***hiragana*** 'plain *kana*' ひらがな (平仮名) or ***katakana*** 'side *kana*' カタカナ (片仮名); collectively, *hiragana* and *katakana* are known as ***kana***. The etymology of the word *kana* in this context is disputed.

Although the *kana* scripts are usually called syllabaries, they are in fact moraic systems. Each symbol in the *kana* scripts represents one mora. Most of these are CV sequences, but final /N/ or /Q/ count as separate moræ, and vowel length adds a mora. Recall that a mora is a CV unit, a second V (additional vowel length), or a codal C.

4.1.4.2.1 HISTORICAL DEVELOPMENT OF KANA

The text *Man'yooshuu* 'Ten Thousand Leaves' from the eighth century NEW had both morphographic (mostly with *kun*-readings) and phonographic use of characters. Characters were commonly used for both phonetic *kun*- and phonetic *on*-readings. From phonetic uses such as this, *kana* developed.

The early texts written in the Chinese style lacked the affixes present in Japanese. The *katakana* symbols arose from abbreviated characters inserted into academic and administrative texts particularly to indicate the Japanese affixes which were not

Table 4.13 The *kanji* sources for some *hiragana* and *katakana* symbols

Katakana	*Source character*		Hiragana	*Source character*	
フ	不	/hu/	ふ	不	/hu/
テ	天	/te/	て	天	/te/
カ	加	/ka/	あ	安	/a/
チ	千	/ti/	の	乃	/no/

represented in the Chinese-style texts. In general, the *katakana* symbols were formed by writing only a part of a character (table 4.13); the *hiragana* and *katakana* forms are not always derived from the same original character. The *hiragana* symbols arose from the use of characters written cursively in informal and private texts to indicate pronunciation generally.

Over time, *katakana* and *hiragana* developed as similar parallel systems but were used in different contexts.

4.1.4.2.2 MODERN KANA

The complete set of *kana* is shown in table 4.14: *hiragana* in the upper row; *katakana* in the second row. The two *kana* systems are structurally alike. Any Japanese utterance can be written in either *hiragana* or *katakana*, and any utterance in one can be converted into the other.

The diacritic <゛> is used to change a symbol from voiceless to voiced: *hiragana* き <ki> ぎ <gi>, *katakana* キギ. The diacritic <゜> is used to change the <h> series of symbols to the <p> series: *hiragana* ほ <ho> ぽ <po>; *katakana* ホポ; and the voiced diacritic <゛> used with <h> gives the <b> series: *hiragana* ほ <ho> ぼ <bo>, *katakana* ホボ. These diacritics are used for both *hiragana* and *katakana*. Recall that the sequence /tu/ is pronounced [tsɯ], /du/ is pronounced [dzɯ], and /hu/ is pronounced [ɸɯ]. The consonants /s, z, t, d/ are pronounced as [ʃ, dʒ, tʃ, dʒ] respectively when they occur before /i/ or /y/.

The symbol for /Q/ is a smaller version of the symbols for /tu/: *hiragana* /tu/ つ /Q/ っ, *katakana* /tu/ ツ /Q/ ッ.

The sound /y/ occurs only before the vowels /a u o/. Complex onsets with /y/ as the second element occur after all phonemes except /y/ and /w/: e.g., /kya, hyu, ryo/. The clusters with /y/ are written as <Ci_{yV}>, with the <$_{yV}$>-symbol written slightly smaller. Thus, /kyu/ is written as <ki_{yu}> きゅ in *hiragana*, and as キュ in *katakana*, and /nyo/ is written as <ni_{yo}> によ or in *katakana* ニョ.

In *hiragana*, long vowels are written by adding the appropriate single vowel symbol: /okaasan/ 'mother' おかあさん <o-ka-a-sa-n>, /oniisan/ 'older brother' おにいさん <o-ni-i-sa-n>. Most words with /oo/ are written as <ou>: /doozo/ 'please' どうぞ <do-u-zo>, /kinoo/ 'yesterday' きのう <ki-no-u>. However, a few words with /oo/ are written as <oo>: /ooi/ 'many' おおい <o-o-i>, /too/ 'ten' とお <to-o>. You should realize that most of these words could also be written using *kanji*, or a mixture of *kanji* and *hiragana*: *okaasan* お母さん, *oniisan* お兄さん, *kinoo* 昨日, *ooi* 多い, *too* 十.

Table 4.14 The complete *kana* list. *Hiragana* are given above the equivalent *katakana*

あ	い	う	え	お					
ア	イ	ウ	エ	オ					
a	i	u	e	o					
ぱ	ぴ	ぷ	ぺ	ぽ	ば	び	ぶ	べ	ぼ
パ	ピ	プ	ペ	ポ	バ	ビ	ブ	ベ	ボ
pa	pi	pu	pe	po	ba	bi	bu	be	bo
た	ち	つ	て	と	だ	ぢ	づ	で	ど
タ	チ	ツ	テ	ト	ダ	ヂ	ヅ	デ	ド
ta	ti	tu	te	to	da	di	du	de	do
か	き	く	け	こ	が	ぎ	ぐ	げ	ご
カ	キ	ク	ケ	コ	ガ	ギ	グ	ゲ	ゴ
ka	ki	ku	ke	ko	ga	gi	gu	ge	go
さ	し	す	せ	そ	ざ	じ	ず	ぜ	ぞ
サ	シ	ス	セ	ソ	ザ	ジ	ズ	ゼ	ゾ
sa	si	su	se	so	za	zi	zu	ze	zo
な	に	ぬ	ね	の	ま	み	む	め	も
ナ	ニ	ヌ	ネ	ノ	マ	ミ	ム	メ	モ
na	ni	nu	ne	no	ma	mi	mu	me	mo
は	ひ	ふ	へ	ほ	ら	り	る	れ	ろ
ハ	ヒ	フ	ヘ	ホ	ラ	リ	ル	レ	ロ
ha	hi	hu	he	ho	ra	ri	ru	re	ro
や		ゆ		よ	わ				を
ヤ		ユ		ヨ	ワ				ヲ
ya		yu		yo	wa				wo
ん		つ							
ン		ツ							
N		Q							

ぴゃ	ぴゅ	ぴょ	びゃ	びゅ	びょ
ピャ	ピュ	ピョ	ビャ	ビュ	ビョ
pya	pyu	pyo	bya	byu	byo
ちゃ	ちゅ	ちょ	ぢゃ	ぢゅ	ぢょ
チャ	チュ	チョ	ヂャ	ヂュ	ヂョ
tya	tyu	tyo	dya	dyu	dyo
きゃ	きゅ	きょ	ぎゃ	ぎゅ	ぎょ
キャ	キュ	キョ	ギャ	ギュ	ギョ
kya	kyu	kyo	gya	gyu	gyo

[cont'd]

Table 4.14 (*Cont'd*)

しゃ	しゅ	しょ	じゃ	じゅ	じょ
シャ	シュ	ショ	ジャ	ジュ	ジョ
sya	syu	syo	zya	zyu	zyo
にゃ	にゅ	にょ	みゃ	みゅ	みょ
ニャ	ニュ	ニョ	ミャ	ミュ	ミョ
nya	nyu	nyo	mya	myu	myo
ひゃ	ひゅ	ひょ	りゃ	りゅ	りょ
ヒャ	ヒュ	ヒョ	リャ	リュ	リョ
hya	hyu	hyo	rya	ryu	ryo

Table 4.15 Examples showing how non-Japanese sounds are written in borrowed words

[soɸaa]	'sofa'	ソファー	<so-hu $_{a}$-:>
[wiin]	'Vienna'	ウィーン	<u $_{i}$-:-N>
[ʃerii]	'sherry'	シェリー	<si $_{e}$-ri-:>
[ɸonto]	'font'	フォント	<hu $_{o}$-N-to>

In *katakana*, the same rules for writing long vowels apply as with *hiragana*, but only for words of Japanese origin: *okaasan* オカアサン, *oniisan* オニイサン, *doozo* ドウゾ, *ooi* オオイ, *too* トオ. For words of foreign origin, vowel length for any vowel is indicated by a horizontal bar (written as a vertical stroke in vertical writing and transcribed here as <:>): /aisukuriimu/ 'ice cream' アイスクリーム, /kaado/ '(credit) card' カード, /suupu/ 'soup' スープ, /nooto/ 'notebook' ノート, /sooseezi/ 'sausage' ソーセージ.

To transcribe foreign words in *katakana*, certain conventions have been adopted (table 4.15). As an example, take the English word *disco*, which has been borrowed into Japanese as /disuko/. Referring to table 4.14, we see that the basic *kana* system has no way of writing [di]; to write <di> would be to indicate a pronunciation of [dʒi]. The solution for this is somewhat like the writing of the /CyV/ clusters. A *kana* symbol with the correct consonant sound is first written, followed by the appropriate vowel symbol, written small. For this sound, the *kana* symbol for /de/ is used, followed by a small version of the symbol for /i/: ディスコ <de $_{i}$-su-ko>; thus, <de $_{i}$ > is the way to write /di/. To write an initial /w/, the vowel symbol for /u/ is used. Other examples of this type of writing are shown in table 4.15.

Three of the postpositions are written with irregular *hiragana* (table 4.16).

The careful reader will have noted that in five cases, there are alternative ways of writing certain moræ (the *hiragana* forms are given in table 4.17; the *katakana* equivalents would work the same way). The use of these phonetically equivalent forms is lexically determined.

Hiragana 'plain *kana*' has also been called *onnade* 'woman's hand' from its earlier extensive use in literature for women. In Japanese today, it is used for inflectional endings and grammatical particles, and for many native Japanese words.

Table 4.16 Irregular *hiragana*

/wa/	topic marker	は	(normally used for <ha>)
/e/	direction	へ	(normally used for <he>)
/o/	direct object	を	(formerly used for <wo>)

Table 4.17 Potential ambiguities in writing *hiragana*

[zu]	<du>	づ	or	<zu>	ず
[dzi]	<di>	ぢ	or	<zi>	じ
[dʒa]	<dya>	ぢゃ	or	<zya>	じゃ
[dʒu]	<dyu>	ぢゅ	or	<zyu>	じゅ
[dʒo]	<dyo>	ぢょ	or	<zyo>	じょ

Table 4.18 Examples of *katakana* writing

ハーモニカ	/haamonika/	'harmonica'	English borrowing
カエル	/kaeru/	'frog'	animal
ハツカネズミ	/hatukanezumi/	'mouse'	animal
リンゴ	/riNgo/	'apple'	plant
ワンワン	/waNwaN/	'bow-wow'	onomatopoetic
パタン	/pataN/	'sound of slamming'	onomatopoetic
カネ オクレ	/kane okure/	'Send money!'	telegram

Table 4.19 'Kimono' written in *kanji* (below) and in *furigana* (above)

き	もの
着	物
ki	mono

Katakana 'side *kana*' is used for emphasis, non-Chinese loanwords, Chinese loanwords where the *kanji* would be used but for some reason is missing, names of many plants and animals, onomatopoetic words, and telegrams (table 4.18). In modern-day Japan, the use of *katakana* is increasing; it is frequently found in computer work, in filling out forms, in new trade names, and in colloquial expressions. In some dictionaries, *kun*-readings are given in *hiragana*, and *on*-readings in *katakana*.

A special use of *hiragana* is called *furigana*, which is written small next to characters to indicate the pronunciation. In earlier times, when a large number of *kanji* were used, *furigana* were used extensively in popular publications such as newspapers, sometimes to the point where every character was accompanied by *furigana*. In the example in table 4.19 of the word *kimono*, the *furigana* show that the first character is pronounced /ki/ and the second /mono/.

A braille version of Japanese based on *kana* is available for people unable to see ordinary text. *Kanji* are not used in the braille system.

4.1.4.3 SHORT EXAMPLE SENTENCE

Japanese today is normally written in a mixture of *kanji* and *kana*. Although it is possible to use *kana* only, this is normally done only in special cases such as in material for children or foreigners. For a Japanese person to write only in *kana* would be regarded as bizarre, conveying a strong impression of a lack of education.

Word boundaries are not usually written in Japanese; however, *kanji* frequently signals the beginning of a word with *hiragana* representing a suffix or postposition.

The example text in table 4.20 shows the typical mixture of *kanji* (K), *hiragana* (hg), and *katakana* (kk); subsequent abbreviations of the same type of symbol are omitted. The proper name *Hanako* and the verb stem /hatara/ are written in *kanji*. The postpositions /wa/ and /de/ are written in *hiragana* (note the special *hiragana* used for /wa/), as well as the suffixes /ite-iru/ and the common verb /desu/. The English borrowing /biru/ 'building' is written in *katakana*. The English phrase *office lady*, in the meaning 'female clerical employee', has been borrowed as an acronym, written with the Roman (rom) letters <OL> and pronounced as a sequence of the two letters /ooeru/ (Japanese pronunciation of English /ˈow ˌɛl/). A similar example to the last one is <OB> for /oobii/ 'alumnus' derived from English *old boy*.

Like Chinese, Japanese was first written in vertical columns starting at the top right corner of the page; in modern times, horizontal writing from left to right (as in the example in table 4.20) has become very common although vertical writing is still used, particularly for more formal and traditional writing. Signs on a truck often have the names of the company written differently on each side, with the writing on each side starting at the front. Table 4.21 shows the traditional reading order, starting at the top right.

Table 4.20 Example sentence in ordinary Japanese writing (K = *kanji*; hg = *hiragana*; kk = *katakana*; rom = Roman)

K	hg			kk		hg	K	hg				rom		hg	
花子	は	あ	の	ビ	ル	で	働	い	て	い	る	O	L	で	す
Hanako	wa	a	no	biru		de	hatara-i-		te-	i-	ru	ooeru		de	su
Hanako	topic	that		building		at	work-ing					OL		is	

'Hanako is an OL (office lady) working in that building' (Shibatani 1990)

Table 4.21 The traditional way of arranging Japanese characters on a page

9	5	1
10	6	2
11	7	3
12	8	4

4.1.5 Writing reform in Japan

From the mid-twentieth century, many proposals for the simplification of the Japanese writing system have been proposed. Such proposals have been resisted strongly by conservatives desiring to retain the older system. After the Second World War, the time was felt to be particularly ripe for change. In 1949, the government created the *Kokugo Singikai* 'National Language Council' which has issued various instructions about writing for schools and the public at large. Until the mid-twentieth century, virtually any Chinese character could be borrowed into Japanese. In 1981, the Kokugo Singikai issued a list of only 1945 characters for general use and 284 further ones for writing proper names. Older variants of *kanji* and *kana* were dropped. The government also established an official list of *kun-* and *on*-readings, eliminating many less common readings. Needless to say, not everyone follows the government guidelines strictly. Newspapers and most other publications generally follow the official guidelines, and about 99 per cent of the characters in their text is from the official list, but for the other 1 per cent, they need some 1000–1500 characters for proper names. Individuals are more likely to stray from the official guidelines. Frequently, *hiragana* is used if the writer cannot think of the appropriate *kanji*, and writers frequently use *kanji* not on the list, especially for proper names. The older *hiragana* variants might be found on the sign of a country inn where they would convey a traditional, rustic flavour.

Smith and Schmidt (1996) investigated stereotypical attitudes towards the different ways of writing used in Japanese (table 4.22). They investigated the proportion of script type found in several varieties of popular fiction. In general, the stereotypes were confirmed. Comic books and science fiction, aimed at a young audience, had fewer *kanji* and more *katakana*. Business and mystery novels, aimed at adult men, had more *kanji* and less *katakana*. Romance novels, aimed at women, had a greater proportion of *hiragana*.

The government reforms of the mid-twentieth century left the traditional Japanese writing system essentially intact with its mixture of *kanji* and *kana*. The intention of the reforms was a containment of diversity, rather than a thoroughgoing revision of the writing system. It would, of course, be possible to write Japanese entirely in *hiragana* or *katakana* or Roman letters. The writing system, however, is so strongly identified with the Japanese culture that there is little movement at present for a major reformation.

After the reforms of the mid-twentieth century, there was a nationwide increase in literacy reported. Unger (1996) argues that this was due primarily 'to the reform of

Table 4.22 The social connotations of *kanji*, *hiragana*, and *katakana*

	Writer/reader features	*Stylistic features*
kanji	male, middle-aged and older	erudition
hiragana	female, young	softness or femininity
katakana	young, especially male	modernity; pop culture

the EDUCATIONAL system, not the WRITING system. Greater opportunities for women, . . . expansion in high school enrolments, . . . liberalisation of university admission . . . – these were the changes that made a difference' (p. 123; Unger's emphasis).

When computers were first introduced, they required simple input and output methods. In general, *katakana* was used, and at first it seemed as if computing would force the abandonment of characters. In a short time, however, computers became more sophisticated and accommodating. Today, Japanese can be written on a computer with only a small amount of inconvenience (in comparison to entering Roman text). Technology adapted to the writing system, rather than the reverse. Typically the keyboard is set up to accommodate either *kana* or Roman input. The word processor then shows possible *kanji* forms for the input, often examining the context and trying to guess the most likely *kanji* form, presenting it first along with other possibilities; the author then selects the suggested form or chooses another form.

4.1.6 *Psychology of writing in Japanese*

A good deal of research has been done on reading and writing Japanese. For example, Paradis et al. (1985) investigated acquired dyslexia (disability in reading) and dysgraphia (disability in writing) among Japanese native speaker-writers. He found that the ability to use *kana* and *kanji* were independent, and that any combination of difficulties could arise. For example, a person might lose the ability to read *kana*, but retain the ability to read *kanji*, or vice versa, or be able to write one, but not the other.

4.2 Korean

4.2.1 *Background and history*

Korean is spoken by about 70 million people living in North and South Korea, as well as by about five million speakers overseas. The genetic relationship of Korean is not certain. Quite likely it is related to the Altaic (Manchu, Mongolian, Turkic) languages, and possibly to Japanese. Most dialects are mutually intelligible. The standard dialect in the south is that of Seoul, and in the north that of Phyengyang (Sohm 1997).

Some of the phenomena mentioned earlier about Japanese writing have Korean parallels. Part of the reason for this is that it was the Koreans who first took Chinese writing to Japan. More importantly, both countries were strongly influenced by Chinese culture over many centuries. Further, the linguistic structures of Japanese and Korean are similar, and thus both languages faced similar problems in adapting the Chinese writing system.

Korean contact with China was very early; according to King (1996) the Koreans were aware of Chinese writing from before Han times (i.e., before the second century OLD). Although earlier examples of writing in Chinese are found in Korea, the first evidence of writing in the Korean language is an inscription on a stone stele dated to

414 NEW. The writing is entirely in Chinese characters, but several characters on the stele are used phonetically to write Korean names.

In addition to borrowing the writing system, Korean borrowed a large number of words from Chinese; the Sino-Korean vocabulary is still sizeable in modern Korean. In a fashion similar to Japan, Koreans first simply wrote in the Chinese language using Chinese characters. Gradually, the writing was adapted to writing the Korean language using characters. In a form known as ***itwu*** 'clerical writing', the Sino-Korean words continued to be written with their Chinese characters, and certain characters were used for writing native Korean words and the verbal suffixes (phonetic *kun*); Korean word order was used. The earliest surviving *itwu* text is from 754 NEW. In 958 NEW, the Korean civil service was formed, modelled on the Chinese institution; its documents were written in *itwu*, which remained the standard way of writing Korean for centuries, particularly for official, legal, and administrative purposes until it was officially discontinued in 1894.

A second type of writing, known as ***hyangchal*** 'local letters', emerged, reminiscent of the Japanese *man'yogana* type of writing in which the characters are primarily used for their phonetic value; Korean word order was used. *Hyangchal* was mostly used for writing lyric poetry; twenty-five such poems have survived.

A third type of writing was ***kwukyel*** 'oral formulæ', in which simplified forms of characters were developed for writing the Korean grammatical morphemes; Chinese word order was used. This was primarily used for annotating Confucian and Buddhist texts written in Chinese. We can easily see a parallel with Japanese *kana* here.

4.2.2 *Korean lexicon*

The Korean lexicon can be divided into three large groups: native Korean words, Sino-Korean borrowings, and borrowings from other languages (especially recent borrowings from English). During 1910–45, when Japan ruled Korea, many Japanese words were borrowed, but subsequently, there has been a conscious effort to avoid Japanese words. The Sino-Korean words are monosyllabic; native Korean words often have polysyllabic morphemes. The Sino-Korean vocabulary has connotations of tradition, education, and formality; native Korean words have either neutral connotations or ones of informality, warmth, and friendliness. There are some homophones in Korean, but not nearly so many as in Japanese or Chinese.

4.2.3 *Phonology of Korean*

Korean has 21 vowels and 19 consonants. There are two common romanizations for transcribing Korean. The Yale system is used here because it agrees well with the *hankul* writing scheme which we will discuss shortly; in linguistic terms, the Yale system is a deep system, i.e., at a morphophonemic level. The other system, the McCune–Reischauer (M–R) system, is shallower, more at the phonetic level, showing the pronunciation more clearly. The Yale system tends to be used in linguistic publications, and M–R in more popular writing. Both systems are shown in table 4.23. The rules for the M–R system are complex and, for certain contexts, involve other symbols; only the main symbol for each sound is given here.

Table 4.23 The Yale and McCune–Reischauer systems of romanizing Korean; the IPA column at the left shows the phonetic pronunciation (U = unrounded; R = rounded)

IPA				*Yale*				*M–R*			
Front		*Back*		*Front*		*Back*		*Front*		*Back*	
U	*R*	*U*	*R*	*U*	*R*	*U*	*R*	*U*	*R*	*U*	*R*
Vowels											
i	y	ɨ	u	i	wi	u	wu	i	wi	ŭ	u
e	ø	ə	o	ey	woy	e	o	e	oe	ŏ	o
æ		a		ay		a		ae		a	
Consonants											
p	t	tʃ	k	p	t	c	k	p	t	ch	k
p^h	t^h	tʃ^h	k^h	ph	th	ch	kh	p'	t'	ch'	k'
p*	t*	tʃ*	k*	pp	tt	cc	kk	pp	tt	cc	kk
	s		h		s		h		s		h
	s*				ss				ss		
m	n		ŋ	m	n		ng	m	n		ng
	l				l				l		
w		j		w		y		w		y	

Korean has three classes of obstruents: plain, aspirated, and tense. In the consonant chart in table 4.23, the plain stops are given in the top row, the aspirated stops in the second row with the /^{h}/ diacritic, and the tense stops are given in the third row with a diacritic /*/. The fricatives /s s*/ similarly have a plain–tense difference.

The basic syllable shape is (C)V(C)(C). About 2000 syllable shapes occur. Although the glides /w/ and /y/ are included with the consonants here, the writing system treats them as part of the vowel nucleus, i.e., as the glide in a diphthong.

4.2.4 Hankul

In the fifteenth century NEW, a completely new alphabet known as ***hankul*** ['hangul] was developed for writing Korean. This alphabet is attributed to King Seycong, who took a strong personal interest in its development. The original name of the alphabet was *hwunmin cengum* 訓民正音 (훈민졍귬) 'The correct sounds for the instruction of the people'. In North Korean, it is referred to as *chosenkul* 'Korean script'. In South Korea, the name *hankul* 'Korean script' has been used since *ca.* 1900.

Hankul is an example of an invented script. Writing was well known to the Koreans; they had, after all, been writing for centuries. One question is whether or not the development of *hankul* was influenced by other alphabetic scripts. Given that Buddhism was well established in Korea at the time, the inventor of *hankul* would likely have been aware of the Indian scripts (see chapter 11) traditionally associated with Buddhist texts. Further, the Mongolian script was used not far to the north. Any or all of these scripts might have provided some inspiration for the

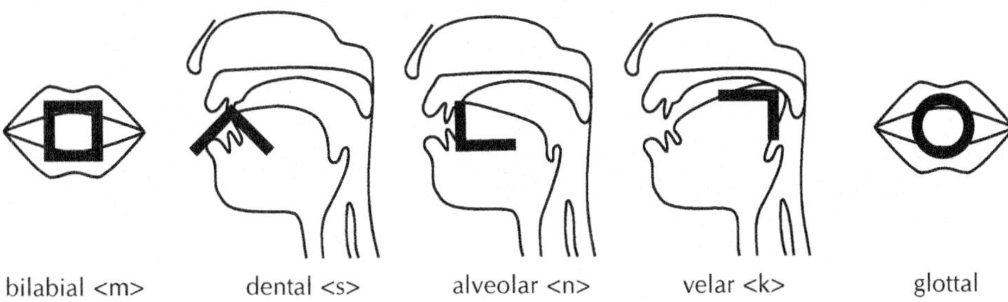

Figure 4.1 The phonetic rationale for the consonant shapes in *hankul*

creation of *hankul*, but there is nothing specific about the shapes of the symbols nor about the conventions of their use which argues clearly for such a connection.

For some time, scholars had thought that the shapes of the consonant symbols might have been based on articulatory positions. Finally, in 1940, a fifteenth-century document *Hwunmin Cengum Haylyey* 'Explanations and examples of the correct sounds for the instruction of the people' was discovered in which the symbols are described as 'depicting the outlines of the forms they represent' (Ahn 1997). Figure 4.1 shows what is meant.

The velar <k> symbol shows the back of the tongue raised to the velum. The alveolar <n> symbol shows the tip of the tongue raised to the alveolar ridge. The dental <s> is said to show the outline of a tooth (Ahn 1997; I must confess, however, that this explanation is not entirely clear to me). The symbol for bilabial <m> shows an open mouth; it is also the same as the Chinese character for 'mouth'. The circular symbol is now used to show the absence of an onset consonant; however, Ahn (1997) suggests that it may have represented a velar fricative at an earlier time. In any case, the circle was chosen because it represents the open vocal folds (a glottal opening). The vowel symbols are said to have been modelled on the neo-Confucian theories of *yang* and *yin*, combining notions of heaven, earth, and man; Martin (1997) suspects that this explanation for the vowels 'may have been elaborated to lend a scholarly air of legitimacy to a system already devised'.

Ledyard (1997) has considered some similarities between the shapes of the *hankul* symbols and those of the 'Phags-pa script. 'Phags-pa is a very square-looking script derived from Tibetan writing (chapter 11). In the thirteenth century NEW during the reign of the Mongolian emperor Kubla Khan, it was used for writing all the major languages of his empire: Tibetan, Uighur, Mongolian, and Chinese. Ledyard concludes, however, that 'the role of the 'Phags-pa script . . . is of relatively modest importance as compared to Seycong's general language strategy and his own creativity and originality'.

Some of the unique features (based on King 1996) of *hankul* are that:

1 It is the only alphabetic script to be written in syllable blocks.
2 The shape of the symbols was original; those for the consonants were based on the shapes of the vocal tract.
3 It was very well designed and is based on an elaborately worked out theory of fifteenth-century Korean phonology.
4 It uses a diacritic structure to derive symbols for phonetically related sounds.

The shapes of *hankul* as originally proposed were quite regular and geometric. Quite soon, the shapes were modified to be more easily written with a brush. Three phonemes have disappeared from the language, and the symbols for these sounds are no longer used.

4.2.5 *Structure of* hankul

The current *hankul* system is given in table 4.24 with the Yale romanization. Each *hankul* letter is a grapheme.

Generally, we can see that the symbols for the aspirated stops are those for the plain stops with an added stroke. The symbols for the tense stops and tense /ss/ are reduplicated forms of the plain symbols. The symbols for /p/ and /t/ seem to be modifications of the corresponding nasal symbols.

The symbol ㅇ is used in two ways: at the beginning of a syllable to indicate the absence of an onset consonant, and at the end of a syllable to indicate [ŋ] in the coda. Since Korean does not have syllables beginning with [ŋ], this creates no confusion.

Table 4.24 The *hankul* inventory

Consonants

p	ㅂ	t	ㄷ	c	ㅈ	k	ㄱ
ph	ㅍ	th	ㅌ	ch	ㅊ	kh	ㅋ
pp	ㅃ	tt	ㄸ	cc	ㅉ	kk	ㄲ
		s	ㅅ			h	ㅎ
		ss	ㅆ				
m	ㅁ	n	ㄴ			#Ø	ㅇ
		l	ㄹ			ng#	ㅇ

Simple vowels

i	[i]	ㅣ	u	[ɨ]	ㅡ	wu	[u]	ㅜ
ey	[e]	ㅔ	e	[ʌ]	ㅓ	o	[o]	ㅗ
ay	[æ]	ㅐ				a	[a]	ㅏ

Diphthongs (IPA symbols showing pronunciation are given in square brackets)

			uy	[ɨj]	ㅢ	wuy	[wi]	ㅟ
						oy	[we]	ㅚ
			ywu	[ju]	ㅠ			
yey	[je]	ㅖ	ye	[jʌ]	ㅕ	yo	[jo]	ㅛ
yay	[jæ]	ㅒ				ya	[ja]	ㅑ
wey	[we]	ㅞ	we	[wʌ]	ㅝ			
way	[wæ]	ㅙ				wa	[wa]	ㅘ

Except for <ey> and <ay>, the simple vowels are written with simple symbols: a single horizontal or vertical main stroke; four of these have an additional short stroke attached to the main stroke. For the <y>-diphthongs where the glide follows the vowel nucleus as in <ey, ay, uy, wuy, oy>, the y-glide is written as the vertical stroke of <i> and is attached to the appropriate vowel. In the past, the vowels [e] and [æ] were both diphthongs; this fact explains their writing as <ey> and <ay>.

Each syllable is normally written as one glyph. A glyph is one square-shaped combination of the individual *hankul* graphemes. Each glyph takes about the same space as one Chinese character. The graphemes of a glyph are combined according to the following rules.

1 The onset consonant is written at the top of the cluster. If there is no onset consonant, the symbol ㅇ is used as a dummy consonant.

/mu/ 므 /u/ 으

2 If the vowel has a main vertical stroke, it goes to the right of the onset consonant.

/ma/ 마 /me/ 머

3 If the vowel has a main horizontal stroke, it goes below the onset consonant.

/mo/ 모 /mwu/ 무

4 Any consonant in the coda is written in a separate layer at the bottom of the cluster. If there are two codal consonants, the first goes on the left, and the second goes on the right.

/mal/	말	/malk/	맑
/son/	손	/hulth/	훑
/ttelp/	떫	/ang/	앙

When *hankul* writing began, it had a fairly simple grapheme–phoneme relationship, but it has become increasingly more complex over time. To pronounce Korean from a *hankul* text today, one must use a number of morphophonemic rules to arrive at the correct pronunciation. These rules underlie much of the difference between the Yale and McCune–Reischauer romanizations. The Yale romanization is similar to *hankul* and represents Korean phonology at a deeper level, whereas the McCune–Reischauer romanization represents Korean at the surface phonological level.

4.2.6 Hanca

Hankul was introduced into a society where Chinese culture was very highly regarded, and the Chinese writing system shared in that esteem. The Korean name for characters is *hanca* [ˈhɑnˌdʒɑ] 'Chinese characters'; this is a borrowing of the Chinese *hànzì* (cf. Japanese *kanji*). The educated people who had spent considerable effort in learning to write Korean with characters were strongly opposed to abandoning traditional writing. They argued that the use of Chinese characters maintained a crucial link to Chinese culture and to the classic Confucian literature. To the privileged literate classes, *hankul* appeared to be a deeply inferior writing system. They referred to it as 'women's letters, monks' letters, children's letters'. Despite its royal endorsement, *hankul* was not really adopted widely until long after its introduction. For the small proportion of the population that was literate, writing continued as before.

Although a certain amount of material was written in *hankul* in the next 400 years, particularly by women, it was only in the mid-nineteenth century with rising literacy that *hankul* began to gain popularity. The system which emerged was in fact a mixed one with the Sino-Korean words written in characters and everything else written in *hankul*. After the political division of Korea in 1948, North Korea eliminated characters entirely, teaching only a few in school for historical interest.

South Korea has continued the mixed form of writing, with students learning about 1800 characters. Only Sino-Korean words are written in characters. However, since 1948, the matter has become highly politicized with government edicts twice eliminating and then reinstating the use of characters. Taylor and Taylor (1995) report that overall the use of characters appears to be decreasing.

4.3 Vietnamese

4.3.1 Background and history

Vietnamese is the first language of most of the 57 million people living in Vietnam. The native speakers of other languages in Vietnam usually also speak Vietnamese as a second language. Vietnamese is a member of the Mon-Khmer group of the Austro-Asiatic family of languages; it is completely unrelated to Chinese, Japanese, or Korean. In structure, Vietnamese is isolating with no affixes; morphemes are monosyllabic.

Vietnam was ruled as a colony by China with brief interruptions from 111 OLD to 939 NEW. Even after this time, Vietnam, although nominally an independent monarchy, was in fact controlled indirectly by China. During the period of direct Chinese colonial rule, education and thus writing were done in Chinese (Nguyễn 1959). After independence in 939, writing continued in Chinese, although a distinct Sino-Vietnamese pronunciation of Chinese developed. By the eleventh century, a new distinctive type of writing had emerged known as **chữ nôm** 'southern script'. In this script, a large number of new characters were developed specifically to write Vietnamese. These were characters unknown in Chinese, which nevertheless had been created along the traditional Chinese principles of character formation, primarily semantic-phonetic compounds.

4.3.2 Chữ nôm

With its monosyllabic and isolating nature, Vietnamese had no need to develop ways to write inflectional affixes, as Japanese and Korean did. It is also not clear why the Vietnamese felt the need to create new characters. We can ask why they could not have adapted Chinese characters to Vietnamese as the Japanese and Koreans did to their languages without changing the shape. Possibly the development of the new Vietnamese characters was a way of expressing cultural independence, although the process of creating the new characters was generally Chinese in its nature. In any case, *chữ nôm* continued into the twentieth century as ways of writing Vietnamese.

Vietnamese borrowed heavily from the Chinese lexicon; Hannas (1997) cites estimates between 30 and 60 per cent of the modern vocabulary as borrowed. The borrowing extended over a long period of time, forming different classes of borrowed words, with the older borrowings being fully assimilated, and the later borrowings having recognized Sino-Vietnamese pronunciations.

The development of *chữ nôm* is somewhat similar to the Japanese situation, and we will use the term we developed for Japanese characters earlier in this chapter. The examples are from Nguyễn (1959) and Hannas (1997).

4.3.2.1 SEMANTIC *ON*

Chinese words were borrowed into Vietnamese and were written with Chinese characters (table 4.25). This is the same process we have seen in Japanese and Korean. These words were perceived as Chinese borrowings.

4.3.2.2 *KUN*

Sometimes, a Chinese character would be borrowed and used for an indigenous Vietnamese word which had the same or similar meaning (semantic *kun*) or sound (phonetic *kun*) as expressed by the character in Chinese (table 4.26).

Table 4.25 Examples of semantic *on* in Vietnamese

	Modern Mandarin	*Modern Vietnamese*	*Chinese meaning*	*Vietnamese meaning*
頭	tóu	đầu	'head, beginning'	'head, beginning'
少	shǎo	thiếu	'few, lack'	'lack'
册	cè	sách	'book'	'book'

Table 4.26 Examples of semantic and phonetic *kun* in Vietnamese

	Mandarin	*Modern Vietnamese*	*Chinese meaning*	*Vietnamese meaning*
Semantic *kun*				
味	wèi	mùi	'flavour, smell'	'smell, odour'
役	yì	việc	'work, labour'	'work, event'
本	běn	vốn	'root, capital'	'capital, funds'
Phonetic *kun*				
沒	méi	một	'not'	'one'
固	gù	có	'strong'	'have'
埃	āi	ai	'dust'	'who'

Table 4.27 Examples of characters invented in Vietnamese

Mandarin			*Vietnamese*		
a	天 + 上	tiān 'sky' + shàng 'up'	𡗶	giời	'sky, heaven'
b	亡 + 失	wáng 'lose' + shī 'lose'	𠅍	mất	'lose'
c	年 + 歲	nián 'year' + suì 'year of age'	𢆫	tuổi	'year of age'
d	美 + 母	měi + mǔ 'mother'	美母	mẹ	'mother'
e	巴 + 三	bā + sān 'three'	𠀧	ba	'three'
f	爲	wéi 'do'	𫜵	làm	'do, make'
g	衣	yī 'sky'	𧘇	ấy	'that, those'
h	羅	lúo 'net'	罗	lạ	'strange'

4.3.2.3 CHARACTERS INVENTED IN VIETNAMESE

Sproat (2000, p. 156) seems to have overlooked the examples of semantic-semantic compounds (table 4.27, forms a–c), when following Nguyễn (1959). He says: 'Exclusively Vietnamese character innovations were found in *chữ nôm*, but these were apparently all semantic-phonetic constructions.' Some semantic-phonetic compounds (table 4.27, forms d–e) are found. Note that these examples are in the phonetic-semantic order rather than the more common Chinese semantic-phonetic order. Sometimes Chinese characters were simplified in shape (table 4.27, forms f–h).

4.3.3 *Quốc ngữ*

In the seventeenth century, a third way of writing Vietnamese arose with the name ***quốc ngữ***. French Christian missionaries developed a version of the Roman alphabet for publishing religious materials in Vietnamese. One of them, Alexandre de Rhodes, published *Dictionarium Annamiticum Lusitanum et Latinum* 'A Vietnamese, Portuguese, and Latin Dictionary' in 1651. He added three letters to the basic Roman alphabet <đ ư ơ> and used diacritics to indicate vowel quality as well as tone. As Vietnam fell more under French cultural and political influence, de Rhodes' alphabet was increasingly used in schools. Haarmann (1991) points out that in the late nineteenth century and at the beginning of the twentieth century, the language and writing system of Vietnam was quite complex with three languages (Chinese, French, Vietnamese) used in schooling and two writing systems in use (*chữ nôm* and *quốc ngữ*).

In 1945, with independence from France, the new communist government proclaimed that *quốc ngữ* would be the only recognized script. The northern dialect of Hanoi is the standard dialect for writing. By now, *quốc ngữ* is strongly identified with the Vietnamese people, and the older scripts are limited to academic and antiquarian interests.

4.4 Further Reading

Taylor and Taylor (1995) cover both Japanese and Korean. Miller (1967, 1986), Seeley (1991), Shibatani (1987, 1990), and Smith (1996) all present basic information about the Japanese writing system. Unger (1996) discusses the history of Japanese writing immediately after the Second World War. Paradis et al. (1985) give an interesting discussion of aphasia and its effect on Japanese writing. For Korean, Sohm (1997) has general information about the language and writing system. Kim-Reynaud (1997) has a number of more technical articles. Vietnamese is less well discussed, but see Nguyễn (1959, 1996), and also Hannas (1997). Hannas has voiced strong criticism to the continued use of characters for writing any Asian language.

4.5 Terms

ateji
chữ nôm
furigana
hanca
hankul
hiragana
hyangchal
itwu
jukujikun
kana
kanbun
kanji
katakana
kokuji
kun-reading
kwukyel
mora
on-reading
phonetic extension
phonetic *kun*
phonetic *on*
quốc ngữ
semantic *kun*
semantic *on*

4.6 Exercises

1 How many pronunciations can you find for the number one <1> in English? (Hint: consider 10, 1^{ary}, etc.)

2 The following words have been borrowed into Japanese from other languages, primarily English. What is the type of script used? Romanize the Japanese writing, and then guess as to the meaning. Some answers have been given for you.

トマト	tomato	'tomato'
ママ		'female bar manager'
マスト		
スマート		
リスク		
マイク		
リスト		'list, Liszt'

マーク
マスク
タイマー
トースト
トースター
スクーター
インク
マトン 'mutton'
リンク
スタントマン 'stunt man'
スーツ
ワルツ
クリスマスツリー
ナッツ
ヨット 'yacht'
クッキー
カルタ 'playing card' < Port. *carta*
カルテ 'medical record' < Ger. *Karte*
カード 'catalogue card' < Eng. *card*
アイスホッケー
マッチ
ハンモック

3 In Chinese, /àn/ 'bank, shore' is written with the character 岸. This Chinese word was borrowed into Japanese as /gan/ 'bank, shore'.

(a) When 岸 is read as /gan/ in Japanese, what is this reading known as?
(b) The same character 岸 was also used for the native Japanese word /kishi/ 'bank, shore'. What is this reading known as?

4 The following words have been borrowed from other languages, primarily English, into Korean. Match each Korean word with the English gloss. (Hint: remember that Korean does not have an /l/–/ɹ/ distinction.)

키스	alibi	오케스트라	restaurant
아이스-크림	boom	칼로리	rucksack
밀크	bulldozer	룩색	spaghetti
알리바이	calorie	레스토랑	stop
캠퍼스	campus	스파게티	tundra
불도저	charisma	디스크-자키	ice cream
스톱	disk jockey	카리스마	kiss
붐	orchestra	둔두라	milk

5 Cuneiform

5.1 Background and History

Cuneiform, the earliest known writing in the world, was done a little over 5000 years ago by the Sumerian people living in southern Mesopotamia (figure 5.1). **Mesopotamia** is the land lying between the Tigris and Euphrates rivers and is now part of modern-day Iraq. A domesticated agricultural life emerged there around 7000 OLD, and cities arose in the fifth millennium with large temples known as ziggurats (a famous one was the biblical Tower of **Babel** – i.e., the ziggurat of Babylon). The Sumerians had an active economy centred around the temples.

5.1.1 Sumerian

The Sumerians settled in this area around 4000 OLD, apparently replacing earlier peoples whose names are unknown to us. The **Sumerian** language is unrelated to any other known language. The phonemes of Sumerian are given in table 5.1 (Hayes 1990). There is some dispute among Sumerologists about several points in this inventory.

Sumerian writing was on clay. When clay is dried, it is extremely durable. Sometimes tablets were baked to preserve them better, but often they were simply allowed to dry. Fire has destroyed many paper and papyrus documents of history; however, with clay, a fire simply bakes it and makes it even more durable. The fact that the Sumerians wrote on clay has meant that the modern world has an unparalleled amount of information about their life at so early a period.

Table 5.1 The phonemes of Sumerian

p b	t d			k g
m	n			ŋ
	s z	ʃ		x
	l r			
		i		u
		e		o
			a	

Figure 5.1 Mesopotamia

The earliest Sumerian documents were bookkeeping records kept by the temples. Later material also included large numbers of administrative and economic texts, as well as legal documents, letters, royal inscriptions, and literary texts (Postgate 1992). The best-known literary text is the *Epic of Gilgamesh*.

5.1.2 Akkadian

The Akkadians, led by Sargon, conquered the Sumerians in 2350 OLD. **Akkadian** is a Semitic language, completely unrelated to Sumerian. The Akkadians adopted much of Sumerian culture, including Sumerian writing. At first, the Akkadians simply wrote in the Sumerian language with the Sumerian writing system; later they adapted the writing system to write Akkadian, but they never entirely gave up writing in the Sumerian language. For the Akkadians, Sumerian was a language of learning, much as

Table 5.2 The phonemes of Akkadian

p	b	t	d		k	g	ʔ		
		ṭ			q				
		s	z	ʃ	x				
		ṣ							
m		n							
		l	r						
w				j					
				i	u			iː	uː
				e	a			eː	aː

Latin was for mediæval Europeans. The names **Akkadian, Babylonian,** and **Assyrian** are all used for this language spoken at different times and places. We can view them simply as dialects of a single language which we will call Akkadian. Akkadian literature is vast, including administrative and economic documents, royal decrees, legal codes, literature, even cookbooks.

The Akkadian phonological inventory is given in table 5.2.

If we compare the Sumerian and Akkadian inventories, we see that Akkadian had more phonemes than Sumerian. The sounds /ṭ q ṣ/ probably involved some sort of pharyngeal, laryngeal, or uvular articulation (see chapter 7). Glottal stop /ʔ/ was present in proto-Semitic, but it was lost during the early stages of Akkadian. Assyriologists (specialists in this area) usually transcribe /ʔ ʃ x j ŋ/ as <’ š ḫ i̯ g̃>.

Sumerian was replaced by Akkadian in the early second millennium OLD. Later, during the first millennium, Aramaic, a different Semitic language, became the lingua franca of the Akkadian world; it was written with an abjad (a system like an alphabet; see chapter 7). In 537 OLD, the Persians conquered the Akkadians. Although the Persians spoke **Old Persian,** an Indo-European language, the administrative language and lingua franca of the area remained Aramaic.

5.2 Tokens and the Invention of Writing

Denise Schmandt-Besserat (1989, 1992) has put forth a very interesting theory as to how writing arose in Mesopotamia. From the period 8500–3000 OLD, a large number of artefacts known as **tokens** have been found. These are small clay objects of simple geometric shapes (figure 5.2): spheres, cones, tetrahedra, cylinders, disks, lens-shaped disks, etc.; tokens of this period are known as *plain tokens.* They are associated with the beginnings of agriculture; Schmandt-Besserat believes that they were used for record-keeping. We can imagine two farmers agreeing: ‘In exchange for the twenty bushels of grain I am giving you now, you will give me two sheep in the spring; I will keep these two tokens as a record of the agreement.’ She argues that the different shapes of tokens were used for different agricultural items: barley, sheep, wool, etc.

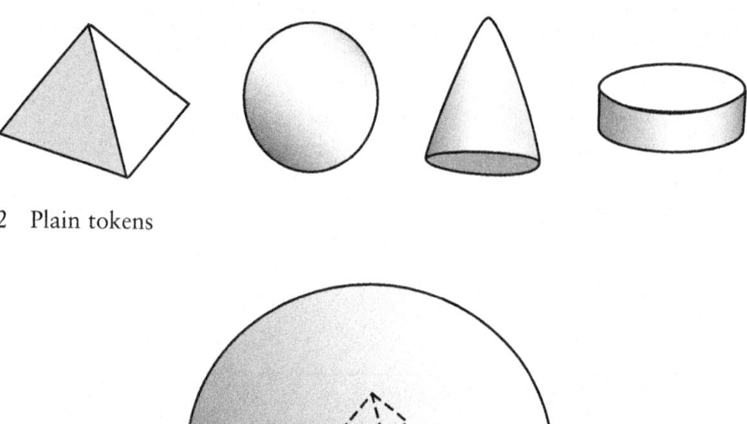

Figure 5.2 Plain tokens

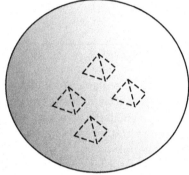

Figure 5.3 Hollow envelope with tokens enclosed

Although the archæological context for many tokens has been lost, some have been found stored inside sealed, hollow clay balls forming envelopes around the tokens (figure 5.3). Schmandt-Besserat argues that these envelopes represented a way of safeguarding the record of the contract. If there was a disagreement, the envelope could be broken, and the evidence of the tokens would be inside.

From the seventh millennium OLD, **seals** were used in the Near East; they were the property of an individual or institution and served as evidence of authenticity (cf. the seals used by corporations and notaries public even today). Mesopotamian seals were cylindrical in shape and were rolled across the clay, leaving the impression of the pattern of the seal. Thus, the early Mesopotamians would have been familiar with the notion of pressing something into the clay to make a record. Schmandt-Besserat suggests that, in order to record a contract, tokens were sometimes similarly pressed into the outer surface of a clay envelope, then they were placed inside the envelope, which was then closed (figure 5.4). This procedure had the advantage of allowing the contract to be consulted without breaking the envelope.

Once the tokens were pressed into the outer surface of the clay, people realized that there was no need to enclose them in the envelope; thus, the envelopes gave way to impressed tablets. A flat tablet of clay was marked with a cylinder seal impression, indicating the party to the contract, and then the tokens were pressed into the tablet to show the content of the agreement.

From about 4400–3000 OLD, more complex tokens (figure 5.5) were found in addition to the plain tokens. These had more complex shapes, sometimes with incised lines on their surface. They are associated with the emergence of cities during

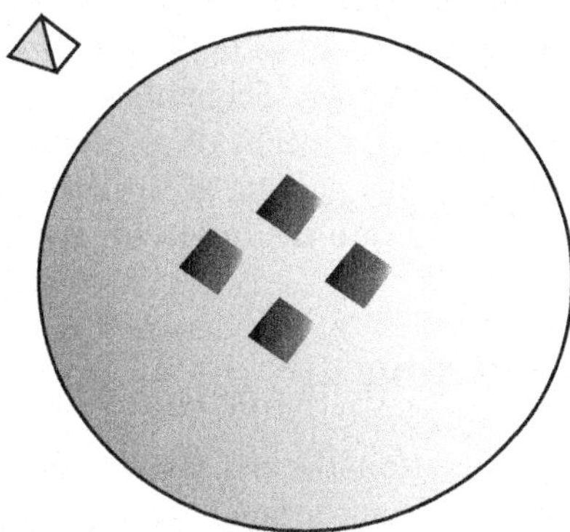

Figure 5.4 Envelope showing where tokens have been impressed; token shown separately

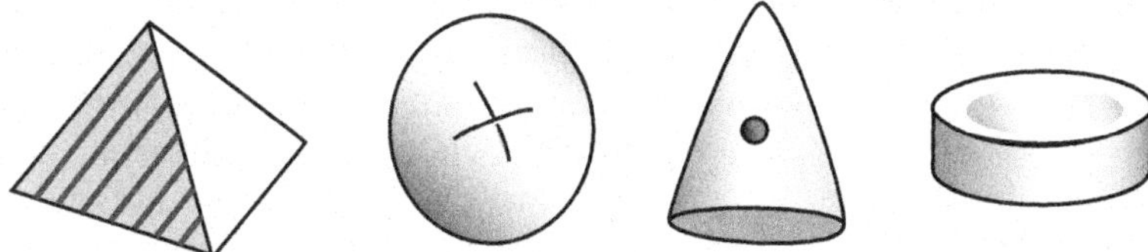

Figure 5.5 Complex tokens

Figure 5.6 Tablet with inscribed signs

this time. Schmandt-Besserat argues that the complex tokens represented the manufactured goods such as cloth, beer, and bread which were traded in the cities.

When complex tokens came into existence, their more complex shapes and particularly the lines in them were difficult to reproduce on the tablet merely by pressing the tokens into the clay. To solve this problem, the shape of the token was drawn into the tablet with a stylus rather than impressed with the actual token (figure 5.6). Special types of impressions came to be used to indicate more than one unit.

From simple documents which recorded different numbers and objects, someone realized that other types of records could be made and ultimately that any utterance in the language could be written down. Schmandt-Besserat's theory that writing developed from the use of tokens as a means of record-keeping is not without controversy, but it seems to be gradually gaining acceptance. If it is true, even partially so, it gives us considerable insight into the origin of writing in Mesopotamia.

5.3 Materials of Writing

The earliest known real writing is from the ancient city Uruk (southern Mesopotamia, near the Euphrates). We presume that the language is Sumerian, but the pictographic nature of the writing does not give any direct evidence for the language of the scribes. The symbols were drawn with a pointed stick, or **stylus**, in soft clay which was allowed to dry. Since pulling a stylus through the clay throws up ridges, a more satisfactory way of writing on clay was found, namely, pressing the stylus into the clay. A triangular stylus was generally used, leaving wedge-like impressions. The name cuneiform 'wedge-shaped' is a nineteenth-century term coined from the Latin word *cuneus* 'wedge'. Numbers were written with a circular stylus (figures 5.6 and 5.9): one impression for 'one', two impressions for 'two', etc. Larger units were written with a larger stylus and also by impressing the stylus at an angle.

A rectangular slab of clay, known as a **tablet** (figure 5.7), was held in one hand and the stylus in the other. Early symbols show strokes in all directions, but soon only the ones which could be made without too much rotation of the stylus were used. For reasons not entirely understood, but no doubt related to the way the tablet was held for writing and reading, symbols were rotated 90° counterclockwise (see figure 5.10).

At first, the scribes wrote the cuneiform symbols by using the triangular stylus to duplicate carefully the same design made by the pointed stylus; however, in time,

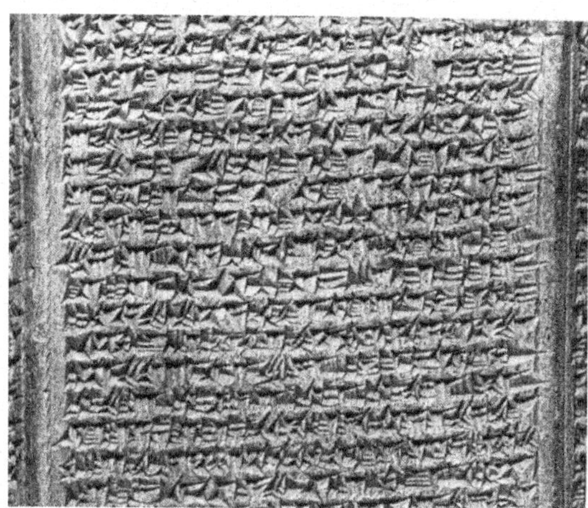

Figure 5.7 Portion of a cuneiform tablet

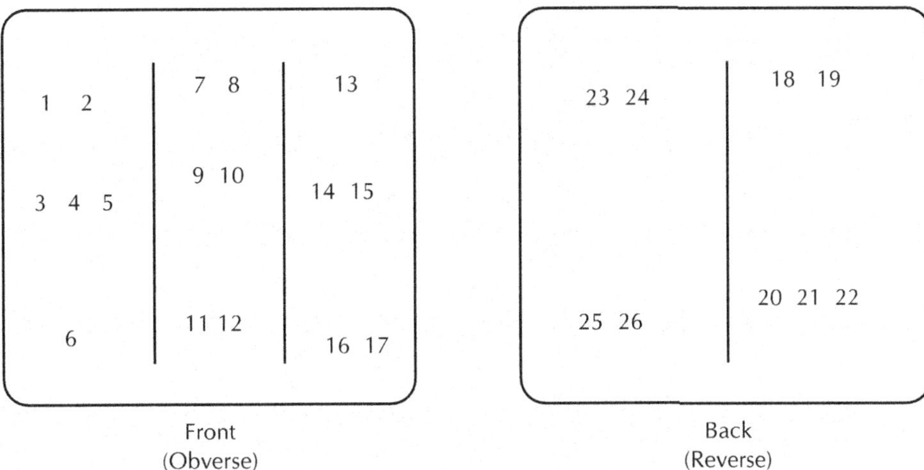

Figure 5.8 The order of writing on both sides of a tablet is shown

the shapes of the symbols became stylized. With the rotation and stylization, continuity with the original representational shape was lost. Later scribes likely had little knowledge of the origin of the symbols.

The shape of clay tablet varied but was typically rectangular, of a size convenient to fit in the hand. The **obverse** (front side) was usually flat, and the **reverse** (back) convex. This design made it easy to find where the writing began. The scribe sometimes wrote in columns beginning at the upper left of the obverse side (figure 5.8). Within a column, the symbols were written horizontally from left to right. At the end of one column, a new column would begin at the right of the last one. When the lower right corner of the obverse was reached, the tablet was turned over, top to bottom. The first column on the reverse started at the right with further columns to the left. Thus, the columns were ordered differently on the two sides. Many tablets have only one column per side, but the tablet would still be turned top to bottom.

We have already mentioned envelopes in the context of tokens; cuneiform tablets were also sometimes written in the form of envelopes. A contract would be written out on a tablet, then sealed inside a clay envelope which would also bear a copy of the same contract. The Akkadians took fraud in contract law very seriously. Seals could also be used to authenticate the author of a tablet.

The standard medium of cuneiform writing is the clay tablet; however, inscriptions were also occasionally made in stone, metal, glass, or ivory. Clay objects in the shape of large ceremonial building nails with inscriptions, even lengthy ones, were sometimes placed in the walls of temples.

5.4 Social Context of Cuneiform Writing

Scribes were an educated elite in Sumerian and Akkadian society. They attended a long and often harsh schooling. In addition to the basics of writing, they also learned about literature and mathematics. Akkadian-speaking students spent a good deal of time learning Sumerian. Tablets exist where the teacher has written a model text on one half of the tablet and the student has copied it on the other. The same school texts are found from different time periods, suggesting that the method of schooling remained much the same for centuries.

One peculiar kind of text was the lexical list. These were lists of semantically related words. At first, the lexical lists were only in Sumerian, but later Akkadian translations were added alongside. Likely these were catalogues of symbols made to help scribal students.

Literacy was not widespread, but there were still many people who could read. Although tablets were usually discarded when they were no longer required, many libraries, some of considerable size, have been found.

5.5 An Early Sumerian Tablet from Uruk

Nissen, Damerow, and Englund (1993) have examined a collection of 82 tablets from ancient Uruk dated to about 3000 OLD. These tablets are among the earliest true writing known to us today. The tablets are mainly bookkeeping records. They were found in dumps where they had been discarded and were no longer in the location where they would have been produced or used. The script of these tablets is known as proto-cuneiform, drawn with a pointed stylus before the introduction of the triangular stylus.

We will look at one of these tablets (figure 5.10) produced by an administrative official with the name Kushim /kuʃim/. Seventeen other tablets in this collection mention Kushim, who appears to be the chief warehouseman for a brewery. His title is Sanga, a senior administrator. His significance is clear from the large quantities of ingredients for which he was responsible.

First, we should look at the counting system for grain. There seems to have been a standard unit of volume of about 24 litres used for barley (figure 5.9). Different symbols indicated multiples of this basic unit (figure 5.9); the multiples did not have a consistent arithmetic relationship to each other. This system was used only for grain, particularly barley. Other objects had different systems of measurement. Nissen et al. (1993) found thirteen different systems for such things as animals, fish, milk products, weight, days, etc. The symbols for numbers appear to have been made with two round styli, one small and one large. With each stylus two different symbols could be made, by pressing the stylus straight down into the clay or by pressing the tip in almost horizontally. This was indicated in the texts by the symbol labelled *a* in figure 5.9. We will label these units as *a*, *b*, *c*, *d*. In figure 5.9, symbols *a* and *b* are made with the small stylus, *c* and *d* with the large one. With symbols *b* and *c*, the tip of the stylus is pressed straight in, and with symbols *a* and *d*, the stylus is pressed in at an angle. Six units of *a* equal 1 unit of *b*; 10 units of *b* equal 1 unit of *c*; and 3 units of *c* equal one unit of *d*.

In the Uruk tablet shown in figure 5.10, the obverse shows four different entries on the left all having to do with barley; on the right, the tablet is signed by Nisa, who appears to be Kushim's second-in-command. The reverse summarizes the information on the obverse and is signed by both Kushim and Nisa.

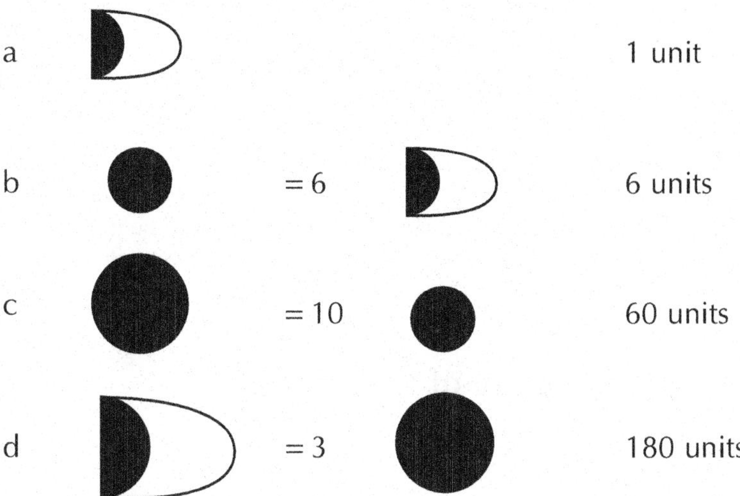

Figure 5.9 Measurement symbols for grain

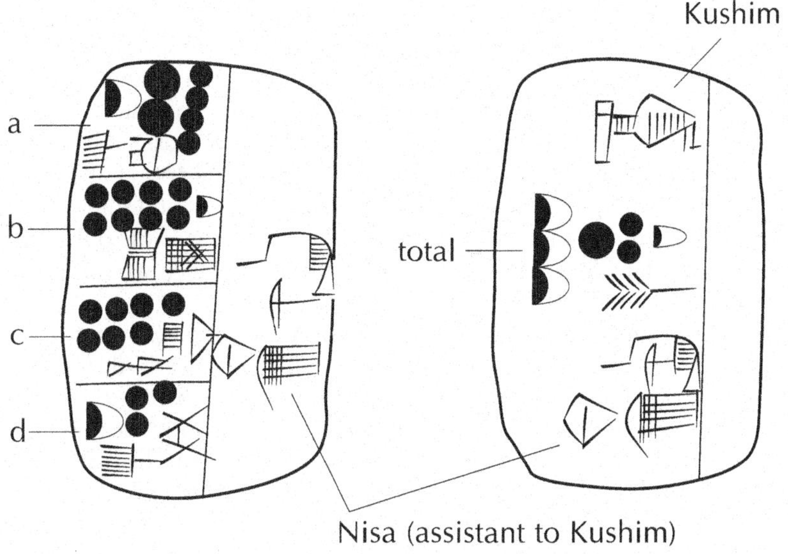

Figure 5.10 An early accounting tablet from Uruk (from Hans J. Nissen et al., *Archaic Bookkeeping*, figure 34, p. 38. Chicago: University of Chicago Press, 1993. © 1986 by University of Chicago Press. Reproduced with permission)

Looking now at the four entries on the obverse, we see that each one contains a number and the title of an official. The first entry shows an amount of 4*b*, 2*c*, 1*d* or a total of 324 units (where 4*b* is 4 occurrences of symbol *b* as shown in figure 5.9); the second entry has 1*a*, 8*b* or a total of 49 units; the third entry has 7*b* or a total of 42 units; and the fourth entry has 3*b*, 1*d* or a total of 198 units. The total number of units on this side is thus 613 units or approximately 14,712 litres.

The reverse shows a number, and the signatures of Kushim and Nisa. The grain-shaped symbol represents 'barley'. The symbol below that has not been deciphered but seems to refer to some kind of distribution. The amount of grain is 1*a*, 2*b*, 1*c*, 3*d* or a total of 613 units; this figure is obviously the total of the four entries on the obverse.

This tablet shows the clear and accurate bookkeeping techniques of the Akkadians. Another tablet shows the amount of various ingredients that the warehouseman would need to have on hand for a certain quantity of beer to be made. One interesting series of tablets shows that a certain person did not have sufficient grain to pay his taxes fully one year and that the shortfall was carried forward to the next year.

5.6 Internal Structure of Cuneiform

5.6.1 Development of symbols

Each cuneiform symbol is a grapheme; graphemes represent both morphological and phonological units in the language (figure 5.11).

The earliest symbols were **pictograms**. In the illustrations in figure 5.11, the symbols for /sag/ 'head' (1), /ki/ 'land' (7: picture of ploughed field), /sal/ 'female sexual organs' (8), and /kur/ 'mountain' (9) are pictograms. In the earliest forms of the symbols (column I) the iconic nature is apparent, but with the rotation and cuneiform stylization, the original pictorial quality has been lost, and the later forms are simply symbolic (column IV). The symbol for /du/ 'go' (5) was originally pictographic, showing a foot, and then extended to the semantically related notion of 'go'. Similarly, a pictograph of a star (6) came to be used for /an/ 'heaven' and /diŋir/ 'god'.

Abstract pictograms are representational, but not exactly of the object itself. The symbol for /a/ 'water' (3) is a picture, not of water itself which would be difficult to draw, but of a stream.

Semantic extension was common. The symbol for /du/ 'go' (5) started as a pictogram of a foot and was then extended semantically to the verb /du/ 'go', and also to the verb /gub/ 'stand'. From its use for /du/ 'go', it was then further extended to the semantically similar morphemes /ra/ and /gin/, all generally meaning 'go'. From its original pictographic shape for a 'star', the symbol for /an/ 'heaven' (6) was also used for /diŋir/ 'god'. The symbol for /ka/ 'mouth' (2) was extended to represent the semantically similar morpheme /dug/ 'speak'. The pictograph for /sal/ 'female sexual organs' (8) became as well the symbol for /munus/ 'woman'.

In the examples, we see **phonetic extension** in the use of the symbol for /a/ 'water' (3) to write the morpheme /a/ 'in', and indeed to write any syllable of the shape /a/. With phonetic extension, the meaning of the original morpheme is irrelevant.

One symbol can be changed to another symbol by **differentiation**, that is, by adding a diacritic. In Akkadian, this process was known as ***gunu***. The symbol for /ka/ 'mouth' (2) was formed by adding a *gunu* mark in the form of diacritic hatch marks to the symbol for head (1) in the area of the mouth. Note that the symbol for /ka/ 'mouth' later underwent semantic extension to be used as the symbol for /dug/ 'speak'.

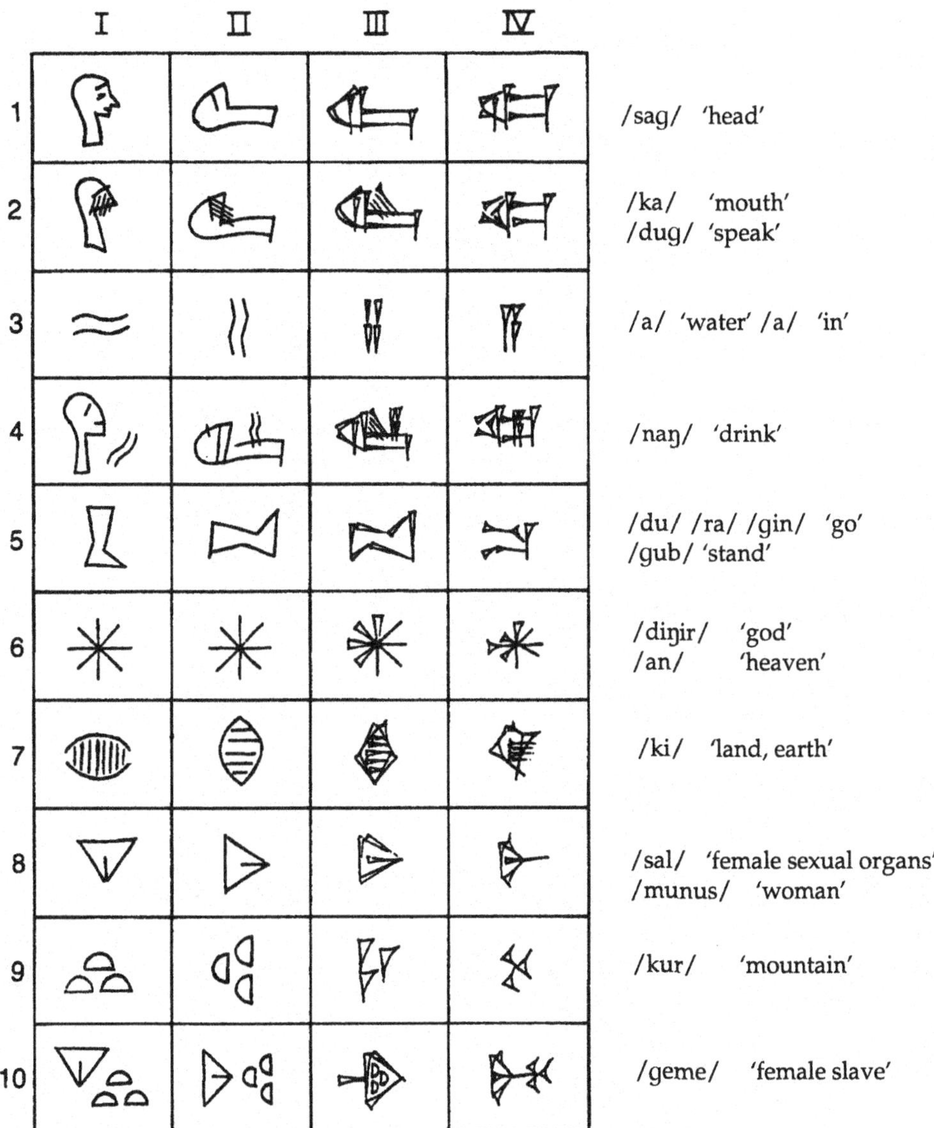

Figure 5.11 Examples of symbols. Different chronological stages of each symbol are shown from left to right (from Edward Chiera, *They Wrote in Clay*, p. 63. Chicago: University of Chicago Press, 1966. © 1966 by University of Chicago Press. Reproduced with permission)

The symbol for /naŋ/ 'drink' (4) is an illustration of a **semantic compound.** The symbol for /sag/ 'head' (1) was combined with the symbol for /a/ 'water' (3) to create a new symbol. Another example of a semantic compound is shown in (10); here, the symbols for /munus/ 'woman' (8) and /kur/ 'mountain' (9) are combined to produce a new symbol for /geme/ 'female slave' (10). The rationale for this was that slaves typically came from the mountain ranges to the East.

The examples so far have been based on Sumerian, which is the period when the processes of creating new symbols emerged. The same principles continued to be used to create symbols required by Akkadian. One complexity during the Akkadian period resulted from the large borrowing of Sumerian vocabulary. A symbol could have both a Sumerian and an Akkadian reading, the same as Japanese *on*- and *kun*-readings (chapter 4). For example, the symbol for 'head' could be given a Sumerian reading /sag/ (*on*-reading) or an Akkadian reading /reːʃum/ (*kun*-reading); similarly, the symbol for 'land' could be read as /ki/ in Sumerian (*on*) or as /ersetu/ in Akkadian (*kun*). Over time, the Akkadian readings became more common, but some Sumerian readings continued throughout the entire Akkadian period.

Phonetic extension could be based on either the Sumerian (phonetic *on*) or the Akkadian reading (phonetic *kun*). For example, the symbol for 'head' could be used both for syllables with the sound /sag/ following the Sumerian pronunciation, or with /reʃ/ following the Akkadian pronunciation.

Semantic extension further complicated the situation by associating a variety of different-sounding morphemes with the same symbol. For example, the symbol for /ka/ 'mouth' was also extended to other morphemes: /zu/ 'tooth', /inim/ 'word', /gu/ 'voice', and /dug/ 'speak'; and by phonetic extension, it was further used for syllables with the sounds /zu/, /gu/, and /du/.

5.6.2 Relationship to language

Some symbols are **morphograms**; for example, the symbol 𒊕 was used to represent the morpheme /sag/ 'head', and 𒀭 is used to represent the morpheme /diŋir/ 'heaven, god'.

Some symbols are **phonograms**; for example, the symbol 𒋧 was used to represent the syllable /ʃum/. Phonographic cuneiform symbols represented moræ or syllables, not single phonemes. A syllable might have had an initial consonant or not, and it might have been open or closed: (C)V(C). Thus, there were different and unrelated symbols for /u/ 𒌑, /ʃu/ 𒋗, /um/ 𒌝, and /ʃum/ 𒋧. The symbol inventory contained symbols for most single vowels, CV, and VC sequences, but not all. There were symbols for only some CVC possibilities. Note that although cuneiform symbols represented syllables, they sometimes represented a single vowel phoneme, where the syllable had no initial or final consonant.

Although Akkadian symbols could represent syllables, not every possible phonological syllable had a corresponding symbol; often two moraic symbols were combined to show a single syllable. Vowel length, for example, was shown irregularly in Akkadian. Sometimes long vowels are simply not indicated at all but have to be inferred from a knowledge of the language. At other times, they were indicated by repeating the vowel with a different symbol. Thus /baː/ could be written just as <ba>, or more explicitly with two moraic symbols as <ba-a>. In a closed syllable, a long vowel such as /baːm/ might be written with two symbols as <ba-am>; it was up to the reader to know whether this represented one syllable with a long vowel

/baːm/ or a two-syllable sequence /ba-am/, or perhaps /bam/. Many consonantal contrasts were neutralized in writing. Thus, the written symbol <ku> might represent /ku/, /gu/, or /qu/.

Some symbols are used as a **semantic complement** – a symbol used to give additional semantic information. For example, the star symbol is used as a morphogram for /diŋir/ 'god'. However, this symbol is also used to accompany the name of any god that is mentioned. In this case the star symbol was not pronounced, but it indicated that the accompanying symbol was to be interpreted as the name of a god. Semantic complements are useful in disambiguating homographs.

Frequently a symbol represented many different things. For example, the symbol 𒄑 was a morphogram meaning 'tree, wood'; as such, it could be pronounced as /giʃ/, the Sumerian (*on*) reading, or as /iṣu/, the Akkadian (***kun***) reading. The same symbols could also be phonograms, ambiguously representing either /is/, /iz/, or /iṣ/. Further, this particular symbol could be used as a semantic complement preceding many words to indicate that the following word is a tree or an object made of wood, in which case the symbol would not have been pronounced at all.

Clearly, in reading Akkadian, context was of great importance in determining which reading was appropriate in each case. As a result of this complexity, Assyriologists have developed certain traditions for romanizing Akkadian texts. They distinguish the terms **transliteration** and **transcription.** A **transliteration** of a text involves giving a symbol-by-symbol rendering of the written Akkadian text. A **transcription** gives the correct pronunciation. Morphemes with a Sumerian reading are transliterated in roman letters, and those with an Akkadian reading are in italics. Morphograms are transliterated in upper-case letters, and phonograms are in lower-case letters. The semantic complements, such as /diŋir/, are transcribed by superscript abbreviations. This semantic determinative is transliterated by a small < ^{d} > (the abbreviation is for Latin *deus* 'god', not /diŋir/).

5.7 Example Text

Ḫammu-rāpi was one of the most famous kings of Babylon, ruling 1792–1750 OLD. He ordered that a collection of laws be publicized, and a copy of these laws is on a large stele now found in the Louvre Museum in Paris. One of the laws is presented in table 5.3, not with the shape of the symbols found on the stele, but in the later form normally used in teaching Akkadian.

The roots for verbs are of the typical Semitic triconsonantal form (see chapter 7). The other vowels and consonants of verbs represent inflectional material. Accents in the transliteration are used to distinguish homophonic graphemes. Hyphens in the transliteration correspond to symbol boundaries; hyphens in the transcription separate lexical morphemes.

An *awi:lum* was a 'first-class citizen', different from a *muʃkenum* 'second-class citizen', or from a slave. The nominative suffix is *-um* and the accusative suffix is *-am*. Note that the word order is SOV (subject–object–verb). In this text, all items are Akkadian phonograms and thus written in lower-case italics. Note the difference between transliteration and transcription.

Table 5.3 Sample Akkadian text: A law from the code of Ḫammu-rāpi

Translit.	*ʃum-ma*	*a- wi- lum*	*a- wi- lam*	*ú- ub- bi- ir- ma*
Transcript.	*ʃumma*	*awi:lum*	*awi:lam*	*ubbirma*
	If	citizen	citizen	accuse
		nom	acc	root /ʔbr/
Translit.	*ne- er- tam*	*e- li- ʃu*	*id- di- ma*	
Transcript.	*ne:rtam*	*eli:-ʃu*	*iddi:-ma*	
	charge of murder	against-him	lay- and	
	acc		root /ndʔ/	
Translit.	*la*	*uk- ti- in- ʃu*		
Transcript.	*la:*	*uktin-ʃu*		
	not	convict-him		
		root /kʔn/		
Translit.	*mu-ub- bi- ir- ʃu*	*id- da- ak*		
Transcript.	*mubbir-ʃu*	*idda:k*		
	accuser-his	kill		
	root /ʔbr/	root /dʔk/		

'If one citizen accuses another and brings a charge of murder against him, but has not convicted him, his accuser shall be executed.'

5.8 Other Cuneiform Writing

Several neighbouring cultures borrowed cuneiform writing from the Akkadians and adapted it to their own languages. As a whole, these borrowings were rather conservative, keeping the general structure of Sumerian and Akkadian writing. We will discuss several of these borrowings briefly, and then examine Ugaritic and Old Persian writing in a little more detail since they show certain interesting innovations.

The state of Elam was in western Iran, north of the Gulf. Elamite texts were written over a very long period of time, from 3100–331 OLD. The Elamite language is not known to be related to any other language. The earliest texts are in an undeciphered pictographic script. A linear script followed which is only partly understood. From the thirteenth century OLD, Elamite texts exist which use a limited number of the phonographic symbols borrowed from Akkadian.

Around 10,000 tablets were discovered in 1964 in Ebla, a site in Syria near Aleppo. The Eblaite texts are dated from the relatively brief period of 2500–2400 OLD. They were partially written in Eblaite, a Semitic language. The texts are mostly administrative in nature. They are largely written in Sumerian with Eblaite interspersed; as a result, much of the structure of the Eblaite language remains unknown.

In northeastern Turkey at Boğhazköy, around 10,000 cuneiform texts were found in 1906, written in Hittite, an Indo-European language (some scholars argue that Hittite and Indo-European together form the Indo-Hittite family). The Hittite scribes used a large number of Sumerian and Akkadian symbols. The texts cover a wide range of subjects: administration, diplomacy, religion, magic, and literature. They are dated from the seventeenth to the thirteenth centuries OLD.

The Hurrians lived in northern Mesopotamia, speaking a language known to be related only to another ancient language of the area, Urartian. An archive of international correspondence in Hurrian was found in Egypt in 1887, with the material dated to the end of the fifteenth century OLD. One of these is the largest known cuneiform tablet. The script is moraic and is an adaptation of the Akkadian script. The Hurrians are known as the people who introduced the horse to the Near East.

As mentioned above, Urartian is related to Hurrian. The Urartians lived around Lake Van in eastern Turkey. The texts are mostly historical in nature, dated from the thirteenth to the seventh centuries OLD. Like Hurrian, it uses a reduced number of Akkadian symbols.

5.8.1 Ugaritic

In 1929, about 1000 **Ugaritic** tablets were found at Ras Shamra (Ugarit) on the coast of Syria (Segert 1984, C. Walker 1987). The language is Semitic, but the script is cuneiform, but unlike any other cuneiform writing. The texts, which have been dated from the fourteenth century OLD, include literary and administrative texts. Rather than representing morphemes or syllables as in Akkadian, the script represents individual segments. In general, only the consonants are written, not the vowels; these characteristics make the Ugaritic script an abjad, a type of script which we will be discussing in chapter 7. The abjad was the typical script for most Semitic languages other than Akkadian.

Each of the consonants has a separate symbol. In addition, there are three moraic symbols for the glottal stop combined with a following vowel: <ʔa ʔi ʔu>; this is an exception to the rule that vowels are not represented. There is also a symbol for a word divider. The order of the symbols is attested, and it is almost identical to the one used for Phœnician and Hebrew scripts (chapter 7).

Essentially, the Ugaritic script is structurally similar to the early Semitic scripts, except that the symbols were of a cuneiform shape written on clay tablets. Presumably, the Semitic Ugaritic speakers were familiar with both the traditional Semitic and Akkadian traditions and incorporated both writing traditions in their script. The internal structure of the Ugaritic script is Semitic, and the external structure is Akkadian.

Table 5.4 shows the Ugaritic symbols in the native order. Where there is a difference between a symbol used in Ugaritic studies and the usual IPA symbol for the reconstructed pronunciation, the IPA symbol is given in brackets. The subscript dot indicates an emphatic consonant; these were common in Semitic languages and

Table 5.4 The Ugaritic cuneiform symbols in the traditional order

𐎀	𐎁	𐎂	𐎃	𐎄	𐎅	𐎆	𐎇	𐎈	𐎉
ʼa [ʔa]	b	g	h	d	ḫ [x]	w	z	ḥ [ħ]	ṭ
𐎊	𐎋	𐎌	𐎍	𐎎	𐎏	𐎐	𐎑	𐎒	𐎓
y [j]	k	ś [ʃ]	l	m	d [ð]	n	ẓ [θ̣]	s	ʿ[ʕ]
𐎔	𐎕	𐎖	𐎗	𐎘	𐎙	𐎚	𐎛	𐎜	𐎝
p	ṣ	q	r	ṯ [θ]	ġ [ʁ]	t	ʼi [ʔi]	ʼu [ʔu]	ŝ [su]

involved some sort of secondary pharyngeal or laryngeal activity. The symbol for /su/ was added late and was quite rare.

5.8.2 *Old Persian*

When the Persians conquered the Akkadians in the sixth century OLD, the administrative language of the Akkadian empire had become Aramaic. The Persians continued to use Aramaic as an administrative and diplomatic language. They themselves, however, spoke **Old Persian**, an Indo-European language. King Darius I (521–486 OLD) ordered a Persian cuneiform to be constructed to give his empire and language a distinctive script. The script had 36 phonographic symbols and a few morphograms, and a word divider (table 5.5). Where there is more than one symbol for a consonant in table 5.5, each alternative was usually used only before cerain vowels. Relatively few texts were written in Old Persian, mostly stone or metal inscriptions, rather than on clay.

Table 5.5 Old Persian cuneiform symbols

Vowel symbols

𐎠	𐎡	𐎢
a	i	u

Consonant symbols

𐎱	𐎲	𐎳	𐎺	𐎻	𐎶	𐎷	𐎸	𐎫	𐎬	𐎭	𐎮	𐎯
p	b	f	v	v	m	m	m	t	t	d	d	d
𐎰	𐎿	𐏀	𐎴	𐎵	𐏃	𐎨	𐎩	𐎪	𐏂	𐏁	𐎹	𐎣
θ	s	z	n	n	h	tʃ	dʒ	dʒ	ç	ʃ	j	k
𐎤	𐎥	𐎦	𐎧	𐎼	𐎽	𐎾						
k	g	g	x	r	r	l						

Table 5.5 (*Cont'd*)

Morphograms				
𐏋	𐏌	𐏎	𐏏	𐏈
xʃajaθija 'king'	dahjāuʃ 'country'	baga 'earth'	būmiʃ 'god'	Auramazdā divine name

Numerals									
𐏑	𐏒	𐏑𐏒	𐏓	𐏓𐏑𐏒	𐏔	𐏔𐏓𐏑𐏒	𐏔𐏔	𐏕	𐏕𐏔
1	2	3	10	13	20	33	40	100	120

5.9 Further Reading

Bottéro (1992), Kramer (1963), Nissen (1988), Postgate (1992), Roaf (1990) all provide background information on Mesopotamia. For more information on the cuneiform script for Sumerian and Akkadian, see Cooper (1996), Green (1989), Michalowski (1996), C. Walker (1987), which all provide relatively easy introductions. Feuerherm (1998) and Huehnergard (1997) are introductions to the Akkadian language with information on the writing system. Schmandt-Besserat (1989, 1992), Jasim and Oates (1986), and Lieberman (1980) discuss tokens. Green (1981), Larsen (1989), Nissen (1986), Nissen, Damerow, and Englund (1993), Picchioni (1985), M. Powell (1981), Reiner (1973), Sack (1981), Vanstiphout (1979) discuss specific points. See Collon (1990), Gibson and Biggs (1977), and Schendge (1983) on seals. For other languages see Bermant and Weitzman (1979, Eblaite), Curtis (1985, Ugaritic), Gragg (1996, general), Gurney (1981, Hittite), Hawkins (1986, Hittite), Kent (1953, Old Persian), Pettinato (1981, Eblaite), Segert (1984, Ugaritic), and Vallat (1986, Iranian).

5.10 Terms

abstract pictogram
Akkadian
Assyrian
Babel
Babylonian
cuneiform
differentiation
gunu
Mesopotamia
morphogram
obverse
Old Persian
phonetic extension
phonogram
pictogram
reverse
seal
semantic complement
semantic compound
semantic extension
stylus
Sumerian
tablet
tokens: plain and complex
transcription
transliteration
Ugaritic
Uruk

5.11 Exercises

1 Examine the development from tokens to fully developed Sumerian writing. At what point can we say that writing first occurred? What development(s) was/were crucial for this change?
2 Using your own familiarity of writing with a pen and ink on paper, consider what changes happened when Akkadian scribes who were accustomed to writing cuneiform on clay first started to write Aramaic on flat surfaces.
3 Using figure 5.9, write the numbers in cuneiform for 36, 87, 23 and then add them together.

6 Egyptian

6.1 Language Family

Egyptian is a member of the Afro-Asiatic language family, a group of languages spoken in northern Africa and the Middle East. There are six branches in the family (table 6.1).

The Egyptian branch has only the Egyptian language, which is known from *ca.* 3000 OLD. The Egyptian language is usually divided into various periods as shown in table 6.2 (Loprieno 1995). Middle Egyptian came to be regarded as the classical language; many texts, particularly religious ones, were written in Middle Egyptian up to 450 NEW, long after Middle Egyptian was no longer spoken. From 1300 OLD, secular texts were written in Late Egyptian, and after 700 OLD, Demotic Egyptian was used for record-keeping and for other texts of a practical nature. The last pre-Coptic Egyptian text written in the old style is dated to about 450 NEW. In the second and third centuries, Egypt became predominantly Christian; from Christian times, the Egyptian language is called **Coptic**. Coptic died out around 1500 although it continues to be used as a liturgical language in the Coptic Church. The term *Coptic* is related to the Greek term for Egypt, *Aigyptos*; note the similar consonants – <c p t> of Coptic and <g p t> of *Aigyptos*.

Table 6.1 The Afro-Asiatic language family; only the better-known languages are listed

Afro-Asiatic

Egyptian	Semitic	Berber	Chadic	Cushitic	Omotic
Egyptian	Akkadian	Tuareg	Hausa	Sidamo	
(Coptic)	Phœnician	Tamazight	Bura	Somali	
	Hebrew	Mandara			
	Aramaic	Sokoro			
	Arabic	Masa			
	South Arabian				
	Amharic				

Table 6.2 Periods of the Egyptian language

Old Egyptian	3000–2000 OLD
Middle Egyptian	2000–1300 OLD
Late Egyptian	1300–700 OLD
Demotic	700 OLD–300 NEW
Coptic	300 NEW–1500

6.2 Background and History

The inhabited part of Egypt is a long thin area consisting of the banks of the Nile and its delta (figure 6.1). The land outside this area is mostly uninhabited desert with only the occasional oasis. The ancient Egyptian empire arose out of the union

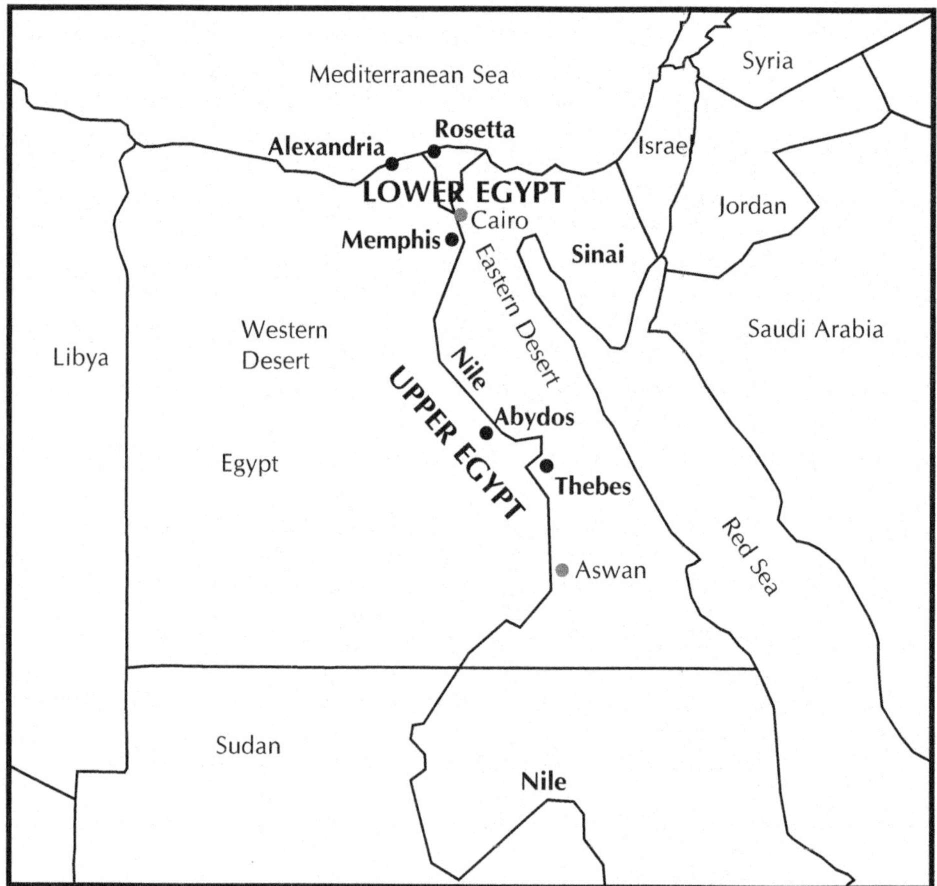

Figure 6.1 Map of ancient Egypt

Table 6.3 The cultural periods of Egypt

3100–2680 OLD	Archaic period
2680–2160 OLD	Old Kingdom
2060–1780 OLD	Middle Kingdom
1570–1085 OLD	New Kingdom
650–332 OLD	Late Dynastic Period
332–30 OLD	Greek
30 OLD–284 NEW	Roman
284–640	Coptic
700–1100	Arabization of Egypt
1250	Turkish
1516	Ottoman
1882–1919	British
1919–1952	Independent, bound by treaty to Britain
1952	Independent Republic

of two kingdoms: lower Egypt (the Nile delta) and upper Egypt (the main part of the river, roughly from modern-day Cairo to Aswan). Memphis (near modern Cairo) was the capital of lower Egypt, and Thebes (near modern Luxor) the capital of upper Egypt. The main part of ancient Egyptian history is usually divided into four periods (table 6.3): Old Kingdom, Middle Kingdom, New Kingdom, and Late Dynastic Period. The Greeks and then the Romans conquered Egypt but generally maintained the traditional Egyptian culture, including the writing system. From the third century NEW, however, Egypt became Christian and turned its back on the old culture. From this time, the people and the language came to be known as Coptic, and the language was written in the Coptic alphabet, based on the Greek alphabet (chapter 8). Egypt became predominantly Muslim after the Islamic conquest in the seventh century. Between the eighth and eleventh centuries, Egypt gradually became Arabized. Today, Arabic is the normal language of most Egyptians. There are also small Greek- and French-speaking communities in Egypt.

6.3 Phonology of Old Egyptian

The inventory in table 6.4 shows the phonemes for Old Egyptian. Many points about the phonology of Egyptian are uncertain.

Table 6.4 Phonemes of ancient Egyptian (adapted from Loprieno 1995)

p b		t d			c ɟ		k g	q		ʔ
f		s z	ʃ		ç			χ		ʕ h
m		n								
w		r l			j					
	i	u			iː	uː				
			a			aː				

6.4 Origin of Egyptian Writing

The emergence of writing in Egypt presents an interesting problem for scholars: was Egyptian borrowed from Mesopotamian cuneiform, or did it develop independently? The traditional view has been that writing was first attested in Mesopotamia around 3300 OLD and in Egypt around 3000 OLD.

From this time difference, many scholars have assumed that cuneiform writing developed first and was borrowed to create Egyptian writing. The borrowing was clearly not a close imitation. The structures of the two writing systems differ considerably, as do the shapes of the symbols. This type of borrowing is known as **stimulus diffusion**: the underlying idea is borrowed, although not the superficial details. Recent evidence, from Abydos, however, suggests that Egyptian writing dates back to 3500 OLD (Cruz-Urube 2001). The texts are primarily of an administrative nature, similar to the kind of early documents found in Mesopotamia. Clearly, this new Egyptian evidence argues that Egyptian and cuneiform writing developed simultaneously. The fact that they were both used for similar purposes suggests that there may have been some contact between the two peoples in the development of the two writing systems. Although these early Egyptian texts were used for administrative and mercantile purposes, writing became associated with the upper class. Writing in Egypt has been particularly associated with scribes, who were drawn from the upper classes; writing itself became a marker of social status in Egypt (Cruz-Urube 2001).

6.5 Styles of Writing

There are three major styles of Egyptian writing, known by their Greek names. The earliest, and best-known, form is called **hieroglyphic** 'sacred carving' from its early use in religious texts. **Hieratic** 'priestly' writing was a cursive type of writing, first appearing about the same time as hieroglyphic. Hieroglyphic and hieratic writing styles were largely in complementary distribution, with hieroglyphic used for more formal purposes, and hieratic for less formal ones. Around 600 OLD, a third type of writing called **demotic** 'popular' arose, and hieratic writing was confined to religious texts (hence the Greek name *hieratic* 'priestly'). Demotic was an even more cursive form of the script and was widely used in administrative and personal documents. Examples of hieratic and demotic styles are shown in figure 6.2 with a hieroglyphic transcription. Note that the hieroglyphic and hieratic styles continued alongside demotic, although it became customary to write certain types of texts in only one of the three forms of writing. The last known piece of writing in ancient Egyptian is a demotic graffito in the temple of Philae, dated 450 NEW. A **graffito** (pl. *graffiti*) is an informal text, especially on a wall.

Hieroglyphic writing has a strong pictorial aspect. A picture of a bird, although stylized, looks like a bird. This pictorial aspect was never lost in hieroglyphic writing throughout its history. In hieratic and demotic writing, which were written cursively, the pictorial aspect is generally absent. In the hieroglyphic style, individual

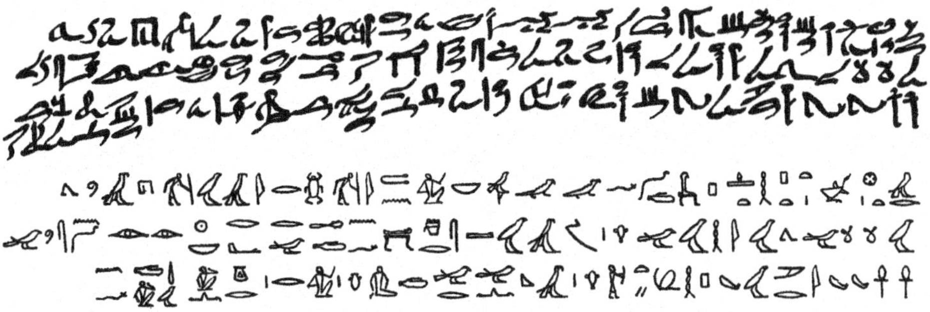

Literary hieratic of the twelfth dynasty, with transcription

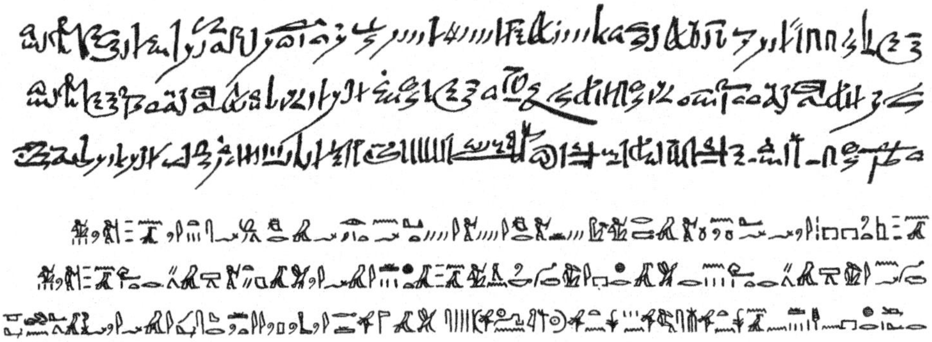

Official hieratic of the twentieth dynasty, with transcription

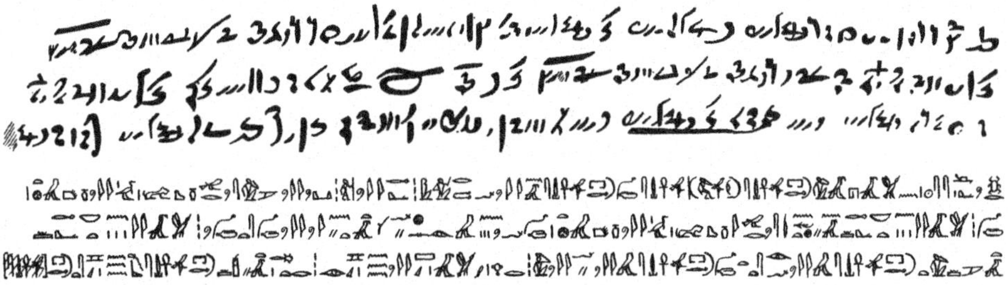

Literary demotic of the third century OLD, with transcription

Figure 6.2 Some examples of hieratic and demotic writing with hieroglyphic transcription (from Sir Alan Gardiner, *Egyptian Grammar*, plate 2. Oxford: Griffith Institute, Oxford University Press, 1950. © 1950 by Griffith Institute. Reproduced with permission)

graphemes were written as separate units, but in hieratic and demotic styles, many ligatures were used.

6.6 Social Context of Writing

6.6.1 *Materials*

Hieroglyphic writing was frequently inscribed in stone, but hieroglyphs were also painted on walls and other surfaces. Most writing, however, was done in hieratic or demotic on papyrus. **Papyrus** is a reedy plant growing in warm, wet locations. Thin slices can be laid together with overlapping edges to form an excellent writing surface, looking somewhat like a sheet of paper. For longer works, the sides of sheets of papyrus were attached together to form a scroll which could be rolled up for storage. In the very dry climate of Egypt, many objects such as papyrus have been preserved which would have decayed elsewhere. As a result of the climate, Egypt has an enormously rich archæological record. Many documents in other languages are preserved simply because they happened to have ended up in Egypt.

Scribes carried reed pens in a special case. Most writing was in black ink, but red was also used on occasion. Hieroglyphic inscriptions were probably drawn in ink by a scribe and then cut by a stonecutter.

6.6.2 *Literature*

Early records which mention a name may have shown ownership of an object or honoured the person named. This use of language is found in many places where writing is first used. Among the earliest Egyptian documents showing writing is the Narmer palette (figure 6.3), a ceremonial cosmetic palette from around 3000 OLD. (Cosmetics were used in certain ritual situations, and the palette served as a surface for mixing different substances.)

Egyptian religion provided an unusual use for writing. Egyptians believed in an afterlife. As long as a person's name was regularly mentioned, that person would continue to have a life after death. Writing provided a permanent way of invoking someone's name. By putting someone's name in a funerary inscription, that person was ensured of a continuing afterlife regardless of the possible neglect of descendants. Conquerors who wanted to be particularly vindictive would chisel away the name of the conquered king off inscriptions, effectively ending his life forever.

Beyond religion, Egyptian literature has a very wide range of material: personal and administrative letters; medical, dental, veterinary guides; economic and diplomatic reports; prose, poetry, epics; wisdom literature (etiquette books); and moralistic books.

6.6.3 *Scribes and literacy*

Scribes occupied an important place in Egyptian life. Being able to read and write was a matter of considerable prestige. It is difficult to estimate how widespread

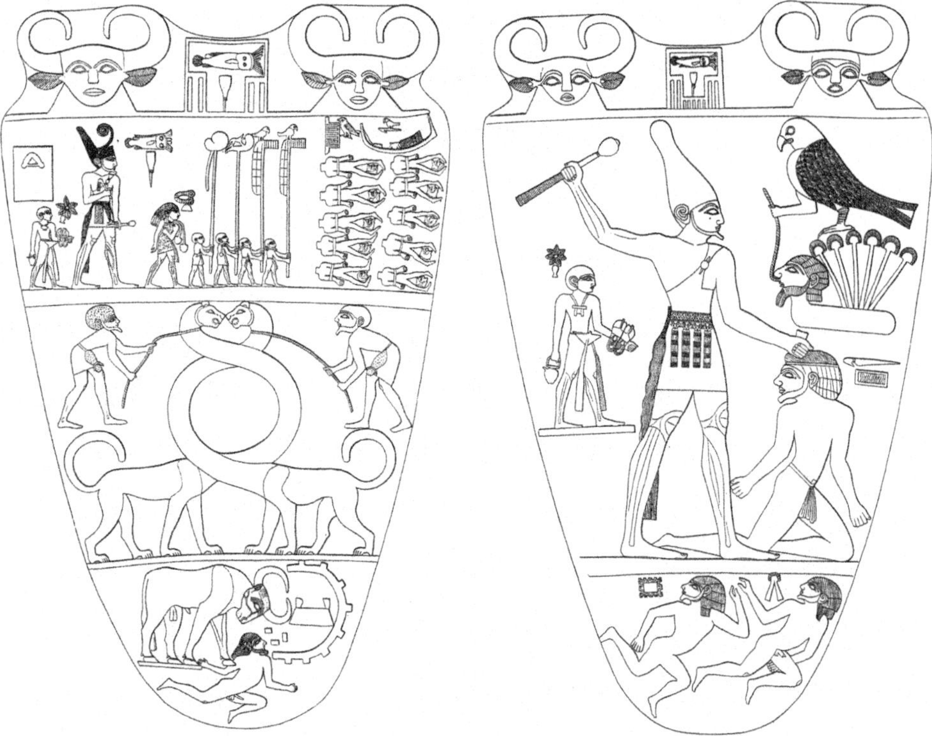

Figure 6.3 The Narmer palette

literacy was in ancient Egypt: the lower classes were probably uniformly illiterate, although literacy was likely somewhat common among the upper classes. For the middle classes, literacy existed where it was necessary for work. No doubt, when people needed to write a letter or when they received one, they often went to a scribe who, for a fee, would write or read the document.

6.7 Structure of Egyptian Writing

6.7.1 *Phonographic writing*

Egyptian writing has a large phonographic component. Only consonants were written; vowels were not written. There are different graphemes for all the consonants except /l/, which according to Loprieno (1995) was written ambiguously in a variety of ways. In principle, all Egyptian writing could have been done phonographically, but that was not the practice; Egyptian writing also had a significant morphographic component.

The absence of written vowels presents a difficulty for modern scholars. The Egyptians themselves, of course, spoke the language and knew what vowels went

Table 6.5 The monoconsonantal symbols of Egyptian

Grapheme	*Transliteration*	*Sound value*	*Object depicted*
𓄿	ꜣ	ʔ	vulture
𓇋	ỉ	i or ʔ	reed
𓇌	y/j	j	two reeds
𓂝	ʿ	ʕ	arm
𓅱	w	w	quail chick
𓏲	w	w	(alternative form for <w>)
𓃀	b	b	foot and leg
𓊪	p	p	mat or stool
𓆑	f	f	horned viper
𓅓	m	m	owl
𓈖	n	n	water
𓂋	r	r	mouth
𓉔	h	h	plan of courtyard
𓎛	ḥ	ħ	wick of twisted flax
𓐍	ḫ	x	placenta
𓄡	ẖ	ç	animal's belly with teats
𓊃	s	s	door bolt
𓋴	s	s	folded cloth
𓈙	š	ʃ	pool
𓈎	ḳ	q	hill
𓎡	k	k	bowl with handle
𓎼	g	g	stand for pot
𓏏	t	t	loaf
𓍿	ṯ	c	tether
𓂧	d	d	hand
𓆓	ḏ	ɟ	snake

where. For us today, the writing does not tell us when a vowel occurred nor what that vowel was. For example, when a form was written <pt>, it could have represented a variety of shapes: /pt, Vpt, pVt, ptV/ (where /V/ represents any vowel), or other combinations, and further, different vowels could have filled the V position.

By using a variety of evidence, such as other Afro-Asiatic languages, internal reconstruction, knowledge of Coptic, and Egyptian loanwords in Greek, scholars have made some headway in determining the vowels of ancient Egyptian, but a great deal is unclear. In pronouncing Egyptian, Egyptologists often insert the vowel [e] simply to make the word pronounceable: for example, the word for 'house' is <pr>, and scholars usually pronounce this as [per] without necessarily meaning that the ancient Egyptian vowel in this word really was [e]. The written transliteration remains, however, <pr>.

6.7.1.1 MONOCONSONANTAL GRAPHEMES

Every Egyptian consonantal phoneme (except /l/) had a specific grapheme; these are shown in table 6.5. The traditional transliteration used by Egyptologists is given; the column 'Sound value' is a guess as to how the phonemes of ancient Egyptian sounded. Most graphemes are fairly clear as to what object they depict, but some are uncertain; the names for the objects depicted here are traditional in Egyptology.

The symbol <3> represents a glottal stop which is sometimes transliterated as <a>. A curled top is used with <ỉ> to emphasize that it is not a vowel. The graphemes <w> and <s> have allographic variation. The spiral allograph of <w> was a cursive hieratic form which came to be used in hieroglyphic writing as an alternative for the quail chick. The two allographs for the sound /s/ were in free variation; these originally represented two different sounds, possibly /s z/, which fell together early on. There were four different [h]-type sounds transcribed <h ḥ ḫ ẖ]>; the phonetic values given are reasonable guesses as to how they actually sounded. The Egyptians had no fixed order for their graphemes; the order given here was developed by nineteenth-century scholars and is universally used by Egyptologists in dictionaries and other lists.

6.7.1.2 BICONSONANTAL GRAPHEMES

In addition to the **monoconsonantal graphemes** representing one consonant, the Egyptians also had graphemes which represented two- and three-consonant sequences. Note that these did not necessarily represent consonant clusters. The **biconsonantal grapheme** <mn> could represent /men/, /mun/, /min/, or /mn/, or any other combination in which the consonants /m/ and /n/ might have occurred in that order. Not all phonologically possible consonant sequences have graphemes. If the monoconsonantal graphemes are taken as basic, then bi- and triconsonantal graphemes can be regarded as diphones and triphones in our terminology. Some of the biconsonantal symbols are given in table 6.6. The transliteration is given alongside; the sound values can be determined by reference to the preceding chart. (Not all biconsonantal graphemes are given here.)

Table 6.6 Some biconsonantal symbols of Egyptian

Grapheme	*Transliteration*	*Object depicted*
	3w	spine and spinal cord
	w3	lasso
	wḏ	cord wound on stick
	b3	jabiru (kind of stork)
	mr	hoe
	nb	basket
	ḥm	laundry club
	s3	pintail duck
	sw	sedge
	k3	two arms
	ḏ3	fire drill
	ỉr	eye
	wr	fork-tailed swallow
	mn	gameboard
	ms	three foxskins
	ns	tongue
	ḥn	cloth receptacle
	sn	arrowhead
	mt	penis
	tỉ	pestle
	ḏd	reed column

Table 6.7 Some triconsonantal symbols of Egyptian

Grapheme	*Transliteration*	*Object depicted*
	ỉwn	column with tenon
	w3ḥ	swab
	nṯr	flag
	nḏm	pod
	ḥtp	bread loaf on mat
	ḫrw	oar
	tyw	buzzard
	ʕnḫ	sandal strap
	nfr	heart and trachea
	ʕḥʕ	mast
	rwḏ	bowstring
	ḫpr	scarab beetle
	šmʕ	flowering sedge
	ḏʕm	staff with animal head

6.7.1.3 TRICONSONANTAL GRAPHEMES

There are also **triconsonantal graphemes** for three-consonant sequences. Some of these are given in table 6.7. Note that Egyptian typically had triconsonantal roots; that is, a root consisted of three consonants. Thus, a root could always be written with the same triconsonantal grapheme.

6.7.2 Phonological complements

A **phonological complement** is a grapheme that repeats phonological information already given by a previous grapheme. The previous grapheme can be a phonogram or a morphogram. Phonological complements were commonly used in Egyptian writing to repeat or reinforce phonological information given by a bi- or triconsonantal grapheme. Consider, for example, the word /nfr/ 'beautiful, good'. There is

Table 6.8 Examples of phonological complements. In these examples, the bi- or triconsonantal grapheme is at the left or top, and the phonological complement is at the right or bottom. The phonological complement is written in parentheses

	ȝw (w)		wȝ (ȝ)
	wr (r)		bȝ (ȝ)
	mn (n)		wȝḥ (ḥ)
	nḏm (m)		ḫpr (r)

a triconsonantal grapheme for the sequence <nfr>. In principle, this word could be written with this symbol alone; normally, however, this word was written where the graphemes for <f> and <r> do not add new information, but merely reinforce part of the information already present in . One problem in reading an Egyptian text is to distinguish the phonographic graphemes presenting new information from the phonological complements which merely repeat information already given by the bi- and triconsonantal graphemes. In the examples in table 6.8, the phonological complement is shown in parentheses.

6.7.3 *Morphographic writing*

Although in principle Egyptian could have been written completely phonographically, it was normally written as a mixture of **phonographic** and **morphographic** graphemes.

Many graphemes could be used as both morphograms and phonograms. The grapheme for /pr/ 'house' is (table 6.9). Frequently, a small vertical stroke was added to a grapheme to indicate that it was used as a morphogram, i.e., as a symbol meaning 'house'. To indicate the plural in older writing, a grapheme would be repeated three times. Later for the plural, the symbol would be written only once, and three strokes or three circles would be added. Since the word for 'house' was pronounced /pr/, this grapheme was also used phonographically for the consonant sequence /pr/ generally; this use is an example of **phonological extension**, a process by which many graphemes derived their phonological value.

Table 6.9 Examples of morphemic writing. Note that the same symbol could be used morphographically for 'house' or phonographically for the sequence /pr/

morphogram 'house'	older plural 'houses'	later plural 'houses'	phonogram /pr/

6.7.4 *Semantic complements*

Semantic complements, graphemes which are used to give additional semantic information, were common, particularly with nouns and verbs. In general, they relate to the general semantic area of the form. In English, we sometimes clarify the meaning of the word 'funny' by saying 'funny weird' or 'funny ha-ha'; here, 'weird' and 'ha-ha' function as semantic complements. In Egyptian, semantic complements were normally written at the end of a word and were not pronounced. Table 6.10 shows some of the common semantic complements.

The word /ptr/ means 'see, behold'. It is written 𓊪𓏏𓂋𓁹 <ptr> with three phonographic graphemes, <p> <t> <r>, and the eye at the end is a semantic complement showing that the word has to do with vision.

Semantic complements are often useful in distinguishing homonyms (table 6.11), but they are by no means limited to such situations. For example, there are several words /mn/: 'be firm', 'be ill', 'a sick man'. Remember that although these words were written the same, we do not know if they were pronounced the same; i.e., they may have had different vowels. These words are written with the same phonographic elements, but are distinguished by the semantic complements. The scroll indicates an action or state. The specific bird in the second one always shows something bad or wrong. The third word, for 'a sick man', has two semantic complements: the bird shows that the meaning is bad, and the seated figure refers to a man.

Another set of examples is shown (table 6.12) by the homonyms /šsp/ (the grapheme itself is a pictograph of a fence). The square mat □ is a phonological complement repeating the /p/ of the basic symbol.

6.7.5 *Internal structure of Egyptian writing*

The direction of writing varied. Figure 6.4 shows the same text written in different ways. In the top part, the same hieroglyphic text is written in three ways: top left – written left to right; just below – right to left; top right has two vertical arrangements showing how the same text would be written on each side of a door. Numbers in the top left example show the order in which the individual symbols would be written and read. In the text below, the **transliteration** shows a symbol-by-symbol romanization; the transcription shows the consonantal text. Next comes the translation, and the conventional Egyptological reading.

Most commonly, writing went from right to left. In the hieratic and demotic styles this was always the case. In the hieroglyphic style, left to right was also used. One can easily tell the direction of writing by looking at a symbol of a living figure. If an animal looks to the left, writing goes from left to right; if the animal faces to the right, writing goes from right to left. It is as though the reader walks along encountering the animals going in the opposite direction. In some cases, such as next to doors, writing was vertical, going from top to bottom; in such cases, writing goes from the outside in: that is, glyphs of animals face away from the door. In texts for modern readers, the hieroglyphic style is usually given left to right since that is the normal way users of the Roman alphabet read.

Table 6.10 Examples of semantic complements

Grapheme	*Use as semantic complement*	*Notes*
𓀀	man, person	
𓁐	woman	
𓀭	god, king	note beard
𓀜	force, effort	
𓂡	force, effort	replaced previous allograph in later texts
𓀏	enemy, foreigner	man with elbows tied behind back
𓁹	eye, see, vision	eye
𓂻	walk, run	
𓄹	limb, flesh	piece of flesh
𓄛	skin, mammal, leather	piece of skin with flesh attached
𓅪	small, bad, weak	sparrow, note rounded tail
𓆱	wood, tree	branch
𓇳	sun, light, time	
𓈓	copper, bronze	piece of metal
𓊖	town, village	layout of village
𓈉	desert, foreign country	
𓉐	house, building	one-room building seen from overhead
𓏛	book, writing, abstract object	scroll, bound and sealed
𓊛	boat	
𓊜	capsize	

Table 6.11 Homonyms having the same phonological symbols /mn/ but different semantic complements

𓏠𓈖[illegible]	/mn/	'be firm'
𓏠𓈖𓅪	/mn/	'be ill'
𓏠𓈖𓅪𓀀	/mn/	'a sick man'

Table 6.12 Homonyms having the same phonological symbols /šsp/, but different semantic complements

Graphs	*Sound value*	*Meaning*	*Notes on semantic complement*
	/ʃsp/	'accept'	force or effort
	/ʃsp/	'palm (unit of length)'	pictorial origin of semantic complement uncertain
	/ʃsp/	'statue'	upright mummy
	/ʃsp/	'white, bright, dawn'	sun with rays

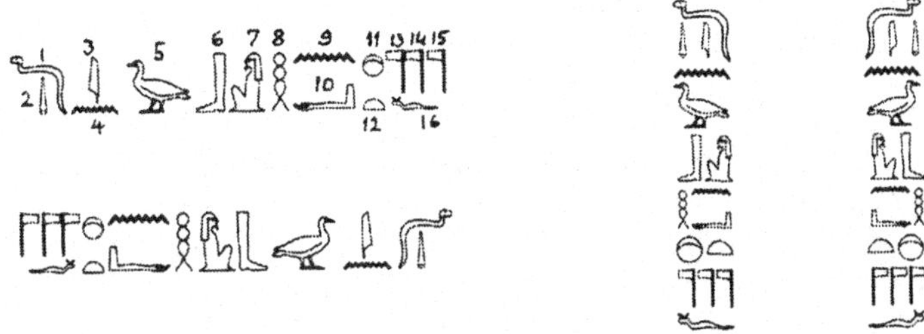

TRANSLITERATION: [1]*ḏ* [2]MDW [3]*j* - [4]*n* [5]*gb* - [6]*b* - [7]"GOD" [8]*ḥ* - [9]*n* - [10]ʿ [11]PSḎ - [12]*t* - 13-14-15"GODS" - [16]*f*

TRANSCRIPTION:	*ḏ(d)*	*mdw(.w)*	*jn*	*gbb*	*ḥn*ʿ	*psḏ.t=f*
TRANSLATION:	"To say	the words	by	Geb	with	his Ennead"

CONVENTIONAL READING: [ɟed me'duu in 'gebeb 'ḥena peseɟe'tef]

Figure 6.4 The same text in different orientations (from Anthony Loprieno, *Ancient Egyptian: A Linguistic Introduction*, p. 16. Cambridge: Cambridge University Press, 1995. © 1995 by Cambridge University Press. Reprinted with the permission of Cambridge University Press)

Within a line of text, graphemes are arranged to fit the space suitably. Graphemes are often made to fit into an imaginary square. Thus two graphemes with a generally horizontal shape would be written on top of each other rather than in a horizontal sequence. Rearrangement is normal with names which include the name of a god, where the grapheme for the god is always written first no matter where it actually occurs in the name. Very occasionally, graphemes are written in the wrong order for æsthetic reasons. In /t3/ (table 6.13), the <t> symbol is placed above the bird to fill the space more evenly.

Over time, new graphemes were added and older ones abandoned. There was little, if any, attempt at simplifying the writing system over time. Although a word might potentially be written in a variety of ways, normally one way prevailed.

Table 6.13 Examples of æsthetic rearrangement

	not		/tȝ/ 'this'
	not		/wḏ/ 'command'
	not		/mr/ 'pyramid'

Table 6.14 Egyptian sample text

< nfr	f.r.t	fem	tn	m	sn	n.t	fem	ỉ >
/ nfr-t			tn	m	sn-t-i /			
beautiful-fem			this-fem	is	sister-my			

'This beautiful woman is my sister;

< n	ḏ.d	n	s	ḏw-	w	t .bad	nb.t >
/ n	ɟd-n-s			ɟw-t			nb-t /
not	say-not-she			evil-fem			any-fem

she cannot speak any evil.'

6.8 Example Text

In the first line of the sample text in table 6.14, /nfr/ is a triconsonantal phonogram, reinforced by two monoconsonantal phonological complements /f/ and /r/. (Periods in the transliteration separate symbols written vertically; in the transcription hyphens separate morphemes.) This is followed by a phonogram /t/, which represents a feminine suffix. At the end of the word is the semantic complement for a woman. The second word is /tn/, the feminine form for 'this', written phonographically. The third word is /m/ used to form a copulative sentence, i.e. 'is'. In the word /snti/ 'my sister', the biconsonantal grapheme for /sn/ is reinforced by a phonological complement /n/. This is followed by the feminine suffix /t/, and then the semantic complement for a woman. The /i/ is a suffix meaning 'my (masc.)'; it is written with the grapheme which is also commonly used as the semantic complement for 'man', but here is a morphogram pronounced /i/.

In the second line, a morphogram for /n/ 'not' is the first word. The verb /ɟdns/ 'she did not say' is written with four monoconsonantal phonograms. The noun /ɟwt/ 'evil' is written with the biconsonantal phonogram for /ɟw/ followed by the feminine suffix marker /t/ (abstract nouns are frequently feminine). The semantic complement at the end of the word is the sparrow indicating something 'small' or 'bad'. The adjective /nbt/ 'any (fem.)' modifies /ȷwt/; it is written with the biconsonantal phonogram /nb/ followed by the feminine suffix /t/.

6.9 Decipherment

The **decipherment** of Egyptian is an extremely interesting story (Parkinson 1999). When the Egyptians became Christian, they turned away from the ancient Egyptian culture which they regarded as heathen. As a result, knowledge of the writing system was lost. The existence of Egyptian writing was obvious to anyone visiting Egypt, but it had become unreadable. In Europe, it was commonly believed that the symbols were ideographic, that is, that they represented ideas, not linguistic entities.

In 1799, a French soldier came across a large stone in the Mediterranean town of Rashid (Rosetta). The stone contained the same text in two languages (Egyptian and Greek) and three scripts (hieroglyphic, demotic, and Greek). The Rosetta Stone, as it came to be known, quickly found its way to England where it can be seen today in the British Museum. Copies of the text were sent to scholars around Europe. The Greek was easily read. The stone records a decree of 196 OLD: the priests were to establish a cult in honour of King Ptolemy V in return for favours he had granted them.

An Englishman, Thomas Young (1773–1829), took some steps towards deciphering the text; however, the French scholar Jean-François **Champollion** is generally credited with using the stone to decipher the Egyptian script. In the hieroglyphic portion of the text, he found several occurrences of a grapheme enclosed in an oval, called a **cartouche.** In 1761, the Rev. Jean-Jacques Barthélemy had suggested that these cartouches contained the names of rulers. Champollion was fortunate in that these names were written almost entirely phonographically, and furthermore the Egyptians had made some attempt to include the vowels in these foreign-sounding Greek names. (Recall that Egypt was ruled by the Greeks after Alexander's conquest of the fourth century OLD.) With this foothold, Champollion was able to make considerable headway in deciphering the entire language. By the end of the nineteenth century, Egyptian texts were once more understood.

6.10 Further Reading

Allen (2000) provides an excellent modern introduction to the language and writing system, with many interesting cultural essays; Hoch (1996) is another good modern text for beginners. Gardiner (1973) is the standard reference grammar. Loprieno (1995) is a good introduction to the language, but with little on writing. Faulkner (1988) is a useful dictionary; it is also an example of handwritten books, common before computer printing of Egyptian. Davies (1990) is a short introduction to the writing system. Quirke and Andrews (1988) gives a life-size reproduction of the Rosetta Stone; the decipherment is described in the recent work by Parkinson (1999). The readily available reprints of works by Wallace Budge are to be avoided as unreliable and outdated.

6.11 Terms

biconsonantal grapheme
cartouche
Champollion
Coptic
decipherment
demotic
graffito
hieratic
hieroglyphic
monoconsonantal grapheme
morphographic writing
papyrus
phonographic writing
phonological complement
phonological extension
semantic complement
stimulus diffusion
transliteration
triconsonantal grapheme

6.12 Exercise

The following cartouches show the names *Cleopatra* and *Ptolemaios* written in Egyptian. Without looking at the values in table 6.5, try to decipher the writing of these names. The cartouches contain additional symbols that you will not be able to decipher.

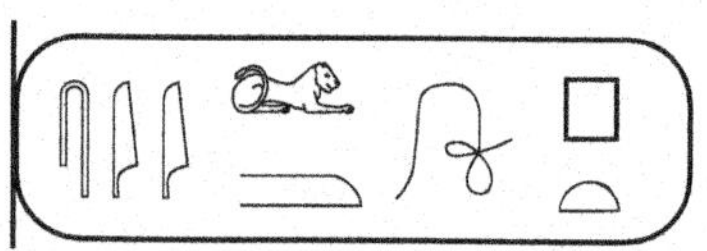

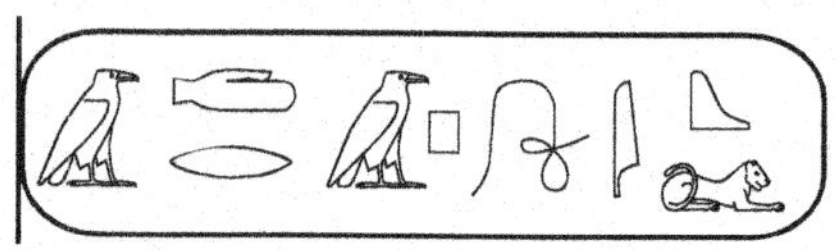

7 Semitic

7.1 The Semitic Language Family

The **Semitic** family of languages is a branch of the Afro-Asiatic family already introduced in chapters 5 and 6. The Semitic languages are particularly important for the history of writing because the Semitic Akkadians were among the very first people to write, and because an early West Semitic speaker invented the **abjad**, from which ultimately descend all the non-Chinese writing systems in use today. Recall from chapter 2 that an **alphabet** is a writing system in which all phonemes, both consonants and vowels, are represented by a distinct symbol; an abjad is like an alphabet, but only consonants are written, not vowels; the term 'abjad' was introduced by Daniels (1996a). One of the Semitic scripts, Ethiopic, has a somewhat different structure, which Daniels calls an **abugida**; in an abugida, the vowels are written as diacritics on the consonants, and one vowel is not explicitly written. (Abugidas are discussed in more detail in chapter 11.)

The classification of Semitic languages presented in table 7.1 is based on Hetzron (1987) and Faber (1997). The Semitic language family as a whole is divided into

Table 7.1 The Semitic language family

- **East Semitic**
  - Akkadian, Babylonian, Assyrian
  - Eblaite
- **West Semitic**
  - Central West Semitic
    - Northwest Semitic
      - Ugaritic
      - Canaanite
        - Old Canaanite
        - Phœnician, Punic
        - Hebrew
        - Moabite, Amorite
      - Aramaic, Syriac
    - Arabic
  - Southern West Semitic
    - Old South Arabian
    - Modern South Arabian
    - Ethiopic
      - Ge'ez, Amharic, Tigrinya, Tigré

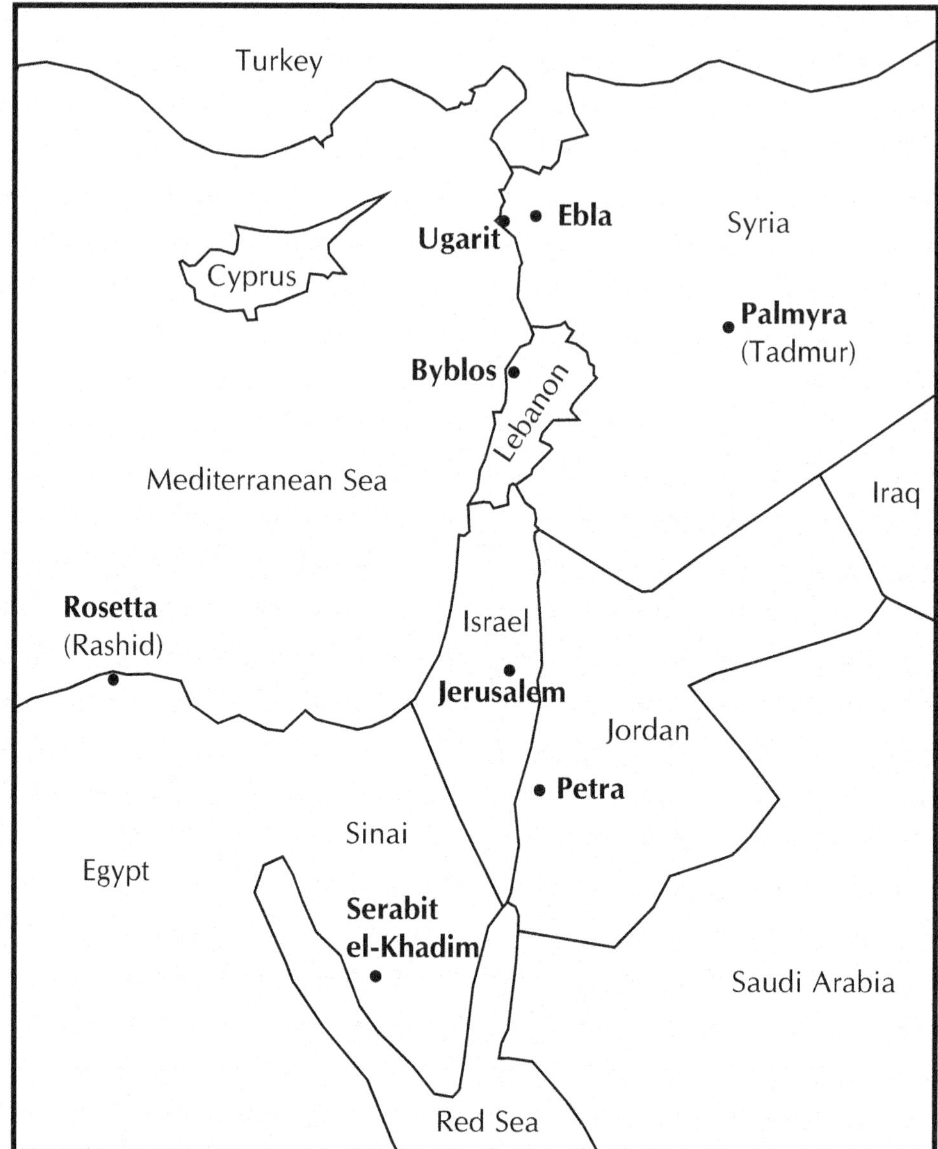

Figure 7.1 Linguistic sites of importance in the Middle East

East and West Semitic. We have already seen that **Akkadian**, the main language of East Semitic, used cuneiform writing. West Semitic is divided into Central West and Southern West Semitic. Central West Semitic consists of two branches: Northwest Semitic and **Arabic**. Northwest Semitic languages include Ugaritic (see chapter 5), Canaanite, and **Aramaic**. Canaanite includes Old Canaanite (a few early inscriptions),

Phœnician (and its later form **Punic**, spoken in Carthage), Hebrew, and a few other poorly attested languages. Southern West Semitic includes the South Arabian languages and a number of languages spoken in Ethiopia and Eritrea. The South Arabian languages are spoken at the southern end of the Arabian peninsula (note that the South Arabian languages are different from Arabic). We have ancient South Arabian inscriptions, but the languages of those inscriptions are not the ancestors of the South Arabian languages that are spoken there today.

The Semitic abjad emerged about 1500 OLD. We have already seen that the East Semitic speakers lived in Mesopotamia (chapter 5). In this chapter we are concerned with the West Semitic peoples who by this time had established themselves in the **Levant** (the eastern end of the Mediterranean; figure 7.1). To get a picture of the Semitic language situation in this area around 1500 OLD, we see that Akkadian is spoken in Mesopotamia. In the Levant, Eblaite, once spoken around Aleppo in Syria, has died out. The Ugaritic peoples are living at Ras Shamra (in modern-day Syria) and the Canaanites are farther south. The Aramæans (who spoke Aramaic) are to the northeast. Soon, the Canaanites will divide into Phœnicians in the north and Hebrews in the south. We know little about the ancestors of the Arabic speakers at this time, but they are later found at Petra (in modern-day Jordan) and in the northern Arabian peninsula. The South Semitic peoples are living in southern Arabia and will soon cross to northeastern Africa.

7.2 Origin of the Semitic Abjad

The West Semitic abjad appeared around 1500 OLD. An interesting and difficult question for us is how this system came about. Very likely the Semitic peoples did not invent the abjad out of nothing. The Levant was a crossroads between the two important empires of the Akkadians and the Egyptians, each empire with its own writing. Anyone living there could easily have learned about both types of writing.

Both Egyptian and Akkadian had a **morphographic** component in their writing systems which the Semitic writing did not adopt; the abjad was completely **phonographic.**

The Akkadian system of writing is a less likely ancestor for the abjad. Akkadian writing was structurally quite different from the Semitic abjad. The phonographic component of Akkadian was syllabic, not phonemic, and it indicated both consonants and vowels. In the Semitic abjad, writing was consonantal and did not include vowels.

The Egyptian writing system had greater similarity to the Semitic abjad. It would have been possible in Egyptian to use only the monoconsonantal symbols. Further, Egyptian did not write vowels. Thus, the Egyptian writing system is structurally like the Semitic abjad in two crucial aspects: only consonants were written, and a word could be written consonant by consonant. On balance, I choose Egyptian over Akkadian as the more likely ancestor of the abjad on the basis of systemic similarities.

In the creation of the Semitic abjad, the system used in Egyptian was greatly simplified. All Semitic writing was phonographic, and all symbols were used to represent single consonants only. The morphographic and multiconsonantal usages of Egyptian, as well as the phonological and semantic complements, were discarded. Sass (1992) points out that it was common in Egypt during the Middle Kingdom period (2060–1780 OLD) to write foreign names phonographically. It is also quite possible that Egyptian scribes were taught by learning to write phonographically first and then later to substitute the appropriate morphographic symbols. Japanese children learn *kana* first in this way and then gradually substitute the appropriate *kanji*. We can imagine that an Egyptian writing instructor might explain to a Semitic speaker how phonographic writing was done, but not get to the morphographic explanation.

The Semitic symbols were used acrophonically. In **acrophony**, a symbol is used to represent the first phoneme in the object portrayed. For example, if, in English, I use a picture of a tulip to represent /t/ or one of a daisy to represent /d/, I have used these symbols acrophonically. The relevance of acrophony for the history of the Semitic abjad will be made clear shortly.

Gardiner (1916) analysed the Proto-Canaanite material found in 1905 in turquoise mines in the Sinai at Serābîṭ el-Khâdem. The mines were operated by the Egyptians with Canaanite slaves. Several objects were found there with short inscriptions. The reading of these inscriptions remains problematic, but many scholars (Gardiner 1916, Albright 1966, Cross 1989, Naveh 1982) have seen them as the forerunners of the Semitic abjad.

Gardiner saw a resemblance between some of the symbols and Egyptian phonograms (figure 7.2). Possibly a Semitic speaker, who was familiar, at least to some degree, with Egyptian writing, tried to apply Egyptian writing to the Semitic language. Gardiner believed that rather than using the Egyptian value of a symbol, the Semitic speaker translated the Egyptian term into Semitic and then used the symbol acrophonically to represent the first phoneme in the Semitic word. For example, the Egyptian symbol for house is 𓉐. This symbol can be used in Egyptian as a morphogram for 'house', but also phonographically for a /pr/ sequence. Gardiner's view was that this symbol was used in writing Semitic, but not with the Egyptian sound value. Rather, the Egyptian symbol meaning 'house' was translated into Semitic /bēt/, and the symbol was used acrophonically as the symbol for /b/ in writing Semitic. Note that although a symbol may have been bi- or triconsonantal in Egyptian, all symbols were used monoconsonantally in Semitic. Subsequent discoveries were made in the Sinai, and Albright (1966), who reanalysed the material, claimed to have deciphered the majority of it. Figure 7.2 gives some of the identifications that Gardiner and Albright made. Other symbols of the Semitic abjad may have simply been invented.

Although the matter is not decided fully, and the Gardiner–Albright theory may not turn out to be correct in all respects, it appears that the Semitic abjad was at least partially based on a simplified application of Egyptian writing.

Naveh (1982) summarizes the development of the **Proto-Canaanite** script as follows:

1 It was invented around 1700 OLD by Canaanites who had some knowledge of Egyptian writing.

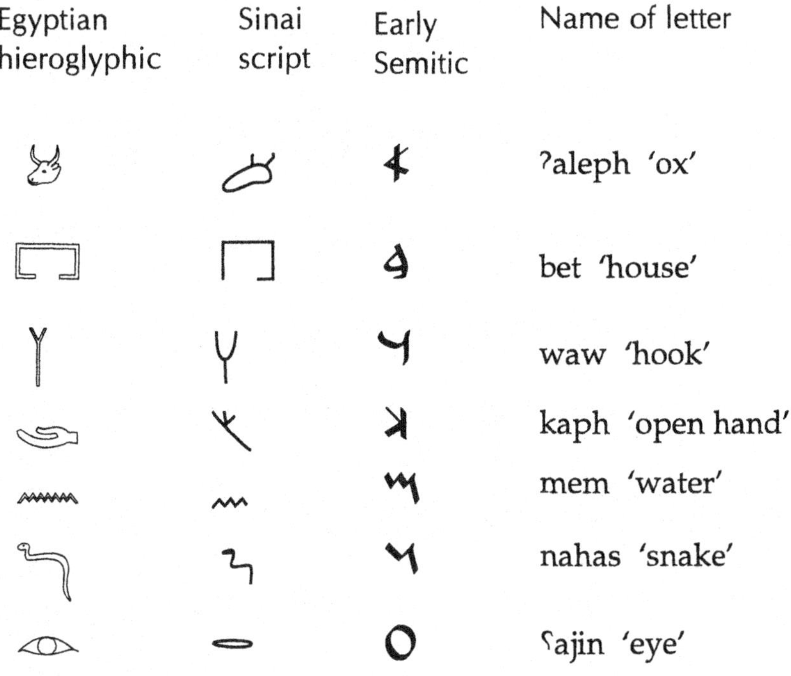

Egyptian hieroglyphic
Sinai script
Early Semitic
Name of letter
ʔaleph 'ox'
bet 'house'
waw 'hook'
kaph 'open hand'
mem 'water'
nahas 'snake'
ʕajin 'eye'

Figure 7.2 Some examples of the Egyptian sources of Semitic letters according to Gardiner (1916) and Albright (1966)

2 The number of letters representing the consonantal system was initially twenty-seven. By the thirteenth century, it was reduced to twenty-two.

3 The original signs were pictographs and most developed acrophonic values. These evolved into linear letters.

4 The pictographic conception permitted writing in any direction: from right to left, from left to right, in vertical columns, and even horizontal or vertical boustrophedon (lines in alternating directions; see §8.3). Vertical writing effectively disappeared around 1100 OLD.

7.3 Development of the Semitic Abjad

Figure 7.3 gives a timeline of the development of the Semitic abjad starting with Proto-Canaanite. Many of the dates shown are uncertain. We will discuss the Semitic abjad in historical order. During the Proto-Canaanite period, South Semitic speakers used the abjad to write their languages; they established a South Semitic script which took its own course (§§7.3.1 and 7.6). The Greeks borrowed the Semitic abjad next, but we will delay the history of Greek writing until chapter 8. In the northern Levant, Phœnician is the direct descendant of Proto-Canaanite, in both language

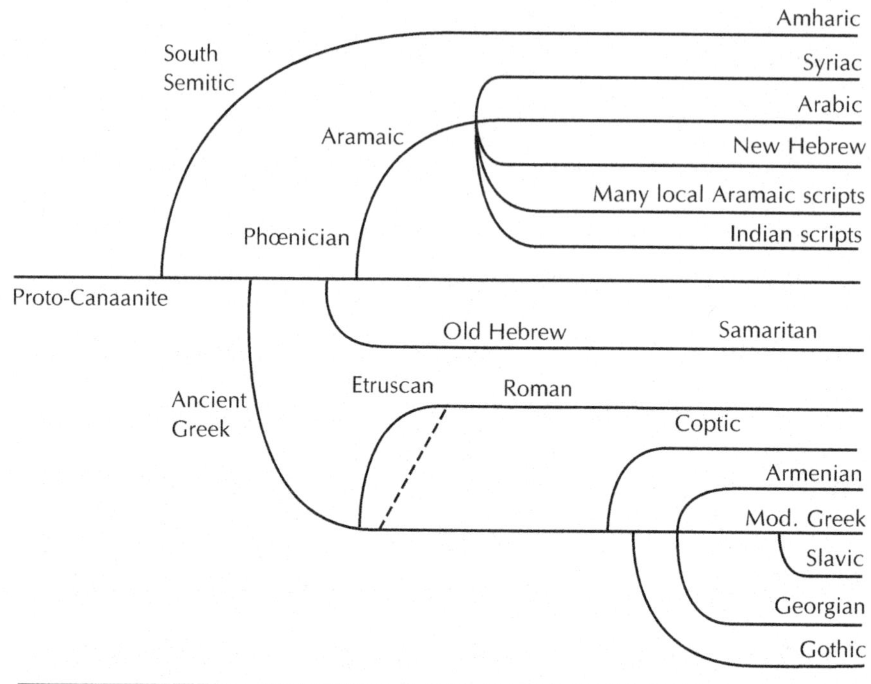

Figure 7.3 Timeline of the development of the Semitic abjad

and script. The Phœnician script was used first to write Phœnician and then Hebrew and Aramaic.

7.3.1 *Southern West Semitic*

The Southern West Semitic languages are spoken by small numbers of people in the southern part of the Arabian peninsula (the South Arabian languages) and by much larger numbers of people in northeastern Africa (**Ge'ez**, Amharic, Tigré, Tigrinya). (Be sure not to confuse South Arabian with Arabic; see table 7.1.) The Semitic abjad became known in this area quite early, possibly by 1400 OLD, and was used for the old South Arabian languages. A large number of South Arabian inscriptions are found in the southwestern area of the Arabian peninsula in a monumental script, dating from the eighth century OLD. The South Arabian script had 29 letters as opposed to the Proto-Canaanite inventory of 27. The two additional letters were added to write new phonemes which had emerged in the South Arabian languages.

The South Arabian abjad travelled from the Arabian peninsula across the narrow stretch of water to Africa. Originally, the Ethiopic script was a purely consonantal abjad, like South Arabian. However, the script was eventually modified to an abugida, probably through contact with Indian scripts (Daniels 1996a). The Ethiopic abugida is presented in more detail in §7.6.

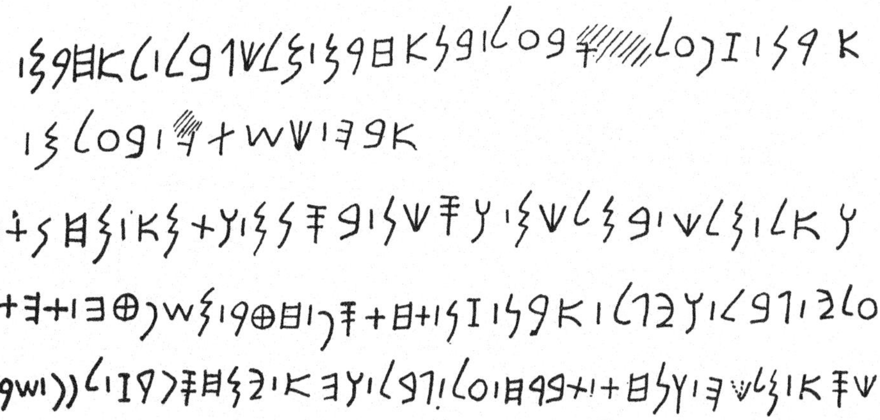

Figure 7.4 Phœnician inscription of Aḥiram. Byblos, eleventh century OLD. 'This sarcophagus was made by Et(?)baʿal, son of Aḥiram, King of Gebal, for Aḥiram his father; here he laid him down for eternity.'

7.3.2 *Phœnician*

After 1050 OLD, the Semitic peoples in the northern Levant came to be known as the Phœnicians. They left a considerable body of material in the Phœnician language. The Phœnicians were important traders in the Mediterranean; they founded a number of colonies, notably at Carthage on the coast of north Africa. The language of these colonies was known as Punic; it continued to be spoken and written after the language disappeared in Phœnicia proper. The last Punic writing is from about 200 NEW. The Phœnician script is written only right to left, and the symbols no longer have a pictographic quality. An inscription of the sarcophagus of Aḥiram (figure 7.4) shows an early form of the Phœnician script.

The Phœnician abjad was adopted by the Aramæans to the northeast and by the Hebrews to the south. The Aramæans lived in northern Mesopotamia and spoke Aramaic, a Northwest Semitic language. By the tenth century OLD, they had borrowed the Phœnician abjad and used it for their own language. By around 750 OLD, the Aramaic abjad had developed an identifiable form, distinct from its Phœnician origin.

The Hebrews borrowed the abjad from the Phœnicians and developed a new form known as the **Old Hebrew abjad**. Early Hebrew inscriptions have been dated to the ninth century OLD. The longest text is the Hebrew Bible, composed between the fifteenth and fifth centuries OLD, although preserved in manuscript copies only from a much later time. The earliest existing manuscripts of the Hebrew scriptures are portions of the **Dead Sea Scrolls** dating from the second to first centuries OLD (plate 2). Hebrew at this time had more consonants than Phœnician which meant that some letters were used ambiguously.

In 586 OLD, the **Babylonians** conquered the Hebrews, holding a large number of them in **captivity** in Babylon, especially the more educated upper classes. Up to that

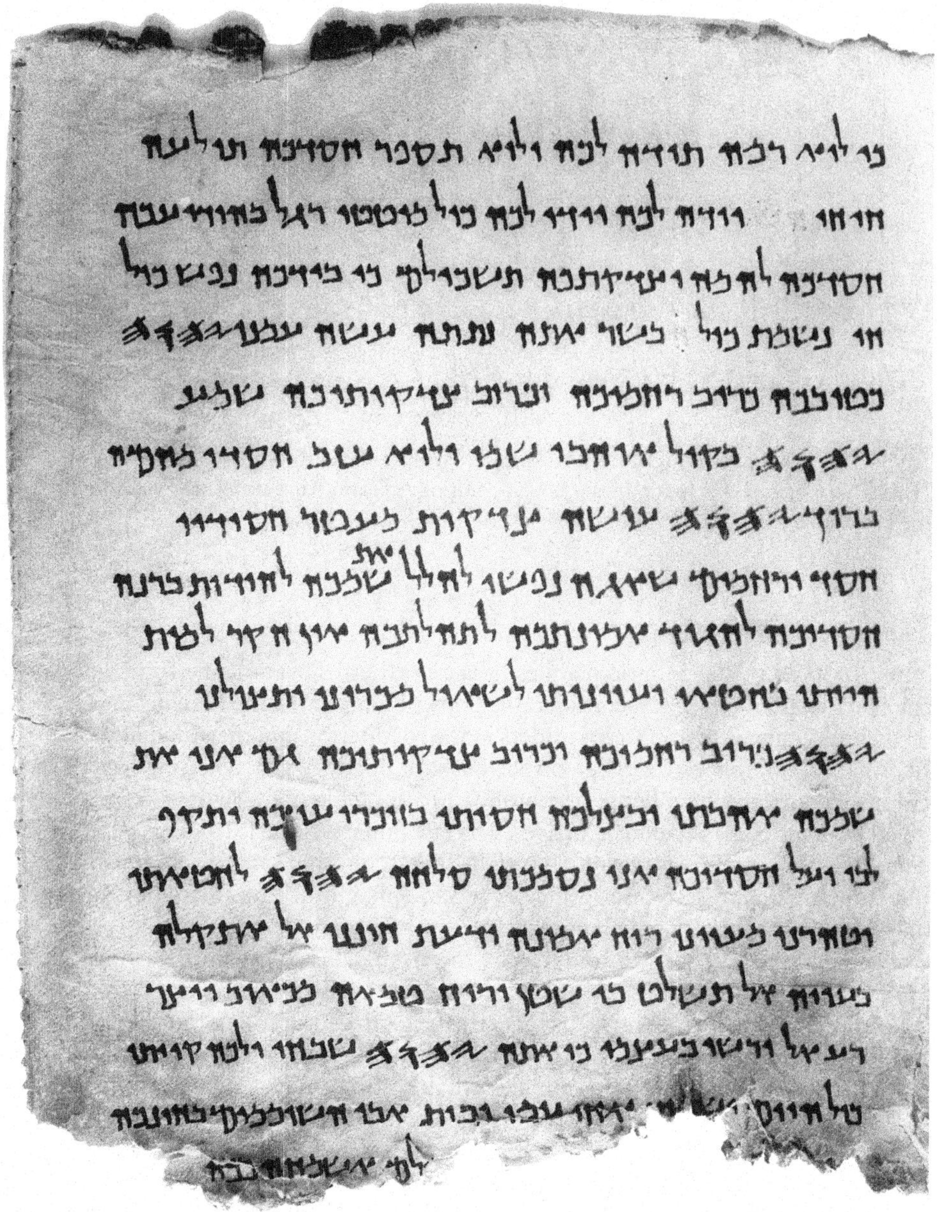

Plate 2 Dead Sea Scroll version of a psalm not included in the Bible. The body of the text is written in the New Hebrew abjad, but the name of God is written in the Old Hebrew abjad. This name occurs six times on this page: the first occurrence is the leftmost word in line 4. 30–40 NEW. Reproduced courtesy of the Israeli Antiquities Authority, Jerusalem

point, the Hebrews had been speaking Hebrew and using the Old Hebrew abjad. By this time, Aramaic had replaced **Babylonian** (Akkadian) as the spoken language of the Babylonian empire and the lingua franca of the entire Middle East. Because of its international importance, the Hebrews were likely familiar with Aramaic before the Babylonian captivity; but during the sixth century OLD, while they were in Babylon, the Hebrew people began speaking Aramaic and using the Aramaic abjad. After their return to Israel in 538 OLD, Hebrew became increasingly restricted to religious purposes, and Aramaic became the ordinary spoken language. Parts of the biblical books of Ezra and Daniel are written in the Aramaic language; and later, Jesus' native language was Aramaic.

In writing as well, an Aramaic form of the abjad, the **New Hebrew abjad**, replaced the Old Hebrew abjad, descended from the Phœnician abjad. The Hebrews were a conservative people; thus the switch from the Old Hebrew abjad to the New Hebrew abjad is hard to explain (Naveh 1982). Goerwitz (1996) notes the fact that the Hebrew-speaking area had been ruled by a series of powers who used Aramaic. Since the two abjads have equivalent inventories of letters, no structural change was involved. In one of the Dead Sea Scrolls (plate 2), the main text is written in the New Hebrew abjad, but the name of God is written in the Old Hebrew form. Coins were occasionally minted with the Old Hebrew letters. But for reasons that are not entirely clear, religious leaders took a dislike to the Old Hebrew abjad and insisted on the New Hebrew form. Jewish theologians continued to write in both Hebrew and Aramaic using the New Hebrew abjad for both languages. The Samaritans, a group who separated from the mainstream Jews, have continued to use the Old Hebrew abjad. The New Hebrew abjad developed its own characteristics in time; it is still in use today as the normal way to write Hebrew.

7.3.3 *Aramaic*

Aramaic was spoken in Syria and northern Mesopotamia. The Aramæans borrowed the Phœnician script by the eleventh or tenth century OLD, but specific Aramaic characteristics do not appear in the script until the mid-eighth century (Naveh 1982). By the sixth century OLD, Aramaic had become the script used for administrative purposes of the Babylonian Empire. When the **Achæmenid** Persians, who spoke Old **Persian**, an Iranian language of the Indo-European family, conquered Babylon in 549 OLD, they took over the existing civil service which was functioning in Aramaic. Although the Persians created an Old Persian cuneiform system for writing their language (Testen 1996), it was used rather little, primarily for monumental purposes (see chapter 5). Correspondence, contracts, and records continued to be written in Aramaic in the Aramaic abjad. During the Persian period, the script maintained a strong uniformity throughout the empire.

The Assyrians adopted Aramaic as the official language of their empire, as did the Akkadians and Babylonians, and later the Persians. As a result, Aramaic became one of the most important languages in the history of the world, spoken as a first or second language by enormous numbers of people in the ancient Middle East. The Aramaic abjad developed a large number of local variants, several of some linguistic and cultural importance.

< J H A > < l t J H A > < n j l t J H A >

Figure 7.5 Aramaic morphograms in Middle Persian writing. In the transliteration, the Aramaic morphograms are in upper case, and the Middle Persian suffixes are in lower case

At first, the situation was bilingual diglossia. The people spoke Middle Persian, and writing was in Aramaic. By the second century OLD, Middle Persian words, written in the Aramaic script, gradually began to appear in writing; i.e., the Aramaic script was borrowed for writing Middle Persian (Skjærvø 1996). In time, a curious mixture of language and writing emerged. From bilingual diglossia, writing came to be conceived of as entirely in Middle Persian. Many words, however, were still written in the Aramaic language, but were pronounced in Middle Persian. For example (figure 7.5), the Middle Persian word for 'brother' is /brād/; however, rather than spelling /brād/ out in the Aramaic script, which would have been easy to do, the practice was to write the Aramaic word for <AHJ> 'brother' but to pronounce it /brād/. Such Aramaic words, thus, came to be **morphograms** for the Persian scribe. Middle Persian suffixes could be added to Aramaic morphograms: e.g., the nominative plural of brother /brādar/ was formed by writing the Aramaic logogram <AHJ> and then attaching the Middle Persian suffix <-tl> which represents the sounds /-dr/. The genitive plural was formed by adding the further suffix <-jn> /-īn/ giving <AHJ-tl-jn> pronounced /brādarīn/ (Skjærvø 1996). The Middle Persian use of Aramaic morphograms is a remarkable example of the conservatism in borrowing writing systems that we often encounter. Note that these morphograms are different from Chinese characters borrowed into Japanese or Korean, since their pronunciation was transparent to the Persian scribe as they were written in the Aramaic script. In English, we have a similar situation where we write *lb.* (an abbreviation for the Latin word *librum*) but pronounce it as *pound*. By adding an English suffix to this abbreviated Latin word, we form the plural as *lbs.*, in a manner similar to the addition of Middle Persian suffixes to the Aramaic writing of the word. Similarly, we often write other Latin abbreviations as *etc.*, *e.g.*, or *i.e.* but pronounce them in English as 'and so on', 'for example', or 'that is'.

In 330 OLD, Alexander the Great conquered the Achæmenid empire of Persia and established Greek as the official language. Aramaic continued as a lingua franca, but the central authority which gave uniformity to the Aramaic script disappeared, and many local varieties arose.

In the west, two local scripts emerged. We have already seen that a Hebrew version of the Aramaic abjad came to be used in Israel, and the Nabatæan empire around Petra (in modern-day Jordan) also developed its own variant, which ultimately led to the Arabic abjad.

In Mesopotamia, the Hatran script was used in the north and Mandaic in the south. A number of scripts arose in Persia (Persian, Parthian, Sogdian, Khorazmian),

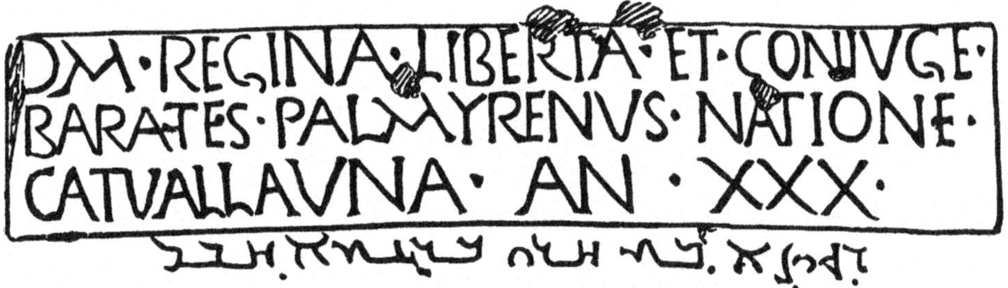

Figure 7.6 Palmyrene Aramaic inscription from Britain. The inscription reads <rgjnʔ bt xrj brʕtʔ xbl> 'Regina, the freedwoman of Barates: woe!'

all derived from the earlier Aramaic. The Sogdian script was adopted by peoples living farther east. It is the ancestor of the Uighur, Mongolian, and Manchu scripts (chapter 11).

In India, King Aśoka was a powerful king in the third century OLD. As a convert to Buddhism, he erected a number of Buddhist monuments around the country. Those on the northwestern edge of his empire (modern Afghanistan) were written in Greek and Aramaic so as to be more easily understood by the people there. In chapter 11, we will see that the Aramaic script is likely the ancestor of the many Indian and southeast Asian scripts.

Palmyra (modern Tadmur) is an oasis in Syria between the Mediterranean and the Euphrates River. The inhabitants spoke Aramaic and developed a local Palmyrene version of the Aramaic abjad. An interesting inscription is found in England written in the Palmyrene abjad. Apparently a man named Barates from Palmyra decided to seek his fortune at the other end of the Roman empire. In South Shields, in northeastern England near Newcastle, he erected a monument (figure 7.6) in the late second century NEW in Palmyrene letters to the memory of his late wife, Regina.

With the spread of Islam, Aramaic was replaced by Arabic as the lingua franca of the Middle East. Today Aramaic is still spoken by about 200,000 people, with the largest group of speakers in an area where Turkey, Iraq, and Syria meet. Aramaic today is usually written with the Syriac abjad, of which there are three versions: Estrangelo, Serto, and Nestorian.

7.4 Hebrew

7.4.1 Background and history

The linguistic situation of **Hebrew** is unique. As we have already noted, by the second century OLD, Hebrew had died out as a spoken language, and Jews were speaking mainly Aramaic or Greek. As they later spread out to various parts of the world, they spoke the local language where they were living. Nevertheless, Hebrew remained the liturgical language, and scholars continued to write in Hebrew (and in Aramaic) and occasionally used Hebrew for spoken communication with visitors. In the nineteenth century NEW, a movement arose to revive Hebrew as a spoken language. This movement succeeded and coincided with the establishment of the modern state of Israel where it has become the native language of native-born Israelis. This is the only known case of the successful revival of a dead language to a language spoken natively by a sizeable group of people.

7.4.2 Phonology of Tiberian Hebrew

The **Bible** is the only large text of ancient Hebrew. It contains material written over several centuries and from different dialect areas. The text as we know it today was fixed around the seventh century NEW, long after Hebrew was no longer a spoken language. The editors were known as Masoretes, and the text is known as the **Masoretic** text. Since the editing was done in Tiberias, the dialect of Hebrew used is referred to as **Tiberian** Hebrew. In the various parts of the Jewish world, different ways of pronouncing Biblical Hebrew arose. None of these is exactly the same as what we now believe ancient Hebrew sounded like, nor the same as the Tiberian Masoretes in the seventh century NEW would have used, nor the same as that which emerged in modern Hebrew in Israel today. In order to talk about the Hebrew writing system, we will use a reconstructed form of what scholars believe to be the Tiberian pronunciation (Khan 1997).

The consonant phonemes of Tiberian Hebrew are presented in table 7.2. The stops /p t k b d g/ had fricative allophones [f θ x v ð ɣ] which occurred after vowels. The phonemes /ṭ ṣ/ were distinct from /t s/. Proto-Semitic had a series of obstruents referred to by Semiticists as emphatic sounds. The exact phonetic nature of these obstruents during the early stages of Semitic is difficult to determine as they turn up differently in different Semitic languages. Generally, however, the emphatic stops seem to have involved a secondary articulation at the back of the oral tract (i.e., velarization, uvularization, pharyngealization, or laryngealization). We will simply note here that Tiberian Hebrew had these two emphatic phonemes /ṭ ṣ/, distinct from /t s/.

A variety of analyses exist for Tiberian Hebrew phonology, particularly for the vowels. The one given here is only one of various possibilities. In this analysis, Tiberian Hebrew had eight vowels (table 7.3).

The Tiberian Masoretes explicitly indicated certain variations in the vowel system which are regarded here as allophonic and predictable. For example, although scholars today generally view vowel length as allophonic and predict it from the syllable structure, the Tiberian scholars indicated length in the writing as though

Table 7.2 Consonant phonemes of Tiberian Hebrew

p b	t d		k g	q		ʔ
	ṭ					
	ṣ					
	s z	ʃ			ħ ʕ	h
m	n					
w	l	j		ʁ		

Table 7.3 Vowel phonemes of Tiberian Hebrew

i		u
e	ə	o
ɛ		ɔ
	a	

it were phonemically contrastive. The Tiberian theory of phonotactics held that a syllable could end only in a consonant or a long vowel. Thus, /CVC/ or /CVː/ would constitute syllables, but /CV/ alone would not; as a result, the sequences /CVCVː/ and /CVCVC/ were treated as single syllables. The first vowels in these complex syllables are referred to as reduced vowels; the relevance of this analysis for the writing system will be discussed below. In this chapter, I have omitted vowel length when citing Hebrew words generally, but I have included it when discussing the writing of a word to make it easier for the reader to relate a cited item to traditional writing.

In modern Hebrew, /t/ and /ṭ/ have merged as /t/; /k/ and /q/ have merged as /k/; [ð ɣ θ] have merged with the stops [d g t], respectively; /w/ has become [v]; /ṣ/ has become /ts/; /e ɛ ə/ have merged as [ɛ]; and /a/ and /ɔ/ have merged as [a] (Bolozky 1997). For some speakers, the sounds /ʔ/, /ʕ/, and /h/ have disappeared. Despite these historic phonological changes, modern Hebrew writing has tended to retain traditional Biblical spelling.

7.4.3 Hebrew abjad

At first in early Semitic, only the consonants were written and no vowels. Later, some long vowels came to be written using consonant letters. This system began with the Aramæans and spread to the other Semitic users of the abjad (except the Phœnicians). In Hebrew, the symbol י, originally used only for the consonant /j/, was used to write long vowels /iː eː/; ו, originally used only for the consonant /w/, was used for long /uː oː/; and sometimes the consonantal symbol ה <h> was used for /aː/. Thus /ʃoːreʃ/ 'root' was earlier written שרש <ʃrʃ>, with no vowel marking the long /oː/; later it was written as שורש <ʃwrʃ> where the <w> shows the long vowel /oː/. A consonant symbol used in this manner to indicate a vowel is known as a ***mater lectionis*** (Latin for 'mother of reading', pl. ***matres lectionis***). *Matres lectionis* were common for long vowels in Hebrew, but they were not always used; short vowels were not indicated at all. By the seventh century NEW, even with the *matres lectionis*, concern arose that knowledge of the correct pronunciation of the Hebrew scriptures might be lost. By this time, Hebrew scholars were familiar, of course, with the Greek method of using ordinary letters for vowels; however, they did not wish to alter the sacred text by inserting vowel symbols between the existing letters. Their solution was to indicate vowels by means of a set of diacritic marks over or below the consonantal letters. This use of diacritics in Hebrew is known as **vowel pointing**, and texts with vowels indicated are called **pointed texts**. Actually, three different systems of pointing developed, but in the end the system from Tiberias in Palestine won out. A few other

Table 7.4 Letters of the Hebrew abjad. The sound values given for the abjad are those reconstructed for Tiberian Hebrew; parentheses indicate transcriptions appropriate for modern Hebrew. The super- or subscript macron is used to show a fricative pronunciation: <b̠ d̠ ḡ p̄ ṯ k̠> = [v ð ɣ f θ x]

Printed	*final form*	*Cursive*	*final form*	*Sound value*	*Name*	*Modern pron. of name*	*Numeric value*
א		א		ʔ	ʔalep̄	/ˈalɪf/	1
ב		ב		b	beṯ	/bɛt/	2
ג		ג		g	gimel	/ˈgɪməl/	3
ד		ד		d	daleṯ	/ˈdalət/	4
ה		ה		h (Ø)	he	/heː/	5
ו		ו		w (v)	waw	/vav/	6
ז		ז		z	zayin	/ˈzajin/	7
ח		ח		ħ (Ø)	ħeṯ	/xɛt/	8
ט		ט		ṭ (t)	ṭeṯ	/tɛt/	9
י		י		j	jod	/jʊd/	10
כ	ך	כ	ך	k	kap̄	/kɔf/	20
ל		ל		l	lameḏ	/ˈlaməd/	30
מ	ם	מ	ם	m	mem	/mɛm/	40
נ	ן	נ	ן	n	nun	/nʊn/	50
ס		ס		s	samek̠	/ˈsaməx/	60
ע		ע		ʕ (Ø)	ʔayin	/ˈajɪn/	70
פ	ף	פ	ף	p	pe	/peː/	80
צ	ץ	צ	ץ	ṣ (ts)	ṣade	/ˈtsadi/	90
ק		ק		q (k)	qup̄	/kuf/	100
ר		ר		ʀ	reʃ	/ʀɛʃ/	200
ש		ש		s/ʃ	sin/ʃin	/sɪn, ʃɪn/	300
ת		ת		t	taw	/tav/	400

marks were added to remove ambiguities in pronunciation, and a set of symbols known as cantillation marks were also added to indicate the liturgical tune.

Hebrew is written from right to left like all Semitic abjads. Five letters have special allographs which are used only at the end of a word. Various calligraphic styles exist. In table 7.4, the letterforms at the left are typical of those used in modern printed matter. The forms to their right are typically used in handwriting. Letters are written separately and not joined, even in handwriting.

The order of letters in the Semitic abjad, given in table 7.4 has a very long tradition. As we have seen in chapter 5, the Ugaritic cuneiform abjad had essentially the same order in the late second millenium (O'Connor 1996a). Today, the Hebrew, Roman, and Greek alphabets still have essentially the same ordering of symbols. Arabic and the Indian scripts stand out in having reorganized this order: Arabic slightly, and the Indian scripts, thoroughly. We have no idea how this early Semitic order arose. (Hebrew had no special symbols to represent numbers, but used letters with **numeric values**, as shown in table 7.4.)

Table 7.5 Sibilant letters of Hebrew

Letter	*Faber's Proto-Semitic reconstruction*	*Early Hebrew pronunciation*	*Tiberian pronunciation*	*Name*
ס	ts	s	s	samek̠
שׂ	ɬ	ś	s	sin
שׁ	s	ʃ	ʃ	shin

Table 7.6 *Dagesh* letters of Hebrew. Where the modern pronunciation differs, it is given in parentheses

b	בּ	v	ב	p	פּ	f	פ
d	דּ	ð (d)	ד	t	תּ	θ (t)	ת
g	גּ	ɣ (g)	ג	k	כּ	x	כ

Originally, Semitic had three sibilants (table 7.5). The reconstruction of the pronunciation of these has been problematic. Faber (1981; see also Daniels 1999) has reconstructed them as [s], [ɬ], and [ts]. The traditional view for Hebrew has been that early Hebrew had three kinds of s-sounds /s ś ʃ/ which were written with two letters ס and ש; the letter ס was pronounced /s/, and the letter ש had two different pronunciations /ś ʃ/. By Masoretic times, <ś> had come to be pronounced as /s/. The Masoretes maintained the traditional writing of both ס and ש, and, in pointed Hebrew, they distinguished the two pronunciations of ש by putting a dot over the left or right side.

In pointed Hebrew, the *dagesh* (a dot inside the letter) is used in two ways. First, it is used to indicate a geminate consonant: עַמִּים <ʕammīm> 'peoples', שַׂקִּים <śaqqīm> 'sacks'. Second, Hebrew historically underwent a process of lenition, changing single stops to fricatives intervocalically. Although this was an allophonic change, Tiberian scholars used the *dagesh* to indicate that the letter was pronounced as a phonetic stop [b d g p t k]; without a *dagesh*, the letter was pronounced as a fricative [v ð ɣ f θ x] (table 7.6). In Modern Hebrew, the stops without a *dagesh* are pronounced as [v d g f t x] (older Hebrew [ð ɣ θ] have become modern Hebrew [d g t]). The dual function of the *dagesh* is facilitated by the fact that single stops do not occur between vowels. Thus, an intervocalic stop without a *dagesh* represents a fricative, and an intervocalic stop with a *dagesh* represents a geminate cluster.

7.4.4 *Hebrew vowels*

The Tiberian writing of Hebrew vowels is fairly complex. As we have already noted, early Hebrew writing did not indicate vowels. Some long vowels came to be indicated by adding י, ו, and in some cases ה as *matres lectionis*. A major purpose of the Tiberian edition of the text was to fix the pronunciation of the Bible by indicating all vowels. This was accomplished by using the existing *matres lectionis* in combination with a new set of diacritics known as points (table 7.7). The diacritics

Table 7.7 Tiberian Hebrew vowel pointing, shown with the letter מ <m>

Short			*Long/diphthong*					*Reduced*		
ħîreq	i	מִ	ħîreq jōḏ	ī		מִי		ʃəwa	ə, Ø	מְ
səḡol	e	מֶ	ṣere	ē	ēj	מֵ	מֵי	ħaṭep̄ səḡol	ĕ	מֱ
paṯax	a	מַ	qameṣ	ā		מָ		ħaṭep̄ paṯaħ	ă	מֲ
qameṣ xatup̄	o	מָ	ħolem(-wāw)	ō	ōw	מֹ	מוֹ	ħaṭep̄ qameṣ	ŏ	מֳ
qibbuṣ	u	מֻ	ʃūreq	ū		מוּ				

Table 7.8 Hebrew personal names

שרה h r ś	שָׂרָה h r̄ ś ā ā	<ś r h>	<ś ā r ā h>
יוסף נתן	יוֹסֵף		

are written with the consonant that they phonologically follow. As an example, the earliest writing of /dawid/ [daːwiːð] 'David' would have been דוד <dwd> (the <w> here is consonantal, not a *mater lectionis*), later with <j> as a *mater lectionis* for the long vowel /iː/ דויד <dwjd>, and finally with points דָוִיד <dāwīd>.

As we have said, vowel length was indicated although this was essentially allophonic. The writing of the diphthongs and corresponding long vowels is sometimes conflated. The reduced vowels were given special symbols. One of the reduced vowels is known as **schwa** (literally 'nothing'; this is the source of the name of the phonetic symbol [ə]). The written diacritic for schwa indicates either the presence of the reduced vowel [ə] or the absence of any vowel. The names of the points are given in table 7.7; vowels are often referred to by these names. Examples are shown with the letter מ <m>.

Note that <o> and <ā> are written with the same diacritic. Knowledge of Hebrew is necessary to determine which is intended. Romanization schemes sometimes use a circumflex to indicate that a long vowel is written with a *mater lectionis*. Readers should be aware that a number of different romanizations for Hebrew exist.

Although these symbols for vowels exist, as we have just seen, Hebrew today is not generally written with vowel points although *matres lectionis* are regularly written. Biblical texts are normally written with points although the scrolls used in a synagogue are unpointed. Texts for children or learners of the language are pointed to give extra help. Poetry is sometimes pointed since it often contains unusual words. For other material in Hebrew, the reader is expected to know the language well enough to supply the appropriate vowels.

Like all Semitic abjads, Hebrew is written right to left. In pointed texts, the vowels are written with the consonant which they phonologically follow. For example, the name *Sarah* (table 7.8) is written as <śrh>. The reader sees the consonantal sequence <śrh> and given the context of the word, interprets this as the name Sarah. See if you can guess the second name in table 7.8; the third may be harder since it is not pointed.

Hebrew originally had no special numerals. Ordinary letters were used as numbers. In table 7.4, the numeric value of each letter is given. Today, Arabic numerals are used in most situations. One interesting sociolinguistic phenomenon is that the number of a year, according to the Jewish calendar, is written with Hebrew letters and then interpreted as an ordinary word, to predict what kind of year it will be.

7.4.5 Reading the Bible

God is referred to by several names in the Hebrew scriptures, but the most sacred was יהוה <jhwh>, likely pronounced /jahweh/. In the course of time, this name came to be regarded as too holy to be spoken, except once a year by the High Priest in a part of the prayers on the Day of Atonement. Note that in the Dead Sea Scroll text shown in plate 2, the text is written in the New Hebrew abjad, but the name of God is written in the Old Hebrew abjad. When reading the Bible where this word appears, the reader is supposed to substitute the word אֲדֹנָי /ădōnāi/ 'my Lord'. To remind readers to make this substitution, the vowel points of /ădōnāi/ are written with the consonants <jhwh>, the result being written as יְהֹוָה or יְהוָֹה (with ħāṭēp̄ paṯaħ < ֲ > predictably changed to schwā < ְ >). This form is a mnemonic and not intended to be pronounced as written. Mediæval Christian translators of the Bible, with a somewhat shaky understanding of Jewish tradition, rendered this literally as *Jehovah*, a word which does not exist in Hebrew.

Tradition also says that the readers must not touch the holy name in a scroll with their fingers. To avoid this, scrolls have handles for rolling and unrolling them, and readers use a special pointer to keep their place in the text. The book of Esther often has only one handle, since it is the only book in the Bible not containing the holy name.

Another interesting sociolinguistic point is that if a reader in a synagogue believes that the scroll contains an error, the service is to stop until the matter is clarified. A young boy is called forward, one old enough to have learned the Hebrew letters, but not experienced enough to understand the meaning of the words. He is asked to decide what the letter in question is. If his decision shows that the scroll is in error, it must be taken away to be corrected or destroyed (Elan Dresher, personal communication).

7.4.6 Other languages written with the Hebrew script

After the destruction of the temple in 70 NEW, the Jews were forced to leave Israel and spread out widely. They generally came to speak the language where they were living. For example, those living in the Middle East and North Africa came to speak Judæo-Arabic, a form of Arabic with many Hebrew and Aramaic loanwords. The Jews wrote this language using the New Hebrew abjad. Similar phenomena happened elsewhere (Hary 1996). In northeastern Europe, Jews spoke a form of German which developed into **Yiddish**, also written with the New Hebrew abjad. In southern Europe, the same thing happened in the Spanish (Ladino, Judezmo) and Italian (Judæo-Italian) areas.

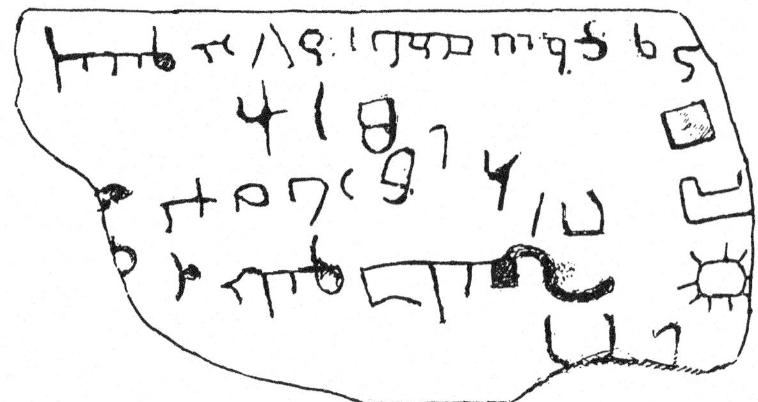

Figure 7.7 Inscription from Jabal Ramm (near Aqaba), late fourth century NEW; the oldest Arabic inscription so far discovered (*Revue biblique* 45.91, 1936)

7.5 Arabic

7.5.1 *Background and history*

Very little is known about pre-Islamic Arabic writing (i.e., before 622 NEW). A considerable body of pre-Islamic poetry has been preserved, but this was passed on orally and not written down until Islamic times. We know that the Nabatæan kingdom of Petra spoke Arabic, but the Nabatæans normally wrote in Aramaic, or they wrote Arabic texts in non-Arabic scripts. The **Nabatæan** variety of the Aramaic script is believed to be the ancestor of the Arabic script. Only five clear examples of pre-Islamic Arabic inscriptions exist (Bellamy 1989). The text in figure 7.7 is the oldest known. Bellamy analyses it as 'a boast made by an energetic man who went out into the world and made money; this he announces to all those who are so world-weary that they cannot do likewise'.

With the advent of Islam (622 NEW), Arabic experienced an explosion of writing. Tradition holds that Mohammed himself was illiterate and dictated the *Qur'ān*, the Islamic sacred text, to scribes. By 650 NEW, his writings had been collected and published. Subsequently, many copies of the *Qur'ān* were made, and other writing, both religious and secular, ensued. Wealthy families amassed large libraries.

As Islam spread, some converts began to speak Arabic, and others used the Arabic script to write their own language. Today, many languages spoken in areas where Islam is a common religion are written with the Arabic script, notably Persian and Urdu, and many other languages across central Asia. In the past, other languages, such as Turkish, Swahili, and Hausa, were written using the Arabic alphabet.

Like other Semitic abjads, Arabic writing does not show vowels fully. Long vowels are regularly indicated by *matres lectionis*, but not short vowels. Some centuries after the *Qur'ān* was written down, Islamic scholars developed a way of indicating short vowels. They did this partly to facilitate their missionary work among non-Arabic speakers, and also because they were concerned that the sacred text might be altered. They introduced diacritic marks to indicate short vowels and other matters; these symbols are considered to be secondary symbols and are not used in writing ordinary text, but they are regularly used in writing the *Qur'ān*, and in texts for children or students of Arabic; they are also occasionally used for decorative purposes, as on the cover of a book. There are interesting structural and sociolinguistic parallels between the Arabic and Hebrew writing of vowels.

Arabic is highly diglossic. Throughout the Arabic-speaking world, everyone speaks a local dialect, often referred to as colloquial Arabic. Writing, however, is almost entirely done in the dialect known as **Standard Arabic**, which is generally not mutually intelligible with local dialects. Today, this dialect is similar to, but not exactly the same as, the classical Arabic of the *Qur'ān* and other older literature. Although everyone speaks colloquial Arabic, Standard Arabic is highly regarded. Modern Standard Arabic can on occasion be spoken, but it is more usually read aloud. University lectures, the news on television, and formal speeches are usually composed in Standard Arabic and then read aloud. It would, however, be quite unusual for an Arabic speaker to use Standard Arabic for any extended period of time in an informal situation. Normally, all Arabic speakers, no matter what their social status, converse in their local dialect. Written Arabic has the advantage that it is the same for all Arabic speakers. To become literate in Arabic means learning this dialect of Arabic. Although it is quite possible to write colloquial Arabic, this is rarely done outside of special situations such as in a comic book, popular advertising, or in a play to show a local pronunciation.

Over time a large number of calligraphic styles of Arabic have emerged. Islam discouraged the drawing of living beings. As a result, calligraphy gained a special significance as a permitted artistic endeavour. Sometimes, the decorative value of the writing became supreme. During the Ottoman Empire, an official signature known as a ***tughra*** (plate 3) was created for each Sultan; these were so ornate that they had to be written by scribes.

7.5.2 Phonology of Modern Standard Arabic

Arabic is spoken by about 150 million people living primarily in the Middle East and northern Africa. The dialect described here is Standard Arabic. It has 28 consonants and 6 vowels (table 7.9). The subscript dot indicates the emphatic consonants.

Table 7.9 The phonemes of Modern Standard Arabic

			t	ṭ		k	q		ʔ
b			d	ḍ	dʒ				
f	θ		s	ṣ	ʃ	x		ħ	h
	ð	ð̣	z			ɣ		ʕ	
			l						
			r						
w					j				
m			n						
i	u		iː	uː					
	a			aː					

Plate 3 Imperial edict with *tughra* of Sultan Ahmed II, Turkey, 1694 NEW. Reproduced with permission from Freer Gallery of Art, Smithsonian Institution

7.5.3 *Arabic abjad*

Arabic is written from right to left with an abjad of 28 letters plus a number of additional, optional symbols. The letters indicate consonants and long vowels. Although there are diacritics to indicate the short vowels, they are normally not written. The consonant symbols of each word are generally connected to each other; words are divided from each other. The short vowels and other optional marks, when written, are written as diacritics above or below the consonants.

Arabic is always written **cursively**, i.e., with the letters joined. There is nothing equivalent to our hand printing with separate letters. Most letters are connected to any preceding and following letters within a word; these letters have four shapes: initial, medial, final, and isolated. Six letters <ʔ d ð r z w> are connected to the preceding letter, but not to the following letter; they have only two shapes: isolated and final. The letters are given in table 7.10 in the traditional Arabic order.

The sequence *la:m–:alif* is never written as لـا, but always as a ligature ﻻ. This ligature is sometimes considered as a letter in its own right; it is then ordered second-last, after *wa:w*.

The order of the letters in Arabic is a modified version of the traditional Semitic ordering, with letters of a similar shape placed near each other. This reordering must have been the result of thoughtful planning, not simply a gradual development. A slightly different order is used in northwestern Africa.

The terms initial, medial, final, and isolated refer to a **writing group**. A writing group starts at the beginning of a word or after a non-connecting letter <ʔ d ð r z w>. A writing group ends at the end of the word or with a non-connecting letter. If a writing group consists of only one letter, the isolated form is used. Otherwise, the initial, medial, or final form is used depending on the position in the writing group. Some nonsense examples (table 7.11) with a connecting letter <b> and a non-connecting letter <d> will illustrate this. The vowel /a/ is understood, but not written.

7.5.4 *Vowels and diphthongs*

The three short vowels are known as /a/ *fatḥah*, /i/ *kasrah*, and /u/ *ḍammah*; vowels are optionally written with the consonant they follow. *Fatḥah* and *ḍammah* are written above the consonant; *kasrah* is written below the consonant:

/ba/ بَ /bi/ بِ /bu/ بُ

Long vowels are written by ا /a:/, ي /i:/, or و /u:/; the corresponding short vowel symbol is optionally written with the preceding consonant:

/ba:/ با or بَا = ب + ا

/bi:/ بي or بِي = ب + ي

/bu:/ بو or بُو = ب + و

Table 7.10 The Arabic abjad

Isolated	*Final*	*Medial*	*Initial*	*Name*	*Value*
ا	ـا			ʔalif	ʔ, a:
ب	ـب	ـبـ	بـ	baʔ	b
ت	ـت	ـتـ	تـ	ta:ʔ	t
ث	ـث	ـثـ	ثـ	θa:ʔ	θ
ج	ـج	ـجـ	جـ	dʒi:m	dʒ
ح	ـح	ـحـ	حـ	ħa:ʔ	ħ
خ	ـخ	ـخـ	خـ	xa:ʔ	x
د	ـد			da:l	d
ذ	ـذ			ða:l	ð
ر	ـر			ra:ʔ	r
ز	ـز			zajn, za:ʔ	z
س	ـس	ـسـ	سـ	si:n	s
ش	ـش	ـشـ	شـ	ʃi:n	ʃ
ص	ـص	ـصـ	صـ	ṣād	ṣ
ض	ـض	ـضـ	ضـ	ḍa:d	ḍ
ط	ـط	ـطـ	طـ	ṭa:ʔ	ṭ
ظ	ـظ	ـظـ	ظـ	ð̣a:ʔ	ð̣
ع	ـع	ـعـ	عـ	ʕajn	ʕ
غ	ـغ	ـغـ	غـ	ɣajn	ɣ
ف	ـف	ـفـ	فـ	fa:ʔ	f
ق	ـق	ـقـ	قـ	qa:f	q
ك	ـك	ـكـ	كـ	ka:f	k
ل	ـل	ـلـ	لـ	la:m	l
م	ـم	ـمـ	مـ	mi:m	m
ن	ـن	ـنـ	نـ	nu:n	n
ه	ـه	ـهـ	هـ	ha:ʔ	h
و	ـو			wa:w	w (u:)
ي	ـي	ـيـ	يـ	ya:y, ya:ʔ	y (IPA [j])/(ī)

Table 7.11 Arabic nonsense examples showing connecting <b> and non-connecting <d>

ب	د	بد	دب	بب	دد
ba	da	bada	daba	baba	dada
ببب	ببد	بدب	بدد	دبب	دبد
bababa	babada	badaba	badada	dababa	dabada
				ددب	ددد
				dadaba	dadada

In the remainder of the section on Arabic, short vowels are explicitly indicated with the understanding that this would not ordinarily be done.

7.5.5 Hamzah

Glottal stop is a phoneme in Arabic; it appears in all positions – initial, medial, and final. In the original Semitic abjad, glottal stop was written with an *ʔalif* ا. The *Qur'ān* was written much later in the dialect of Medina of western Arabia. By the time the *Qu'rān* was written, the glottal stop sound had been lost in word-medial and word-final position in the Medina dialect. As a result, glottal stop was written in the *Qu'rān* only in initial position. Early scholars from other dialect areas were troubled by this loss and wanted to indicate the glottal stops in the *Qur'ān* which the Medina scribes had omitted; however, they were unwilling to change the sacred text. In the end, the scholars solved their dilemma by creating a new mark ء, called ***hamzah***, to represent glottal stop. The *hamzah* was added as part of the secondary layer of symbols and thus was not considered to alter the sacred (i.e., consonantal or primary) layer of the text of the *Qur'ān*.

In modern Arabic grammar, the *hamzah* itself is now considered to be the symbol which indicates a glottal stop and the *ʔalif* is viewed merely as a 'seat' for the *hamzah* (or as marking long /a:/ in other contexts) (Bellamy 1989, Bauer 1996). The complete rules for writing *hamzah* are quite complex; only the basics are given here.

In word-initial position, a glottal stop is written with an *ʔalif* and an accompanying *hamzah*. If the vowel following the glottal stop is /a/ or /u/, the *hamzah* is written above the *ʔalif*; with /i/, it is written below:

/ʔakala/	'he ate'	أَكَلَ	/ʔumm/	'mother'	أُمّ
			/ʔibn/	'son'	إِبْن

This case of *hamzah* shows a situation where a straightforward relationship (glottal stop written as an *ʔalif*) has been drastically altered (glottal stop is written as a *hamzah*, sometimes with an *ʔalif*, whose placement is quite complex) because of dialect variation and a desire to preserve a cultural value, namely a sacred text in its traditional form.

Table 7.12 The writing of Arabic nouns. Note the special *tanwīn* diacritics for the indefinite endings

Indefinite				*Definite*		
Nom.	/–un/	كِتَابٌ	/kita:bun/	/–u/	اَلْكِتَابُ	/al-kita:bu/
Acc.	/–an/	كِتَابًا	/kita:ban/	/–a/	اَلْكِتَابَ	/al-kita:ba/
Gen.	/–in/	كِتَابٍ	/kita:bin/	/–i/	اَلْكِتَابِ	/al-kita:bi/

7.5.6 *Other symbols*

Other optional diacritics are not normally used, but they are found in the *Qur'ān* and in material for learners. A doubled consonant is written only once, and an optional diacritic like a small round *w* is written above, to show consonant doubling (seen in the example /ʔumm/ above). The absence of a following vowel is shown by a superscript circle:

عَلَّقَ /ʕallaqa/ خُمْسْ /xums/

Arabic has three cases: nominative, accusative, and genitive. The cases are indicated by suffixes, which are illustrated in table 7.12 with the word كتَاب /kitāb/ 'book'. The indefinite suffixes are written with special symbols called ***tanwīn*** (left side, table 7.12), which are essentially doubled forms of the simple vowel diacritics. The indefinite accusative is written with a silent *ʔalif*.

The definite article is the prefix /al-/ 'the' which is always written as a prefix ...ال before the noun (table 7.12) even though the /l/ assimilates to a following dental or postalveolar consonant.

7.5.7 *Numerals*

The numerals from 0 to 9 in Arabic are ٠ ١ ٢ ٣ ٤ ٥ ٦ ٧ ٨ ٩ <0 1 2 3 4 5 6 7 8 9>. Arabic numbers are written from left to right: ١ ٩ ٦ ٥ '1965'. The so-called 'Arabic numerals' used in English are actually from India (see chapter 11) and are called 'Indian numerals' in Arabic. They are often used in modern Arabic writing.

7.6 The Ethiopic Abugida

The early South Arabian abjad and its development into an **abugida** have already been discussed in §7.3.1. The Ethiopian abugida was first used for Ge'ez, the classical language of Ethiopia. It was originally spoken in northern Ethiopia. Most texts from the early period are translations of Christian literature from Greek. Ge'ez died out as a spoken language around 1000 NEW. Since the mid-twelfth century, Amharic

Table 7.13 Phonemes of Amharic

p b	t d	tʃ dʒ	k g	kʷ gʷ	ʔ	
p′	t′	tʃ′	k′			
f v	s z	ʃ ʒ			h ʕ	hʷ
	ts					
m	n	ɲ				
w	l r	j				

i		ə		u
	e		o	
		ɜ		
		a		

Table 7.14 Selected symbols from the Ethiopic abugida. Symbols in the same row have the same consonant; those in the same column have the same vowel

	ɜ	u	i	a	e	ə	o
h	ሀ	ሁ	ሂ	ሃ	ሄ	ህ	ሆ
l	ለ	ሉ	ሊ	ላ	ሌ	ል	ሎ
m	መ	ሙ	ሚ	ማ	ሜ	ም	ሞ
q	ቀ	ቁ	ቂ	ቃ	ቄ	ቅ	ቆ
b	በ	ቡ	ቢ	ባ	ቤ	ብ	ቦ
qʷ	ቈ		ቊ	ቋ	ቌ	ቍ	

has been the main spoken language of Ethiopia, but Ge'ez retained great importance as a liturgical and cultural language. Until the nineteenth century, virtually all writing in Ethiopia was done in Ge'ez, and it remains the language of the Ethiopian church. The Jewish Falasha of Ethiopia also produced a small amount of material in Ge'ez. Now we will examine how the modern Ethiopic abugida, the script of Amharic and neighbouring languages, works. (For more details on abugidas, see chapter 11 on the Indian scripts.)

The phonemic inventory of Amharic is given in table 7.13 (C′ indicates an ejective consonant).

Recall that in an abugida, the consonants are the main symbols, and the vowels are written as diacritics. Also, in an abugida, one vowel is not explicitly indicated. In the Ethiopic abugida, the vowel /ɜ/ is not explicitly indicated; thus, the absence of a diacritic shows the presence of /ɜ/. The other six vowels are indicated by diacritics. The shapes of the diacritics are almost, but not quite, predictable. As an example, consider the second row for /l/ in table 7.14: ለ /lɜ/, ሉ /lu/, ሊ /li/, ላ /la/, ሌ /le/, ል /lə/, ሎ /lo/. By comparing these forms with those in other rows, we can see that ለ is the basic consonant shape for /l/, and thus that /ɜ/ is the vowel that is not explicitly indicated. The other vowels are indicated by diacritics attached to this symbol.

Table 7.15 Ethiopic numerals. These are borrowed from Greek

፩	1	፮	6	፳	20	፸	70
፪	2	፯	7	፴	30	፹	80
፫	3	፰	8	፵	40	፺	90
፬	4	፱	9	፶	50	፻	100
፭	5	፲	10	፷	60		

The symbols with the diacritic for the vowel /ə/ are also used to show the absence of a vowel, thus allowing consonant clusters to be written. Whether a <Cə> symbol represents /C/ or /Cə/ can only be determined by a knowledge of the language. Geminate consonants are not indicated although they are phonetically distinctive. Labialized consonants are written with special diacritics. The writing system preserves certain contrasts no longer existing in the present-day language.

The order of the letters in the Ethiopic abugida is different from the usual northern Semitic order. The reason for the Ethiopic ordering is not known. In certain religious contexts, the northern Semitic order is used, and the name *abugida* comes from this order; cf. aleph, beth, gimel, daleth in Hebrew.

The numerals (table 7.15) were borrowed from the Greek alphabetic numerals; see chapter 8 for the use of Greek numerals as letters. Horizontal strokes are written above and below the numerals. Today, Arabic numerals are used in most situations.

7.7 The Distinctiveness of Abjads

Semitic morphology is unusual among languages, consisting of two interlocking patterns. One pattern represents the root, which typically consists of three consonants: for example /ktb/ 'write' or /fˤl/ 'do'. The other pattern is the inflectional morphology; different inflectional patterns are marked by inserting different vowels between the consonants of the root. Prefixes and suffixes may also be part of the inflectional morphology. The examples from Arabic (table 7.16) show this structure. In the last column, the phonemes of the root are in upper case (/ˤ/ is to be included here), and those of the affixes in lower case to highlight the two different patterns. If you examine the phonological forms, you will see that the forms for 'write' all have /ktb/, and those for 'do' have /fˤl/.

If we look at the writing system, we see that the consonants of the stem are always written, and the inflectional morphology is written only to the degree that it contains consonants. Quite frequently, two forms are exactly alike, and the correct reading can only be determined by the context. The forms in table 7.17, for example, would all be written exactly the same.

In English, we are much less commonly faced with this sort of homography. Where it does occur, the context in English, as in Arabic, usually distinguishes the possible readings: *bow* /bow/ and /baw/, or *lead* /lid/and /lɛd/. One might expect forms such as *read* /ɹid/ and /ɹɛd/ to be more problematic since they distinguish the present and

Table 7.16 Examples of Arabic showing Semitic morphology. The root consonants are shown in upper-case letters. The inflectional morphemes consist of the medial vowels, prefixes, and suffixes

كتب	kataba	'he wrote'	KaTaBa
فعل	faˤala	'he did'	FaˤaLa
كتبن	katabna	'they (fem.) wrote'	KaTaBna
فعلن	faˤalna	'they (fem.) did'	FaˤaLna
يكتب	yaktubu	'he was writing'	yaKTuBu
يفعل	yafˤalu	'he was doing'	yaFˤaLu
يكتبن	yaktubna	'they (fem.) were writing'	yaKTuBna
يفعلن	yafˤalna	'they (fem.) were doing'	yaFˤaLna

Table 7.17 Homography in Arabic. These words, although phonologically different, would be written the same

فعلت	<f ˤ l t>	faˤaltu	'I did'
فعلت	<f ˤ l t>	faˤalta	'you (masc.) did'
فعلت	<f ˤ l t>	faˤalti	'you (fem.) did'
فعلت	<f ˤ l t>	faˤalat	'she did'

past tense of the same verb, either of which could easily occur in the same syntactic position. Even though *read* is a rather common verb in English, my own experience, however, is that I have little sense of misreading this word, certainly not very often. Similarly, Arabic speakers do not have frequent difficulties in reading Arabic.

Some people have claimed that Semitic languages are ideally suited for an abjad since writing only the consonants highlights the lexical root. Sometimes this argument is stated as though the inflectional morphemes are of no consequence. Most people, however, feel that there is some significance in the difference between 'I will die' and 'I have died'. Rather than saying that the inflectional information is not so important, perhaps it would be closer to the truth to say that it is likely to be more redundant or more easily recovered from the context. In this sense, the Semitic abjad emphasizes the lexical and less redundant parts of words.

7.8 Further Reading

This chapter covers a great deal of territory with an enormous literature. Healey (1990) is a good short general introduction. The various articles in Daniels and Bright (1996) are all useful studies of the individual scripts: O'Connor (1996a, 1996b), Goerwitz

(1996), Daniels (1996b), Skjærvø (1996), Bauer (1996), Haile (1996), Hary (1996), Kaye (1996). Bellamy (1989) and Cross (1989) are also very useful. Driver (1976), Naveh (1970, 1982 – the most accessible), and Sass (1992) are more technical treatments. Versteegh (1997) is an interesting introduction to Arabic with a good deal on writing. Abbott (1939) and Gruendler (1993) deal with the history of Arabic writing. Brustad et al. (1995) is a modern introduction to Arabic writing. Mitchell (1954) is quite detailed, but will repay the efforts of a serious student to learn authentic Arabic handwriting. Bender et al. (1976) and Weninger (1993) give more information on Ethiopic writing.

7.9 Terms

abjad
abugida
Achæmenid
acrophony
Akkadian
alphabet
Arabic
Aramaic
Babylonian
Babylonian Captivity
Bible
cursive
Dead Sea scroll
Ge'ez
hamzah
Hebrew
Levant
Masoretic
mater lectionis
morphogram
morphographic
New Hebrew abjad
Old Hebrew abjad
Persian
Phœnician
phonographic
pointing, pointed text
Proto-Canaanite
Punic
Qur'ān
schwa
Semitic
Standard Arabic
tanwīn
Tiberian
tughra
vowel pointing
writing group
Yiddish

7.10 Exercises

1 This exercise involves Hebrew names which have been borrowed into English. For each of the following items, transcribe the Hebrew name cursively. Transliterate the name in Roman letters using the chart in table 7.4. Don't forget to reverse the Hebrew order so that your transliteration is in the correct order for English. There will usually be some discrepancy between the Hebrew and English forms of the names. Note that the Hebrew consonants ו י may represent glides /j w/, but they may also be *matres lectionis* for long /i: e:/ or /u: o:/. The consonantal value of Hebrew ו is likely to be /v/ in English, and Hebrew י will often be /dʒ/. Hebrew tav ת often turns up in English as <th>.

(a) Each of the names in italics below is contained in the following Hebrew list (there is one extra name); write the English name for each Hebrew name in the appropriate row.

Daniel, David, Dinah, Esau, Esther, Rachel, Reuben

	Hebrew	Cursive	Transliteration	English Name
e.g.	ראובן	ראובן	<r ? w b n>	Reuben
a.	רחל			
b.	דניאל			
c.	דינה			
d.	אסתר			
e.	דוד			

(b) For each of the following items, transcribe the Hebrew name cursively. Transliterate the name in Roman letters. Write the English name for each Hebrew name at the right.

	Hebrew	Cursive	Transliteration	English Name
a.	רות			
b.	אברהם			
c.	מיכאל			
d.	רבקה			
e.	נעמי			
f.	אדם			
g.	בנימין			

(c) The following Hebrew names are a little harder:

	Hebrew	Transliteration	English Name
a.	איוב		
b.	נבכדנאצר		
c.	איזבל		
d.	מתושלח		

2 The following words are important proper names primarily from the Arabic or Muslim worlds. Transcribing the words in Roman letters first may help. Most of the words are given as they are ordinarily written in Arabic – that is, without vowels. The first one is done for you. Note that some proper nouns in Arabic are preceded by the article /ʔal–/ ال. (Note: item (g) is named after a famous Greek general who founded this city. Two things happened to this name in Arabic: (1) two consonants are reversed (metathesis), and (2) it has been reanalysed as containing the article.)

Iraq	<ʔl ʕ r ā q>	العراق	a.
ألنيل	c.	السودان	b.
الباكستان	e.	إسطمبول	d.
الإسْكَنْدَرِيَّة	g.	الإسلام	f.
الكويت	i.	بيروت	h.
مكة	k.	كندا	j.
بغداد	m.	ليبيا	l.
		مالطة	n.

3 A number of words have been borrowed into English from Yiddish and Hebrew. Try to guess the word written beside.

Yiddish orthography is slightly different from Hebrew. Note that אַ represents /ɑ/; ע is /ɛ/; a double ײ represents /ej/; and a double װ represents /v/. The superscript horizontal line indicates a fricative pronunciation. Note that the English meaning of a borrowed word is not always the same as the original Yiddish. The infinitive of Yiddish verbs ends in /-n/.

	Yiddish meaning	English meaning (where different)
בײגל	doughnut-shaped bread	
שמאַלץ	(chicken) fat	excessive sentiment
שלימזל	an unlucky person	a mess
קוועטשן	to press, complain	
מזל טוב̄	congratulations	
חוצפה	impertinence, nerve	
שלעפן	to drag	
משוגענער	a crazy person	
קיבעצן	chat	
נאַשן	to snack	

4 Suppose that English speakers had borrowed Egyptian writing and used it in the same way that early Semitic writers did. What would be the phonological value of the first three symbols of the English alphabet in this situation?

5 How do modern Hebrew and modern Arabic differ from each other structurally (not just in having different-shaped symbols) in the way vowels are written?

6 Write your own name and city in the Hebrew and Arabic scripts, paying attention to the sound, not English spelling.

8 The Greek Alphabet

8.1 Background and History

Greek is the only language of the Greek branch of the Indo-European language family. Although many of us today are familiar with the Greek alphabet which has existed for almost 3000 years, early texts in several scripts have been discovered in the Greek area. The earliest texts in the Greek language date from the Mycenæan period, 1550 to 1200 OLD. The Mycenæan texts are in an early form of Greek in a script known as Linear B. Linear B died out around 1200 OLD and knowledge of the system was later lost to the Greeks. Other very old undeciphered scripts exist; we are generally uncertain of the language in the undeciphered texts. Only in the eighth century OLD do we find texts written in the ancestor of the modern Greek alphabet.

The Greek language can be divided into the periods shown in table 8.1.

The Greek poet Homer composed the epics *Iliad* and *Odyssey* in the eighth century OLD. These are the oldest post-Mycenæan Greek texts that we have. Classical Greek from 600 OLD is well known with a vast literature that forms a major component of European cultural history. Ancient Greek had a great deal of dialect variation although the Attic (i.e., Athenian) dialect has a certain prestige.

Ancient Greece (figure 8.1) included a much larger area than the modern country of Greece; in particular, a large portion of what is today Turkey was earlier Greek. Greek colonies existed in Cyprus and southern Italy. Thus, Greek was the native language of many people living beyond the boundaries of modern Greece. Following Alexander the Great's conquests in the late fourth century OLD, Greek became an important lingua franca throughout the eastern Mediterranean and the Middle East, as far as India. In large part, Greek supplanted Aramaic in this role. The Hebrew

Table 8.1 Periods of the Greek language

Mycenæan	1500–1200 OLD
Homeric	*ca.* eighth century OLD
Classical	600–300 OLD
Hellenistic (Koiné)	300 OLD–300 NEW
Byzantine	300 NEW–1100
Mediæval	1100–1600
Modern	1600–present

Figure 8.1 Map of ancient Greece

Bible was translated into Greek for Greek-speaking Jews. This translation is known as the Septuagint after the Greek word for '70' because of the 70–72 translators involved. Early Christians were largely Greek-speaking Jews, and their sacred text (the New Testament) was composed in Hellenistic (Koiné /ˌkɔjˈnej/) Greek. Greek was the language of the Byzantine Empire in Constantinople and continues as the language of Greece today.

Modern Greek is an example of a diglossic language situation. Although the language had changed over time, many mediæval and modern authors attempted to write in Classical Greek. The result is that two forms of Greek developed: ***katharevousa*** (καθαρεύουσα 'purifying' /ˌkaθaˈɹevuˌsa/) is conservative and more like Classical Greek (although not completely the same) and is used for more formal purposes; the other variety is ***demotike*** (δημοτική 'popular' /ˌdiˈmatɪˈki/), which is based on current speech and used in less formal situations. Up to the twentieth century, writing was generally only done in *katharevousa*. Since 1900, the tendency has been to increase the use of *demotike*.

Greek pronunciation has changed considerably since classical times. In Greece today, however, Classical Greek is pronounced as though it were modern Greek. Students of Greek elsewhere have tended to use the pronunciation reconstructed by Erasmus in the fifteenth century NEW. Modern scholars disagree with many details of Erasmus' reconstruction.

8.2 Greek Scripts before the Alphabet

8.2.1 *Linear B*

The oldest known writing in Greek consists of clay tablets in an early form of Greek known as **Mycenæan** Greek in a script known as **Linear B** (figure 8.2). Texts have been found primarily at Pylos and Mycenæ on the Greek mainland, and at Knossos in Crete. They have been dated to 1550–1200 OLD. The texts were written horizontally left-to-right on the tablets with a pointed stylus. Most are accounting records. Apparently a disaster struck the society around 1200 OLD, in which the palaces were burnt down. As a result, the clay tablets were baked. There is no later evidence of the Linear B script.

The discovery and decipherment of Linear B is an interesting story (Chadwick 1967). Mycenæan sites were discovered around 1900 and work began soon thereafter on the tablets. The decipherment was particularly difficult; the script was otherwise unknown, and at this time, almost no one thought that the language was Greek.

In the mid-twentieth century, an English architect, Michael **Ventris**, began working on the decipherment using a purely formal approach. Ventris felt that the inventory of signs was too large for the system to be alphabetic and that it was more likely moraic.

Alice Kober (1945) had previously identified a number of related triplets (the three forms in each column) which share symbols. For example, in table 8.2, the first two symbols in each column are shared. Further, in the top two rows, the last two are shared, and in the bottom row, the last symbol is shared. Kober's thinking was that each triplet represented different inflected forms of the same stem and each row represented forms of different stems with the same inflectional ending. Thus, in each form the stem consists of the two leftmost symbols, and the inflectional endings comprise the rest.

Figure 8.2 Example of a Linear B tablet (from Fred Woudhuizen, *The Language of the Sea Peoples*, p. 70. Amsterdam: Najade Press, 1993. © 1993 Jan Best. Reproduced with permission)

Table 8.2 Examples of Kober's Triplets. The transcription (as we now know it, but unknown at the time to Kober) is shown below

𐀬𐀑𐀴𐀊	𐀞𐀂𐀴𐀊	𐀶𐀪𐀯𐀊	𐀒𐀜𐀯𐀊	𐀪𐀍𐀛𐀊
𐀬𐀑𐀴𐀍	𐀞𐀂𐀴𐀍	𐀶𐀪𐀯𐀍	𐀒𐀜𐀯𐀍	𐀪𐀍𐀛𐀍
𐀬𐀑𐀵	𐀞𐀂𐀵	𐀶𐀪𐀰	𐀒𐀜𐀰	𐀪𐀍𐀜
ru.ki.t–i.ja	pa.i.t–i.ja	tu.ri.s–i.ja	ko.no.s–i.ja	ri.jo.n–i.ja
ru.ki.t–i.jo	pa.i.t–i.jo	tu.ri.s–i.jo	ko.no.s–i.jo	ri.jo.n–i.jo
ru.ki.t–o	pa.i.t–o	tu.ri.s–o	ko.no.s–o	ri.jo.n–o

However, we see that the inflectional endings are not exactly the same: the second-last symbols of rows 1 and 2 are the same, but the last symbols of these rows are different, and the last symbols of row 3 are different from each other. If the system is moraic, these latter differences can be explained as follows. The stem ends in a consonant (which falls in the third mora in these examples); the suffixes in rows 1 and 2 have the shape VCV; and the suffix in row 3 has the shape V. The nature of a moraic writing system would mean that the symbols representing a mora which is entirely a part of the stem would be written the same (the first two symbols in these examples); hence the vertical similarity in each column. Similarly, the symbols which represent moræ entirely a part of the suffix would be written the same; hence the horizontal similarity between the columns in rows 1 and 2. Differences would occur at the stem–suffix boundary (the third mora in these examples) where the symbols would represent different CV combinations (the third symbol in these examples). Kober's work started this type of analysis and Ventris built on it.

Using Kober's work, Ventris tried organizing the symbols into patterns (figure 8.3) where the symbols in the same column have the same vowel, and those in the same row have the same consonant. On a whim, he tried reading the texts as an early form of Greek and met with success. However, the Linear B forms did not look like Homeric Greek, the earliest form of Greek known at that time. Partly, this was due to the fact that the Greek language had changed in the time between the Mycenæan era (1200 OLD) and Homeric times (early ninth century OLD). But the differences are also due to the fact that Linear B is written with moraic symbols (table 8.3), and not the alphabetic symbols used for Homeric or Classical Greek. The use of a moraic system made it look unusual for two reasons. Since there were not symbols in Linear B for vowelless consonants, final consonants in Linear B were generally omitted, and consonant clusters were written with a dummy vowel: e.g., a cluster /ksa/ would be written <ka-sa> using two symbols repeating the vowel. John Chadwick was a young Greek scholar who immediately recognized that Ventris was on the right track. Unfortunately, Ventris was killed in an automobile accident, but his work remains an outstanding accomplishment.

The Linear B writing system is a mixture of moraic and morphographic writing. Most of the writing moraic, but a number of morphographic symbols were used as well, particularly in inventory lists and as numerals.

LINEAR SCRIPT B SYLLABIC GRID (2ND STATE) — WORK NOTE 15

DIAGNOSIS OF CONSONANT AND VOWEL EQUATIONS IN THE INFLEXIONAL MATERIAL FROM PYLOS: — ATHENS, 28 SEPT 51

THESE 51 SIGNS MAKE UP 90% OF ALL SIGN-OCCURRENCES IN THE PYLOS SIGNGROUP INDEX. APPENDED FIGURES GIVE EACH SIGN'S OVERALL FREQUENCY PER MILLE IN THE PYLOS INDEX.

	vowel 1	vowel 2	vowel 3	vowel 4	vowel 5
	'Impure' ending typical syllables before - & - in Case 2c & 3	'Pure' ending typical nominatives of forms in Column I	Includes possible 'accusatives'	Also, but less frequently, the nominatives of forms in Column I	
	THESE SIGNS DON'T OCCUR BEFORE - -	THESE SIGNS OCCUR LESS COMMONLY OR NOT AT ALL BEFORE - -			
	MORE OFTEN FEMININE THAN MASCULINE?	MORE OFTEN MASCULINE THAN FEMININE?			MORE OFTEN FEMININE THAN MASCULINE?
	NORMALLY FORM THE GENITIVE SINGULAR BY ADDING -		NORMALLY FORM THE GENITIVE SINGULAR BY ADDING -		
pure vowels?	30.3				37.2
a semi-vowel?				34.0	29.4
consonant 1	14.8	32.5	21.2	28.1	18.8
2	19.6	17.5			13.7
3		9.2		3.3	10.0
4	17.0	28.6			0.4
5	17.7	10.3		4.1	10.2
6	7.4	20.5		14.8	14.4
7	4.1	44.0			
8	6.1	6.1		13.5	15.2
9		33.1		32.3	2.4
10	22.2		38.2	3.5	2.2
11	31.2	33.8	34.4	8.3	0.7
12	17.0			37.7	24.0
13		9.4	14.2		
14	5.0				
15	12.6				

MICHAEL VENTRIS

Figure 8.3 A sample page from Ventris' notebooks. His working hypothesis was that the symbols represent CV sequences; those in each row share the same consonant, and those in the same column share the same vowel (from John Chadwick, *The Decipherment of Linear B*, 'Ventris grid, 28 September 1951', figure 13, p. 59. Cambridge: Cambridge University Press, 1967. © 1967 by Cambridge University Press. Reprinted with the permission of Cambridge University Press)

Table 8.3 Some Linear B symbols

Phonographic (moraic) symbols

a	e	i	o	u
pa	pe	pi	po	pu
ta	te	ti	to	tu
ka	ke	ki	ko	ku
qa	qe	qi	qo	
da	de	di	do	du
sa	se	si	so	su
za	ze		zo	
ma	me	mi	mo	mu
na	ne	ni	no	nu
ra	re	ri	ro	ru
wa	we	wi	wo	
ja	je		jo	ju

Examples of morphographic symbols

wheel	grain	bronze	
wine	100	200	1000

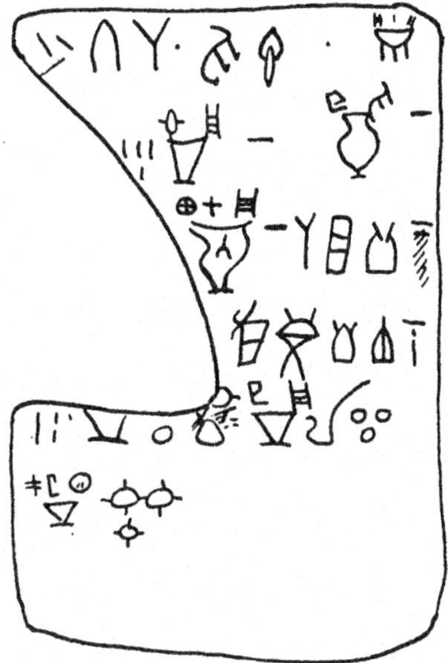

Figure 8.4 Linear A tablet (from Jan Best and Fred Woudhuizen (eds.), *Lost Languages from the Mediterranean*, figure 1, p. 2. Leiden: E. J. Brill, 1989. © 1993 by Jan Best. Reproduced with permission)

8.2.2 *Other early Greek scripts*

Other texts have been found on Crete in scripts known as **Linear A** (figure 8.4). To date, these texts have not been deciphered.

Sometime around 1700 OLD, a clay disk about 18 cm in diameter was made in Crete (figure 8.5). This **Phaistos Disk** has figures in a spiral order on both sides which appear to be writing. The symbols were not written individually, but were impressed with stamps; there are 242 separate impressions made with 45 different stamps. The impressions are made in boxes with two to seven impressions in each box. Unfortunately, the Phaistos Disk has resisted all attempts at decipherment.

Two possibly related ancient scripts have been found on Cyprus. The older group is known as the Cypro-Minoan script from 1500–1200 OLD. It has not been deciphered. The later **Cypriot** script from about 800–200 OLD has been deciphered, and the texts are in Cypriot Greek (figure 8.6). The script is moraic. Although the symbols have different shapes from the Linear B symbols, the orthographic conventions are very similar. See the discussion in the next section of Woodard's claim for the importance of Cyprus in the history of Greek writing.

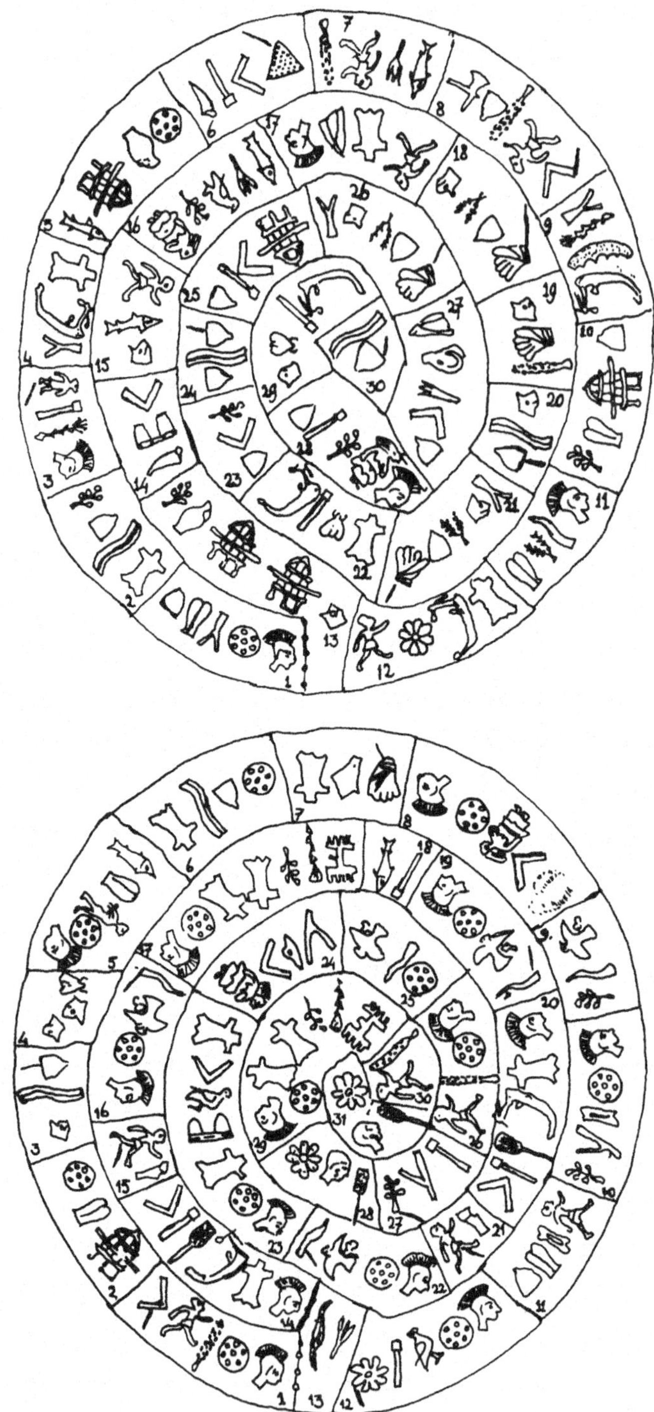

Figure 8.5 Phaistos Disk (from Jan Best and Fred Woudhuizen (eds.), *Ancient Scripts from Crete and Cyprus*, pp. 32–3. Leiden: E. J. Brill, 1988. © 1993 by Jan Best. Reproduced with permission)

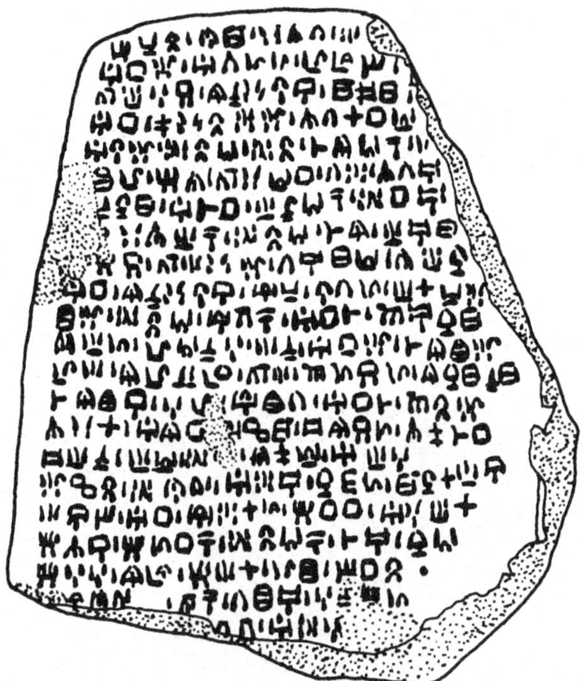

Figure 8.6 Example of a Cypriot Greek text (from Jan Best and Fred Woudhuizen (eds.), *Ancient Scripts from Crete and Cyprus*, p. 106. Leiden: E. J. Brill, 1988. © 1993 by Jan Best. Reproduced with permission)

8.3 Development of the Greek Alphabet

The Semitic abjad was brought to Greece probably by Phœnician traders. Several facts make it clear that the Greek **alphabet** was borrowed from the Semitic abjad. First, the ordering of the Greek letters is basically the same as in Semitic. Second, the Greek names of the letters are obviously similar to the Semitic (cf. Greek /alpʰa/ – Sem. /ʔalif/, Greek /bɛːta/ – Sem. /beːt/, etc.; the actual Greek forms of the names may have been borrowed from Aramaic). Third, these names are meaningful and acrophonic in Semitic, but meaningless in Greek: likely, the Greeks borrowed the letters with their names even though they did not understand those names. Fourth, the shapes of the letters are similar to those of older Phœnician writing. And fifth, ancient Greek texts refer to the letters as φοινικεῖα γράμματα 'Phœnician letters' and as καδμεῖα γράμματα 'Cadmean letters' (named after Cadmus, a legendary Phœnician hero).

Although the fact that the Greek alphabet derives from Phœnician writing is clear, the date of the borrowing is problematic (Naveh 1982, 1988). The earliest Greek texts date from only the eighth century OLD; however, the form of early Greek writing is more like that of Phœnician writing of the eleventh century OLD. If borrowing took place in the eleventh century, then why do we not have texts until the eighth

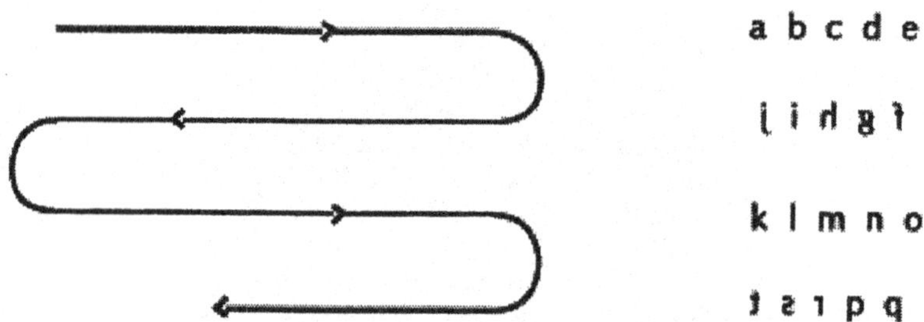

Figure 8.7 Boustrophedon. Note that in boustrophedon, the direction of the letters is reversed as the line direction changes

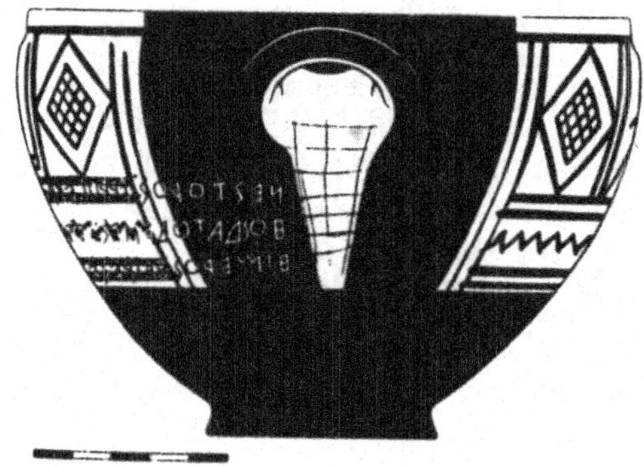

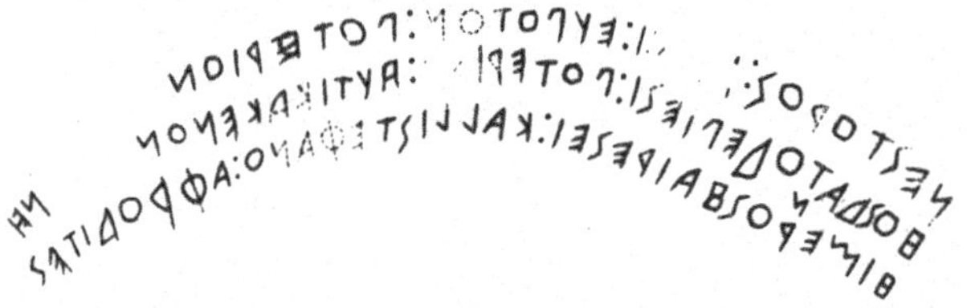

Figure 8.8 Inscription on Nestor's cup (from John Boardman and N. G. L. Hammond (eds.), *The Cambridge Ancient History*, *3.3*, figure 16, p. 100. Cambridge: Cambridge University Press, 1970, © 1970 by Cambridge University Press. Reprinted with the permission of Cambridge University Press)

century? On the other hand, if the borrowing did not take place until the eighth century, then two aspects of Greek writing must be explained. One, the shapes of the letters resemble older Phœnician forms. And two, older Greek texts are sometimes written in **boustrophedon** (βουστροφηδόν 'as an ox ploughs' /ˌbustɹəˈfidən/), that is, lines written alternatingly left to right and right to left (figure 8.7). Early Phœnician texts are often boustrophedal, but by the eighth century OLD, Phœnician writing was only done right to left (only later did Greek writing become exclusively left to right). I am inclined to agree with Naveh (1988) and opt for the earlier date of borrowing, but the dating of the Greek script remains an open question. (Sproat (2000) notes that there are regular reports that with boustrophedon the reversal of letters as shown in figure 8.7 is optional. He says, however, that he has found no examples where the letters are not reversed.)

Woodard (1997) has argued that Cyprus played an important role in the borrowing of the script for Greek. He claims that it is likely that Cyprus was the site of the borrowing and that Greek scribes familiar with Cypriot writing were crucially involved in the process. Woodard places the Cypriot borrowing of the Phœnician script in the ninth century.

Whereas the early evidence for writing is associated with bookkeeping in Mesopotamia or in Mycenæan Greece, or with religion for Hebrew and Arabic, or with oracular predictions for Chinese, such associations for Greek are less clear. One suggestion is that writing was at least in part an affectation that upper-class young men used to show off and amuse themselves. For evidence of this theory, we can examine an example of an early Greek inscription, the dipylon wine jug of Athens, known as Nestor's cup and dated to 740 OLD (figure 8.8). The text is written right-to-left, and reads 'I am the delicious drinking cup of Nestor. Whoever drinks from this cup swiftly will the desire of fair-crowned Aphrodite seize him'.

8.4 Abjad to Alphabet

The phonemic inventories of Phœnician and Greek were different. Greek had sounds not found in Phœnician and did not have all the sounds of Phœnician. Thus, it needed a somewhat different inventory of symbols for writing. How the Greeks dealt with these differences led to a significant change in the nature of the writing system.

The Classical Greek phonemic inventory (Attic dialect of the fifth and fourth centuries OLD) is shown in table 8.4. (Notes: /w/ was lost early in some dialects of Greek. There is also some evidence to consider the clusters /ps/, /ks/, and /zd/ as single phonemes, or at least as tightly bound phonological units.)

Table 8.4 The phonemes of ancient Greek

p	t	k			
b	d	g			
p^h	t^h	k^h			
m	n				
	s		h		
(w)	l, r				
i, iː		y, yː		uː	aj
oj					
e, eː				o	
ɛː				ɔː	
				a, aː	

Table 8.5 The development of the Greek alphabet from the Phœnician abjad. Faber's (1981) proto-Semitic reconstructions are used for the Phœnician sibilants, and the traditionally posited Phœnician forms are in parentheses. The symbols in parentheses in the Modern Greek column were not used in Classical Attic Greek or later except for their numeric values

Phœn. sound	*Phœn. shape*	*Early Greek 8th–7th centuries*	*Greek name*		*Early Greek sound*	*Modern Greek shape*	*Numeric value*
ʔ	𐤀	A	ἄλφα	alpha	a, a:	Α α	1
b	𐤁	8	βῆτα	beta	b	Β β	2
g	𐤂	Λ	γάμμα	gamma	g	Γ γ	3
d	𐤃	Δ	δέλτα	delta	d	Δ δ	4
h	𐤄	Ǝ	ἐ ψῖλόν	epsilon	e	Ε ε	5
w	𐤅	ꟻ	ϝαῦ	wau digamma	(w)	(Ϝ)	6
dz (z)	𐤆	I	ζῆτα	zeta	zd	Ζ ζ	7
ħ	𐤇	H	ἦτα	eta	ɛ:	Η η	8
ṭ	𐤈	⊗	θῆτα	theta	t^h	Θ θ	9
j	𐤉	ϟ	ἰῶτα	iota	i, i:	Ι ι	10
k	𐤊	ꓘ	κάππα	kappa	k	Κ κ	20
l	𐤋	⅃	λάμβδα	lambda	l	Λ λ	30
m	𐤌	ꟽ	μῦ	mu	m	Μ μ	40
n	𐤍	ᴎ	νῦ	nu	n	Ν ν	50
ts (s)	𐤎	Ξ	ξῖ	xi	ks	Ξ ξ	60
ʕ	𐤏	O	ὃ μῖκρόν	omikron	o	Ο ο	70
p	𐤐	Γ	πῖ	pi	p	Π π	80
ts (ṣ)	𐤑	M	σάν, σάμπι	san, sampi	(z)	(ϡ)	900
q	𐤒	Ϙ	κόππα	koppa, qoppa		(ϙ)	90
r	𐤓	ꟼ	ῥῶ	rho	r	Ρ ρ	100
s (ʃ)	𐤔	Ƹ	σίγμα	sigma	s	Σ σ ς	200
t	𐤕	T	ταῦ	tau	t	Τ τ	300
		Y	ὖ ψῖλόν	upsilon	u, u:	Υ υ	400
		Φ	φῖ	phi	p^h	Φ φ	500
		X	χῖ	chi	k^h	Χ χ	600
		ꓘ	ψῖ	psi	ps	Ψ ψ	700
			ὦ μέγα	omega	ɔ:	Ω ω	800

Table 8.5 shows the development of the Greek alphabet from the Phœnician abjad. For most of the consonants, the Phœnician symbol was simply used for a similar-sounding Greek consonant. Some symbols, however, were reallocated. Phœnician <ṭ> (*ṭe:t*) was used for Greek /tʰ/. The symbols <w> (*waw*, also known as *digamma*), <ṣ> (*sampi*), <q> (*koppa*) were kept, but used only in some dialects. New symbols for /pʰ kʰ ps/ were created. Following the Semitic tradition, ordinary letters were used to represent numbers. For this special purpose, the older letters <Ϝ ϙ ϡ> were kept as numerals.

Table 8.6 The traditional view of the borrowing of the Greek sibilants from Phœnician

Symbol				*Sound*	
Phœnician		*Greek*		*Phœnician*	*Greek*
zaj	I	zeta	I	z	dz > zd
semk	≢	xi	‡	s	ks
ṣade	h	san	M	ts	z
shin	W	sigma	ξ	ʃ	s

Table 8.7 The implications of Faber's reconstruction of the early Semitic sibilants for the borrowing of the Greek

Symbol				*Sound*	
Phœnician		*Greek*		*Phœnician (Faber)*	*Greek*
zaj	I	zeta	I	dz	dz > zd
semk	≢	xi	‡	ts	ks
ṣade	h	san	M	ts?	z
shin	W	sigma	ξ	s	s

The borrowing of the Phœnician sibilants has been troublesome for scholars. The traditional view has the correspondences of table 8.6 (early Greek /dz/ became Classical /zd/).

These correspondences seems odd. Why would the Greeks not have used *semk* (instead of *shin*) for /s/, and ṣade for /dz/ (instead of *zaj*)? The role of *san* in Greek is uncertain. It is commonly transcribed as /z/, in which case, why would the Greeks not have used *zaj* for /z/; however, *san* and *sigma* seem to be in complementary distribution in most dialects of Greek, with both retained for their different values in the numeric system.

Faber (1981) has reanalysed the reconstructions of the proto-Semitic sibilants (table 8.7). Her analysis is based on Semitic evidence, but it helps considerably in resolving the problem of the borrowing of the Phœnician sibilant letters into Greek (Daniels 1999).

If Faber's pronunciations for the proto-Semitic sounds are valid for Phœnician (table 8.7), the borrowings make much better sense. *Zeta* /dz/ and *sigma* /s/ are straightforward. *San* is an alternative for *sigma*, but retained for its value of 900 in the numeric system. The only syllable-final consonant clusters in Greek are /ps/ and /ks/. The creators of the Greek alphabet felt the need for separate symbols for these clusters; they created a new symbol *psi* for /ps/ and borrowed *semk* for *xi* /ks/.

With this understanding, the types of adjustment which we have just seen are rather typical of what happens when one language borrows the writing system of another language. The real change that occurred in Greek was that some unneeded Semitic letters were used for vowels, thus changing fundamentally the way in which the writing system related to the language. The abjad became an alphabet. The reasons for this change are not clear. English-speaking students of Semitic languages such as Hebrew or Arabic find the absence of vowel indications very frustrating; perhaps some Greeks, trying to learn to write Phœnician, were also frustrated and thought that they could do better. The Aramaic model of using *matres lectionis* may have also been an influence.

Perhaps a Semitic speaker, demonstrating the way the abjad worked, pointed to an *ʔalif* and said /ʔa/ to indicate a glottal stop. The Greek listener, however, paid no attention to the glottal stop, which did not exist in Greek, but rather thought that *ʔalif* was the way to write the vowel /a/. Generally, however, we find that borrowers of a writing system tend to be very conservative. They often keep the old methods, no matter how inconvenient they may be. Certainly, the Semitic abjad spread to many other languages without becoming an alphabet. Note that the Greeks borrowed writing, they did not borrow the Phœnician language or culture generally; perhaps with this detachment, they felt little need to preserve the system intact. In any case, the Greeks created a new type of writing system, the alphabet, which spread vigorously and is considered the norm today when we want to create a new writing system for an unwritten language.

Almost all vowel distinctions of Classical Greek were written; only the long–short differences for /i iː y yː a aː/ were not indicated. Table 8.8 shows how the Phœnician consonant symbols were reassigned to the Greek vowels.

Note that the spellings <EI> and <OY> reflect an earlier period when these vowels were diphthongs, hence the use of digraphic writing.

Table 8.8 Phœnician origin of Greek vowel symbols

Phœnician letter	*Phœnician consonant sound*	*Early Greek letter*	*Greek vowel sound*	*Modern Greek letter*	
𐤉	j	≀	i	I	
		≀	iː	I	
𐤄	h	Ǝ	e	E	
		Ǝ≀	ei > eː	E I	
𐤇	ħ	H	ɛː	H	
𐤀	ʔ	A	a	A	
		A	aː	A	
			ɔː	Ω	new symbol
𐤏	ʕ	O	o	O	
		OY	ou > uː	O Y	
𐤅	w	Y	y	Y	derived from
		Y	yː	Y	waw <w>

Table 8.9 Dialectal variation in the early Greek alphabet

Modern Greek shape	*Ionia*	*Athens*	*Corinth*	*Eubœa (borrowed by Etruscans)*
Α	A	A	A	A
Β	B	B	ᘉ	B
Γ	Γ	Λ	C	C
Δ	Δ	Δ	Δ	▷
Ε	E	E	B	E
Ϝ (digamma)		F	F	F
Ζ	I	I	I	I
Η (/eː/)	H	—	—	—
(/h/)	—	H	H	H
Θ	⊗	⊗	⊗	⊗
Ι	I	I	Σ	I
Κ	K	K	K	K
Λ	Λ	L	Λ	L
Μ	M	M	M	M
Ν	N	N	N	N
Ξ	ǂ	Xᛊ	ǂ	X
Ο	O	O	O	O
Π	Γ	Γ	Γ	Γ
ͳ (sampi)	—	—	M	M
ϙ (qoppa)	Ϙ	Ϙ	Ϙ	Ϙ
Ρ	P	P	P	P
Σ	Σ	ᛊ		ᛊ
Τ	T	T	T	T
Υ	Y	Y	Y	Y
Φ	Φ	Φ	Φ	Φ
Χ	X	X	X	Ψ
Ψ	Ψ	Φᛊ	Ψ	Φᛊ
Ω	Ω	—	—	—

The letters <Ϝ>, <ϙ>, <ͳ> were used as regular letters only in archaic times; their use as numbers, however, continued. In mediæval times, *sigma* developed two lower-case allographs: <ς> occurs word-finally, and <σ> occurs elsewhere.

Different versions of the Greek alphabet emerged in different areas of Greece (table 8.9). In the fourth century OLD, the Ionic alphabet generally replaced the other local varieties of script; however, in terms of language the Attic dialect increasingly became recognized as the standard. The early Attic dialect had used the Semitic letter *he*: <h> for the sound /h/. The Ionic dialect, however, had lost the sound /h/ and used <h> for the vowel /ɛː/. Thus, to write Attic /h/, a new device had to be found: diacritics, known as **breathings**, developed (probably from divided versions of <H> ⊢ and ⊣). The rough breathing over an initial vowel (<ἁ . . . > /ha . . . /) indicated that the word began with /h/, and the smooth breathing over an initial vowel (<ἀ . . . > /a . . . /) indicated that it did not.

Early Greek apparently had a pitch accent system, and diacritics were developed by the third century OLD to indicate these pitch accents. Later, this pitch accent system turned into a stress accent system, and the same symbols continued to be used to indicate the stress accents. Recent spelling reform has simplified the writing of these accents and has removed other diacritics.

8.5 The Relationship of Language and Writing in Greek

We will use **Classical Greek,** as written in modern times, as an example of how grapheme–phoneme relationships can be formulated systematically. The relationship is fairly straightforward, yet with enough complexity to make it interesting. The phonemes of Classical Greek have already been given in table 8.4. Note that the arrow can be read as 'is written as'.

1 Simple phoneme–grapheme relationships:

/b/	→	β	/p^h/	→	φ	/i, iː/	→	ι
/d/	→	δ	/t^h/	→	θ	/e/	→	ε
/g/	→	γ	/k^h/	→	χ	/ɛː/	→	η
/p/	→	π	/l/	→	λ	/a, aː/	→	α
/t/	→	τ	/r/	→	ρ	/ɔː/	→	ω
/k/	→	κ	/m/	→	μ	/o/	→	ο
			/n/	→	ν	/y, yː/	→	υ

2 Two digraphs are used:

/eː/ → ει /uː/ → ου

3 Three diphones are found:

/zd/ → ζ /ps/ → ψ /ks/ → ξ

4 /n/ before /k ɡ k^h ks/ assimilates to [ŋ]; in these cases, it is written as <γ>: γκ γγ γχ γξ.
5 /s/ → ς at the end of a word, and → σ elsewhere.
6 /h/ occurs only initially and is written with a diacritic known as a rough breathing over the following vowel: ἱ ἑ ἡ ἁ ὡ ὁ ὑ. If a word begins with a vowel, a diacritic known as a smooth breathing is written over that vowel (indicating that no initial /h/ occurs): ἰ ἐ ἠ ἀ ὠ ὀ ὐ. Note that every word-initial vowel must have either a rough or a smooth breathing. With diphthongs, breathings are written over the second vowel /hairéoː/ αἱρέω 'seize'.
7 In initial position, /r/ is written with a rough breathing ῥ; a sequence of /rr/ is written ῤῥ; otherwise, /r/ is written as ρ: ῥῖγος 'frost', Πύῤῥος 'Pyrrhus'.
8 In modern pedogogical texts, long /aː iː yː/ are sometimes written with a macron as ᾱ ῑ ῡ.

9 Historically, there were long diphthongs /a:j ɛ:j ɔ:j/ which were written as αι ηι ωι. Later these diphthongs were simplified to /a: ɛ: ɔ:/. Although no longer pronounced, the iota of these diphthongs was still written, but in a special shape known as iota-subscript; this is small and written beneath the preceding vowel: ᾳ ῃ ῳ: e.g., Διονυσίῳ /dionysiɔː/ from earlier /dionysiɔːj/ 'to Dionysius'.

10 Three accents are written in Classical Greek: **acute** <´>, **circumflex** <ˆ>, and **grave** <`>. Every word, with the exception of a few very common short words (which have no accent), has one and only one accent. The position of the stress is determined by a combination of lexical and phonological rules, but it always falls on one of the last three syllables. The exact phonetic manifestation of the ancient tone marks is not entirely clear.

(a) The circumflex accent occurs only on long vowels and only on one of the last two syllables in the word: ῖ ῆ ᾶ ῶ ῦ.
(b) The acute accent occurs on both short and long vowels: ί έ ή ά ώ ό ύ.
(c) The grave accent falls only on the last syllable. It occurs when a word which would ordinarily have an acute on its last syllable is followed by another word in the sentence; in such a case, the acute turns into a grave:

e.g., μετά τήν μάχην → μετὰ τὴν μάχην 'after the battle'

(d) A circumflex accent is written over a breathing: ἆ ἧ: ὧδε 'thus'.
(e) An acute or grave accent is written after a breathing: ἔ ἓ: ἄνθρωπος 'person'.
(f) With an initial diphthong, accents are written on the second vowel: αἱρέω, Αἱρέω.
(g) Accents and breathings are written before an initial upper-case vowel (except with a diphthong as in (f) above): Ἡ Ἐ Ἄ Ὧ: Ὅμηρος 'Homer'.

8.6 Scripts Derived from the Greek Alphabet

8.6.1 Coptic

The main language of Christianity in the eastern Mediterranean was Greek. As a result, the Greek alphabet was adapted to many languages in order to write translations of the Christian Bible and other religious material. As we have already seen, Egyptians were known as Copts after they became Christian in the third century NEW (chapter 6). The **Coptic** language was written in a version of the Greek alphabet. The names of the letters and the numeric values show the Greek origin (table 8.10). Six letters were probably adapted from demotic Egyptian writing. Coptic died out as a spoken language in the sixteenth century, but it continues as a liturgical language in the Coptic Church.

Six symbols were apparently borrowed from demotic Egyptian (table 8.11).

Table 8.10 The development of the Coptic script from the Greek

Coptic name	*Coptic sound*	*Coptic shape*	*Greek shape 3rd–5th centuries*	*Greek name*	*Numeric value*
alfa	ʔ	ⲁ	Α	alpha	1
ve:ta	b	ⲃ	Β	beta	2
kamma	g	ⲅ	Γ	gamma	3
talta	d	ⲇ	Δ	delta	4
ei	h	ⲉ	Є	epsilon	5
sou		ⲋ			6
sata	z	ⲍ	Ζ	zeta	7
hata	ħ	ⲏ	Η	eta	8
thita	ṭ	ⲑ	Θ	theta	9
io:ta	j	ⲓ	Ι	iota	10
kappa	k	ⲕ	Κ	kappa	20
lauta	l	ⲗ	Λ	lambda	30
me:	m	ⲙ	Μ	mu	40
ne	n	ⲛ	Ν	nu	50
ksi	s	ⲝ	Ξ	xi	60
ou	ʕ	ⲟ	Ο	omicron	70
pi	p	ⲡ	Π	pi	80
ro:	r	ⲣ	Ρ	rho	100
se:mma	ʃ	ⲥ	Ϲ	sigma	200
tau	t	ⲧ	Τ	tau	300
he	i, y	ⲩ	Υ	upsilon	400
fi	f	ⲫ	Φ	phi	500
khi	x	ⲭ	Χ	chi	600
psi	ps	ⲯ	Ψ	psi	700
o:	o:	ⲱ	ω	omega	800

Table 8.11 The six symbols in the Coptic script borrowed from demotic

Name	*Sound*	*Shape*	*Demotic*	
ʃai	ʃ	ϣ	ȝ	
fai	f	ϥ	7	(numeric value 90)
hori	h	ϩ	9	
dʒandʒia	dʒ	ϫ	ɣ	
qima	q	ϭ	ϭ	
ti	ti	ϯ	t	

8.6.2 *Gothic*

Gothic is the only member of the East Germanic language family. It was spoken in eastern Europe in the first millennium NEW; the main surviving texts are fragments of a translation of the Christian Bible from the fourth century NEW, made by Wulfila. Possibly the Gothic alphabet was influenced by other alphabets, but contemporary Greek was clearly the major source (table 8.12).

Table 8.12 The Gothic alphabet

Gothic shape	*Gothic sound*	*Early Greek shape*	*Transliteration*	*Numeric value*
𐌰	a/aː	A	a	1
𐌱	b	B	b	2
𐌲	g	Γ	g	3
𐌳	d/ð	Δ	d	4
𐌴	e/eː	Є	e	5
𐌵	k^w		q	6
𐌶	z	Z	z	7
𐌷	h	H	h	8
𐌸	θ	Θ	þ	9
𐌹	i/iː	I	i	10
𐌺	k	K	k	20
𐌻	l	Λ		30
𐌼	m	M	m	40
𐌽	n	N	n	50
𐌾	j		j	60
𐌿	u/uː		u	70
𐍀	p	Π	p	80
𐍁				90
𐍂	r	P	r	100
𐍃	s	Ϲ	s	200
𐍄	t	T	t	300
𐍅	w/y	Y	w	400
𐍆	f		f	500
𐍇	k^h	X	x	600
𐍈	ʍ		hw	700
𐍉	o/oː		o	800
𐍊				900

Note that Gothic created several letters for sounds that Greek did not have: /k^w j f k^h ʍ/ (by this time the Classical Greek /k^h/ had become a fricative /x/). Some symbols are used only for numbers, such as 𐍊. When letters are used for numbers, they are written between raised dots or marked by horizontal strokes: ·𐍄· or 𐍄̄ '300'.

Table 8.13 The Armenian alphabet. Western sound values are indicated where they differ from Eastern

Minuscule	*Majuscule*	*Eastern sound value*	*Western sound value*	*Numeric value*
ա	Ա	a		1
բ	Բ	b	p	2
գ	Գ	g	k	3
դ	Դ	d	t	4
ե	Ե	jɛ		5
զ	Զ	z	jɛ/ɛɛ	6
է	Է	e		7
ը	Ը	ə		8
թ	Թ	t^h		9
ժ	Ժ	ʒ		10
ի	Ի	ɪ		20
լ	Լ	l		30
խ	Խ	x		40
ծ	Ծ	ts	dz	50
կ	Կ	k	g	60
հ	Հ	h		70
ձ	Ձ	dz	ts	80
ղ	Ղ	ɣ		90
ճ	Ճ	tʃ	dʒ	100
մ	Մ	m		200
յ	Յ	h/j		300
ն	Ն	n		400
շ	Շ	ʃ		500
ո	Ո	vo/o		600
չ	Չ	$tʃ^h$		700
պ	Պ	p	b	800
ջ	Ջ	dʒ	tʃ	900
ռ	Ռ	r		1000
ս	Ս	s		2000
վ	Վ	v		3000
տ	Տ	t	d	4000
ր	Ր	ɹ		5000
ց	Ց	ts^h		6000
ւ	Ւ	v/w		7000
փ	Փ	p^h		8000
ք	Ք	k^h		9000
ու	ՈՒ	u		
օ	Օ	o		
ֆ	Ֆ	f		

8.6.3 *Armenian*

In the early fifth century NEW, Bishop Mesrop created the **Armenian** alphabet, known as the ***aybuben***, primarily based on a Greek model. The Armenian alphabet is known for its strong one-to-one relationship between phonemes and graphemes. Armenian is a member of the Indo-European language family. The two dialects East Armenian and West Armenian use the same alphabet. The vowels for the two dialects are the same, but the consonant inventories differ.

The Armenian alphabet is shown in table 8.13.

8.6.4 *Georgian*

The **Georgian** alphabet, or ***mxedruli***, is the only Caucasian language with its own writing system. Other Caucasian languages have been written in the Cyrillic or Arabic alphabets. The creation of the Georgian alphabet has sometimes been attributed to the Armenian Bishop Mesrop, but this attribution has been refuted by Gamkrelidze (1984). The earliest text is from 430 NEW; the alphabet itself was probably created in the early fourth century NEW.

The Georgian letters are given in table 8.14.

Table 8.14 The Georgian alphabet

Georgian	*Sound*	*Numeric value*	*Georgian*	*Sound*	*Numeric value*
ა	ɑ	1	რ	r	100
ბ	b	2	ს	s	200
გ	g	3	ტ	t′	300
დ	d	4	ჳ	u	400
ე	e	5	ფ	p^{h}	500
ვ	v	6	ქ	k^{h}	600
ზ	z	7	ღ	ɣ	700
ჱ	e	8	ყ	q′	800
თ	t^{h}	9	შ	ʃ	900
ი	i	10	ჩ	tʃ	1000
კ	k′	20	ც	ts	2000
ლ	l	30	ძ	dz	3000
მ	m	40	წ	ts′	4000
ნ	n	50	ჭ	tʃ′	5000
ჲ	—	60	ხ	x	6000
ო	o	70	ჴ	q	7000
პ	p′	80	ჯ	dʒ	8000
ჟ	ʒ	90	ჰ	h	9000

Table 8.15 The Glagolitic and Cyrillic Slavic alphabets. An older form of the Greek alphabet is given at the left for comparison

Greek	*Old Cyrillic*	*Glagolitic*	*Value*	*Modern Russian Cyrillic*
Α	А	Ⰰ	a	А а
	Б	Ⰱ	b	Б б
Β	В	Ⰲ	v	В в
Γ	Г	Ⰳ	g	Г г
Δ	Д	Ⰴ	d	Д д
Є	Є	Ⰵ	e	Е е
				Ё ё
	Ж	Ⰶ	ʒ	Ж ж
	Ѕ	Ⰷ	dz	
Ζ	З	Ⰸ	z	З з
Η	И	Ⰺ	i	И и
Ι	І	Ⰹ	i:	И и
				Й й
Κ	К	Ⰽ	k	К к
Λ	Л	Ⰾ	l	Л л
Μ	М	Ⰿ	m	М м
Ν	Н	Ⱀ	n	Н н
Ο	О	Ⱁ	o	О о
Π	П	Ⱂ	p	П п
Ρ	Р	Ⱃ	r	Р р
Ϲ	С	Ⱄ	s	С с
Τ	Т	Ⱅ	t	Т т
ΟΥ	ОУ	Ⱆ	au, ou	У у
Φ	Ф	Ⱇ	f	Ф ф
Θ	Ѳ	Ⱚ	θ	
Χ	Х	Ⱈ	x	Х х
Ω	Ѡ	Ⱉ	o	
	Щ	Ⱋ	ś	
	Ц	Ⱌ	ts	Ц ц
	Ч	Ⱍ	tʃ	Ч ч
	Ш	Ⱎ	ʃ	Ш ш
	Щ	Ⱎ	ç	Щ щ
	Ъ	Ⱏ	ŭ	ъ
	ЪІ	ⰟⰉ	ɯ	Ы ы
	Ь	Ⱐ	ĭ	ь
	Ѣ	Ⱑ	e	Э э
	Ю	Ⱓ	y	Ю ю
	Ꙗ	—	a	Я я

8.6.5 *Slavic*

In the early 860s NEW, two brothers, Cyril and Methodius, undertook a Christian mission from Constantinople to the Moravian Slavs. Cyril is credited with the creation of the Slavic alphabet, and the Cyrillic alphabet is named after him. The actual historic situation, however, is not clear. Early Slavic had two different alphabets: **Glagolitic** and **Cyrillic** (table 8.15). Structurally the two alphabets are equivalent. The Cyrillic alphabet is clearly based on Greek. The Glagolitic alphabet, however, is particularly puzzling because its letter shapes do not obviously resemble those of any other alphabet. Cubberley (1996) feels that Glagolitic was likely older and based on Greek cursive. After the ninth century, Glagolitic was gradually replaced by Cyrillic, although it survived in some Polish and Czech areas until the sixteenth century, where it was seen as a sign of independence from the Roman Church.

The Cyrillic alphabet became the normal alphabet for languages in the Eastern Orthodox Slavic areas; the Roman Catholic Slavic peoples, such as the Poles, Czechs, and Slovaks, used the Roman alphabet. In the early eighteenth century, Peter the Great of Russia instituted reforms which slightly simplified the writing system and westernized the shapes of letters. The communist revolution of 1918 made further reforms. Russian, Belorusian, Ukrainian, Bulgarian, and Macedonian are normally written in the Cyrillic alphabet. During the communist period of a unified Yugoslavia, Serbo-Croatian was written in both the Cyrillic and Roman alphabets. With the separation of Serbia and Croatia, the language tends to be written in Cyrillic in Serbia and in Roman in Croatia. There are minor variations in the symbol inventory of Cyrillic for all these languages to accommodate differences in their phonological systems (Cubberley 1993, 1996; Comrie 1996a, 1996b).

In addition to the Slavic languages, many non-Slavic languages of Eastern Europe and Asia are written in the Cyrillic alphabet (Comrie 1996a): to name a few – Moldovan, Tajik, Komi, Azeri, Turkmen, Tatar, Kazakh, Uzbek, Kirghiz, Abkhaz, Kabardian, Avar, Chuckchee, and Mongolian. Since the fall of the Soviet Union, there has been some movement to return to scripts used in earlier times, principally Arabic and Mongolian.

8.7 Further Reading

Chadwick (1967) is a fascinating account of the decipherment of Linear B. Stroud (1989) is a short general introduction to early Greek writing, and Chadwick (1987) is a short introduction to Linear B. Chadwick et al. (1986–98), Bennett (1996), and Woodward (1997) are sources for the more advanced student for preclassical writing in Greece. Naveh (1988), Swiggers (1996), Daniels (1999), Faber (1981), and Woodard (1997) discuss the transmission of Phœnician writing to Greece. Palmer (1980) discusses the ancient Greek language generally; Jeffrey (1961) is a thorough treatment of dialect variation in Greek writing; Woodhead (1981) presents Greek inscriptions. For the scripts derived from Greek, see: Ritner (1996) for Coptic, Ebbinghaus (1996) for Gothic, Gamkrelidze (1984) and Holisky (1996) for Georgian, Sanjian (1996) for

Armenian, Cubberley (1993, 1996), Comrie (1996a), Schenker (1995) for Slavic. Ullman (1980) is an interesting treatment of the cultural importance of Greek and Latin writing by an eminent American classicist.

8.8 Terms

acute accent
alphabet
Armenian
aybuben
boustrophedon
breathings
circumflex accent
Classical Greek
Coptic
Cypriot
Cyrillic
demotike
Georgian
Glagolitic
Gothic
grave accent
katharevousa
Linear A
Linear B
mxedruli
Mycenæan
Phaistos disk
Ventris, Michael

8.9 Exercises

1 Archæologists have just returned from Lower Eulalia with the following text written in Roman letters. The lines are shown here exactly as they were found in the original. Determine the direction of writing used in the text. (Hint: look for recurring sequences occurring at one edge or the other.)

pe odyjr yor gpt upiyjoml shppf rmm
yp yjsystueo sof pg styu ejrm fop yjsy
rmmyp djsrtsrtm naditoy nr ypfsu upiyj
oml

2 The following are names of famous Greek people, gods, and places. Give the normal English equivalent for each name. The first is done for you.

Πλάτων	Plato
Περικλῆς	
Σπάρτη	
Ὅμηρος	
Σαπφώ	
Ἀθῆναι	
Ζεύς	
Ἡρόδοτος	
Εὐριπίδης	
Κωνσταντίνου πόλις	

3 When Ventris first deciphered Linear B, many Greek scholars argued that the language was not Greek. What might have led them to this conclusion?
4 Describe and contrast the history of the following letters: *beta*, *epsilon*, *digamma*, *theta*, *xi*, *psi*.
5 Write your own name and city in the Greek script, paying attention to the sound, not English spelling. Do the same in some of the other scripts of this chapter such as Gothic, Armenian, Georgian, Cyrillic (modern and old), and Glagolitic.

9 The Roman Alphabet

9.1 From Greece to Italy

Greece had colonies in Italy, and it is through this contact that the alphabet came from Greece to Italy during the seventh century OLD. At this time, the Latin-speaking Romans were a small group of people living in and around Rome. Their neighbours to the north were the Etruscans, who first borrowed the alphabet from the Greeks.

Eventually the Etruscans were conquered and absorbed by the Romans, who borrowed the alphabet from them. In the Greek alphabet each letter is a grapheme, and this situation continued with the Etruscan and Roman alphabets.

9.2 Etruscan

Etruscan is a language unrelated to any other known language. Until recently it has been undeciphered, and even the recent claims of decipherment (Bonfante 1990) are disputed. Since Etruscan is written in a familiar alphabet, we have been able to read the inscriptions in the sense of knowing roughly how they would have been pronounced, but we have not understood them.

Etruscan was usually written from right to left. We have an early Etruscan writing tablet (figure 9.1) with an abecedary written across the top. An **abecedary** is the inventory of letters in order. It is easy to see from this figure that the Etruscan order is essentially the Greek order. We should note that it is the West Greek version of the alphabet that was borrowed; cf. the Eubœian (West Greek) version of the alphabet in table 8.9, not the eastern Ionic version which predominated later in Greece.

The Etruscan alphabet is shown in table 9.1 along with the letters of the Western Greek alphabet and a Roman transliteration. A comparison of the Etruscan and Greek alphabets reveals how accurately the Etruscans preserved the Greek alphabet including the letters which have since disappeared in Greek: *digamma* <𐌅>, *sampi* <𐌑>, and *qoppa* <𐌒>. *Omega* <Ω> is not included here as it was not used in the West Greek alphabet. Note that the West Greek letter <𐌗> was a diphone representing /ks/, not /kʰ/ as in other versions of the Greek alphabet. Note also that the Etruscan letters face to the left as was normal in right-to-left writing; later, when Roman writing went from left to right, the orientation of the letters was reversed. I have transliterated the letter <𐌂> as <C> (instead of <G> as it would have been transliterated for Greek) for reasons that will be explained below.

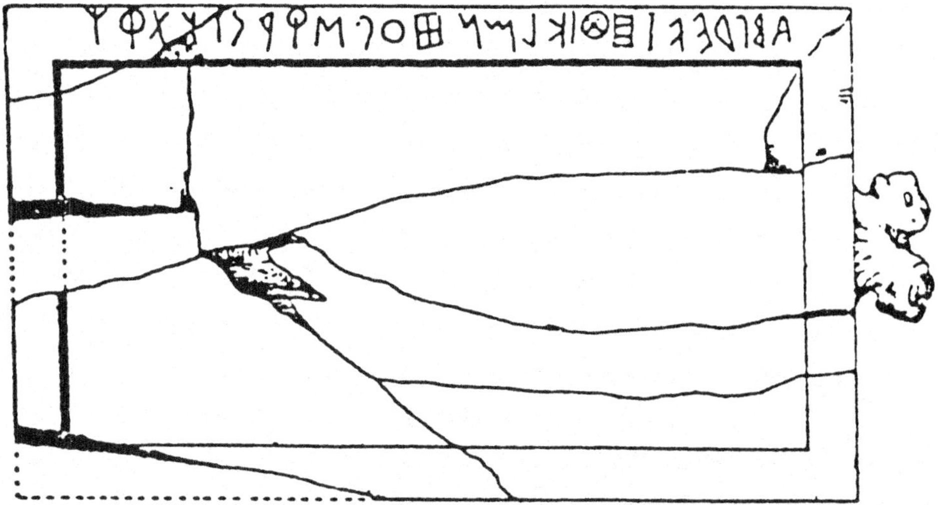

Figure 9.1 Etruscan writing tablet with alphabet written at top from right to left (see Bonfante 1990) (from Giuliano Bonfante and Larissa Bonfante, *The Etruscan Language: An Introduction*, no. 12, p. 132. Manchester: Manchester University Press, 1983. © 1983 by Manchester University Press. Reproduced with permission)

Table 9.1 The Etruscan alphabet. Etruscan in the top row, early West Greek in the middle row, Roman transliteration in the bottom row

𐌌	𐌋	𐌊	𐌉	𐌈	𐌇	𐌆	𐌅	𐌄	𐌃	𐌂	𐌁	𐌀
𐌌	𐌋	𐌊	𐌉	𐌈	𐌇	𐌆	𐌅	𐌄	𐌃	𐌂	𐌁	𐌀
M	L	K	I	T^h	H	Z	V	E	D	C	B	A
𐌙	𐌘	𐌗	𐌖	𐌕	𐌔	𐌓	𐌒	𐌑	𐌐	𐌏	𐌎	𐌍
	𐌘	𐌗	𐌖	𐌕	𐌔	𐌓	𐌒	𐌑	𐌐	𐌏	𐌎	𐌍
PS	P^h	KS	U	T	S	R	Q	S	P	O	S	N

Etruscan did not have voiced stops, aspirated stops, nor a vowel /o/. Nevertheless, the Greek graphemes for /b d g t^h p^h k^h o/ were dutifully included in the Etruscan inventory of graphemes. These graphemes were borrowed because the alphabet was seen as a whole, a single cultural entity. We have previously mentioned the conservatism which often accompanies the borrowing of a writing system. The Etruscan borrowing of the Greek alphabet is a clear example of this. Over time, the need to be faithful to the original weakens as it did with Etruscan, and the letters <B D T^h P^h K^h O> were dropped.

In the northern Etruscan area, three different letters <C K Q> were used for the single Etruscan voiceless stop /k/, with the distribution shown in table 9.2. It is not clear why this situation developed. Quite possibly, the distribution corresponded to different allophones of /k/ preceding different vowels. These three letters appear to be in complementary distribution and to be allographs of the same grapheme.

Table 9.2 Etruscan allographs for writing /k/

𐌂	<C>	/k/ before /e, i/
𐌊	<K>	/k/ before /a/
𐌒	<Q>	/k/ before /o, u/

In any case, keep this point in mind as we will return to it later in discussing the Roman alphabet.

9.3 Latin

9.3.1 Background and history

Latin is the best-known member of the Italic family of Indo-European. Other Italic languages were Oscan, Umbrian, and Faliscan, all spoken in ancient Italy. Latin survives today as the Romance languages: Italian, French, Spanish, Portuguese, and Romanian. Table 9.3 shows the various historical stages of Latin.

Latin-speaking peoples settled the area around Rome in the early first millennium OLD. Politically, they were among the most successful societies in the history of the world. First, they extended their control to the entire Italian peninsula by the early third century OLD, and ultimately the Roman Empire extended from Britain to the Middle East and north Africa. The Latin spoken by ordinary people is known as **vulgar** ('popular') **Latin** as opposed to the classical style used by the more educated elite. The Romance languages developed from late vulgar Latin, not Classical Latin. Even after the classical period, schools continued to teach Classical Latin with the result that during the Late Latin period, the language became increasingly diglossic. For much of the early Middle Ages, people spoke local Romance dialects while writing was done in Latin. In the early Middle Ages, Latin was the normal language for writing in all of western Europe because of its role as the language of the western Christian Church, although in the later Middle Ages vernacular writing became increasingly common. Until the seventeenth or eighteenth centuries, Latin was the pre-eminent language of learning throughout western Europe, and it remains an important part of European cultural heritage even today. The terms 'Latin alphabet'

Table 9.3 Historical stages of Latin

753 OLD	Traditional date for the founding of Rome (no certain evidence for this)
seventh century OLD	earliest inscriptions
before 150 OLD	Early Latin
150 OLD–150 NEW	Classical Latin
150 NEW–sixth century	Late Latin
sixth–fifteenth century	Mediæval Latin
fifteenth century–	Neo-Latin

Table 9.4 The phonemes of Classical Latin

p	t		k	k^w	i iː		u uː
b	d		g		e eː		o oː
f	s		h			a aː	
m	n						
	r	l					
w	j						

and '**Roman alphabet**' are often used interchangeably. I will use 'Roman' for the alphabet and 'Latin' for the language.

The earliest Latin inscriptions date from the seventh century OLD. By the early sixth century, examples of writing are found in major centres around Rome. In time, literacy became moderately common, at least for men. Literacy was normal for upper-class men, and often for women. Schools were common, and children of wealthy families were usually taught by household slaves. The **graffiti** at the ruins at Pompeii suggest that fairly ordinary people could write. For boys, a knowledge of Greek was a desirable refinement; those families who could sent their sons for advanced study in Greece.

9.3.2 *The phonology of Latin*

The phonological inventory of Classical Latin is given in Table 9.4.

9.4 The Roman Alphabet

Perhaps envying the cultural achievements of their Etruscan neighbours, the Romans borrowed the Etruscans' alphabet. However, the structures of the sound systems of the two languages were different. Unlike Etruscan, Latin did have voiced consonants and the vowel /o/. The Romans used the graphemes for /b/, /d/, and /o/ just as if they had borrowed the alphabet directly from the Greeks. This usage suggests that although the Romans primarily borrowed the Etruscan alphabet, they were nevertheless aware of the Greek alphabet and the sound values of its letters.

As we noted above, the northern Etruscans used three different allographs <C K Q> to write the single phoneme /k/. The Romans retained this system. They used <Q> to write /k^w/. The grapheme <K> was used for only a few words (all with /a/ after the /k/), and <C> became the normal way to write /k/. Interestingly, although the allograph <K> was not important for Latin, it was never dropped from the Roman alphabet.

In Greek, <C> had been used to write /g/, but the Etruscan alphabet used this symbol as one of the ways of writing /k/. The Romans had a sound /g/ and needed a way to write it. They could, of course, have used <K> for /k/ and <C> for /g/ as in Greek. The Romans chose rather to keep <C> for /k/, and to create a new symbol for /g/ by adding a lower stroke to <C> to create <G>, and they placed the new grapheme after <F> in the alphabet. The abbreviations for the common Roman men's names

Gaius /gajus/ and *Gnaeus* /gnajus/ were always <C> and <CN>, respectively, using <C> in its older Greek value of /g/.

The Romans were less conservative than the Etruscans in their borrowing. They discarded letters that they did not need, e.g., <Z> and the symbols for the aspirated consonants, as well as other Greek letters. For Cicero, the alphabet would have ended in <X>: <A B C D E F G H I K L M N O P Q R S T V X>. The grapheme <I> was used for /i/, /iː/, and /j/; similarly, <V> was used for /u/, /uː/, and /w/. The modern letters <J U W Y> were mediæval additions, unknown to the ancient Romans. The sequence /ks/ could, in principle, have been written <CS> or <KS>, but the Romans retained the West Greek diphone <X> for /ks/. Only rarely was vowel length indicated by an accent on the vowel symbol.

At first, the Romans discarded <Z> as unnecessary since Latin did not have a /z/ sound. However, in time they had borrowed so many Greek words which contained the sound /z/ that they found <Z> useful for writing this Greek sound, so they resumed the use of <Z>, but they placed it at the end of the alphabet. The emperor Claudius (*ca.* 50 NEW) proposed three new letters for /ps, y, w/; they were used slightly during his reign but disappeared soon after his death.

As you can see, the Romans kept the Greek-Etruscan ordering of the alphabet reasonably intact, but they did not borrow the letter names. Rather, they created new names based on the sound of the letters. For vowels, the sound of each vowel was used as its name. The names of the consonants were made with the sound of the consonant plus /e/; for <f l m n r s x>, the /e/ was pronounced before the consonant. Thus, the Latin alphabet would have been pronounced /a be ke de e ef/ etc. When <Z> was reintroduced at the end of the alphabet, its Greek pronunciation /zeta/ was used; this gives modern English /zɛd/. The nineteenth-century American lexicographer Noah Webster advocated the regularizing of this to /zi/ like /bi si di/ etc. His preference for /zi/ has become the norm in the United States, probably producing the form that would have occurred had the Romans not removed <Z> from the alphabet in the first place.

Unlike Etruscan, Latin writing was always left-to-right. This direction is perhaps further evidence that the Romans took the Greek alphabet as a model in creating the Roman alphabet, since by the fifth century OLD, Greek writing was regularly left-to-right.

9.5 Examples of Roman Writing

The form of writing used on public monuments erected in ancient Rome is strikingly readable by us today. This monumental form of the letters has had such prestige in the history of the Roman alphabet that it has continued for two millennia. The Trajan monument (plate 4) in the Roman Forum is often cited as a fine example of this sort of writing. Even if we know no Latin, we have no difficulty in recognizing the letters.

Lest you think that all ancient Latin writing is easy for us to read today, consider the example of ancient cursive handwriting in figure 9.2.

The oldest Latin inscriptions date from the late seventh century OLD. Among them are two inscribed wine vessels (Wallace 1989) dated 620–600 OLD. One has the

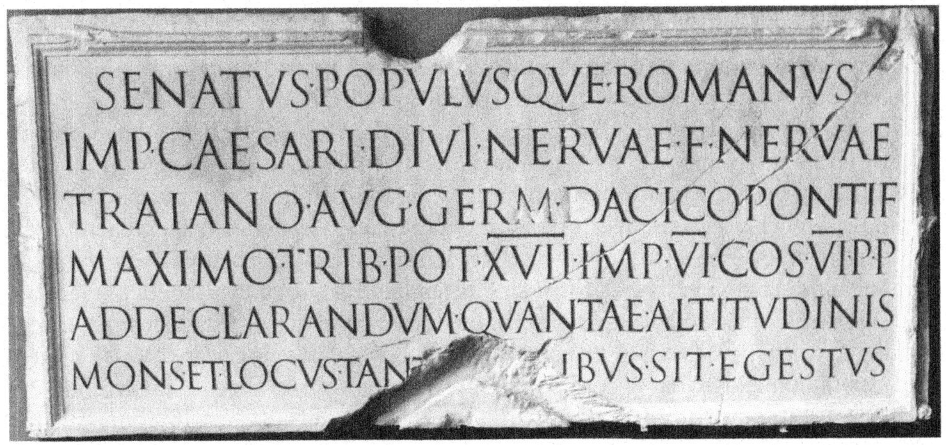

Plate 4 Trajan inscription, 113 NEW. Roman Forum (photograph of a full-size replica created by Edward Catich; reproduced courtesy of R. R. Donnelley & Sons, Chicago)

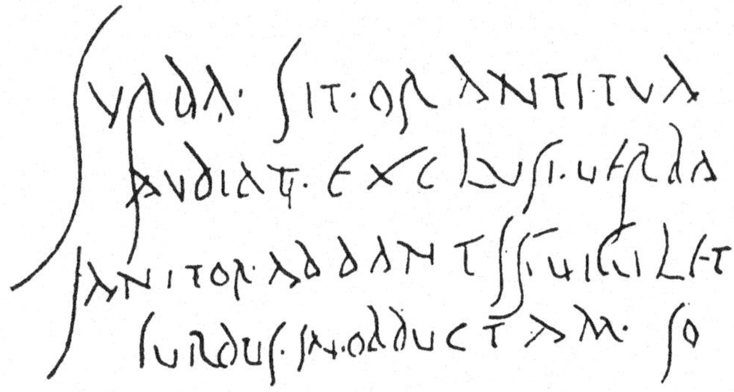

Figure 9.2 Example of ancient Roman cursive handwriting

wording: SALVETOD TITA 'May Tita be in good health' (Classical Latin: *salveto tita*). The other is ECO URNA TITA VENDIAS MAMAR[COS M]ẸḌ ṾḤẸ[CED] 'I am the urn of Tita Vendia; Mamarcos made me' (Classical Latin: *ego urna titae vendiae. mamarcus me fecit*). The portions in brackets are lost and have been reconstructed; the portions with subscript dots are partially obscured.

9.6 Later History of the Roman Alphabet

Over the course of time the Roman alphabet developed into many local **calligraphic** varieties. Some are difficult for us to read today without extensive training. Nevertheless, these local forms were always considered to be forms of a single Roman alphabet shared by all western European cultures, and the classical monumental forms of the letters retained their status as the standard shape for letters. If we compare this with the Greek situation, we note that when the alphabet was used for other languages, those variants frequently became independent scripts: Coptic, Gothic, Cyrillic, etc. In chapter 11, we will see that in India a single early script gave rise to a very large number of different scripts. Western Europe, however, maintained a sense of cultural unity which preserved the Roman alphabet intact.

Very rarely does a particular language using the Roman alphabet have a completely different grapheme beyond the basic twenty-six. Rather, new graphemes have usually been created by modifying an existing grapheme with a diacritic. For example, French uses a number of diacritics: <é è ê ç>. German has one diacritic, the **umlaut**, as in <ä ö ü>. The umlaut derives from a small <e> written over the main symbol; although the umlauted forms are normal and required in all types of German, if the writer is unable to write an umlaut (perhaps using an English typewriter), writing <ae oe ue> is a recognized alternative. A few proper names are always written without the umlaut, *Goethe* for example. German also uses the special symbol <ß> instead of <ss> in certain situations; this symbol is used in Germany and Austria, but not in Switzerland. Writing <ss> is a recognized alternative to <ß> if it is not available. The symbol <ß> is etymologically a ligature of <ſ> (an old form of <s> – see chapter 10) and <z>; it is known in German as /es tset/ 'S-Z'.

Of the few new symbols which are not simply diacritics, Polish has a plain <l> /l/, and one with a slanted cross-bar <ł>. This cross-bar could be considered a diacritic, but it occurs nowhere else in Polish, nor is it otherwise used with the Roman alphabet in other languages. Icelandic uses two symbols for /θ/ and /ð/ – <θ ð> (upper-case <Þ Đ>).

One of the great difficulties in using the Roman alphabet is that Latin did not have any postalveolar or palatal consonants. For /ʃ/, English uses the digraph <sh> whereas French uses <ch>, and Italian uses <sci>. The Slavic languages have a number of these sounds and different languages have solved the problem in different ways; some of these are shown in table 9.5.

Late Latin had a palatal nasal /ɲ/ (e.g., *senior* /seɲor/ 'older, elder' and title of respect) and a palatal lateral /ʎ/ (e.g., *filia*) /fiʎa/ 'daughter'. The different Romance languages arrived at different solutions for writing these (table 9.6). Italian uses <gn gl> for the palatals, and Portuguese uses <nh lh>. French uses <gn> and <ll>, and Spanish uses <ñ> and <ll>. In Spanish, the Romance palatal /ʎ/ has become /h/, e.g., *hija* /iha/ 'daughter', but the palatal /ʎ/ has been reintroduced in other words such as *amarillo* 'yellow'. In French, the earlier palatal lateral [ʎ] has become a palatal approximant [j].

Table 9.5 Ways of writing postalveolar obstruents and the palatal nasal in different Slavic languages

	Polish	*Czech*	*Croatian*
/ʃ/	sz	š	š
/tʃ/	cz	č	č
/ʒ/	ż, rz	ž	ž
/ɲ/	ń	ň	nj

Table 9.6 Different ways of writing the palatal nasal and lateral in Romance languages

	Italian	*French*	*Spanish*	*Portuguese*	
/ɲ/	signore	seigneur	señor	senhor	'sir, Mr'
/ʎ/	figlia	fille	(amarillo) 'yellow'	filha	'daughter, girl'

9.7 Orthographic Depth: Two Examples

In this section and the next, we will compare two somewhat different orthographies, both using the Roman alphabet: Finnish and Scots Gaelic. The two systems differ rather strongly in what is known as **orthographic depth**. Finnish writing is shallow, Scots Gaelic is deep. By orthographic depth, we are talking about the relationship of writing and language. (You may at this point need to review phonemic and morphophonemic levels in Appendix A on linguistic concepts.) In a writing system which is orthographically **shallow**, graphemes represent phonemes; in a writing system which is orthographically **deep**, graphemes represent morphophonemes. Languages are often inconsistent in that they may represent some things at one level and other things at another or at an intermediary level. One commonly sees the term 'phonetic' used to mean shallow, as in 'Finnish writing is phonetic'. This is a poor choice of words on two grounds. First, in linguistics, 'phonetic' implies subphonemic, allophonic, which is clearly not meant here. Second, 'phonetic' suggests an absolute type of relationship between the writing system and language, whereas 'deep' suggests one end of a continuum, a much more realistic appraisal, in my opinion.

9.7.1 Finnish: A shallow orthography

Finnish (called Suomi in Finnish) is a Finno-Ugric language spoken in Finland. The earliest Finnish text goes back to the thirteenth century NEW, and more plentiful material is found from the sixteenth century. The phonemes of Finnish are given in table 9.7.

Finnish orthography almost perfectly agrees with the phonemic representation except in three respects: the final glottal stop is not written, /ŋ/ is written as <n> before /k/, and long /ŋŋ/ is written as <ng>. Finnish writing is a strikingly strong example of a shallow orthography. Other letters are found in recent loans from other languages: <b g f z>.

9.7.2 Scots Gaelic: A deep orthography

Scots Gaelic provides a contrasting example of a deep orthography. Scots Gaelic is a Celtic language spoken in the northwestern part of Scotland. Gaelic came to Scotland from Ireland in the fifth century NEW and formed a continuous linguistic and cultural area with Ireland until the fifteenth–sixteenth centuries. Although a

Table 9.7 The phonemes of Finnish. The doubled vowels are long

Consonants							
	p		t		k		ʔ
			d				
			s				h
	v						
	m		n		ŋ		
			r				
			l		j		
Vowels							
		i	y	u	ii	yy	uu
		e	ö	o	ee	öö	uu
		ä		a	ää		aa
Diphthongs							
			yi	ui			
		ei	öi	oi			
			äi	ai			

Table 9.8 The consonant phonemes of Scots Gaelic

p		t	tʃ	kʲ	k	
b		d	dʒ	gʲ	g	
f		s	ʃ	ç	x	h
v, ṽ				j	ɣ	
m	n̵	n	nʲ			
	ɫ	l	lʲ			
	rʷ	r	rʲ			

few early texts exist in the ogham script (see chapter 13), the vast majority of Irish and Gaelic texts have been written in the Roman alphabet. During the Middle Ages, Middle Irish became established and fixed as the written form of the language in both Ireland and Scotland. Although the languages continued to change, the writing system did not, and the situation became increasingly diglossic. In the fifteenth and sixteenth centuries this situation broke down, and the modern languages came to be written. It was at this point that Irish and Scots Gaelic writing became distinct from each other. However, certain writing conventions which had been established in Middle Irish have substantially continued in both languages to the present time.

The consonant phonemes of modern Scots Gaelic are shown in table 9.8.

At the morphophonemic level, there is a considerably simpler inventory shown in table 9.9.

Two historic phonological changes account for much of the discrepancy between the phonemic and morphophonemic inventories. First, consonants between vowels

Table 9.9 The consonant morphophonemes of Scots Gaelic

p	t		c	
b	d		g	
f	s			h
m	n			
	l	j		
	r			

Table 9.10 The effect of lenition in Scots Gaelic. The non-lenited forms are shown above and the lenited forms below

Sound									
non-len.	p	b	t	d	k	g	f	s	m
len.	f	v	h	ɣ	x	ɣ	Ø	h	ṽ
Writing									
non-len.	p	b	t	d	c	g	f	s	m
len.	ph	bh	th	dh	ch	gh	fh	sh	mh

underwent **lenition**: i.e., generally, stops became fricatives, and fricatives were further weakened or lost. Orthographically, lenition was earlier shown by writing a dot over the letter, and in modern writing with an <h> after the consonant. In this section, I will indicate morphophonemic transcriptions in curled brackets { }. Thus, in the word *màthir* 'mother', the {t} is lenited as shown by the writing of <th>; a lenited {t} is pronounced as /h/, so the word is pronounced as /ma:hir^{j}/ (an accent indicates a long vowel). Over time, the original intervocalic conditioning environment of lenition has changed so that lenition is partly lexical (as here) and partly morphological. Modern Scots Gaelic spelling, however, is clear about indicating lenition with an <h>; with a few exceptions at the beginning of a word, the letter <h> does not occur in any other use. Table 9.10 shows the lenited form of some of the consonants.

Note that {d} and {g} both lenite to /ɣ/, and {s} and {t} both lenite to /h/; {f} disappears in lenition.

The second phonological change which affected Scots Gaelic was **palatalization** (table 9.11). Roughly, consonants before a front vowel were palatalized. Again, the conditioning factor for this change has been lost over time, and the process has become lexical or morphological. For example, some plurals are formed by palatalization:

singular	plural	written forms		
/baːs/	/baːʃ/	*bàs*	*bàis*	'death'
/ɛx/	/eç/	*each*	*eich*	'horse'

Table 9.11 Scots Gaelic masculine vocative. The initial consonant of a man's name is lenited, and the final consonant is palatalized

	Spoken forms		*Written forms*	
	Nominative	*Vocative*	*Nominative*	*Vocative*
'James'	/ʃeməs/	/ə hemiʃ/	*Seumas*	*a Sheumais*
'Donald'	/dõəl/	/ə ɣũilʲ/	*Domhnall*	*a Dhomhnuill*

Table 9.12 Examples of the writing of palatalization. Note that B is always next to b, and N is always next to n [b = broad, n = narrow; upper-case for consonants, lower-case for vowels]

cadal /kadəɫ/ 'sleep' (noun)	c a d a l B b B b B
cadail /kadil/ gen. of *cadal*	c a d a i l B b B b n N
caidil /kadʒil/ 'sleep' (verb)	c a i d i l B b n N n N
cinnich /kʲinʲiç/ 'grow'	c i nn i ch N n N n N

The vocative of masculine names is formed by an initial particle /ə/, which lenites the initial consonant, and in addition the final consonant of the name is palatalized (a neighbouring vowel is also sometimes affected by palatalization) (table 9.11).

The writing of palatalization is an unusual feature of Scots (and Irish) Gaelic. The example /baːs/ is written *bàs*; the plural /baːʃ/ is written *bàis*. Palatalization is indicated here by inserting an <i> before the palatalized <s>. The general rule is that a non-palatalized consonant must always be next to a back vowel <a o u>, and a palatalized consonant must always be next to a front vowel <i e>. With 'horse', the singular is spelled *each* and the plural *eich*. First, in both forms, the spelling <ch> represents a lenited {k}. In the singular, the <a> is a back vowel showing that the <ch> is not palatalized; in the plural, the <a> is replaced by <i> to show palatalization. These letters <a> and <i> are present to show pronunciation not of the vowel, but of the adjacent consonant. Interpreting the function of a vowel letter presents a difficulty in learning to read Gaelic.

In Scots Gaelic, palatalized consonants and front vowels are called 'narrow', and non-palatalized consonants and back vowels are called 'broad'. To describe the writing of palatalization, there is a saying *Leathann ri leathann's caol ri caol* 'Broad to broad and narrow to narrow'; i.e., broad consonants only occur next to broad vowels, and narrow consonants only occur next to narrow vowels. The examples in table 9.12 illustrate the writing of palatalization. The label below each consonant identifies the type. In the noun *cadal* /kadəɫ/ 'sleep' , all three consonants are 'broad', and both vowels are the broad vowel <a>. Thus, each broad consonant is only next to broad vowels. In *cadail* /kadil/, the genitive of 'sleep', the {l} is palatalized (/ɫ/ becomes [l]); this is indicated by inserting an <i> before the <l> giving *cadail.* Notice now that the first two consonants are broad and are both next to broad vowels; the final consonant is narrow and is next to a narrow vowel. In *caidil* /kadʒil/ 'sleep' (verb), the first consonant is broad, but the other two are palatalized. Here an <i> appears before the second consonant to show that it is narrow, and the <a> of the second syllable disappears as it is no longer needed to show a broad consonant. The final example is *cinnich* /kʲinʲiç/ 'grow' with all consonants palatalized; here an <i> appears in both syllables. Broad consonants are always next to broad vowels, and narrow consonants next to narrow vowels; however, broad and narrow vowels may be next to each other.

Scots Gaelic spelling conventions are decidedly different from those of English or Finnish or most languages using the Roman alphabet. However, they allow the writing system to represent a morphophonemic level of the language quite elegantly. In doing so, a much smaller number of symbols is needed than if a shallow writing system representing phonemes were used.

9.8 Further Reading

Bonfante (1990, 1996) and Bonfante and Bontante (1983) provide an introduction to recent work in Etruscan. Wallace (1989) discusses the development of the Roman alphabet. Comrie (1996b), Senner (1996), and Tuttle (1996) discuss the use of the Roman alphabet for other languages; McManus and Hamp (1996) and Rogers (1972) specifically discuss Scots Gaelic. Ullman (1980) is an interesting cultural discussion, and Harris (1989) treats literacy in Rome and Greece.

9.9 Terms

abecedary
calligraphy
deep
Etruscan
graffiti
Latin
lenition
orthographic depth
palatalization
Roman alphabet
shallow
umlaut
vulgar Latin

9.10 Exercises

1 Discuss the question: Does Italian have a letter W?
2 Why is Czech written in the Roman alphabet, but Bulgarian in the Cyrillic alphabet?
3 In Scots Gaelic, how would you expect the following words to be pronounced?

cóig 'five' [<ó> represents /oː/]
mór 'large (masc. sg. nom.)'
mhór 'large (fem. sg. nom.)'
mhóir 'large (masc. sg. gen.)' [the vowel is still /oː/]
MacThòmais 'Thomson' [the <a> is /a/; <ò> represents /ɔː/; the final vowel is /i/]
Sasunnaich 'English people' (cf. *Saxons*) [the vowels are /a, ə, i/]

4 German was previously written in a form of the Roman alphabet known as *Fraktur* /ˌfɹɑk'tuɹ/:

aß	/a:s/	'ate'	außen	/awsən/	'outside'
äußere	/ɔjsərə/	'exterior'	eſſen	/esən/	'eat'
Fluß	/flus/	'river'	Flüſſe	/flysə/	'rivers'
Fuß	/fu:s/	'foot'	Füße	/fy:sə/	'feet'
groß	/gro:s/	'big'	Haus	/haws/	'house'
Häuſer	/hɔjzər/	'houses'	heiße	/hajsə/	'am called'
heißen	/hajsən/	'are called (3 pl.)'	Meſſe	/mesə/	'fair'
muß	/mus/	'must (3 sg.)'	müſſen	/mysən/	'must (1,3 pl.)'
paſſen	/pasən/	'fit'	ſaß	/za:s/	'sat'
Schoß	/ʃo:s/	'lap'	Schuß	/ʃus/	'shot (n.)'
Schüſſe	/ʃysə/	'shots'	ſechs	/zeks/	'six'
ſein	/zajn/	'be'	ſenden	/zendən/	'send'
ſowieſo	/zo:vi:zo:/	'anyhow'	ſpäteſtens	/ʃpe:testens/	'at the latest'
Straße	/ʃtra:sə/	'street'	ſüß	/sy:s/	'sweet'

(a) In Fraktur, there are three forms of the lower-case letter *s*: <s ſ ß>. Note that there is a difference between *s* <s> and *f* <ſ>. The difference between the use of <s> and <ſ> is simply orthographic, depending on its position in the word. Examine the data above, and complete the rules below by stating the appropriate environment as simply as possible at the end of each rule. The rules should describe when <s> occurs and when <ſ> occurs. Do not worry about doubled <ſſ> or <ß> or upper-case S <S>.

i. /s/ → <s> / (/ = in the environment)
ii. /s/ → <ſ> /

(b) The difference in the use of <ſſ> and <ß> is more complex. Only one of these occurs at the end of a word. Complete the following rule by writing <ſſ> or <ß> as appropriate:

iii. /s/ → < > / at the end of a word

(c) Note that long vowels are indicated by a /:/ after the vowel in the phonemic transcription. German orthography does not directly show vowel length. The diphthongs /aw/, /aj/, and /ɔj/ are considered to be long vowels. Examine the words having either <ſſ> or <ß> in the middle. Complete the following rules by stating the environment as simply as possible. (State the environment after the /-sign.)

iv. /s/ → <ſſ> /
v. /s/ → <ß> /

5 Italian has (among others) the following consonants:

	tʃ	k
	dʒ	g
s	ʃ	
	j	

and the consonant cluster /sk/. For this exercise, we will assume a five-vowel system: /i e a o u/.

The writing of these consonant sounds is somewhat complex in Italian. From the following examples, try to figure out the system.

acciughe	/atʃːuge/	'anchovies'
amiche	/amike/	'(female) friends'
amici	/amitʃi/	'(male) friends'
broccoli	/brok:oli/	'broccoli'
bruschetta	/brusket:a/	a type of hors d'œuvres
buchi	/buki/	'holes'
cacciatore	/katʃ:atore/	'hunter'
canolli	/kanol:i/	a type of pasta
ceco	/tʃeko/	'Czech'
cello	/tʃel:o/	'cello'
che	/ke/	'that, what'
Chiara	/kjara/	a woman's name (= Eng. Clara)
concerto	/kontʃerto/	'concerto'
faccia	/fatʃ:a/	'face'
funghi	/fuŋgi/	'mushrooms'
fungo	/fuŋgo/	'mushroom'
gallo	/gal:o/	'chicken'
gelato	/dʒelato/	'ice cream'
ghetto	/get:o/	'ghetto'
ghiaccio	/gjatʃːo/	'ice'
ghiotto	/gjot:o/	'gluttonous'
Gina	/dʒina/	a woman's name
gioielli	/dʒojel:i/	'jewels'
Giorgio	/dʒordʒo/	a man's name (= Eng. George)

Giovanni	/dʒovanːi/	a man's name (= Eng. John)
maggiorana	/madʒːorana/	'marjoram'
maraschino	/maraskino/	'preserved cherry'
santa	/santa/	'holy'
scarola	/skarola/	'escarole'
scena	/ʃena/	'scene'
scherzo	/skerdzo/	'light musical movement'
schiavo	/skjavo/	'slave'
sciabla	/ʃabla/	'sabre'
scienza	/ʃenza/	'science'
si	/si/	'yes'
spaghetti	/spagɛtːi/	'spaghetti'
viaggio	/vjadʒːo/	'trip'
zucchini	/dzukːini/	'zucchini'

10 English

The English language has arguably become the most important international language and the most widely studied second language in the world today. In view of its world importance and also by the fact that as a reader of this book you obviously have some familiarity with and interest in English writing, we will devote some time to exploring the English writing system. English orthography is interesting in its own right, particularly because of its reputation for complexity. We will investigate the nature and development of this complexity.

10.1 Background and History

Britain was conquered by the Romans in 43 NEW and became the westernmost region of the ancient Roman Empire. The British inhabitants at that time spoke a Celtic language, the ancestor of modern Welsh. Although the senior Roman soldiers were literate, there is little evidence that the Britons borrowed writing from the Romans. In the early fifth century NEW, the Romans had difficulties at home and recalled their troops from Britain, with the withdrawal completed by 426 NEW. In the ensuing political vacuum, Germanic-speaking peoples invaded from the continent, taking over the area we now call England and southern Scotland. Their language came to be known as English.

Latin-speaking Christian missionaries reintroduced the Latin language and the Roman alphabet to England around 600. Somewhat later the Norse invaded parts of Britain. Many runic inscriptions (chapter 13) have been found in England in the Norse language as well as a few in Old English. Although the early Middle Ages are sometimes called the 'Dark Ages' in reference to the collapse of learning after the fall of the Roman empire, this term is somewhat misleading, especially for England. Winchester emerged as the capital of England at this time, and with the sponsorship of King Alfred, its monastery became a recognized centre of learning in Europe with a large library. Other monasteries throughout England followed Winchester's lead.

During the Old English period, Latin held sway as the preferred language for writing. Documents of both church and state were normally in Latin, as was the case throughout western Europe; nevertheless, English was written to a limited extent in fairly early times. Portions of the Bible, prayers, and other religious material were translated into English for the devotional needs of the people. Wills were sometimes written in English; presumably, people were more comfortable if the arrangements for their inheritance were made in their native language. Certain other works were also either written in English, such as the *Anglo-Saxon Chronicles*, or translated into English from Latin, such as the Venerable Bede's *Ecclesiastical History of the English People*. The best-known Old English literary work is *Beowulf*.

In 1066, England was conquered by William of Normandy, who quickly installed his own French-speaking people into positions of authority. Latin remained the language for much writing, but Norman French emerged as the court language, and many documents came to be written in French. The nobility spoke French, but ordinary people continued to speak English. For about 200 years, until 1250, very little was written in English.

By the late thirteenth century, the nobility had begun to speak English. English began gradually to replace both Latin and French in almost all contexts. By 1350, English was used in schools, and in 1384, Wycliffe's English translation of the Bible had appeared. In 1420, English replaced French as the official language of Parliament. English survived as the ordinary spoken language of England, but it had changed considerably. As well as changes in the phonology and grammar, an enormous number of French words had been borrowed into English: often words of government and warfare – *duke*, *judge*, *government*, *county*, *general*, *army*, but also very ordinary words – *table*, *very*, *single*, *beef*. London was the capital, and the dialect of the London court became the standard spoken form of Middle English although there was considerable variation throughout the country. Whereas Old English spelling was relatively uniform, following the Winchester standard, Middle English spelling was quite diverse, often following the local pronunciation. The best-known literary work in Middle English is Chaucer's *Canterbury Tales*.

In the fifteenth century, a standard form of English, based on court usage, emerged as the official style of writing for government and spread throughout Britain. It also became the standard form used for all types of written communication, gradually displacing local variation.

The English language is usually divided into three periods:

500 NEW–1100	**Old English** or **Anglo-Saxon**
1100–1500	**Middle English**
1500–present	**Modern English**

The boundary between Old and Middle English is marked by the Norman conquest and the introduction of French; the boundary between Middle and Modern English is less dramatically marked by a set of sound changes. In the mid-fifteenth century, English underwent what is known as the Great English Vowel Shift (described in more detail below) which affected the quality of all long vowels. Shakespeare is the best known of the early Modern English writers.

Printing came to Britain in the late fifteenth century and was established by the mid-sixteenth century. The Reformation encouraged every English family to read the Bible; printing made Bibles widely available, if not to every family, at least to those of moderate means. The Renaissance, with its interest in the classical world, introduced large numbers of words of Latin and Greek origin. Printers tended to use uniform spelling, and by the reign of Elizabeth I in the mid-sixteenth century, English spelling had become fairly standardized.

Since the sixteenth century various minor modifications have been made to English spelling, but the basic structure remains. As Venezky (1999, p. 115) remarks: 'The amount of orthographic change that has occurred since 1600 is small, and the amount that has taken place since 1700 is minuscule.' Dictionaries had considerable influence in propagating the standard. **Samuel Johnson**'s dictionary of 1755 was particularly important in England, and **Noah Webster**'s dictionary of 1806 set a slightly different standard for the United States. English has never had an official **language academy** to regulate the language, such as those found in France, Sweden, Portugal, and other European countries; quite possibly, the effectiveness of these dictionaries reduced the need for a regulatory body. The fixed nature of spelling since 1600, of course, did not mean that the language did not change. In fact the phonological changes that have occurred since that time have meant that the relationship between written and spoken English has grown more complex.

10.2 Old English

Old English had the phoneme inventory as shown in table 10.1.

For many sounds there was a one-to-one correspondence between grapheme and phoneme. All of these were straightforward adaptations of the Roman alphabet to the sounds of Old English.

<p>	/p/	<plegian>	/plejian/	'play'
<b>	/b/	<blod>	/blo:d/	'blood'
<t>	/t/	<tunge>	/tunge/	'tongue'
<d>	/d/	<deaþ>	/de:aθ/	'death'
<f>	/f/	<folc>	/folk/	'people'
<m>	/m/	<mus>	/mu:s/	'mouse'
<n>	/n/	<nama>	/nama/	'name'
<l>	/l/	<lufian>	/lufian/	'love'
<r>	/r/	<read>	/re:ad/	'red'

In Old English, [h] and [x] were allophones of the same phoneme /h/ in complementary distribution, with [h] used word-initially, and [x] used elsewhere. The letter <h> was used for both allophones.

Table 10.1 The phonemes of Old English

p	b		t	d	tʃ	dʒ	k	g	i	y	u	i:	y:	u:
f		θ	s		ʃ		h		e		o	e:		o:
m			n								ɑ			ɑ:
			l											
w			r		j									

<h>	/h/	[h]	<hat>	/ha:t/	[ha:t]	'hot'
		[x]	<riht>	/riht/	[rixt]	'right'

The letters <c>, <g>, and <s> were used with their expected Latin values to represent /k/, /g/, and /s/, but they were also used to represent other sounds not present in Latin. The letters <c> and <g> were also used to represent /tʃ/ and /j/ respectively; further, the digraphs <cg> and <sc> were used for the sounds /dʒ/ and /ʃ/.

<c>	/k/	<corn>	/korn/	'grain'
<c>	/tʃ/	<ceap>	/tʃe:ap/	'cheap'
<g>	/g/	<guma>	/guma/	'man'
<g>	/j/	<geard>	/jeard/	'yard'
<s>	/s/	<sæ>	/sæ/	'sea'
<cg>	/dʒ/	<brycg>	/brydʒ/	'bridge'
<sc>	/ʃ/	<scip>	/ʃip/	'ship'

The sound /θ/ which was not found in Latin was first written as <th>. Later, however, the symbols <þ> and <ð> were used more or less interchangeably for /θ/. The symbol <þ> is 'thorn' from the runic alphabet (chapter 13), and the symbol <ð> is a modified form of <d>.

<þ ð>	/θ/	<þancian, ðancian>	/θankian/	'thank'

In early Old English, a runic symbol <ƿ>, known as 'wynn', was used for <w>. Later, wynn was replaced by <u>, <uu>, or <w>. Note the three similar symbols: thorn <þ>, wynn <ƿ>, and modern lower-case <p>.

<ƿ>	/w/	<ƿæpen>	/wæ:pen/	'weapon'

Vowel length was not marked in Old English. The ligature <æ> was used for the low front vowel. In later Old English, the vowels /y, yː/ merged with /i, iː/ and were written as <i>.

		short		*long*	
<i>	/i/	<sittan>	'sit'	<wif>	'woman, wife'
<y (i)>	/y (i)/	<yfel (ifel)>	'evil'	<fyr (fir)>	'fire'
<e>	/e/	<bern>	'barn'	<swete>	'sweet'
<æ>	/æ/	<fæder>	'father'	<hælan>	'heal'
<a>	/ɑ/	<wacian>	'be awake'	<gan>	'go'
<o>	/o/	<god>	'god'	<mod>	'heart, spirit'
<u>	/u/	<lust>	'desire'	<þu>	'thou'

A portion of the Lord's Prayer is shown in figure 10.1. The first line is in Latin; the next two are in Old English. Note that the upper-case form of <ð> is <Ð>.

PATER NR· QVIES INCELIS	pater n[oste]r qui es in celis
ÐVVRE FÆDER.	Ðu ure fæder
þeeart onheofenu seoþinnama	þe eart on heofenu seo þin nama

Figure 10.1 The beginning of the common Christian prayer known as the Lord's Prayer. The first line is in Latin; and the next two lines are in Old English (eleventh century)

Table 10.2 The phonemes of Middle English

p b		t d	tʃ dʒ k g	i iː		u uː
f v	θ ð	s z	ʃ h	eː	ə	oː
m		n		ɛ ɛː		ɔ ɔː
		l				a aː
		r				
w			j			

10.3 Middle English

The phonemic inventory for Middle English is given in table 10.2.

Unlike Old English, the fricatives in Middle English had contrastive phonemes distinguished by voicing: /f v/, /θ ð/, /s z/. The letters <f> and <v> were used for the phonemes /f/ and /v/ respectively. Both /þ/ and /ð/ are spelled <th>; thorn <þ>, however, was retained in a few common words: <þe þat þou þen> 'the, that, thou, then'. This limited use of thorn survived into the eighteenth century, giving the quaint forms such as *þe olde shoppe*. Commonly, the thorn was written as a superscript: <ᵖe>; the thorn was later misunderstood as <y>, and this antiquated writing of *the* is commonly misread today as /ji/.

The letter <s> was used for both /s/ and /z/. Furthermore, two lower-case allographs of <s> arose: <s> and <ſ>, with no set pattern for their distribution although there was a tendency to use <ſ> word-initially and -medially, and <s> word-finally. Instead of double <ss> or <ſſ>, a form <ß> was common, a combination of <ſ> and <z>. The long <ſ> continued to be used into the early nineteenth century when it was replaced entirely by <s>.

As a result of the influence of French borrowings, such as *cellar*, <c> came to be used for both /k/ and /s/. The French use of <c> for /s/ was extended to some native words such as *lice* and *mice*. French <qu> replaced Old English <cw> for /kw/: OE *cwen* MidE *quene* 'queen'. The digraph <sh> was used for /ʃ/: OE *scamu* MidE *shame*; <ch> was used for /tʃ/: OE *ceap* MidE *cheap*; and <gh> was used for /x/: OE *riht* MidE *right*.

The letters <i> and <j> were in free variation: *tiim tijm* 'time', *iuge juge* 'judge', as were <u> and <v>: *up vp* 'up', *euen even* 'even'. The letter <y> was considered an allograph of <i>.

One phonological change involving vowels also affected the relationship of language and writing. In Middle English unstressed vowels were neutralized to /ə/, and sometimes lost; the writing, however, retained the etymological vowel. Thus in writing today, one needs to know the etymological spelling of a word. For example, the first and third syllables of the words *serene* and *divine* were both unstressed and the vowel in these syllables became /ə/: Mid. Eng. /səˈreːnə/ and /dəˈviːnə/. The final syllable is spelled <e> in both cases, but the first syllable is spelled differently in the two words, <se-, di->, reflecting the history of the words. Today, English speakers often stumble over pairs such as *affect* and *effect*; both words are normally pronounced /əˈfɛkt/, but distinguished in spelling by the etymological vowel.

In Late Middle English, unstressed <e> /ə/ was lost in word-final syllables: /dəˈviːnə/ > /dəˈviːn/, and /səˈreːnə/ > /səˈreːn/, but again the spelling did not change to reflect this change in pronunciation. The situation of a long vowel being written as <VCe> was so common that in Modern English the convention has arisen that this is a normal way to spell tense vowels: e.g., *bite*, *made*, *rose*, *cute*.

10.4 Modern English

Between Middle and Modern English, various changes occurred in the language which altered the relationship between writing and pronunciation. During the Middle English period, a sound change known as trisyllabic shortening occurred (table 10.3), which shortened long antepenultimate vowels. This shortening resulted in many morphemes having different allomorphs with long and short vowels. Since the writing system did not distinguish long and short vowels, no change to the writing of these words was indicated.

Table 10.3 Trisyllabic shortening in Middle English. Antepenultimate vowels are shortened. The addition of the suffix (right column) to the root causes the long vowel to occur in the antepenultimate syllable and thus become shortened. Except in the first example, only the affected vowels are shown

MidE	*Long*		*Short*	
/i/	*divine*	/(dəv)iː(nə)/	*divinity*	/(div)i(niti)/
	derive	/iː/	*derivative*	/i/
/e/	*serene*	/eː/	*serenity*	/e/
	supreme	/eː/	*supremacy*	/e/
/a/	*sane*	/aː/	*sanity*	/a/
	explain	/aː/	*explanatory*	/a/
/u/	*profound*	/uː/	*profundity*	/u/
	abound	/uː/	*abundance*	/u/

Table 10.4 Great English Vowel Shift. The long high vowels became diphthongs, and the others shifted upwards

/iː/	>	/ʌj/	/uː/	>	/ʌw/
/eː/	>	/iː/	/oː/	>	/uː/
/ɛː/	>	/eː/	/ɔː/	>	/oː/
			/aː/	>	/ɔː/

In late Middle English times, after trisyllabic shortening was complete, the long vowels, but not the short ones, underwent a sound change known as the **Great English Vowel Shift** (table 10.4) in which the high vowels became diphthongs, and the other long vowels were shifted upwards.

For morphemes having allophones with long and short vowels, the Great English Vowel Shift greatly accentuated the phonetic difference between the two allomorphs. English orthography could have revised the spelling to reflect these sound changes, perhaps with forms like **serine–serenity*, **sene–sanity*. Such a change would have maintained the relationship between language and writing much as it had been, i.e., a fairly close phoneme–grapheme correspondence. However, this did not happen. The spelling of these words remained as before. The retention of these spellings greatly changed the relationship between English writing and pronunciation. For this type of alternation in Modern English, morphemes were given a single spelling, and allomorphic variations had to be supplied by the reader. The effect today of the Great English Vowel Shift is shown in the following examples:

	serene	*serenity*	*sane*	*sanity*
Middle English	/e:/	/e/	/aː/	/a/
Early Mod. English	/i:/	/e/	/e:/	/a/
Later Mod. English	/i/	/ɛ/	/ej/	/æ/

Thus, we can see that from a relatively simple relationship between grapheme and phoneme in Middle English, various forces combined to create a much more complex relationship by Modern English times. In particular, it frequently became necessary to know which morpheme one was writing. Thus, Modern English spelling is deeper (cf. discussion of orthographic depth in chapter 9) than Middle English spelling because of the larger number of cases where the spelling is morphophonemic or morphemic.

One incidental effect of the Great English Vowel Shift was that English tense vowels today are pronounced differently from the way they are pronounced in the great majority of languages using the Roman alphabet: cf <a e i o u> in English /ej i aj ow u/ and in German /ɑ e i o u/. English regularly uses a number of digraphs. Some digraphs like <ch> /tʃ/, <sh> /ʃ/, and <th> /θ, ð/ are used in a fairly consistent fashion. Other digraphs are used only in certain environments. The sound /dʒ/ is usually spelled <j> at the beginning of a word, but <dge> at the end, cf. *jay*, *edge*, *judge*. The sound /k/ is usually spelled <k> or <ke> after tense vowels or after two vowel sequences, but <ck> after lax vowels: *seek*, *eke*, *break*, *take*, *soak*, *smoke*,

Luke, *like*; *lick*, *deck*, *rack*, *duck*. The diphone <x> has the same value /ks/ that it had in Latin: *axe*, *six*; in the few words with <x> in word-initial position, it is usually pronounced /z/: *xylophone*, *Xavier*.

For most words borrowed into English in Modern English times from languages using the Roman alphabet, the original spelling has been retained. For example, from French, we have *soufflé*, *ballet*, *lingerie*, *cul-de-sac*; from German: *Kindergarten*, *Fahrenheit*, *Gesundheit*, *Umlaut*; from Italian *spaghetti*, *concerto*, *bologna*. Although the pronunciation of a borrowed word is regularly altered to fit English patterns, sometimes there are other unpredictable changes: *lingerie* /ˈlɑnʒəˌrej/, where one might expect a final /-i/, or *bologna* /bəˈlowni/ instead of /*bəˈlownjə/; compare *Einstein* /ˈajnˌstajn/ and *Holstein* /ˈhowlˌstin/, both borrowed from German.

Spelling pronunciations (or **reading pronunciations**) arise by guessing at the pronunciation of a word by applying the regular orthographic conventions of English. This is common with foreign words. The surname *Samaranch* is pronounced /sɑmɑrɑŋ/ in Catalan, but it is regularly heard as /ˈsæməɹæntʃ/ in English; French *déshabillé* /dezabije/ is sometimes heard as /ˈdejʃəbil/.

A somewhat different situation involves the Chinese capital *Beijing* /ˌbejˈdʒɪŋ/, which is often heard as /ˌbejˈʒɪŋ/. Note that <jing> is a perfectly ordinary spelling in English for /dʒɪŋ/; the syllable /ʒɪŋ/ is, in fact, unusual in English. Probably, the mistaken pronunciation /ʒɪŋ/ for the Chinese city is used in English because it sounds more foreign and exotic and thus more appropriate for a foreign word. Similarly, one occasionally hears *Copenhagen* /ˈkopənˌhejgən/pronounced with /-hɑg-/ (the Danish is quite different: *København* /køβənhawn/); presumably, the vowel /ɑ/ is assumed to sound foreign. The television character named *Bucket* who insisted that her name was pronounced /ˌbuˈkej/ gives us an example of manipulating the different spelling conventions of English in an attempt to achieve elegance.

10.4.1 Orthographic dialect variation

In the nineteenth century, particularly because of the spelling preferences of Noah Webster's dictionary, two standard spelling variations arose, which we may term **orthographic dialects**. Most of the English-speaking world generally follows what we can call 'British usage'; the United States, however, follows 'American usage'. The actual number of words affected is not large, but the differences often assume a patriotic and symbolic significance. Some examples of these orthographic dialectal variations are given in table 10.5.

These differences are never significant enough to impede anyone's reading; however, their symbolic significance is enough that popular novels are frequently re-typeset to reflect the appropriate market; film titles are also often similarly altered.

Canada, having an inherited tradition of British spelling, yet widely exposed to American media, often shows an interesting mixture of the two traditions. The word *cheque*, for the bank instrument, is almost never spelled *check* in Canada; *check* is the spelling everywhere for the meanings 'inspect, obstruct, intersecting pattern', etc. The *-re* words occur in Canada with British spelling fairly consistently. With the other types of words, there is a good deal of variation. The *-our* spelling is

Table 10.5 Examples of English dialect differences in spelling

American	*British*
color, favor, honor, humor, glamor	*colour, favour, honour, humour, glamour*
center, theater, fiber, liter (but *acre, ogre*)	*centre, theatre, fibre, litre, acre, ogre*
(*bank*) *check*	*cheque*
traveling, leveling	*travelling, levelling*
enroll, enrolled, enrollment	*enrol, enrolled, enrolment*
license, practice	*licence, practice* (*noun*); *license, practise* (*verb*)
defense, offense	*defence, offence*
judgment	*judgement* (but *judgment* in legal contexts)
catalog, cigaret	*catalogue, cigarette*

more widely used in Central and Eastern Canada and in British Columbia than in the prairie provinces (Pratt 1993). The spelling of other words takes on a somewhat random appearance. Most Canadian newspapers use some variant of British spelling; yet, despite the best efforts of editors, oddities still occur. Overcorrections are not uncommon. *Honour* and *honourable* both have a <u>; *honorary* is not supposed to have one – in any tradition – but Canadian newspapers have nevertheless recorded many an *honourary degree*. In the food section, one often sees a reference to the herb as *summer savoury*, which in all dictionaries is given as *savory*; *savoury* is the general adjective meaning 'tasty'. Editors almost always get *Minister of Defence* right (cf. the American *Secretary of Defense*), but the sport section of newspapers often extols a strong *defense*. At my own university, the official document for examiners to register their decision for a PhD examination contained both spellings *defence/defense* on the same sheet of paper. By the same token, American editors complain that they have constant battles to keep the <e> out of *judgement* and the <u> out of *glamour*.

In the twentieth century, English became widely used in international affairs. The increase of political and economic importance of the United States in this period has led to an increasing use of American orthographic usage, not only in areas where English is a foreign language, but also in Canada, Australia, New Zealand, etc., and at times even in Britain itself.

10.4.2 *Creative spelling*

Since the Second World War, there has been a marked popularity of what Venezky (1999) calls **creative spellings**. Forms such as *Kids "R" Us*, *Molson Lite Beer*, *E-Z-Kleen* demonstrate playful, inventive spellings to give greater differentiation to the name; for marketing, this often gives greater brand recognition to a company or product. The umlauts in *Häagen Dazs* ice cream or the music group *Moxy Früvous* are apparently purely decorative. Spellings such as *nitelite* substitute a more common spelling convention for another slightly less common one. *Ye Olde Clocke Shoppe* uses (pseudo-)archaic spelling to suggest old-world charm and value (see discussion above in §10.3).

Computer usage has led to many creative spelling variations, such as *PostScript*, *theglobeandmail*, *DVORAK*. The internet revived the almost defunct @-sign as part of an internet address. The punctuation mark <.> traditionally has dialectal pronunciations, being known both as 'period' and 'full stop'; in internet addresses, however, it is universally read as 'dot', as in *www.widgetville.com*. (Note: the @-sign arose in the Middle Ages as an abbreviation of the Latin word *ad* 'to' (Ullman 1980). The vertical stroke of the <d> was enlarged and curved over the <a>, eventually resulting in the present form. In later times, the abbreviation was used for English *at* in commercial phrases such as '10 apples @ 12¢ each'.)

10.5 Spelling and Sound Changes

Frequently, sound changes occur without a corresponding change in the spelling. We have already seen examples of this in trisyllabic shortening and the Great English Vowel Shift. In Middle English, the words *see* /se:/ and *sea* /sɛ:/ were written and pronounced differently. With the Great English Vowel Shift, the vowels were raised to *see* /si:/ and *sea* /se:/ in early Modern English, still pronounced and spelled differently. In the eighteenth century, *sea* /se:/ was raised to /siː/, neutralizing the pronunciation with *see*, but the spelling difference was maintained. This is an example of the later tendency of English to retain spelling differences where they distinguish morphemes.

Old English had initial clusters of /hl, hn, hr/ spelled respectively as <hl, hn, hr>. By Middle English times, the /h/ of these clusters had been lost and the spelling revised to reflect the change in pronunciation. This is an example of the earlier tendency of English to revise the spelling to reflect changes in pronunciation.

French, of course, is a descendant of Latin. Over the centuries, French has undergone many sound changes. By the eleventh century, the Latin words *debitum* 'debt' and *dubitum* 'doubt' had lost the /b/ and the final /m/ and were written in French as *dette* and *dout*. The Norman conquerors brought these words with them to England, and they were borrowed into Middle English as *dette* /dɛt/ and *dout* /duːt/. In Renaissance times, scholars showed off their knowledge of Latin by inserting an etymological <b> into the spelling, giving the modern forms *debt* and *doubt*. Here we have a spelling change with no sound change. These words have never been pronounced with a /b/ in English.

Similarly, the Latin *falconem* 'falcon' was borrowed into Middle English in its French form as *faucon* with no /l/. Note the proper name *Fawkner* (alongside *Falconer*); the <l> was added to the spelling following the Latin spelling *falcon-*, like the <b> in *debt* and *doubt*. In modern times, falcons have not figured prominently in most people's lives, although those who used the word usually pronounced it in the traditional way without an /l/ as /ˈfɑkən/ (or /ˈfɔkən/, depending on their dialect). In the twentieth century, the Ford Motor Company introduced an automobile with the name *Falcon*. By this time, the word was sufficiently unfamiliar that a spelling pronunciation /ˈfælkən/ became the norm, at least in North America. As a side note, automobile manufacturers seem to like fast birds. Toyota found a rather rare term for a kind of falcon – *tercel*. Dictionaries regularly give this word with a stress on the first syllable /ˈtəɹsəl/. Toyota, however, stressed the second syllable as /təɹˈsɛl/, perhaps thinking that this sounded more French, more exotic, and worth more money.

English place-names, notably in Britain, often have unusual spellings. Often, the spelling reflects an older pronunciation and has not kept pace with sound change. Some examples of these are *Thames* /tɛmz/, *Gloucester* /ˈglɑstəɹ/, *Towcester* /ˈtowstəɹ/, *Kirkcudbright* /kəɹˈkubɹi/, Cholmondeley /ˈtʃʌmli/, and my personal favourite *Featherstonehaugh* /ˈfænˌʃɑ/.

10.6 Spelling Reform

10.6.1 The nature of reform

Because of the complex relationship of writing and language in English, there have been many proposals for **spelling reform**, ranging from the scientific and well-thought out to the amateurish and confused. Various arguments can be made for spelling reform in English, but the strongest is that a phonemically based system would allow children to learn to read and write more quickly. Different spelling reformers have proposed different approaches to reforming English spelling, but certain themes recur.

Most of these schemes aim to spell English with a one-to-one grapheme–phoneme relationship in which each sound would be represented by a single symbol. Where the same sound is now spelled in different ways, only one spelling would be used, a single grapheme where possible. For example, the use of <c> for both /k/ and /s/ would be eliminated, by using either <k> or <c> consistently for /k/, and <s> for /s/. The sound /dʒ/ would be consistently spelled as <j>, eliminating spellings such as <dge>.

Silent sounds would be removed in such words as *debt*, *indict*, *right*, *hymn*, *sign*, *knee*, *sword*. Many schemes would eliminate the final silent <e> in words such as *kite*, *late*, *flute*. The digraphs <sh zh ch> would be used to spell /ʃ ʒ tʃ/; /θ/ would be written as <th>, and /ð/ as <dh>. These digraphs would be useful since no reasonable single symbol is otherwise available. The one diphone <x> would be replaced by <ks>. The large number of English vowels creates a problem since the Roman alphabet has only five vowel letters. However, doubled vowel symbols and vowel digraphs could be used.

A basic way to spell English phonemically would be to remove morphemically based heterography. Thus, pairs such as *blue–blew*, *scene–seen*, *wood–would*, *ring–wring*, *meat–meet* would each have the same spelling. Further, words with irregular spellings such as *is*, *was*, *of*, *one* would be respelled to reflect their pronunciation.

10.6.2 Problems with spelling reform

Despite the efforts of various people with a variety of schemes to reform English spelling, the last successful reforms were the minor reforms of Noah Webster some 200 years ago, and his influence outside the United States has been very limited.

Why has spelling reform in English not met with greater success, considering the number of proposals for reform? One reason is the natural conservatism of people. Reformed spelling looks strange. Some people, of course, are attracted to novelty, but more seem to be put off by unusual spellings. Millions of people have learned to spell English. Indeed, the expectation today for most native speakers of English is that they will become literate. We have little sense that English-speaking countries, in relation to others in the world, have been held back in science, the arts, or commerce because of any extra time spent in school learning to read and write English. With this success rate, the general public reaction is to invoke the adage: 'If it ain't broke, don't fix it.'

If we take a more scholarly, scientific view of spelling reform, other problems emerge. One, English is widely spoken with many dialects. Which dialect would be chosen as a standard? Should *car* be spelled with an <r> or without? English speakers can be divided into two large dialect groups: one which pronounces /ɹ/ in such a word, the other which does not. The present situation is that words like *car* are spelled with an <r>, and the large group of English speakers who do not pronounce the /ɹ/ have to learn when to insert the <r> in spelling. If the <r> were to be omitted in spelling, the large group of English speakers who do pronounce /ɹ/ would have to learn not to write a consonant which they pronounce. Either way, the fundamental notion of a simple one-to-one equivalence between phonemes and graphemes is violated. This problem becomes enormous as we go through the various other dialectal variations: most dialects distinguish the vowels of *cot* and *caught*, but many do not. Should *path* have the same vowel as *pat* or *palm*? Should *solder* have an <l> to reflect the British pronunciation, or no <l> to reflect the North American pronunciation? Quite simply, the dialectal variation of English means that no transcription system can be devised which would not require a large number of arbitrary rules and considerable memorization for many people, precisely the problem that spelling reform set out to avoid.

The second concern is that evidence from psychology suggests that some of the so-called irregularities of English actually serve to facilitate reading, especially for the experienced reader. Experienced readers tend to perceive words as single units and do not 'read' them letter by letter. Evidence suggests that we process the information slightly faster when homophonous morphemes are spelled differently: *pair–pear–pare*. On the other hand, when we see the word *well*, we have to spend a slightly longer time figuring out which morpheme is intended.

Phonemic transcription may be useful to the inexperienced writer in that the spelling can be accurately determined from the pronunciation. For the reader, however, especially for the experienced reader, the English tendency of spelling different morphemes differently is useful.

Other objections to spelling reform also have some validity. The amount of literature in the current English orthography is enormous. Most people, certainly university students, would have to learn to read both systems for at least 50–75 years; for scholars, knowledge of both systems would be required for much longer. Moreover, the political likelihood of persuading all English-speaking countries and publishers to use a single revised system is unlikely. Even if the political will for revision existed, it is not unimaginable that a hodgepodge of new standards would emerge.

Certain arguments against spelling reform are less persuasive. Sometimes we take false pride in difficulty: 'If I could do it, so can you.' A bad system need not be perpetuated just because it is workable. Having mastered a difficulty, we sometimes ascribe greater attributes to ourselves than is warranted: 'People who can spell *chrysanthemum* correctly are of a higher moral character and have a greater intelligence than those who cannot.' We should not forget the purported saying of Andrew Johnson, a president of the United States and a poor speller: 'It takes a poor mind not to be able to think of more than one way to spell a word.' Sometimes the argument is made that our current spelling system keeps us in touch with the past: 'Writing a <g> in *gnaw* keeps us aware of our glorious history.' Just exactly how much glory are we talking about here?

In summary, spelling reform in English would offer some help to writers and those learning to read; the present system, however, has virtues useful to the experienced reader. The extensive dialect variation, the complex international situation, and the enormous amount of material existing in the present system work to make change impracticable. There is a danger of fragmenting a stable system. At present, there is no viable movement to reform English spelling.

In other countries, writing reform has been successful. For Dutch, the social situation was very different. First, Dutch is spoken by many fewer people than English. Second, although it is spoken in two countries, the Netherlands and Belgium, there is a strong desire to maintain uniformity in linguistic matters wherever possible.

The character simplification in China succeeded for different reasons. Although Chinese is spoken by a very large number of people, China has been ruled by a strong central government for centuries with the authority to make significant changes. The communist government of the People's Republic of China imposed enormous changes on Chinese society, of which writing reform was simply one of many. In Táiwān and elsewhere outside the PRC, Chinese speakers have resisted character simplification, partly out of conservatism and partly because of a dislike of the communist government in the PRC. However, as more material is printed using the simplified characters, and with the handover of Hong Kong to the PRC, a slow drift of other users towards the simplified characters seems inevitable.

10.7 Further Reading

Lass (1987), Millward (1988), Wakelin (1988) are recent treatments of the history of English. English orthography is specifically discussed in Carney (1994), Deighton (1972), Parkes (1993), Scragg (1974), Vallins (1954), and Venezky (1970, 1999).

10.8 Terms

Anglo-Saxon
creative spelling
Great English Vowel Shift
Johnson, Samuel

language academy
Middle English
Modern English
Old English
orthographic dialect variation
reading pronunciation
spelling pronunciation
spelling reform
Webster, Noah

10.9 Exercises

1 Give the British/American alternative spelling for the following words.

(a) program
(b) pyjamas
(c) jail
(d) maneuver
(e) sulphur
(f) plow
(g) woolen
(h) kerb
(i) esophagus

2 Why would *acre* and *ogre* not be spelled *acer* and *oger* in the United States like *center* and *scepter*?

3 Find examples showing three different ways of spelling each of the English vowels: /i ej ɑ ʊ/

4 Look up the standard pronunciation of the following words in a dictionary. Consider why each would be considered an unusual or problematic spelling. Where two different pronunciations are in common use, dictionaries typically give the one considered more standard first.

(a) boatswain
(b) brooch
(c) cotoneaster
(d) diocese
(e) dour
(f) gaoler
(g) gunwale
(h) stele
(i) victuals

11 The Indian Abugida and Other Asian Phonographic Writing

11.1 Background and History

This chapter examines several interesting phonographic writing systems of Asia, particularly those found in South Asia, but also in Tibet, Mongolia, and Manchuria; we have already looked at *kana* of Japan and *hankul* of Korea in chapter 4.

South Asia is an area of great diversity and complexity. It comprises six countries (figure 11.1): India, Pakistan, Bangladesh, Nepal, Bhutan, and Sri Lanka; India is expected soon to have the largest population of any nation in the world. As a result of the partition in the mid-twentieth century, British India was divided into three countries with Muslim Pakistan and Bangladesh in the west and east, and mainly Hindu India in the middle. Four major religions have their origins here: Hinduism, Buddhism, Jainism, and Sikhism. Christianity came to India quite early and was reinforced by the European colonization much later. Moreover, in the sixteenth century NEW, the Mughals from Persia brought Islam. As we will see, religion in India has often been connected to the use of different scripts.

There are two major language groups in South Asia (figure 11.1 and table 11.1): **Indo-Aryan** in the north and **Dravidian** in the south. Since the nineteenth century, English has become an important second language for many people throughout this area. The Indian Government recognizes fifteen official languages. Most of these languages have their own script.

Sanskrit and its later form **Prakrit** are the ancestors of the modern Indo-Aryan languages. Sanskrit was spoken in northern South Asia around 1500–600 OLD. The

Table 11.1 The major languages of South Asia

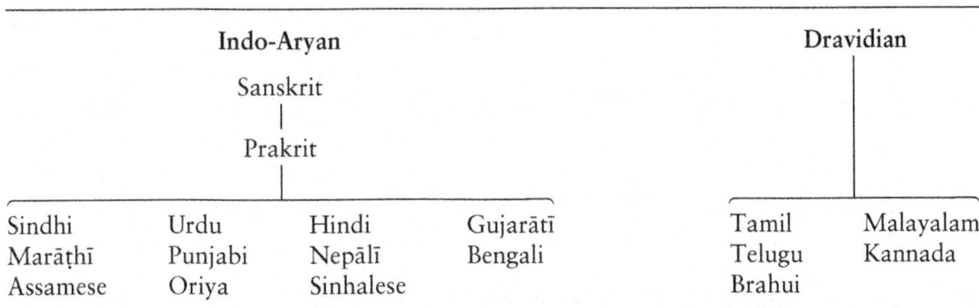

Indo-Aryan				**Dravidian**	
Sanskrit					
Prakrit					
Sindhi	Urdu	Hindi	Gujarātī	Tamil	Malayalam
Marāṭhī	Punjabi	Nepālī	Bengali	Telugu	Kannada
Assamese	Oriya	Sinhalese		Brahui	

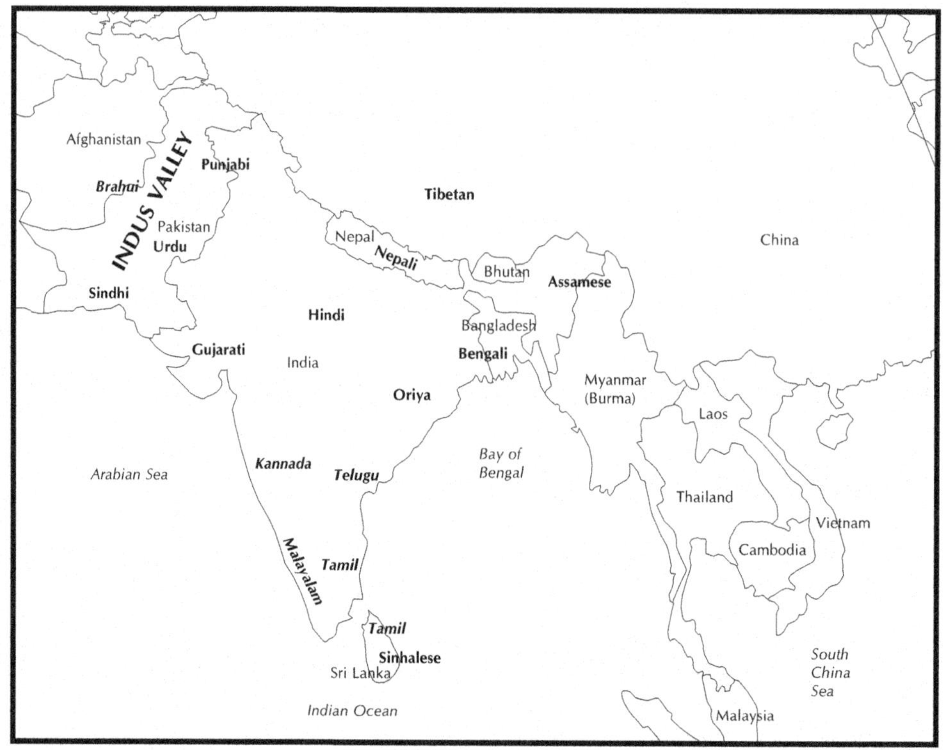

Figure 11.1 Languages of South Asia. The Indo-Aryan languages are shown in roman type; the Dravidian in italics

earliest form of the language is known as Vedic Sanskrit, in which the oldest Sanskrit text, a collection of hymns, known as the Rigveda, was composed around 1200 OLD. A later form of the language is known as classical Sanskrit which has a vast literature. The successor to Sanskrit is known as Prakrit, followed by gradual dialect diversification which led to the various Indo-Aryan languages we have today.

Sanskrit has continued to be used to the present day as a language of learning, literature, and religion. It is the source of learned vocabulary in South Asian languages, especially in the non-Muslim areas. It has also been the source of much lexical borrowing into other languages where Buddhism has been influential, such as Tibetan, Burmese, Thai, Laotian, and to some degree Chinese and Japanese. Sanskrit still functions as a language of learning in India much as Latin did in Europe in the Middle Ages; there is even a daily newspaper published in Sanskrit.

The Indo-Aryan languages are spoken in the north (figure 11.1), with the exception of Sinhalese, which is spoken in Sri Lanka. As a whole, the main group of Indo-Aryan languages form a dialect continuum without clear geographic boundaries between them. Hindi is the most widely spoken native language of India.

The Dravidian languages were probably distributed throughout South Asia in early times. The Indo-Aryan speakers, however, arrived around 1700–1400 OLD and conquered the northern area, pushing the Dravidians to the south (see figure 11.1) leaving only small groups of speakers in the north.

South Asia has had a strong tradition of oral transmission of texts. Even when writing did appear, the early Hindu and Buddhist traditions were wary of writing religious material. Neither Hindu nor Buddhist sacred texts were written down until writing had been used fairly extensively for other purposes. It is interesting to note that by the time Sanskrit texts were first written down around 300 NEW, Sanskrit itself was no longer a living language.

11.2 Indus Valley Writing

Before we examine the history of Sanskrit writing, we must look at a phenomenon which developed before the Indo-Aryans arrived. Plentiful archæological evidence remains of an **Indus Valley** culture which existed along the Indus River (modern-day Pakistan) dating from about 2500–1900 OLD. Some 1000 sites are known; the larger ones such as Mohenjo-daro and Harappa housed at least 40,000 people each.

The Indus culture proper began in the Bronze Age around 3600 OLD. By 2500 OLD, the Indus people had developed complex cities with systematic planning and a strongly centralized administration. Streets were laid out in straight lines with a good water supply and a sewage system. The houses were of baked bricks. There was a fairly high standard of living with a rather even distribution of wealth.

Indus writing developed around 2500 OLD (Parpola 1996). The texts that have been found are short, mostly on stamp seals which were pressed into clay. Around 1900 OLD, the Indus culture collapsed. The reason for this demise is not clear, but the script died with the culture. Not long after the fall of the Indus society, an Indo-European people known as the Indo-Aryans migrated into the Indus Valley.

The Indus sites were essentially forgotten until the nineteenth century. Unfortunately, some sites had been plundered for building materials, and the British destroyed some sites by using rubble as ballast for over 100 miles of railway track. The main excavations were in the first half of the twentieth century, and unexcavated sites still remain.

Of the some 4000 inscribed Indus Valley objects with writing, 60 per cent are seal inscriptions, typically square, about an inch on a side, with a line of text at the top and a picture below (plate 5). The shortest texts consist of only one sign; the average length of a text is about five signs; and the three longest texts have 14, 17, and 28 signs each. There is no evidence of word division. We assume that writing also occurred on perishable material, such as cloth or bark, which was lost over time.

11.2.1 Decipherment of the Indus script

The decipherment of an unknown language has a romantic aura about it and often attracts many devoted workers, some luckier or more gifted than others. In evaluating a proposed decipherment, a degree of scepticism is not out of place. The essential part of a successful decipherment is uncovering principles which apply to all texts in a regular manner.

Plate 5 Indus seal from Mohenjo-daro. National Museum, Karachi. Reproduced with permission from Harappa.com.

Anyone attempting to decipher the Indus writing faces the worst possible decipherment task (Bright 1990a). For the Indus script, neither the language nor the script is known. No bilingual text exists, such as the Rosetta Stone which helped in deciphering Egyptian. At the present time, the tentative attempts at decipherment by Parpola (1994, 1996) seem most plausible; however, even he admits that there is no general agreement that any attempts at decipherment of the Indus writing have been successful. Possehl (1996) has an extensive discussion of the various attempts at deciphering the Indus script.

11.2.2 The language of the Indus writing

Indus writing has about 400 symbols; these have a generally geometric, stick-figure quality to them. The clear iconic nature of some signs suggests a pictographic origin, such as those appearing to represent a person, fish, or bird. The most frequently occurring sign, however, is not clear. It appears to be a cup with two handles on each side, but this identification is likely incorrect since the pottery found in the Harappan sites does not include any such vessels. An alternative interpretation is that it represents the head of a horned animal.

Ligatures appear to exist, i.e., composite signs composed of two different signs. A few of these ligature parts do not occur as independent signs and are bound graphemes. The script shows no development over time except for stylistic variation. There is little geographic variation in the script throughout the area in which it was used. Scholars generally agree that the direction of writing is right to left.

An inventory of 400 different signs is far too large a number for a purely phonemic or moraic system. A phonemic system is likely to have fewer than fifty symbols, and a moraic one around 50–100 symbols. For a completely morphographic system, we would expect, however, a larger figure, perhaps closer to a thousand. Parpola (1994, 1996) concludes that the Indus writing system is most likely a mix[illegible] morphemic-moraic system. Of the 400 different signs, perhaps some 80–100 [illegible] moraic symbols representing consonant–vowel sequences, with the rest b[illegible] morphographic signs representing morphemes. A mixed morphemic-moraic s[illegible] would also be consistent with the short length of texts; a typical five-sign tex[illegible] contain two to four words, suitable for a seal text containing possibly on[illegible] names plus a title.

One of the most important questions in deciphering the Indus writing [illegible] mine what language was written, or at least to try to limit the choice[illegible] likely candidate language for the Indus writing is Dravidian. Today, th[illegible] languages are mostly found in the southern part of India; however, Brahui is sp[illegible] on the Pakistan–Afghanistan border, and a number of small groups of Dravidian speakers are found scattered in northern India.

Was the Indus writing a local invention, or was it borrowed from some other writing system? At the time of the development of Indus writing around 2500 OLD, the existing writing systems were cuneiform in Mesopotamia and Western Persia, Egyptian hieroglyphics, and Chinese. There is no evidence for any cultural contact at this time with China or Egypt. There seems to have been no direct contact at the time with Mesopotamia, but the Indus people would likely have known about cuneiform writing from their trade with the Gulf area. And even more likely, they would also have been aware of writing through their contacts with their western neighbours in Persia. Knowing as little as we do now about the Indus writing system, we can say little with certainty, but if the writing was borrowed, it is likely that the borrowing was an example of stimulus diffusion, with only the most rudimentary notion of writing being borrowed, not the details.

11.3 Brāhmī and Kharoṣṭhī

11.3.1 Aśokan inscriptions

After the demise of Indus writing around 1700 OLD, there is a gap of 1400 years before writing again appeared in South Asia. Aside from the Indus material, the earliest writing in South Asia dates from the third century OLD. The Emperor Aśoka

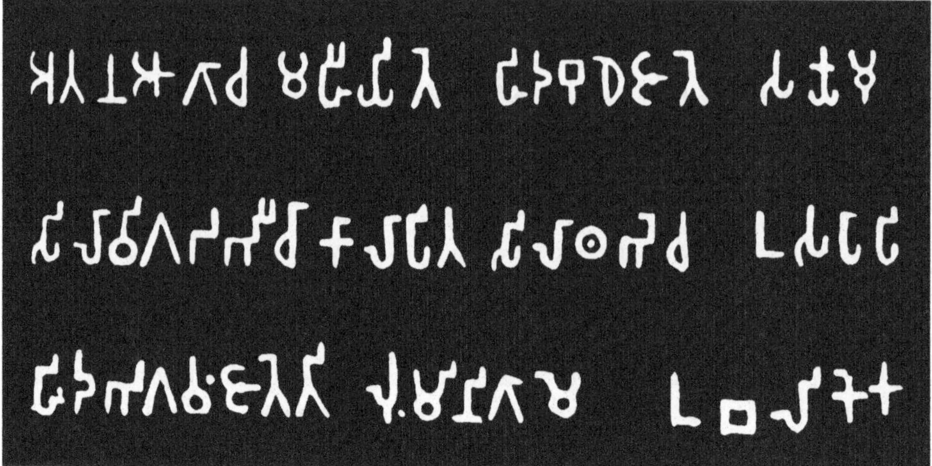

Figure 11.2 An example of an Aśokan Brāhmī inscription

(264–223 OLD; /ə'ʃowkə/) converted to Buddhism and caused a number of inscriptions to be erected throughout the land with texts urging Buddhist moral values on his people (figure 11.2).

By Aśoka's time, Sanskrit was no longer spoken although it was still a widely known language of learning. People ordinarily spoke Prakrit, a descendant of Sanskrit. The Aśokan inscriptions were in Prakrit, not Sanskrit, presumably so that they could be more widely understood by the people. Texts written in Sanskrit later became quite common, but the earliest date for Sanskrit texts is from around 150 NEW, some 400 years after the Aśokan inscriptions, a time when Sanskrit was no longer a spoken language. The Aśokan texts were written in two somewhat similar scripts – Brāhmī and Kharoṣṭhī, discussed below.

The climate of South Asia is not conducive to preserving writing on bark, palm leaves, or other soft material for any length of time. We might reasonably conclude that writing existed for some 100–200 years before the Aśokan inscriptions, which were written on stone.

Prior to Aśoka's reign, an oral tradition of linguistic analysis had arisen in South Asia. The best-known work of this tradition is the grammar of Pāṇini (probably fourth century OLD) which has detailed descriptions of the phonetics and morphology of Sanskrit. Pāṇini's work was held in high esteem and widely studied. However writing in South Asia may have arisen, it is clear that the writing system took its particular shape in the light of this linguistic analysis.

The Brāhmī script gradually changed shape over time with many local variants. These changes were eventually sufficient that knowledge of how to read the early Brāhmī texts was lost. The knowledge of Kharoṣṭhī was also lost. The early texts were not deciphered until the nineteenth century, principally by an Englishman, James Princep. By 1900, a large number of texts had been published from all areas and periods of South Asian history.

Table 11.2 Some Brāhmī and Kharoṣṭhī symbols. The last three symbols show consonant clusters

	Brāhmī	*Kharoṣṭhī*
ka	𑀓	𐨐
ki	𑀓𑀺	𐨐𐨁
ku	𑀓𑀼	𐨐𐨂
ta	𑀢	𐨟
ti	𑀢𑀺	𐨟𐨁
tu	𑀢𑀼	𐨟𐨂
ra	𑀭	𐨪
ri	𑀭𑀺	𐨪𐨁
ru	𑀭𑀼	𐨪𐨂
va	𑀯	𐨬
vi	𑀯𑀺	𐨬𐨁
vu	𑀯𑀼	𐨬𐨂
tva	𑀢𑁆𑀯	𐨟𐨿𐨬
rva	𑀭𑁆𑀯	𐨪𐨿𐨬
rvi	𑀭𑁆𑀯𑀺	𐨪𐨿𐨬𐨁

11.3.2 *The scripts*

The early scripts, Kharoṣṭhī and Brāhmī (/kə'ɹɑʃti/, /'brɑhmi/), are both abugidas, a type of writing which we have already encountered in §7.6. An **abugida** is similar to an alphabet: all vowels are indicated, but normally, vowels are written as diacritics, and one vowel is not written. The Kharoṣṭhī and Brāhmī abugidas have very similar structures (table 11.2). In both scripts, all consonants are written. Vowels generally have two allographs: one is a free allograph used only in word-initial position; the other allograph is bound, and is used word-medially and -finally. Further, the vowel /a/, the most common vowel in Sanskrit, is not written in word-medial and -final position; the absence of any vowel diacritic predicts the presence of /a/. Thus, /a/ has only one allograph, the one occurring in word-initial position. The Indian tradition considers /a/ to be inherent in the consonant symbol. Vowels, other than short /a/, are shown by diacritics on the preceding consonant (table 11.2). Consonant clusters are written as ligatures. The abugida came to dominate Indian writing and remains the organizing principle of the indigenous scripts of South Asia today.

The question arises whether the Kharoṣṭhī and Brāhmī scripts could be analysed as a moraic system rather than as an abugida. Recall that in a true moraic system, such as Japanese *hiragana*, each symbol represents one mora; however, the various *hiragana* symbols have no internal structure. For example, the symbols representing any particular consonant or vowel share no graphic feature. By contrast, the symbols of the Brāhmī abugida do have an internal structure; for example, the symbols for /ka ki ku/ all share the symbol **+**, and the symbols for /ki ti ri/ all share the diacritic ¬. This difference of internal structure is precisely the difference between a moraic system and an abugida (cf. the discussion of Cree in chapter 13).

In the ligatures, the first consonant is written above the second (see /tva rva rvi/ in table 11.2). The first consonant is fully formed, and the second may be somewhat attenuated. In early Brāhmī, the ligatures are generally transparent; in Kharoṣṭhī, there are some opaque ligatures (cf. <tva> in table 11.2) whose source is not clear. In some instances, the consonants may be written in the reverse order; thus, the same symbol may ambiguously represent /sra/ or /rsa/.

11.3.2.1 KHAROṢṬHĪ

The Kharoṣṭhī script existed primarily in the northwestern part of South Asia (northern Pakistan and eastern Afghanistan) where it was used to write the Prakrit dialect known as Gāndhārī. In this area, Kharoṣṭhī is well attested from the Aśokan period to the third century NEW, when it was replaced by Brāhmī, leaving no descendants. Kharoṣṭhī is probably slightly older than Brāhmī (Salomon 1998).

Kharoṣṭhī material has also been found from the second and third centuries NEW in the Tarim Basin of western China (Xinjiang-Uighur Autonomous Region), Uzbekistan, and neighbouring areas, where Kharoṣṭhī may have survived until the eighth century NEW (Salomon 1996).

Kharoṣṭhī is written from right to left. In this script, the free vowel allographs were all variants of the free allograph of <a>; e.g., the free form for <i> was formed by adding the diacritic of <i> to the free allograph of <a>. Kharoṣṭhī underspecified the phonological system by not distinguishing the contrastive short and long vowels.

11.3.2.2 BRĀHMĪ

Brāhmī was used to write Prakrit, and later Sanskrit, in most of India outside the northwestern Kharoṣṭhī area. Ultimately, it is the ancestor of all Indic scripts, of Tibetan writing, and of most of the scripts of southeast Asia.

Generally, the Brāhmī symbols are made with lines of uniform width, without serifs or headlines; each symbol is distinct with little tendency towards cursiveness. In appearance, Brāhmī is monumental and more formal than the more cursive Kharoṣṭhī. Brāhmī is written from left to right, and the free and bound vowel allographs do not physically resemble each other.

Even though the later variants of Brāhmī were adapted to the various spoken languages, the cultural importance of Sanskrit meant that all the scripts were conservative in retaining the ability to write Sanskrit. Even the scripts adapted for Dravidian languages with different phonological inventories maintained the symbols for writing Sanskrit, the notable exception being the Tamil script which followed Dravidian phonology. On the one hand, this conservatism maintained a relatively consistent relationship of language and writing for all of India generally and created there a common cultural understanding of how a script works. On the other hand, this loyalty to conservatism has made the relationship of each spoken language and its writing more complicated.

11.3.3 Origin of Kharoṣṭhī and Brāhmī

The origin of writing systems presents certain interesting problems, not the least of which is the obvious fact that little can be known about writing before writing itself exists. As we saw in chapter 1, writing systems come about in various ways: independent invention of writing, borrowing of a writing system, or the development of a new script. We will investigate the history of Kharoṣṭhī and Brāhmī in light of these methods.

To show that writing was independently invented is largely a negative endeavour. One must show that for the script in question any similarities between the shape of its symbols or the conventions for using them and those of any other writing system can only have emerged by chance. Further, cultural contact at the relevant time with any existing writing system must be ruled out.

To show that one writing system was borrowed from another, one must show that cultural contact existed at the appropriate time. This alone would allow for the possibility of stimulus diffusion. To show a closer degree of borrowing, one must show that similarities in the external shape of symbols or in the convention of their use are greater than random chance would allow.

In many cases, with the evidence available, it is not possible to demonstrate clearly whether a writing system was borrowed or independently invented. The Indian situation is frustrating in this regard with its paucity of early historical information.

Most scholars agree that Kharoṣṭhī is derived from Aramaic (table 11.3): 'A connection between Kharoṣṭhī and the Semitic scripts . . . , particularly Aramaic, has been evident to scholars from an early period' (Salomon 1998, p. 52). For many of the symbols, formal similarities can be found between Kharoṣṭhī and Aramaic. The symbols for Kharoṣṭhī /b g v k n r t/ seem reasonably close to their Aramaic counterparts. Structural similarities exist as well. In Aramaic, as in other Semitic writing, only consonants are written; vowels are not usually indicated. The Kharoṣṭhī practice of not writing short /a/ is reminiscent of this Aramaic convention. Culturally, Kharoṣṭhī was a local script of the northwest, an area which from the sixth century OLD was controlled by the Persian empire which used Aramaic as its chancery script. People living in the area where Kharoṣṭhī developed would have been familiar with Aramaic writing. Despite its Aramaic beginnings, it is obvious that the internal structure of Kharoṣṭhī has been thoroughly reworked in accordance with the linguistic theory of the Sanskrit grammarians. For example, the symbol inventory fits Prakrit closely, and the order of the symbols follows the logical phonetic order worked out by the **Indian grammarians**. (Note the sytematic ordering of stops in table 11.4.)

The origin of Brāhmī has proved a more difficult question to answer. There is no direct information about its early history. The Aśokan inscriptions appear in the mid-third century OLD with a fully developed writing system. The pre-Aśokan (composed orally, written down later) religious and linguistic texts have been interpreted as

Table 11.3 Comparison of Aramaic and early Indic symbols

Semitic sound	*Phœn. shape*	*Aramaic*	*Indic sound*	*Kharoṣṭhī*	*Brāhmī*
ʔ	𐤀	𐡀	a	𐨀	𑀅
b	𐤁	𐡁	b	𐨧	𑀩
g	𐤂	𐡂	g	𐨒	𑀕
d	𐤃	𐡃	d	𐨡	𑀤
h	𐤄	𐡄	h	𐨱	𑀳
w	𐤅	𐡅	v	𐨬	𑀯
z	𐤆	𐡆	j	𐨗	𑀚
ħ	𐤇	𐡇	gh		𑀖
ṭ	𐤈	𐡈	th	𐨠	𑀣
y	𐤉	𐡉	y	𐨩	𑀬
k	𐤊	𐡊	k	𐨐	𑀓
l	𐤋	𐡋	l	𐨫	𑀮
m	𐤌	𐡌	m	𐨨	𑀫
n	𐤍	𐡍	n	𐨣	𑀦
ts	𐤎	𐡎	s	𐨯	𑀲
ʕ	𐤏	𐡏	e		𑀏
p	𐤐	𐡐	p	𐨤	𑀧
ts (ṣ)	𐤑	𐡑	c	𐨕	𑀘
q	𐤒	𐡒	kh	𐨑	𑀔
r	𐤓	𐡓	r	𐨪	𑀭
s (ʃ)	𐤔	𐡔	ś	𐨭	𑀰
t	𐤕	𐡕	t	𐨟	𑀢

having a few references to writing, but they are not clear. Some commentaries by early Greek visitors to India mention writing, but they have conflicting comments about the existence of writing. The presence of the Indus writing complicates the situation further: is there a relationship between it and Brāhmī?

No other writing system (except Kharoṣṭhī) was in use in the third century OLD which offers a transparent resemblance to Brāhmī. The diacritic way of writing vowels is strongly reminiscent of the way they are written in the Ethiopic languages, but this feature of Ethiopic writing seems to have been borrowed from an Indian writing system, not the other way around.

Various theories about the origin of Brāhmī have been proposed. The most important of these are considered below in turn.

11.3.3.1 BRĀHMĪ IS AN INDIGENOUS INDIAN INVENTION

The indigenous theory holds the view that writing in the form of Brāhmī was invented in South Asia independently of the Indus Valley writing, Semitic writing, Chinese, or any other writing system. This view was originally advanced by Cunningham (1877), who thought that Brāhmī had developed from an earlier pictographic script. No evidence exists, however, for an earlier pictographic script in South Asia.

More recently, some have argued that the Brāhmī script was invented in India during the period of Aśoka. These theories are speculative and not based on evidence (Salomon 1998).

Even those who are not persuaded by the indigenous theory agree that Brāhmī was the result of considerable reworking in South Asia in light of the phonological framework developed by the early Indian linguists (Bright 1990a).

11.3.3.2 BRĀHMĪ IS BASED ON THE INDUS VALLEY WRITING

With the discovery of Indus writing in the early part of the twentieth century, some scholars, most recently Sircar (1971), have attempted to show that the Indus Valley writing is the ancestor of Brāhmī; however, Parpola, a leading scholar on the Indus script, says that there is 'no positive evidence whatsoever for a [Indus] origin of the Brāhmī script' (1994, p. 57). This hypothesis has been widely rejected for three reasons. At present, we have not deciphered the Indus writing system; any comparison between it and Brāhmī can be made only on the shape of symbols. Comparisons of this sort are very shaky because of the high likelihood that something in one set of marks will outwardly resemble something in a different set of marks. A comparison of the symbols of Indus writing and Brāhmī reveals no obvious connection that could not be due to coincidence.

A second difficulty is that most scholars believe that the Indo-Aryans were not yet in South Asia until after the Indus society collapsed.

Third, if the Indo-Aryans borrowed the Indus writing system, there is a very long period between 1700 OLD and 300 OLD with no writing. The best explanation which has been put forward for this gap is that writing during this period was done on perishable materials which have disappeared. Bright points out that this is not very plausible. Given that Indus writing was widely done on stone and other hard materials, it is likely that the Indo-Aryans would have continued this tradition.

The fact that the indigenous hypotheses described in this and the preceding section have been held primarily by South Asian scholars, and rejected generally by scholars from elsewhere, raises the awkward question of patriotism over evidence. Some doubt always arises about a theory which tends to glorify the ancestors of the proponent of the theory. This scepticism overlooks the very fine scholarship and sensitivity to evidence that some of those proposing the indigenous or Indus hypotheses about the origin of Brāhmī have shown. At times, concern has been expressed that outsiders view South Asia through foreign eyes and from a foreign perspective, undervaluing its real accomplishments and, consciously or unconsciously, want to see a European connection to the origin of Indian writing. This position, however, overlooks the fact that all scholars of European background posit a non-European origin for their own writing.

Issues such as these usually settle themselves, not by a sudden, clear-cut victory on the academic battlefield, but by a gradual drifting of the troops into one camp or the other. At the moment, the non-indigenous view seems to be winning.

11.3.3.3 BRĀHMĪ IS BASED ON A SEMITIC MODEL

The notion that Brāhmī is based on a Semitic model goes back to the nineteenth century (Salomon 1998). According to this theory, the Indo-Aryans were aware of Semitic writing in the west, borrowed the system, and thoroughly reworked it with Brāhmī as the result.

The Indo-Aryans had ample opportunity to learn of Aramaic writing from the contact from the sixth century OLD with the Persian empire in the northwest. A few of the Aśokan inscriptions in this area were written in Aramaic. However, a comparison of the letter shapes of Aramaic and Brāhmī (table 11.3) does not show enough formal similarity in the symbols to provide very persuasive evidence.

Bright (1996) and Salomon (1996) have stressed the typological connections between the Aramaic abjad and the Brāhmī abugida. As we have seen, with the Aramaic abjad, consonants are always written, but vowels are written only sporadically. In the Brāhmī abugida, the consonants are always written and form a primary class of graphemes with the vowels written as diacritics.

Salomon suggests that the Semitic system of not writing vowels was continued for Sanskrit /a/, the most common vowel, and the other vowels were indicated in a secondary fashion keeping the consonants primary. He argues that it would be hard to arrive at such a system starting completely from scratch, or from a morphographic system.

According to the theory of a Semitic origin, a possible scenario for the introduction of writing is that during the period in which Gāndhāra belonged to Persia, an Indo-Aryan speaker observed the way in which Aramaic was written down. This person decided to apply the same principles to Sanskrit or Prakrit. This adaptation, however, required a larger number of symbols than was available in the Aramaic abjad. Unnecessary Aramaic letters were redeployed with different values, although often retaining some phonetic similarity. For example, from the Indo-Aryan point of view, Aramaic had two symbols *kaph* and *qōph* available for /k/. One of these was used for Indo-Aryan /k/ and the other for /kh/. Other extensions were made by tinkering with symbols for related sounds.

Within South Asia, the existing linguistic analysis of the phonology of Sanskrit recognized the **akṣara** or open syllable as a primary unit. For the adapter of the alphabet, there was a strong correspondence between the unit written by a Semitic letter and an Indo-Aryan *akṣara*. The linguistic analysis of Sanskrit, however, clearly recognized both consonants and vowels. In order to preserve the principle that one *akṣara* equals one symbol, and yet fully to acknowledge the vowels of the linguistic analysis, diacritics were added to the consonant symbols for all the vowels except short /a/. Further, the symbols were ordered according to the logical sequence of the linguistic analysis and were given new logical names based on their Indo-Aryan pronunciation.

Differences between Semitic and Indo-Aryan writing are to be explained as follows: (1) the borrower did not feel constrained to maintain the exact shapes of the

Semitic symbols – possibly the shapes were not learned or remembered perfectly; (2) Indo-Aryan had more consonants than Aramaic and some new symbols had to be invented; (3) the rules governing the Aramaic use of the symbols were thoroughly reworked in accordance with the principles of the Indian linguistic tradition: this involved primarily maintaining the *akṣara* as the primary unit of writing, and the diacritic indication of vowels; (4) the direction of writing was changed to left to right, a not uncommon type of change; Falk (1993) views this change as possibly a Greek influence.

On balance, a direct Semitic origin for Brāhmī seems possible, but nothing like clear evidence for this hypothesis exists.

11.3.3.4 BRĀHMĪ IS BASED ON KHAROṢṬHĪ

A final possibility is that Brāhmī is derived from Kharoṣṭhī. This theory has been advanced by Falk (1993) and considered at least plausible by Salomon (1998). The structure of the two scripts is virtually identical: particularly, the manner in which vowels and consonant clusters are written. The most obvious differences are the different directions of writing, the absence in Kharoṣṭhī of different graphemes for short and long vowels, and generally, the different shapes of the symbols.

As we have seen, Kharoṣṭhī is generally agreed to have been derived from Aramaic; further, Kharoṣṭhī seems to have appeared somewhat earlier than Brāhmī. A possible scenario for Brāhmī is that, after Kharoṣṭhī emerged in the northwest, the system was taken to the northeastern area, where several modifications were made. Possibly a conscious effort was made to produce a different-appearing script, possibly with some reference to Aramaic letters. Or, Brāhmī is possibly a revision of an earlier script bringing it more into line with Kharoṣṭhī.

In my view, the Kharoṣṭhī hypothesis seems the most attractive of the existing possibilities. The advantage of this theory is that it explains the great similarity between Kharoṣṭhī and Brāhmī, and it requires no great leap of faith to move from Aramaic to Kharoṣṭhī to Brāhmī. The additional letters in Brāhmī can be seen as the result of correcting certain flaws in the earlier Kharoṣṭhī. The change of direction is not uncommon in the history of writing. The different shapes of the individual letters may have been the result of an intentional effort to distinguish the two scripts.

11.3.4 Later development of Brāhmī

Although Kharoṣṭhī died out, Brāhmī survived to become the ancestor of all the indigenous scripts of South Asia as well as those of Tibet and many Southeast Asian countries. Within South Asia, this type of development was evolutionary, very much parallel to the common diversification of dialects into distinct languages. Local varieties of the Brāhmī script emerged and were identified with local varieties of the spoken language. Just as the varieties of the spoken language evolved often into mutually unintelligible languages, so the varieties of script diverged until they often could no longer be recognized by all readers.

In general, all the scripts of India maintained the same basic structure as the original Brāhmī. This was partly due to the fact that the scripts were commonly used to write not only the contemporary language, but also Sanskrit. The prestige of Sanskrit acted as a strong conservative force on the evolution of the scripts. Just as we saw with Chinese that, although the shapes of characters changed over time, the basic structure of writing did not change, so also in India, the internal structure of the various writing systems stayed much the same, but the shapes of the letters changed, sometimes drastically.

In general, the northern scripts maintained a moderate simplicity, but the southern scripts became quite ornate and elaborate. By and large, the north–south division in scripts corresponds to the divide between the Indo-Aryan and Dravidian languages; however, the Sinhalese script of Sri Lanka belongs to the southern group although the language is Indo-Aryan.

Hindi and Urdu are sometimes described as a single language divided by two scripts. Typically, Urdu is spoken by Muslims living in Pakistan and is written with the Arabic script, whereas Hindi is spoken by Hindus living in India and is written with the Indian **Devanāgarī** script. For ordinary conversation, however, there is almost no difference between the two languages; they are mutually intelligible. But, for more academic purposes, the two languages diverge somewhat since Urdu has chosen its learned vocabulary from Persian or Arabic (consider how English uses Latin and Greek for this purpose) whereas Hindi has borrowed words from Sanskrit for its learned vocabulary.

Devanāgarī, discussed in detail later in this chapter, is the script used for writing Hindi, Marāṭhī, and Nepālī. Today, Sanskrit is usually written in *Devanāgarī.* Occasionally, languages of India with no traditional script of their own are written in *Devanāgarī.*

The Gujarātī script is used for the Gujarātī and Kacchī language. The Gujarātī script is historically a cursive form of *Devanāgarī*, developed for keeping business records and for personal correspondence. In the past, more formal writing in Gujarātī, such as literary and scholarly texts, were done in the *Devanāgarī* script. Since the beginning of printing in the early 1800s, the Gujarātī script has been used generally for prose writing although verse is still sometimes printed in *Devanāgarī* today. (Texts in Sanskrit are normally written in *Devanāgarī*.) Mistry (1996) reports that the earliest handwritten document in Gujarātī dates from 1592, and the earliest printed record is an advertisement from 1797.

Bengali is spoken by Hindus in the West Bengal state of India and by Muslims in Bangladesh. Although many languages spoken by Muslims have come to be written in the Arabic script (e.g., Persian, Urdu), the Bengali language (Bānglā) continues to be written with the Bengali script by all speakers. The reason for this is that during the period of Muslim domination in India, rather than writing Bengali in the Arabic script, most writing was in the Urdu language using the Arabic script. The Bengali script is also used for Assamese, Manipurī, and some Munda languages.

The Punjabi language is spoken in northern India and in Pakistan. In India, Punjabi speakers are generally members of the Sikh religion and use the Gurmukhi (/'gurməki/) script for writing Punjabi. In Pakistan, Punjabi is sometimes written in the Arabic script. However, the situation there is often bilingually diglossic, with Muslim Punjabi speakers commonly writing in a different language, Urdu, in the Arabic script.

Oriya is the major language of Orissa state. The Oriya script is used for the Oriya language as well as for the numerous other minority languages spoken in Orissa. The tradition of writing Sanskrit in the Oriya script is continued there as well. Although the Oriya script is more closely connected to the northern group of scripts, the large curved lines are similar to those found in the southern scripts.

The Kannada and Telugu scripts are very similar; they are used to write the Dravidian languages Kannada and Telugu of south India. The Malayalam script is used for the Malayalam language of south India. This script is characterized by the large number of special ligature forms.

The Tamil script is used for the Tamil language spoken in south India and in Sri Lanka. The Tamil script is unusual among the Indian scripts in two ways. First, it follows the Dravidian phonology, and in its basic form cannot be used for writing Sanskrit. To do this, several additional letters are used. Second, the use of ligatures has been almost abandoned with the result that the script is more an alphabet than an abugida.

The Sinhalese script is used in Sri Lanka for the Sinhalese language, an Indo-Aryan language spoken in the far south of the South Asian area. The language is strongly diglossic. The distinction of voiceless and aspirated stops and of voiced and breathy voiced stops has been lost, but the different symbols for these sounds have been retained in writing.

Apart from the major borrowing of the Brāhmī script by languages of Southeast Asia which are considered below in §11.5, a considerable number of versions of Indian writing are used or have been used for various languages across the south-eastern area of Asia, particularly in the islands, stretching as far as the Philippines.

In Japan, a script derived from Brāhmī, known as *siddham* or *siddhamātr̥kā*, is used by some Buddhists for religious purposes (Stevens 1995).

11.4 *Devanāgarī* as Applied to Sanskrit

To illustrate the Indian abugida in more detail, we will look at the *Devanāgarī* script as applied to Sanskrit. *Devanāgarī* is the script most often used in modern times for writing Sanskrit although traditionally Sanskrit was written in a variety of local scripts. *Devanāgarī* is also currently used for writing Hindi, Marāṭhī, and Nepālī, and on occasion for writing other languages. It is the most widely used script in India and generally serves as the default Indian script. The name *Devanāgarī* is not entirely clear. The script is often called *Nāgarī*, which seems to mean 'of the city'; *Devanāgarī* would then be 'of the divine city, *nāgarī* of the gods'. The relationship to 'city' is uncertain.

The various abugidas of South Asia all derive from Brāhmī and have continued to function in much the same way. The structure we find for *Devanāgarī* is, by and large, the same for all the scripts of South Asia.

11.4.1 *Sanskrit phonology*

The phonemes of Sanskrit are given in table 11.4 in the order in which they normally appear in grammars.

Table 11.4 The phonemes of Sanskrit, in the traditional order

a	ā		i	ī	u	ū
r̥	r̥̄		l̥	l̥̄		
e	ai		o	au		
ṁ	ḥ					
k	kh	g	gh	ṅ		
c	ch	j	jh	ñ		
ṭ	ṭh	ḍ	ḍh	ṇ		
t	th	d	dh	n		
p	ph	b	bh	m		
y	r	l	v			
ś	ṣ	s	h	(ḷ)		

The romanization scheme used here is frequently used for South Asian languages; the order of the phonemes is the one commonly used in South Asia and reflects the ancient grammatical tradition. Vowels occur, both short and long. Superscript bars indicate length. The subscript circles indicate syllabic (not voiceless!) consonants. Thus, the vowels /r̥ r̥̄ l̥ l̥̄/ are phonetically syllabic consonants; the vowels /r̥̄/ and /l̥/ occur only rarely. Long syllabic /l̥̄/ does not occur in any real Sanskrit word; it was added by the grammarians to make the vowel repertoire symmetrical. The sound /ṁ/ is pronounced as a homorganic nasal, or it nasalizes the preceding vowel; /ḥ/ represents a regular voiceless [h], whereas /h/ indicates breathy voiced /ɦ/.

Note that the stops are ordered according to their place of articulation from back to front. The voiceless aspirated stops [k^h $tʃ^h$ $ʈ^h$ t^h p^h] are romanized as /kh ch ṭh th ph/. The breathy voiced stops [g̤ d̤ʒ̤ ɖ̤ d̤ b̤] are romanized as /gh jh ḍh dh bh/. The subscript dot under /ṭ ḍ ṇ ṣ ḷ/ shows a retroflex place of articulation; without the dot, /t d n s l/ are dental. The retroflex lateral /ḷ/ is found only in Vedic texts; later, it is replaced by /ḍ/. The symbol [ñ] is palatal, and [ṅ] is velar. The postalveolar fricative [ʃ] is romanized as /ś/.

A complicated set of morphophonemic alternations, known as *sandhi*, operate across morpheme boundaries and sometimes even across word boundaries.

11.4.2 Devanāgarī *writing system*

The ancient Brāhmī script was developed for Sanskrit as described earlier. As a successor script to Brāhmī, *Devanāgarī* continues this tradition and follows the phonological structure of the language quite closely. There are several small regional variations in *Devanāgarī* which are described more fully in section 11.4.2.5 below. *Devanāgarī* is written left to right.

The graphemes of the writing system (table 11.5) are given in the same arrangement as the sounds in table 11.4; this arrangement is used for the ordering of words in dictionaries as well. The series of symbols is known as the *varṇamālā* वर्णमाला.

Table 11.5 The basic symbols of *Devanāgarī*

a	ā		i	ī	u	ū
अ	आ		इ	ई	उ	ऊ
r̥	r̥̄		l̥	l̥̄		
ऋ	ॠ		ऌ	ॡ		
e	ai		o	au		
ए	ऐ		ओ	औ		
ṁ	ḥ					
ं	ः					
k	kh	g	gh	ṅ		
क	ख	ग	घ	ङ		
c	ch	j	jh	ñ		
च	छ	ज	झ	ञ		
ṭ	ṭh	ḍ	ḍh	ṇ		
ट	ठ	ड	ढ	ण		
t	th	d	dh	n		
त	थ	द	ध	न		
p	ph	b	bh	m		
प	फ	ब	भ	म		
y	r	l	v			
य	र	ल	व			
ś	ṣ	s	h	ḷ		
श	ष	स	ह	ळ		

11.4.2.1 VOWELS

Vowel graphemes (table 11.6) have two allographs: one free, and the other bound. At the beginning of an orthographic unit (see *akṣara* below), the free allograph is used; otherwise, the bound allograph is used, i.e., the vowel is written as a diacritic on the preceding consonant.

Table 11.6 shows the free and bound allographs and the bound allograph with the consonant क <k>, forming a complex symbol.

Table 11.6 The vowel symbols of *Devanāgarī*

Free	*Bound*	*Bound with* <*k*>	*Free*	*Bound*	*Bound with* <*k*>
a		ka	ā		kā
अ	—	क	आ	ा	का
i		ki	ī		kī
इ	ि	कि	ई	ी	की
u		ku	ū		kū
उ	ु	कु	ऊ	ू	कू
r̥		kr̥	r̥̄		kr̥̄
ऋ	ृ	कृ	ॠ	ॄ	कॄ
l̥		kl̥	l̥̄		kl̥̄
ऌ	ॢ	कॢ	ॡ	ॣ	कॣ
e		ke	ai		kai
ए	े	के	ऐ	ै	कै
o		ko	au		kau
ओ	ो	को	औ	ौ	कौ

Note the following points about vowels:

1 The short vowel /a/ is written only at the beginning of an orthographic unit (*akṣara*); otherwise, it is not overtly indicated. The absence of any vowel diacritic indicates the short /a/: प <p> (=/pa/). To indicate the absence of a following short /a/, the diacritic *virāma*, a short subscript diagonal line (्), is added below the consonant symbol: प् /p/, त् /t/, मप् /map/, thus indicating the absence of a vowel at the end of a word.

2 The diacritic for /i/ precedes the consonant symbol: पि /pi/. The diacritics for /e ai/ are written above the consonant symbol: पे /pe/, पै /pai/. The diacritics for /ā ī o au/ follow the consonant symbol: पा /pā/, पी /pī/, पो /po/, पौ /pau/. Note that the top portions of the diacritics for /o/ and /au/ are the same as the diacritics for /e/ and /ai/, but placed above the vertical stroke of /ā/.

The diacritics for /u ū r̥ r̥̄ l̥ l̥̄/ are written below the consonant symbol: पु /pu/, पू /pū/, पृ /pr̥/, पॄ /pr̥̄/, पॢ /pl̥/, पॣ /pl̥̄/. Note that the diacritics for /u ū/ differ only in their orientation. As mentioned above, the vowels /r̥̄ l̥/ are rare, and /l̥̄/ does not really occur.

3 Certain special forms of consonant + vowel exist: e.g., रु /ru/, रू /rū/, दृ /dr̥/, दॄ /dr̥̄/, हृ /hr̥/.
4 With some vowels, /ś/ श takes the allographic shape श: e.g., शृ /śr̥/, शु /śu/, शू /śū/; but शा /śā/, शि /śi/.

11.4.2.2 CONSONANTS: SINGLE CONSONANTS AND CONSONANT CLUSTERS

A single consonant, as opposed to a consonant cluster, is written with the symbols as given in table 11.5.

A consonant cluster is written as a ligature, with the individual graphemes of the cluster combined into a single symbol. Frequently, special allographs are used; often, a vertical stroke is omitted from an initial grapheme. For example, for <py>, the vertical stroke of प <p> is removed to give the allograph प्; this is then combined with य <y> to give the ligature प्य <py>.

A ligature is treated as a single unit with respect to vowels. The vowel diacritics are attached to this conjunct symbol exactly as to a single consonant symbol. Superscript and subscript vowels are written above or below the last element of the ligature:

प्य	प्या	प्यि	प्यी	प्यु	प्यू	
<py> (=/pya/)	<pyā>	<pyi>	<pyī>	<pyu>	<pyū>	
प्यृ	प्यॄ	प्यॢ	प्ये	प्यै	प्यो	प्यौ
<pyr̥>	<pyr̥̄>	<pyl̥>	<pye>	<pyai>	<pyo>	<pyau>

The complete set of ligatures is quite large. Note that some of the clusters occur only across syllable or word boundaries (word boundaries were not indicated in early texts). Selected examples are given below to show the various methods of forming ligatures. In some cases, more than one form is found in free variation for the same cluster: e.g., च्च or च्च <cc>.

(a) Horizontal combination:

ग्व <gv> < ग + व
च्छ <cch> < च + छ

(b) Vertical combination. The symbols may be adjusted in shape or size to fit the smaller vertical space:

ज्ज <jj> < ज + ज
क्क or क्क <kk> < क + क
ट्ट <ṭṭ> < ट + ट
द्ध <ddh> < द + ध

(c) When <r> occurs as the first consonant of a cluster, it is not written as र, but as a diacritic र् above the final consonant; this allograph of <r> is known as *repha*:

र्त <rt> < र + त
र्झ <rjh> < र + झ

(d) When <r> occurs as a non-initial consonant of a cluster, it is not written as र, but as a diagonal stroke <ˏ> below the first consonant:

ग्र <gr> < ग + र
न्र <nr> < न + र

(e) With some ligatures, the shape of the free allograph is altered slightly:

क्त <kt> < क + त
त्त <tt> < त + त
द्द <dd> < द् + द्

(f) Diphones. Two symbols, <jñ> and <kṣ>, have diphones, where one symbol represents two phonemes:

ज्ञ <jñ> < ज + ञ
क्ष <kṣ> < क + ष

Ligatures made of more than two consonants are constructed according to the same principles as set out above for two-consonant ligatures. Note that many of the clusters occur only across syllable or word boundaries.

ग्ध्य <gdhy> < ग + ध + य
न्स्म्य <nsmy> < न + स + म + य
ङ्ख्य <ṅkhy> < ङ्ख (< ङ + ख) + य
च्छ्व <cchv> < च + छ्व (< छ + व)
ञ्च्म <ñcm> < ञ्च (< ञ + च) + म
त्त्व <ttv> < त्त (< त + त) + व
ष्ट्र्य <ṣṭry> < ष्ट (< ष + ट) + र + य
र्त्स्न्य <rtsny> < र + त + स + न + य

11.4.2.3 *AKṢARA*: THE ORTHOGRAPHIC SYLLABLE

The term ***akṣara*** is used to define an orthographic syllable in Sanskrit. Each initial vowel symbol alone or each consonant symbol with its vowel diacritic plus any final modifier constitutes an *akṣara* or orthographic syllable. Consonant clusters are combined orthographically into ligatures. A ligature counts as a single consonant, and thus a ligature with its vowel diacritic also forms an *akṣara*. An *akṣara* consists of any number of initial consonants (or none) + a vowel (= (C)V).

Frequently, an *akṣara* is also a phonological syllable. For example, the word /bahumānaḥ/ 'esteem' is written बहुमानः. Divided into phonological syllables, this word has exactly the same division as when it is divided into *akṣara*. (The ***visarga*** is considered to be the coda of a syllable.) To divide a word into *akṣaras*, the onsets are absolutely maximized, even over word boundaries; only *visarga* (syllable-final [h]) and *anusvāra* (vowel nasalization) are permitted in the coda.

phonological syllables	/ba-hu-mā-naḥ/	
akṣaras (orthographic syllables)	<ba-hu-mā-naḥ>	ब – हु – मा – नः

However, with a word such as /kūrmaḥ/ 'tortoise' कूर्मः, containing a consonant cluster, the phonological syllables do not correspond to the *akṣaras*. In linguistic terms, the maximization of onsets for *akṣaras* violates the phonotactic constraints of the syllables.

phonological syllables	/kūr-maḥ/	
akṣaras (orthographic syllables)	<kū-rmaḥ>	कू – र्मः

11.4.2.4 WORD DIVISION

In early writing, word divisions were not indicated. Today, word divisions in Sanskrit are indicated where this does not change the way the letters are written. Texts prepared for learners sometimes show all word divisions by using a *virāma* (§11.4.2.1) under final consonants.

The following lines from a well-known Sanskrit story about a King Nala illustrate word division. First the transliteration and translation are given, then the text with all words divided using the *virāma* if necessary, and finally the text as written without word divisions.

āsīd rājā, nalo nama, vīrasenasuto balī
upapanno guṇair iṣṭai, rūpavan, aśvakovidaḥ
atiṣṭhan manujendrāṇāṁ mūrdhni devapatir yathā

'There was a king, Nala by name, the strong son of the army of heroes, endowed with desired virtues, handsome, skilled with horses. He stood superior to princes, just as Indra to gods.'

With word divisions	Without word divisions
आसीद् राजा नलो नम वीरसेनसुतो बली	आसीद्राजानलोनमवीरसेनसुतोबली
उपपन्नो गुणैर् इष्टै रुपवन् अश्वकोविदः	उपपन्नोगुणैरिष्टैरुपवनश्वकोविदः
अतिष्ठन् मनुजेन्द्राणां मूर्ध्नि देवपतिर् यथा	अतिष्ठन्मनुजेन्द्राणांमूर्ध्निदेवपतिर्यथा

Note the differences between the versions with and without word divisions:

Line 1

द् रा = द्रा /drā/

Line 2

र् इ = रि /ri/
न् अ = न /na/

Line 3

न् म = न्म /nma/
र् य = र्य /rya/

11.4.2.5 ALTERNATIVE FORMS

Over time, a few graphemes have developed geographic allographs, known as the Bombay and Northern (or Calcutta) forms. Current government policy favours the Bombay variants. The more obvious differences are shown below. Sanskrit and Hindi have been written with both variants depending on the location and preference of the author or printer. The Marāṭhī language is written with Bombay variants, and the Nepālī language with the Northern variants.

	Bombay	Northern		Bombay	Northern
initial <a>	अ	अ	<jh>	झ	झ
initial <ā>	आ	आ	<ṇ>	ण	ण
<kṣ>	क्ष	क्ष	<kṣy>	क्ष्य	क्ष्य
<tkṣ>	त्क्ष	त्क्ष	<jhy>	झ्य	झ्य
<jjh>	ज्झ	ज्झ	<ṇm>	ण्म	ण्म
<ṇṇ>	ण्ण	ण्ण			

11.4.2.6 NUMERALS

The numerals have special forms. There are also special Bombay and Northern alternative forms for some numerals. It is interesting to note that what are called 'Arabic numerals' in the West are really Indian in origin and in the Arabic language are called 'Indian numerals'.

	1	2	3	4	5	6	7	8	9	0
Bombay forms:	१	२	३	४	५	६	७	८	९	०
Northern forms:	१	२	३	४	५	६	७	८	९	०

11.4.2.7 OTHER SYMBOLS

Anusvāra (vowel nasalization) is written as a diacritic dot above the main grapheme: कं /kaṁ/. A dotted-half-moon diacritic is sometimes used instead of *anusvāra* to show nasalization कँ. The syllable /oṁ/, sacred in Hinduism and in Buddhism, is normally written as ॐ. This is an older form of ओं /oṁ/.

The *visarga* (syllable-final [h]) is written as two dots; it is transcribed as /ḥ/.

Table 11.7 The phonemes of Burmese

Consonants						
	k	kh	g		ŋ̣	
	c	ch	j		ñ	
	t	th	d		n	
	p	ph	b		m	
	y	r	l	w	s	
	h	ḷ	ʔ			
Vowels						
		i		u		
		e		o		
		ɛ		ɔ		
			a			
Tones						
	creaky [´]			low [¯]		high [`]

11.5 Southeast Asian Writing

Buddhism travelled from India to Southeast Asia via Sanskrit or a later language known as Pāli. Buddhism thus brought both the Sanskrit language and the Brāhmī abugida to Southeast Asia. Large numbers of Sanskrit and Pāli words, both religious and secular, were borrowed into the indigenous Southeast Asian languages. There, the Brāhmī abugida developed into the Burmese, Thai, Laotian, Cambodian, and other writing systems. We will not go into these writing systems in detail, but we will point out an interesting aspect of the conservatism of the borrowing, using Burmese as an example. Note that Sanskrit and Burmese are not related languages.

Burmese has the phoneme inventory shown in table 11.7. The romanization is very close to that used for the Indic languages. Note that the Burmese order of consonants follows the Indic tradition.

The basic Burmese symbols are shown in table 11.8.

The basic inventory is quite similar to the Indian systems; however, there is a major difference in the relationship of the consonant symbols and the language. As we have seen above, Sanskrit had a series of retroflex stops with its own symbols in the Brāhmī script. The symbols for these consonants <ṭ ṭh ḍ ḍh ṇ> were retained in the Burmese writing system although the sounds were not present in Burmese. For example, in Burmese, the retroflex series of stops is kept distinct in writing from the series <t th d dh n> even though both series are pronounced as dentals (Roop 1972). The so-called retroflex stops in Burmese are used primarily for words of Sanskrit origin.

Similarly, the letters for the breathy voiced stops of Sanskrit are preserved <gh jh ḍh dh bh>, even though in Burmese they are phonetically identical to the voiced stops <g j ḍ d b>.

Table 11.8 The symbols of the Burmese abugida

	Voiceless stop				*Voiced stop*				*Nasal*	
	Unaspirated		*Aspirated*		*Unaspirated*		*Aspirated*			
Velar	က	k	ခ	kh	ဂ	g	ဃ	gh	င	ṅ
Palatal	စ	c	ဆ	ch	ဇ	j	ဈ	jh	ဉ	ñ
Retro	ဋ	ṭ	ဌ	ṭh	ဍ	ḍ	ဎ	ḍh	ဏ	ṇ
Dental	တ	t	ထ	th	ဒ	d	ဓ	dh	န	n
Labial	ပ	p	ဖ	ph	ဗ	b	ဘ	bh	မ	m
	ယ	y	ရ	r	လ	ḷ	ဝ	w	သ	s
			ဟ	h	ဠ	ḷ	အ	ʔ		

Table 11.9 The writing of the Burmese vowels /i a u/

	Initial with <k>			*Initial with <k>*			*Initial with <k>*		
creaky	ဣ	ကိ	í	အ	က	á	ဥ	ကု	ú
low	ဤ	ကီ	ī		ကာ	ā	ဦ	ကူ	ū
high		ကီး	ìː		ကား	àː	ဦး	ကူး	ùː

In these two examples, we see that the cultural importance of the original language favoured retention of the original inventory. A large number of Sanskrit words were borrowed into Burmese, and this conservatism allowed distinctions made in Sanskrit to be written in Burmese even though no such phonemic distinction existed in Burmese. When a writing system is borrowed, there is a tendency for the inventory of symbols to be considered a single object, and for the entire inventory to be borrowed regardless of how well it fits the new language. Because the entire inventory is borrowed, complex relations between phoneme and written symbol are often introduced at the beginning.

Like the Indian abugidas, the Burmese abugida writes vowels as diacritics unless they occur at the beginning of a word (table 11.9). The vowel /a/ is not written. The Burmese system is different from the Indian systems in using vowel diacritics to indicate not only vowel quality, but tone as well. The entire vowel system is not shown here, but the examples in table 11.9 indicate the basic structure. There are separate symbols when the vowel occurs word-initially. For the non-initial vowels /i a u/, diacritics derived from the Brāhmī short vowel diacritics are used to indicate vowels with creaky tone; diacritics derived from the Brāhmī long vowel symbols are used to indicate vowels with low tone; and the high tone vowels are indicated with the creaky diacritics together with an additional diacritic resembling the Roman colon. Other vowels are written in a somewhat similar way. For a more complete discussion of Burmese writing, see Roop (1972) and Wheatley (1996).

11.6 The Tibetan Abugida

Tibetan is a member of the Tibeto-Burman language family, which is itself a member of the Sino-Tibetan family. It is spoken in Tibet and neighbouring areas (China, India, Nepal, and Bhutan) by about four million people. Tibet has politically been a part of China since 1951.

According to Buddhist tradition, the Tibetan King Srong Btsan Sgam Po (early seventh century NEW) sent his son Thon Mi Sambhoṭa in 632 to Kashmir to learn the art of writing in order that the Buddhist texts could be translated and written down in Tibetan. This account is sometimes disputed, but Tibetan writing is ultimately based on an Indian model and was established by the seventh century NEW. A grammatical treatise was written by Thon Mi Sambhoṭa, of which only portions survive.

The earliest existing Tibetan texts are from the eighth and ninth centuries NEW. The literary language derives from Tibetan of the fifteenth to the eighteenth centuries. The modern dialects differ considerably from literary Tibetan; the dialect of Lhasa of central Tibet is considered standard. In the twentieth century, written Tibetan changed to reflect more closely the spoken language.

A large number of unpronounced consonants are written in Tibetan. Possibly some of these consonants were pronounced at earlier stages in the history of Tibetan, but very likely some of these were never pronounced but were used to distinguish homophonous morphemes. For modern Tibetan, the relationship between the written and spoken forms is complex, and the one cannot be completely predicted from the other.

The Library of Congress (LC) romanization scheme is used here except that <zha sha> is used instead of <z,a s,a>. The romanization present a one-to-one mapping between Tibetan orthography and Roman letters, without regard to pronunciation. Because of the considerable difference in Tibetan between writing and pronunciation, it is important to bear in mind that the romanization is simply a device for showing Tibetan spelling in Roman letters and does not necessarily indicate the pronunciation exactly.

11.6.1 Tibetan phonemic inventory

The phonemic inventory of Tibetan is given in table 11.10.

Tibetan has a general syllable shape of (C)V(C) + tone. Generally, an initial consonant is present. In native Tibetan words there are no consonant clusters within the syllable. The only final consonants are /p k m n ŋ l/. Words borrowed from Sanskrit often do have consonant clusters.

Table 11.10 The phonemes of Tibetan

Consonants							
p	t	ts	ʈ	c	tʃ	k	ʔ
pʰ	tʰ	tsʰ	ʈʰ	cʰ	tʃʰ	kʰ	
ɬ	s	r̥	ʃ		h		
w	l	r		y			
m		n		ɲ		ŋ	
Vowels						**Tones**	
i	y	u				high	´
e	ø	o				low	`
	a						

Table 11.11 The basic graphemes of the Tibetan abugida in the traditional order

ཀ	<ka>	ཁ	<kha>	ག	<ga>	ང	<ṅa>
ཅ	<ca>	ཆ	<cha>	ཇ	<ja>	ཉ	<ña>
ཏ	<ta>	ཐ	<tha>	ད	<da>	ན	<na>
པ	<pa>	ཕ	<pha>	བ	<ba>	མ	<ma>
ཙ	<tsa>	ཚ	<tsha>	ཛ	<dza>	ཝ	<wa>
ཞ	<zha>	ཟ	<za>	འ	<´a>	ཡ	<ya>
ར	<ra>	ལ	<la>	ཤ	<sha>	ས	<sa>
ཧ	<ha>	ཨ	<a>	ཕ༹	<fa>	བ༹	<va>

11.6.2 *The Tibetan abugida*

The Tibetan abugida traditionally consists of thirty basic letters གསལ་བྱེད་ <gsalbyed> /sɛtʃe/ which are ordered as shown in table 11.11; the romanized transcription is also given. The letters for <f v> have been added at the end recently for foreign words.

The structural similarity between the Tibetan and Indian abugidas is obvious. When a consonant is written alone, the vowel <a> is assumed to follow the consonant as shown in the romanization.

The simplest orthographic syllable consists of a single consonant grapheme, possibly accompanied by a vowel grapheme: e.g., ཀ་ སེ་ ངུ་ <ka se ngu>. A raised dot is written at the end of every syllable. Complex syllables involve the addition of one or more graphemes to the basic syllable. The most complicated orthographic syllable consists of seven graphemes – six consonants and a vowel – although it is pronounced as a simple CVC syllable.

བསྒྲུབས་ <bsgrubs> /ḍùp/ 'completed'

The vowels (དབྱངས་ <dbyangs> /yaŋ/) are written above or below the consonant grapheme. Only one vowel occurs per syllable. Three vowels <i e o> are written above the consonant, and <u> is written below. The vowel <a> is not written; a syllable with no written vowel contains the vowel /a/: ཀ <ka>, ཀི་ <ki>, ཀེ <ke>, ཀུ <ku>, ཀོ <ko>.

In the rare cases where a vowel occurs at the beginning of a syllable, it is written with the grapheme <ཨ>. For <a>, <ཨ> is written alone; the other vowels are written with <ཨ> as though it were a consonant, i.e., <ཨ> plus the appropriate vowel diacritic. This way of writing vowels other than /a/ is a departure from the Brāhmī system: ཨ་ <a>, ཨི་ <i>, ཨེ <e>, ཨུ་ <u>, ཨོ་ <o>.

11.6.3 *Complex orthographic syllables*

Figure 11.3 shows the structure of the Tibetan orthographic syllable. The numbers above the names indicate the sequence in which the elements are written. Only the radical is present in every syllable. Only one grapheme can occur in any one box; i.e., a syllable can be written with only one subscript consonant. The vowel of a syllable is written in one of the boxes labelled 5, but not in both. Each

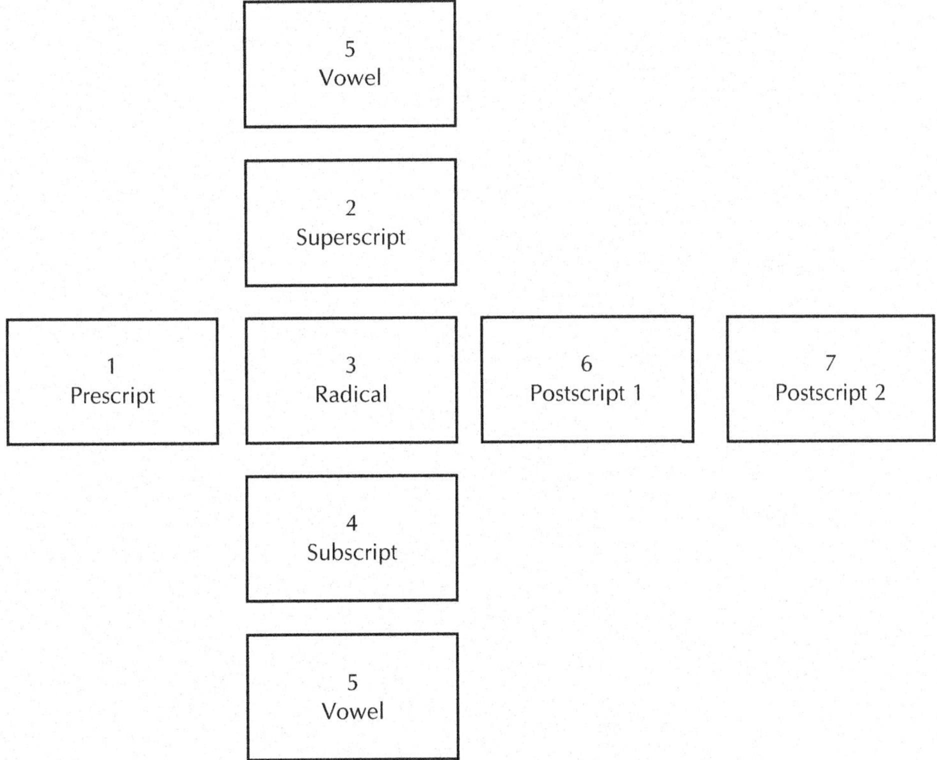

Figure 11.3 The structure of the Tibetan orthographic syllable

orthographic syllable consists of a radical (box 3) and one or more adscript graphemes. An adscript consonant is written to the left (box 1), right (boxes 6 or 7), above (box 2), or below (box 4) the radical (box 3). A vowel diacritic is written in box 5, either at the top or at the bottom, depending on the vowel. Figure 11.3 shows all possibilities.

The following examples show a variety of forms. Note the lack of simple relationship between the writing and the pronunciation: ཐབ་ <thap> /tʰáp/ /'oven'/, ཐབས་ <thaps> /tʰáp/ 'way, means'.

Three graphemes ར ལ ས <r l s> occur as superscript graphemes written above the radical in position 2: ལྦ་ <lb> /bà/, ལྟ་ <lt> /tá/, ལྫ་ <ldz> /tʃà/, ལྔ་ <lng> /ŋá/.

Four graphemes ཡ ཝ ར ལ <y w r l> are written under the radical in position 4. Subscript ཡ <y> appears as a loop ྱ attached under the radical: བྱ་ <bya> /tʃà/, པྱ་ <pya> /tʃá/, ཕྱ་ <phya> /tʃʰá/.

Subscript ཝ <w> appears as a triangle ྭ attached under the radical. This is not pronounced but is used only to distinguish homophonous syllables. Subscript ར <r> appears as a horizontal stroke ྲ at the bottom of the radical. Subscript ལ <l> is written below the radical. Its shape is not changed, although written smaller: དྭ་ <dw> /tà/, བྲ་
 /ʈà/, བླ་ <bl> /lá/.

Superscript /s/ occurs in box 2, and subscript /r/ in box 4: སྤྲ་ <spra> /ʈá/, སྨྲ་ <smr> /má/.

The graphemes བ ད ག མ འ <b d g m ´> occur in the prescript position; that is, they are written as a separate grapheme preceding the radical within the same syllable. Prescript graphemes are not pronounced as such, but they sometimes affect the tone of the syllable or distinguish homophonous syllables: ཡུ་ <yu> /yú/, གཡུ་ <gyu> /yù/; ད་ <da> /dà/, བད་ <bda> /dà/.

The syllable structure allows a maximum of two postscript consonants, known as postscript-1 and postscript-2. Postscript-1 allows a variety of consonants: ཁབ་ <khab> /kʰáp/, དམ་ <dam> /tàm/, གོལ་ <gol> /kœ̀/.

The postscript-2 position may be filled only by ས <s> and only if the postscript-1 position is filled; it is not pronounced: ཁེབས་ <khebs> /kʰep/.

In writing, the consonants appear to hang from an imaginary line. A superscript consonant is written at this line; the radical, any subscript consonant, and an <u> are lowered accordingly. In གྲུབ་ <grub>, the <g> and the <b> both hang from the imaginary top line. The <r> is subscript to the <g>. In སྒྲུབ <sgrub>, the superscript <s> hangs from the same line as the <b> and <gru> is lowered. The vowels <i e o> are written above the imaginary line, as shown in གྲོང <groṅ>.

The raised dot < ་ > /tʃék/ ཚེག་ is placed after every syllable. Word boundaries are not indicated. A vertical stroke <། > /ʃé/ ཤད་ is written at the end of longer grammatical units; it is doubled at the end of the longest grammatical units <༎ >. At the end of a chapter, it may be written four times <༎༎ >. At the end of a large portion of text the following symbol may appear: ༄

The Tibetan abugida has been presented in some detail although many details were omitted. It is obvious that both the internal structure and the relationship of writing and language in Tibetan are quite complex. Further, there are different calligraphic styles in use which do not resemble each other very much.

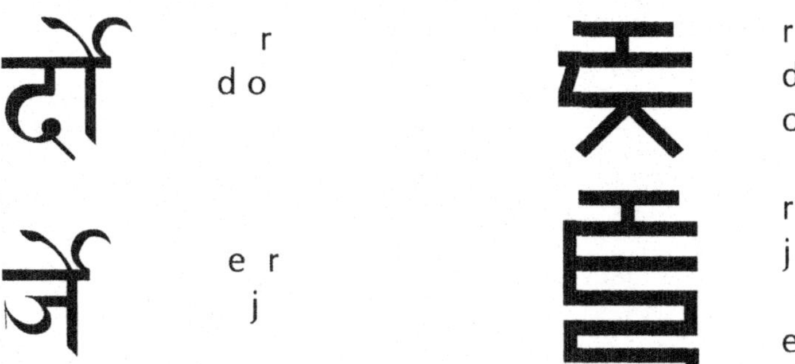

Figure 11.4 Two syllables /rdo rje/ written in Devanāgarī and 'Phags-pa (from Bright 1999)

11.7 The 'Phags-pa Script

The 'Phags-pa (/ˈpɑgzˌpɑ/) script was created by a Tibetan monk in the thirteenth century under instructions from the Mongolian king Kublai Khan who wanted to devise a unified script for writing the most important languages of his empire: Mongolian, Chinese, Tibetan, and Uighur. The script was based on the Tibetan model; the symbols have a generally square shape.

The structure of the 'Phags-pa abugida is very similar to the Tibetan and Indian scripts except that it is written in vertical lines from the top left of the page (cf. Mongolian in §11.8). Symbols for the sounds in all four languages are included.

The 'Phags-pa script was used only sporadically during Kublai Khan's reign and then generally disappeared. It lingered somewhat in the Mongolian area, where it is still used occasionally for ornamental purposes. Some scholars (Ledyard 1997) have suggested that the 'Phags-pa script may have been, at least partially, the model for Korean *hankul*.

In contrast to the Tibetan and Indian models, the non-initial vowel symbols in 'Phags-pa are not diacritics (figure 11.4). Each syllable is written as a connected glyph with the elements proceeding from top to bottom. Consonant clusters are simply written one on top of the other. Thus, the 'Phags-pa system is typologically intermediate between an abugida and an alphabet. Like an abugida, it does not write one vowel, namely /a/. However, as with an alphabet, both consonants and vowels are written with free graphemes, not diacritics.

11.8 The Mongolian and Manchu Alphabets

11.8.1 Mongolian

We saw in chapter 7 that the Aramaic abjad was used in mediæval Persia. One variety, known as Sogdian, was used by Persian speakers living in western China from the third century NEW. The script spread and in the eighth century NEW was

Table 11.12 The symbols of Mongolian

	Initial	*Medial*	*Final*
a	ᠠ‍	‍ᠠ‍	‍ᠠ ‍ᠠ
e	ᠡ‍	‍ᠡ‍	‍ᠡ ‍ᠡ
i	ᠢ‍	‍ᠢ‍	‍ᠢ
o, u	ᠣ‍	‍ᠣ‍	‍ᠣ
ö, ü	ᠥ‍	‍ᠥ‍ ‍ᠥ‍	‍ᠥ
n	ᠨ‍	‍ᠨ‍	‍ᠨ
ng		‍ᠩ‍	‍ᠩ
q	ᠬ‍	‍ᠬ‍	‍ᠬ
ɣ	ᠭ‍	‍ᠭ‍ ‍ᠭ‍	
b	ᠪ‍	‍ᠪ‍	‍ᠪ
(p)	ᠫ‍	‍ᠫ‍	
s	ᠰ‍	‍ᠰ‍	‍ᠰ
ʃ	ᠱ‍	‍ᠱ‍	‍ᠱ
t, d	ᠲ‍	‍ᠳ‍	‍ᠳ
l	ᠯ‍	‍ᠯ‍	‍ᠯ
m	ᠮ‍	‍ᠮ‍	‍ᠮ
tʃ	ᠴ‍	‍ᠴ‍	
(dʒ)	ᠵ‍	‍ᠵ‍	
j	ᠶ‍	‍ᠶ‍	‍ᠶ
k, g	ᠺ‍	‍ᠺ‍	‍ᠺ
r	ᠷ‍	‍ᠷ‍	‍ᠷ
v, w	ᠸ‍	‍ᠸ‍	
(h)	ᠾ‍	‍ᠾ‍	

borrowed and adapted for writing Old Uighur (/ˈwiˌguɹ/), a Turkic language of Central Asia. Subsequently, the Uighur direction of writing changed and Uighur was written in vertical columns starting at the top left of the page. Vowels were more fully written than in the Aramaic tradition, especially in initial position. Uighur is currently written with the Arabic abjad; Uighur is unusual among languages using the Arabic abjad in that it has respelled Arabic words according to the Uighur pronunciation (Kaye 1996).

In the twelfth century NEW, the Mongolians borrowed the Uighur script from which a distinctive Mongolian script emerged. Mongolian is an Altaic language, related to the Turkic languages and possibly to Korean and Japanese. The Mongolian-speaking area is divided into Inner Mongolia, a province of China, and Outer Mongolia, which is the Mongolian People's Republic. In Inner Mongolia, the traditional Mongolian alphabet is used although the language itself is under considerable pressure from the Chinese language. In Outer Mongolia, there is less influence from Chinese, but under the influence of the former Soviet Union, the language has been written there in the Cyrillic alphabet since 1946. Since the breakup of the Soviet Union, there have been discussions of reverting to the traditional Mongolian alphabet in Outer Mongolia, but so far this has not happened.

When the traditional Mongolian alphabet is used, the situation is somewhat diglossic since an older Middle Mongolian dialect is used. The modern language is used when writing with the Cyrillic alphabet.

In the process of borrowing the abjad from Uighur into Mongolian, vowels came to be written fully, thus producing an alphabetic system of writing from the earlier abjad. Visually, Mongolian writing has a strong vertical line forming a backbone with the individual letters appearing as distinctive marks on the side of the backbone (figure 11.5). There are positional variants for initial, medial, and final positions (table 11.12).

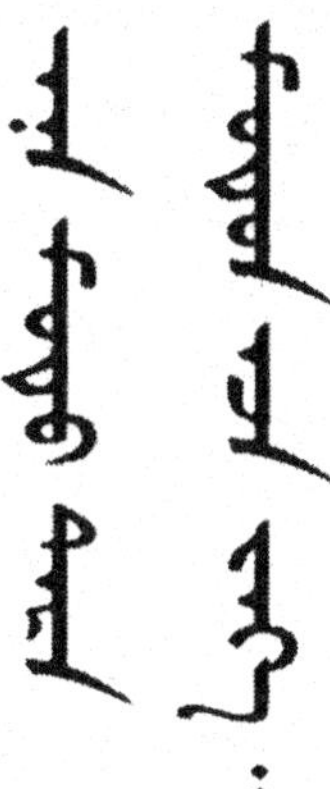

<ene mode tere modun-atʃa yeke.>

Figure 11.5 An example sentence in Mongolian

11.8.2 Manchu

Manchu is an Altaic language, closely related to Mongolian. It was spoken in Manchuria, but is virtually extinct today. Around 1600 NEW, the Manchus borrowed the Mongolian script, adapting it to their own language. The two scripts remain very similar to each other both in appearance and in structure.

The Qīng dynasty (1644–1911), the last imperial dynasty of China, came from Manchuria. Although the Manchu emperors quickly became acculturated to Chinese life, adopting Chinese as their native language, they continued to emphasize their Manchu heritage. The last emperor, Pu Yi (1906–67), in his autobiography (1964), however, admitted that he could speak only a few set phrases in Manchu and that his Manchu calligraphy was very bad. From the outset, the Qīng emperors had all important documents translated into Manchu, a practice that continued until 1911. As a result, there is an enormous amount of historical material preserved in Manchu (G. Li 2000).

11.9 Further Reading

Parpola (1994) is a lavishly illustrated book with a great deal of information about Indus writing; Parpola (1996) is a concise summary of the same information. Salomon (1996) is a brief introduction to the early Indic scripts. Lambert (1953) is a very practical introduction to the details of *Devanāgarī* and other scripts. Daniels and Bright (1996) contains chapters on all the scripts of India and Southeast Asia. Salomon (1998) is a technical description of early Indian inscriptions. Masica (1991) is an introduction to the Indo-Aryan languages. For Tibetan, Miller (1956) and van der Kuijp (1996) are concise descriptions. Roop (1972) is a practical manual for Burmese. See Poppe (1968) for Mongolian; G. Li (2000) provides information on the Manchu script.

11.10 Terms

abugida
akṣara
Devanāgarī
Dravidian
Indian grammarians
Indo-Aryan
Indus Valley
Prakrit
Sanskrit
virāma

11.11 Exercises

1 Write your own name and city in the *Devanāgarī* script, paying attention to the sound, not English spelling.

2 In §11.4.2.4, a short passage of Sanskrit was given in the *Devanāgarī* script. Below, the same Sanskrit passage is given in the Bengali script. Although today Sanskrit is usually written in *Devanāgarī* throughout India, in the past it was written in the local script, as has been done here. Notice that the language here is still Sanskrit; only the script is Bengali.

আসীদ্ রাজা নলো নাম বীরসেনসুতো বলী
উপপন্নো গুণৈর্ ইষ্টৈ" রূপবন্ অশ্বকোবিদঃ
অতিষ্ঠন্ মনুজেন্দ্রাণাং মূর্ধ্নি দেবপতির্ য়থা

(a) Write the Bengali symbols for the following consonants:

k	g
j	ṇ
t	th
d	n
p	b
m	y
s	ṁ
ḥ	l

(b) In one case, a merger in Bengali of two sounds which were distinct in Sanskrit led to the use of one symbol for both sounds in Bengali. What are the Sanskrit sounds and what is the common Bengali symbol?

	Bengali symbol
Sound A in Sanskrit (Roman symbol)	
Sound B in Sanskrit (Roman symbol)	

(c) For the following vowels show the bound and free forms found in the Bengali passage. For the bound forms, show them with the consonant <k>. Not all free forms occur. Bound long /ā/ is given for you.

	Bound	Free		Bound	Free
a			ā	কা	
i			ī		
u					
e			ai		
o					

(d) Make a list of all Bengali ligatures that occur in the text. Show their sound and their form. The ligature for /rū/ is done for you.

Sound (Roman symbol)	Form (Bengali symbol)
rū	রূ

(e) Write the following words in Bengali:

kūdhno
īśvi
iṇai

12 Maya

12.1 Background and History

During the middle of the last millennium OLD, writing was invented in Meso-America, an area of southern Mexico, Guatemala, Belize, and parts of Honduras and El Salvador. This is one of the three clear cases where writing was invented with no prior knowledge of writing. Scholars have identified a number of scripts in this area; most of them, however, have very little textual material. Recent attempts at decipherment appear to be hopeful for the Zapotec and Epi-Olmec writing (Macri 1996). Quite possibly, some of the other scripts are not writing proper, but incipient writing, that is, graphic representation which did not fully develop into writing. One Meso-American society, the **Maya**, however, clearly developed a fully fledged writing system leaving thousands of texts. Some Maya texts are written on small objects, but the majority of material is found on stone monuments, which are unfortunately now subject to weathering and looting. Four texts written on bark survived the Spanish conquest and the humid tropical climate.

The classic Maya period is dated 250–900 NEW; it was a robust, sophisticated culture, organized in interdependent city states with magnificent architecture and art. Maya culture experienced a major reorganization in the tenth century NEW, strong enough that it has often been described as a cultural collapse. Writing after this time was severely curtailed although it survived to the time of the Spanish conquest in the fifteenth century.

In 1549, a severe Roman Catholic priest from Spain, Diego de Landa, arrived in the Yucatán peninsula of Mexico. As part of his missionary work to convert the Maya to his religion, he burnt several Maya books because he considered them 'pagan'. Even the Inquisition considered some of Landa's methods a bit extreme and recalled him to Spain. As part of his defence and rehabilitation Landa wrote a document describing Maya life, which included information on the calendar and the writing system (Tozzer 1941). The document was lost for many years but resurfaced in 1863. After eleven years in Spain, Landa was sent back as a bishop to Mexico where he died. Shortly after the Spanish conquest of Meso-America, the Maya writing system was abandoned and forgotten.

Landa attempted to establish Maya equivalents for the Roman alphabet; this has come to be known as **Landa's alphabet**. This has provided Mayanists with an invaluable, although for many years puzzling, tool for the task of deciphering the Maya script. Landa's main consultant was a Yucatec speaker, Antonio Gaspar Chi, who knew some Spanish. The problem with Landa's alphabet is that the Maya symbols represent moræ, i.e., CV sequences, but Landa expected the symbols to be alphabetic. For example, he described the Maya way of writing <b>, but this is in fact the symbol for the CV-sequence /be/. Probably, Landa asked Chi how he would write the letter <b> which Landa pronounced in Spanish as /be/; thus, Chi wrote down the symbol for the mora /be/, not an alphabetic symbol for /b/ which Landa expected. An interesting example showing this confusion is Landa's report of the Maya writing for 'water'. Presumably Landa knew the Maya word for 'water' /ha/. What we actually find is a nonsense sequence of Maya symbols representing the sounds /a-tʃe-a/. Landa's question to Chi was apparently not 'How do you write /ha/?', but rather 'How do you write <h> <a>?' Landa spelled the word; in Spanish <h> is pronounced /atʃe/, and <a> /a/.

Scholarly interest in the ancient Maya began in the nineteenth century. Early archæologists were able to uncover entire cities abandoned and covered by centuries of tropical growth. This interest grew with new discoveries and continues strong today. Although the area is still populated by Maya-speaking peoples, the language and culture have changed since the time of the ancient Maya. Modern Maya speakers have little or no detailed oral tradition of historical events of the ancient period. Today, there are some 28 Maya languages spoken by four million people in the area.

In the mid-twentieth century, the leading Maya scholar was Sir Eric Thompson. Thompson was a giant in the field, and any modern Maya scholar stands on his shoulders; however, about certain important aspects of Maya culture and writing, Thompson was dead wrong. Thompson believed that the Maya texts were not writing in the sense that they represented language (i.e., phonemes and morphemes), but rather semantic ideas. He also believed that they did not represent historic events. He conceived of the ancient Maya as a peaceful and gentle folk whose priests contemplated the motions of heavenly bodies and constructed an intricate calendar, occasionally making monuments about calendrical observations. We now know that the writing expressed the Maya language, that the ancient Maya were frequently at war with each other, and that the monuments document historic events. Coe (1992) has an interesting discussion of how Thompson with his strong beliefs, persuasive elegance, and control of the pursestrings of Maya research delayed the decipherment of the Maya texts.

The key to the decipherment came when a Russian, Yuri Knorosov (1952), showed that Maya writing represented some words phonetically. Thompson strongly attacked Knorosov's theory, but it has ultimately proved correct. Shortly thereafter, another Russian, Tatiana Proskouriakoff (1960), showed that Maya texts documented historic facts. Again, Thompson criticized her work, but in the end, even he admitted that Proskouriakoff was right. From the 1970s on, enormous strides have been made and continue to be made in deciphering the Maya texts to the point now where we can understand most of them. Research has reached the point where different dialects can be identified in the texts (Vail and Macri 2000).

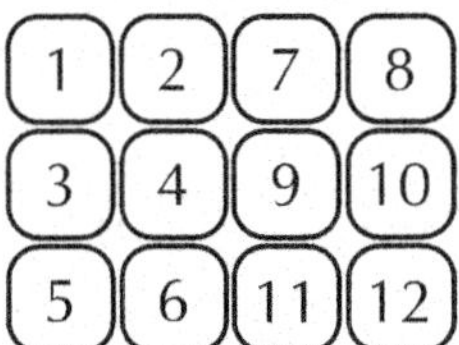

Figure 12.1 The order of reading a Maya text

12.2 Structure of the Maya Writing System

12.2.1 Internal structure

Maya writing is organized graphically as a series of squarish figures known as **glyphs**. A glyph may consist of only one grapheme, but commonly, two or more graphemes are combined into one glyph. Two graphemes may be conjoined by reducing each in size or by using only a part of each grapheme. Graphemes may be combined by attaching one to another; in this case, the **main symbol** is graphically the more prominent one, and the **diacritic** is the less prominent symbol. Diacritics may be positioned to the left, right, top, or bottom of the main symbol. More than one diacritic may occur in a single glyph. Occasionally, one grapheme is infixed or included in the other.

In general a text goes from the top left corner to the bottom right. A typical text is written in double columns and is read in a zigzag motion downwards; the numbered glyphs in figure 12.1 show the order of reading the text. In an inscription, glyphs are usually of equal size although the introductory glyphs may be of double width, i.e., occupying the space normally used by glyphs 1 and 2.

The novice reader of Maya text typically finds the correct interpretation of the symbols very difficult and frustrating. Often the distinguishing part of two different symbols is a relatively small portion; and conversely, two rather different-looking elements may in fact be variants of the same symbol.

Plate 6 is an inscription from around 765 NEW depicting the presentation of captives to a ruler. Note particularly the integration of the several short texts with the picture.

12.2.2 Relation to language

Maya writing has four types of symbols: **morphograms**, **moraic** symbols, **semantic complements**, and **phonological complements**. Morphograms represent morphemes; moraic symbols are phonographic, representing CV sequences. The complements provide additional information to secure the proper reading where it might otherwise be ambiguous. Semantic complements are rather rare, but phonological complements are quite common.

Plate 6 Maya inscription, *ca.* 785 NEW. Presentation of captives to a Maya ruler, Usamacinta River Valley. Kimbell Art Museum, Fort Worth, Texas. Reproduced courtesy of the Kimbell Art Museum

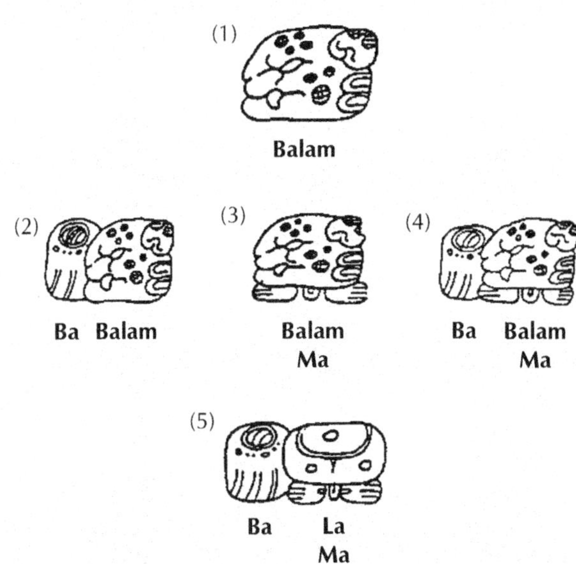

Figure 12.2 Different ways of writing /balam/

The word /balam/ 'jaguar' can be written in a number of different ways (figure 12.2). One way is simply to use the morphographic symbol alone (1). Alternatively, this morphographic symbol could be accompanied by a phonological complements /ba/ written as a prefix (2). Or, a phonological complement /ma/ could be written as a suffix (3). Note that the vowel /a/ is chosen for the suffix since the last vowel of /balam/ is an /a/; the /a/ of the suffix /ma/ in this case is a dummy vowel and not intended to be pronounced – it is there simply because the script only has CV-sized phonographic units. A further possible writing of the word is that both a prefix and a suffix could be written (4). Or, the word could be written entirely phonemically as /ba-la-ma/ (again with the /a/ of /ma/ being a dummy vowel) (5).

Note how the alternative writings of Maya resemble the possibilities in Egyptian. Egyptian, however, tended to pick one alternative and use it regularly. Maya, on the other hand, seemed to enjoy using the available variation.

Aside from the different ways of constructing glyphs just discussed, other kinds of variation occur. Not infrequently, two unrelated graphs are simply two ways of writing the same element; for example, figure 12.3 shows alternative ways of writing 'zero'. Many morphographs have special **head variants**, which tend to be used in more prominent positions. These have some part of the normal variant attached as a diacritic to a human head. For some graphs, there is also a **full-figure variant** involving an entire human body. These are usually double-width glyphs found in introductory material.

Maya scribes tended to exploit different possible ways of writing the same thing. In a text, one frequently sees the same word written differently. Even the names of Maya kings and cities show variation in writing. Perhaps to the Maya, to use the same writing too close together was æsthetically unpleasing, just as in English we tend to avoid using the same word twice too close together.

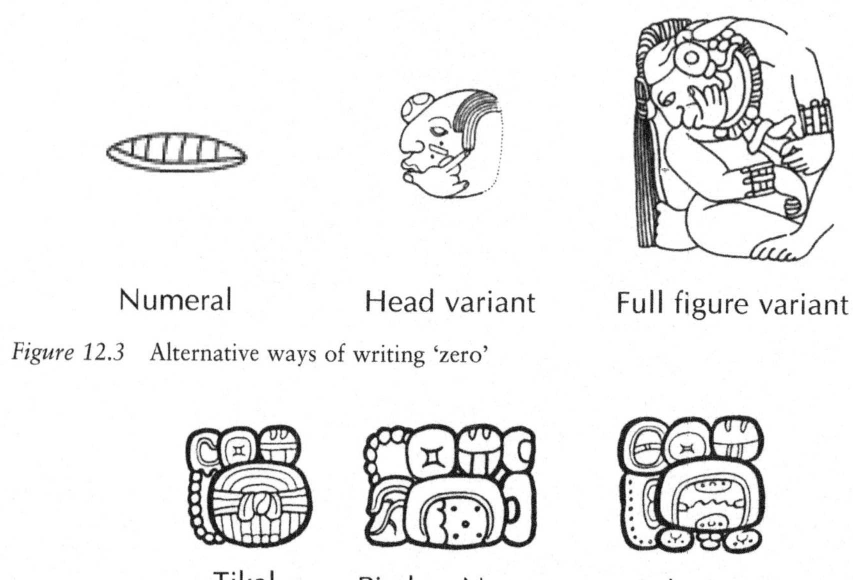

Figure 12.3 Alternative ways of writing 'zero'

Figure 12.4 Emblem glyphs for three Maya cities

Certain kinds of glyphs have received special attention in Maya studies. The verbal glyphs found on monuments provide information about 'birth', 'death', 'accession', 'marriage', 'waging war', 'bloodletting', etc. Some mark the end of a calendrical period. Many verbal affixes have been identified.

Other glyphs give the names and titles of rulers. A common title is *ahaw*, the king of each major site, although *ahaw* could also be part of the title of a lesser dignitary. Names of dignitaries are commonly followed by the names of their parents.

Emblem glyphs (figure 12.4) were recognized in the 1950s. Each is peculiar to a particular city. Typically, they have /ch'ul/ 'holy' (appearing as a string of blood droplets) prefixed, a superfixed form of *ahaw*, and a main symbol which identifies the locality. The Palenque emblem glyph means 'the Holy Lord of Palenque'.

12.3 The Maya Calendar

Dates are a prominent feature of Maya inscriptions; frequently every sentence of a text begins with a date. The Maya had a very complicated calendar which was a part of the general Meso-American culture. In few other ancient cultures do we have the precise dating that we have for Maya history. Rather than saying that something happened between 500 and 550, as we often do for other cultures, for Maya events we can often say, for example, that it happened on 2 August 521.

First, let us consider our own calendar for a moment. We have two independent cycles. One cycle is a weekly cycle of seven days with each day named in turn, Monday, Tuesday, etc. This seven-day cycle continues indefinitely with no variation whatsoever. The other cycle is a yearly one of 12 months: January, February, etc. Again this cycle continues indefinitely. Each month consists of 28, 30, or 31 days according to a set formula. This gives a year of 365 days. Actually, a year is a bit less than 365.25 days long. The Julian calendar assumed that a year was exactly 365.25 days long and added one day to the yearly cycle every four years (a leap year); the seven-day weekly cycle treats the leap day as an ordinary day and is not altered by leap years. To distinguish years from each other, we need an arbitrary reference point. For us, that is midnight between 31 December 1 OLD and 1 January 1 NEW. Years are numbered consecutively before and after this point. Dates before this arbitrary point we call OLD and dates after this as NEW (see note on dates on p. xvii).

Over time, the slight deviation from the 365.25-day year had accumulated, and by the eighteenth century NEW, the Julian calendar was eleven days late. The Gregorian calendar attempts to fix this problem: years divisible by 400 are leap years (as is 2000), but other years divisible by 100 are not (1900, 2100). Most western European countries adopted the revised Gregorian calendar in the late eighteenth and nineteenth centuries. Other countries adopted the Gregorian calendar in the twentieth century. You may be familiar with date differences between the Western and the Orthodox Churches; this is because the Orthodox Church retained the Julian calendar. In the following discussion, Gregorian dates are used.

Next, let's review the Maya numbering system (figure 12.5) which is vigesimal, i.e., based on the number 20. *One* is written as one dot; *two*, as two dots; *three*, as three dots; and *four*, as four dots. *Five* is written as a bar. *Six* is a bar and one dot, and so on up to *ten* which is two bars. *Nineteen* is three bars and four dots. For larger numbers a positional system was used similar to our decimal system. For *one*, we write 1; for *ten*, we write 1 but one position to the left, adding a zero – 10; for a *hundred*, we put the 1 in the third column to the left – 100. The Maya used a similar system but based on twenty (figure 12.5). To write 20, one puts one dot in the second row from the bottom. Two dots would be 40, and so on. Since numbers in any one row extend from 0 to 19, a single dot in the third row would be 400. A single dot in the fourth row would be 8000, etc. There was a special symbol for zero.

Now let's look at the Maya calendar. A day is a *k'in*. *K'ins* are organized into a number of larger units (table 12.1).

The arbitrary first day of the Maya calendar is 13 August 3114 OLD (Mathews 1996). We do not know why this date was selected. It appears to be an imaginary date in Maya history since it predates by far any known Maya settlement in Meso-America. Although there is some disagreement, most scholars use the Goodman-Martînez-Thompson (GMT) correlation of Maya and Gregorian dates.

Table 12.1 Calendar units

20 *k'ins*	=	1 *winal*	=	20 days
18 *winals*	=	1 *tun*	=	360 days
20 *tuns*	=	1 *k'atun*	=	7200 days
20 *k'atuns*	=	1 *bak'tun*	=	144,000 days

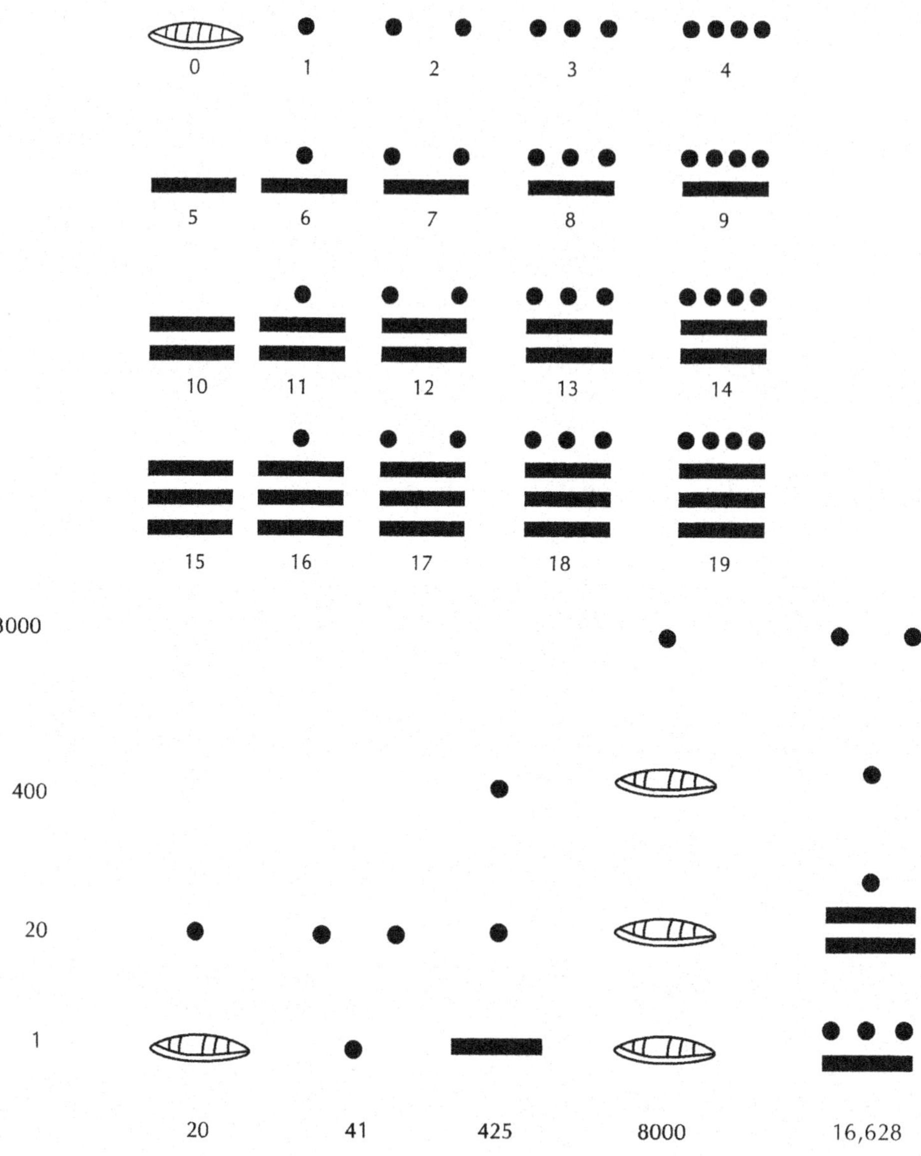

Figure 12.5 Maya numbers

A date can be specified as a certain period of time from the arbitrary first day. For example, the Gregorian date of 26 February 607 NEW would be 9 *bak'tuns*, 8 *kat'uns*, 13 *tuns*, 12 *winals*, 18 *k'ins* after the arbitrary first day. Mayanists abbreviate this as 9.8.13.12.18. The following day would be 9.8.13.12.19, and the day after that would be 9.8.13.13.0 since 20 *k'ins* equal one *winal*. Maya dates recorded like this in reference to the arbitrary first day are known as **long counts**. The system of using long counts was a Maya invention. It lasted until the reorganization of the

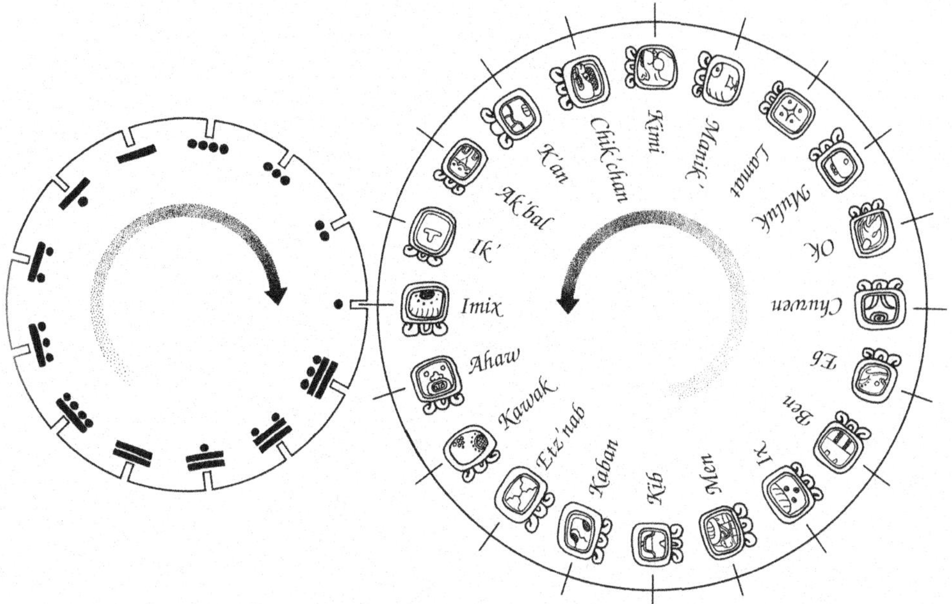

Figure 12.6 Maya calendar showing the *tz'olkin*: the number of the day is determined by the left wheel and the name of the day by the right wheel. The day shown is 1 *Imix*; the next day will be 2 *Ik'*, and the day after that will be 3 *Ak'bal*

classical Maya world in the tenth century NEW. The earliest recorded long count is a decorative pendant dated 8.4.0.0.0 (120 NEW); the last recorded long count was 10.4.0.0.0 (909 NEW) at Toniná (Schele and Freidel 1990).

Independent from the long counts, the Maya, along with other peoples of Meso-America, also had a complex cyclical calendar, known as a **calendar round**, consisting of two parts. One part is known as the *tz'olkin*, which can be portrayed as two interlocking wheels (figure 12.6) turning in opposite directions. One wheel (left) has 13 numbers; the other wheel (right) has 20 named days. The order of the days is shown in the figure from *Imix* to *Ahaw*. Every day, both wheels advance one notch. For example, the first day is 1 *Imix*; the following day is 2 *Ik'*; the third day is 3 *Ak'bal*; the fourth, 4 *K'an*, etc. until 13 *Ben*. The day following 13 *Ben* is 1 *Ix*; the number wheel has returned to 1, but the name wheel still has further names. The twentieth day is 7 *Ahaw*; the day following this is 8 *Imix*; and then 9 *Ik'*, etc. The entire cycle takes 260 days to complete. The 259th day is 12 *Kawak*, the 260th is 13 *Ahaw*, and the cycle starts over with 1 *Imix*. The *tz'olkin* cycle continues indefinitely, repeating every 260 days. In texts, the *tz'olkin* date is represented by a number prefixed to a morphograph of the day name.

The second part of the calendar round is the *haab*. The *haab* can be thought of as another large wheel (not shown) of 365 days (in Maya studies, this is often called a **vague year** since it is about 1/4 day short of the solar year). On this wheel, the year is divided into 19 named months. The first 18 months have 20 days each, and the last month *Wayeb* has 5 days. Within the months, the consecutive days are simply numbered. The first day is 1 *Pohp*, the second is 2 *Pohp*. The last day of *Pohp* is, however, not called 20 *Pohp*, but rather the 'seating of *Wo*', usually written as '0 *Wo*'. The next day is then 1 *Wo*, and then 2 *Wo*, until 0 *Zip*. The second last day of the year is 4 *Wayeb*; the last day is 0 *Pohp*; and the *haab* cycle begins again with 1 *Pohp*. Like the *tz'olkin* the *haab* cycle continues indefinitely, repeating every 365 days. In texts, the *haab* date is represented by a number prefixed to a morphograph of the name of the month.

The calendar round consists of the interaction of the two cycles, the *tz'olkin* and the *haab*. For example, we know that the arbitrary first day of the Maya calendar was 4 *Ahaw* 8 *Kumk'u*. The next day after this was 5 *Imix* 9 *Kumk'u*. The tenth day after this was 2 *Chuwen* 19 *Kumk'u*. The following day would have been 3 *Eb* 0 *Wayeb*. Together, the *tz'olkin* and the *haab* describe a period of 18,980 days or 52 years. At the end of 52 years, the calendar round starts over. The calendar round was not limited to the Maya, but was used throughout Meso-America. In fact, it continues even today in many Maya communities with a local person designated as responsible for keeping track of the date accurately.

In Maya texts, dates are written in different ways. The fullest version is the **initial series** found at the beginning of the text: first the long count date, then the calendar round date. This was often followed by other calendrical information such as the number of days since the last new moon. Later in a text, dates were given as a **distance number** showing a date as a distance from some other date, e.g., '4238 days earlier' or '382 days later'. Distance dates are written in the reverse order of long counts, starting with the smallest unit.

The Maya celebrated the completion of a larger 'round' period, that is the end of a *tun*, *k'atun*, or *bak'tun*, much as we might celebrate the end of century or millennium. If such an end of a period occurs within the timeframe of the text, such a date might be mentioned, e.g., '8 *Ahaw* 13 *Keh*, end of a *bak'tun*'.

12.4 Example Text

We will now examine a short passage of a text from Palenque (/pə'lɛŋkej/), an ancient Maya city in the modern state of Chiapas in Mexico. Palenque is a city of magnificent architecture, and it also contains many records of its important history. In one building, an inscription was found with a design of a cross in the centre. This tablet is known as the Tablet of the Cross. It records a number of important events about various rulers of Palenque. The decipherment of this text was the combined work of several people; I am following the analysis given by Mathews (1996).

Maya scholars use letters to identify the columns and numbers for the rows. We will examine the text S13–S17. Recall that we read a text zigzagging down a double set of columns; the columns relevant for this text are R and S. The syntax in this sentence is distance marker – $verb_1$ – subject – $verb_2$ – date. Roughly this is equivalent to English 'A certain period of time (distance marker) after the date when the subject did $verb_1$, he/she did $verb_2$'.

The easiest place to start a Maya text is with the dates; they are usually quite obvious because they contain numbers, which are easy to recognize. The first three glyphs (S13–S14) contain numbers giving information about a date.

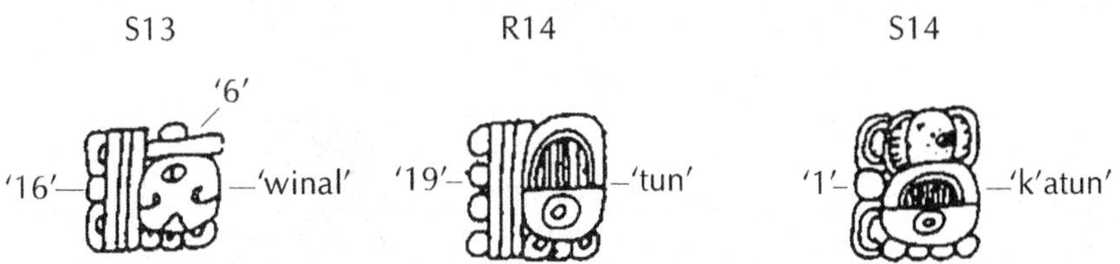

Figure 12.7 The first three glyphs of Text S13–17 showing the date: 1.19.6.16 (in reverse order) (from Dr. Merle Greene Robertson, *The Sculpture of Palenque*, Vol. IV, S13/17 (including R14–R17). Princeton: Princeton University Press, 1991. © 1976 by Merle Greene Robertson. Reproduced with permission)

Table 12.2 Calculation of the distance number 1.19.6.16

k'atuns	*tuns*	*winals*	*k'ins*
1	= 20	= 360	= 7200
	19	= 342	= 6480
		6	= 120
			16
		Total	13,816

The first glyph (S13), in fact, has two numbers (figure 12.7): the first is 16 written vertically at the left. Each of the three bars represents 5, and the central ball is 1. The two handle-like objects at the top left and bottom left simply fill the space around the ball. We will leave aside for the moment what is being counted. The second half of the glyph has the number 6 written horizontally at the top, and a circular element with three balls at the bottom. By consulting a list of calendar units, we can find that the circular element is the symbol for *winal*. Thus, we have '16 X and 6 *winals*'.

The next glyph (R14) gives us 19 *tuns*. Finally, S14 shows 1 *k'atun*. So far, our date reads 16 X, 6 *winals*, 19 *tuns*, 1 *k'atun*. This is not a long count since we have no indication of *bak'tun*. Rather, it is a distance marker showing a certain period of time distant from another date, rather as we might say 'two years, three months, and four days after X'. Now, let's return to the first number 16. We have the units *winal*, *tun*, and *k'atun* explicitly expressed in the order of increasing size. We can see that the day unit of *k'in* would logically occur before *winal*; thus, the number 16 implicitly refers to *k'ins*. The entire distance marker is 16 *k'ins*, 6 *winals*, 19 *tuns*, and 1 *k'atun*. Recall that distance numbers are always written in this order, the reverse of the way they would be written at the beginning of an inscription. Modern scholars abbreviate both types the same way, starting with the largest unit; thus our distance number is 1.19.6.16. If we do the arithmetic (table 12.2), we can see that this is equivalent to 13,816 days or almost 38 years.

The glyph R15 gives the first verb (figure 12.8). Although it may be difficult for neophytes to see, scholars recognize the main element as a frog's head facing upwards.

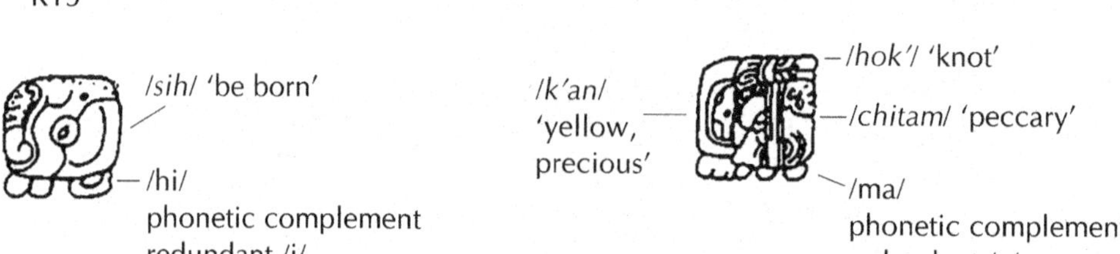

Figure 12.8 The verb and subject of Text S13–17 (from Dr. Merle Greene Robertson, *The Sculpture of Palenque*, Vol. IV, S13/17 (including R14–R17). Princeton: Princeton University Press, 1991. © 1976 by Merle Greene Robertson. Reproduced with permission)

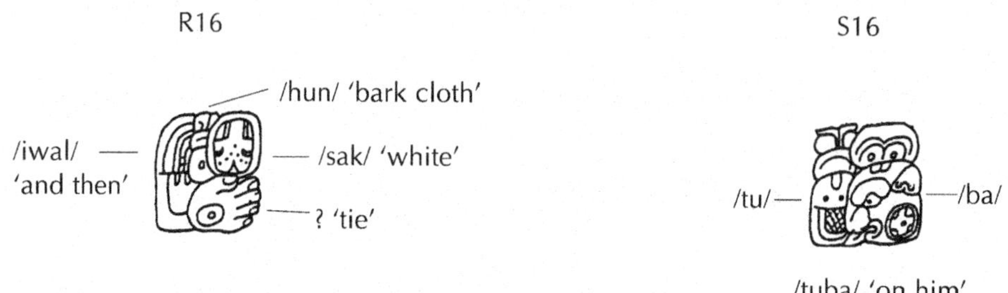

Figure 12.9 The second verbal phrase of Text S13–17 (from Dr. Merle Greene Robertson, *The Sculpture of Palenque*, Vol. IV, S13/17 (including R14–R17). Princeton: Princeton University Press, 1991. © 1976 by Merle Greene Robertson. Reproduced with permission)

It has been identified as meaning 'he/she was born' and had the sound /sih/. The phonetic element /hi/ is suffixed to the main element as a phonological complement. Morphograms are shown in italics, and phonograms in regular type.

The subject of the text is given by the glyph S15. Mathews (1996) identifies this person as the king *K'an-Hok'-Chitam I*. The prefix at the left with the cross is /k'an/ meaning 'yellow' or 'precious' (the latter alternative probably more appropriate here). The main element shows a head with a vertical cloth band tied at the top. The cloth band was a symbol of kingship. Mathews identifies this as /hok'/ meaning 'knot' (metaphorically ascending the throne). The head appears to be that of a peccary /chitam/ (a peccary is a pig-like mammal of Central and South America). Finally, the phonological complement /ma/ is suffixed at the bottom; only the consonant /m/ is intended to be pronounced. Together this gives the name *K'an-Hok'-Chitam*. So far our text reads something like '13,816 days after *K'an-Hok'-Chitam* was born'.

The second verb is given in two glyphs R16–S16 (figure 12.9). R16 means 'and then, he acceded to the throne', literally 'and then, he tied the white bark cloth', although not all details are clear. The main glyph presumably means 'tie' but a clear reading has not yet been made. Three superfixes are found here: from left to right, /iwal/ 'and then'; this shows clearly that the activity of the second verb

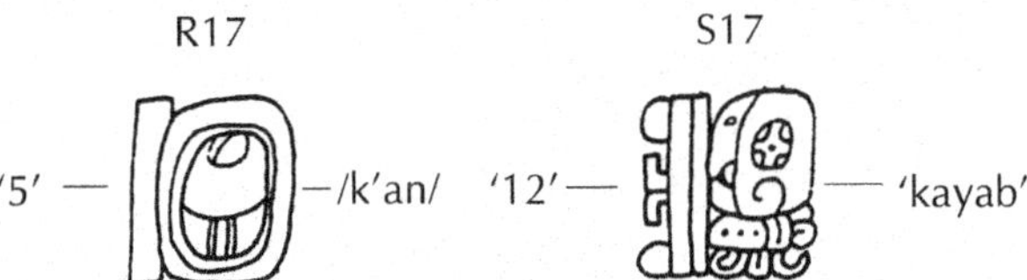

Figure 12.10 Calendar round of the accession date of Text S13–17 (from Dr. Merle Greene Robertson, *The Sculpture of Palenque*, Vol. IV, S13/17 (including R14–R17). Princeton: Princeton University Press, 1991. © 1976 by Merle Greene Robertson. Reproduced with permission)

follows that of the first. The other two prefixes state the object: /sak/ 'white', /hun/ 'bark cloth'. The whole glyph would read /iwal . . . sak hun/ 'and then he [tied] the white bark cloth'.

The second glyph of the second verb S16 is simply /tu-ba/ 'on him'; i.e., 'he tied the cloth on himself'. This is written phonetically: /tu/ is on the left, and /ba/ on the right.

The final two glyphs R17–S17 (figure 12.10) give a calendar round giving the day of the accession to the throne. The *tz'olkin* is *5 K'an*, and the *haab* is 12 *K'ayab*. Remember that a calendar round date recurs every 52 years. From other dates on the text, however, we can be fairly sure that this occurrence of 5 *K'an* 12 *K'ayab* is the day with the long count of 9.4.14.10.4.

Our text now can be translated in full: 'When 16 *k'ins*, 6 *winals*, 19 *tuns*, and 1 *k'atun* had passed after *K'an-Hok'-Chitam I* was born, he then tied the white band on himself [= became king] on 5 *K'an* 12 *K'ayab* [9.4.14.10.4].' According to Mathews (1996), this would have been pronounced as /waklahun, wak winik-hi bolonlahun tun-i hun k'atum sih-i k'an-hok'-chitam iwal . . . -hi sak hun tu-ba ho? k'an lahcha? k'anasi/. We know that *K'an-Hok'-Chitam I* was 1.19.6.16 old when he acceded to the throne on 9.4.14.10.4. Therefore, if we subtract 1.19.6.16 from 9.4.14.10.4, we get the day of his birth – 9.2.15.3.8 (= Wednesday, 21 February 529, in Gregorian).

	9.	4.	14.	10.	4
–		1.	19.	6.	16
	9.	2.	15.	3.	8

12.5 Further Reading

Maya studies has not evolved to the point where there is a good deal of secondary literature which is easily accessible to the uninitiated. Coe (1999) and Sharer (1994) are introductions to Maya culture generally. Montgomery (2002) is the most general treatment of the script. Other information on Maya writing is to be found in Harris and Stearns (1992), Houston (1989), Macri (1996), Lounsbury (1989), Mathews (1996), J. Thompson (1950), and Vail and Macri (2000). Coe (1992) is a fascinating account of the history of the Maya decipherment. The late Linda Schele was central in the decipherment and has a number of works which consider specific texts and provide information on both Maya writing and art: Schele and Freidel (1990), Schele and Miller (1986), and Schele and Mathews (1998).

12.6 Terms

calendar round
diacritic
distance number
emblem glyph
full-figure variant
glyph
haab
head variant
initial series
Landa's alphabet
long count
main symbol
Maya
moraic
morphogram
phonological complement
semantic complement
tz'olkin
vague year

12.7 Exercises

1 What are the structural similarities and differences between the Maya and Egyptian writing systems?
2 Assume that the long count for 1 January 2000 was 12.19.6.15.2. Calculate the long count for today's date.
3 Express the distance between today and 1 January 2000 as a series of Maya units: e.g., XX *tuns*, YY *winals*, ZZ *k'ins*.

13 Other Writing Systems

This chapter describes seven interesting writing systems which do not fit neatly into other chapters. Although most native North American languages have been written by borrowing and adapting the Roman alphabet through contact with the Spanish, French, and English, a number of indigenous scripts have been invented. We will examine three: Cherokee, Cree, and Inuktitut (see W. Walker 1996 for details about other North American writing systems). Later, we discuss two European systems: runic and ogham. Then we look at Pahawh Hmong from Southeast Asia, one of the world's most recently developed writing systems. Finally, we look at Bliss, perhaps the only semantically based writing system.

13.1 Cherokee

13.1.1 Background and history

Cherokee is an Iroquois language spoken in the United States in North Carolina and Oklahoma. Around 1820, Sequoyah (*ca.* 1770–1843), a previously illiterate native speaker of Cherokee, developed a moraic script for his language. Visually, many of the Cherokee symbols are drawn from upper-case Roman letters. Others are alterations of Roman letters or invented symbols. Although the Cherokee symbols may in part resemble Roman letters in their shape, the system differs in two important ways from the Roman alphabet: first, the Cherokee system is moraic, not alphabetic; and second, the values of the Cherokee symbols have no relation to their ordinary values in the Roman alphabet. These facts are consistent with the reports that Sequoyah was previously illiterate and unfamiliar with Roman letters except as graphic symbols.

By 1821, Sequoyah had publicized his writing system, and it spread rapidly amongst the Cherokee. It has been used for a large variety of personal and published writing, particularly for record-keeping of native medical treatments and for Christian publications, including a New Testament and a hymnal.

Shortly after the development of the Cherokee script, an American missionary, Samuel Worcester, arranged to have a type font cast for printing. Worcester also devised the transliteration scheme most often used for Cherokee. Scancarelli (1996) reports that reading pronunciations, based on Worcester's transliteration, are sometimes heard.

Table 13.1 The phonemes of Cherokee

	t		k	k^w	ʔ	i		u
	ts					e	ə̃	o
	tl						a	
	s				h			
	l							
m	n							
w		j						

Table 13.2 The symbols of Cherokee

Ꭰ a, ʔa		Ꭱ e, ʔe	Ꭲ i, ʔi	Ꭳ o, ʔo	Ꭴ u, ʔu	Ꭵ ə̃, ʔə̃
Ꭶ ka	Ꭷ k^{h}a	Ꭸ ke, k^{h}e	Ꭹ ki, k^{h}i	Ꭺ ko, k^{h}o	Ꭻ ku, k^{h}u	Ꭼ kə̃, k^{h}ə̃
Ꭽ ha		Ꭾ he	Ꭿ hi	Ꮀ ho	Ꮁ hu	Ꮂ hə̃
Ꮃ la, hla		Ꮄ le, hle	Ꮅ li, hli	Ꮆ lo, hlo	Ꮇ lu, hlu	Ꮈ lə̃, hlə̃
Ꮉ ma		Ꮊ me	Ꮋ mi	Ꮌ mo	Ꮍ mu	
Ꮎ na	Ꮏ hna	Ꮑ ne, hne	Ꮒ ni, hni	Ꮓ no, hno	Ꮔ nu, hnu	Ꮕ nə̃, hnə̃
Ꮖ kwa, k^{h}wa		Ꮗ kwe, k^{h}we	Ꮘ kwi, k^{h}wi	Ꮙ kwo, k^{h}wo	Ꮚ kwu, k^{h}wu	Ꮛ kwə̃, k^{h}wə̃
Ꮝ s	Ꮜ sa	Ꮞ se	Ꮟ si	Ꮠ so	Ꮡ su	Ꮢ sə̃
Ꮣ ta		Ꮥ te	Ꮧ ti	Ꮩ to, t^{h}o	Ꮪ tu, t^{h}u	Ꮫ tə̃, t^{h}ə̃
Ꮤ t^{h}a		Ꮦ t^{h}e	Ꮨ t^{h}i			
Ꮬ tla	Ꮭ t^{h}la	Ꮮ tle, t^{h}le	Ꮯ tli, t^{h}li	Ꮰ tlo, t^{h}lo	Ꮱ tlu, t^{h}lu	Ꮲ tlə̃, t^{h}lə̃
Ꮳ tsa, ts^{h}a		Ꮴ tse, ts^{h}e	Ꮵ tsi, ts^{h}i	Ꮶ tso, ts^{h}o	Ꮷ tsu, ts^{h}u	Ꮸ tsə̃, ts^{h}ə̃
Ꮹ wa, hwa		Ꮺ we, hwe	Ꮻ wi, hwi	Ꮼ wo, hwo	Ꮽ wu, hwu	Ꮾ wə̃, hwə̃
Ꮿ ja, hja		Ᏸ je, hje	Ᏹ ji, hji	Ᏺ jo, hjo	Ᏻ ju, hju	Ᏼ jə̃, hjə̃

Although the number of speakers of Cherokee is small today, the script continues to be used in newsletters and other publications.

13.1.2 *Phonology of Cherokee*

The phonemes of Cherokee are shown in table 13.1.

13.1.3 *The Cherokee script*

The symbols of the Cherokee script according to Worcester's arrangement are given in table 13.2 with a phonetic transcription.

The Cherokee writing system is essentially moraic except for Ꮝ <s> which is used for /s/ in onset clusters and in coda position. In CV sequences, /s/ is written moraically: **Ꮜ Ꮞ Ꮟ Ꮠ Ꮡ Ꮢ** /sa se si so su sə̃/.

In relation to the phonology, the orthographic system is **underdifferentiated** (some phonemic contrasts are not represented in the writing system) in various ways. A null onset is not distinguished from one with a glottal stop: e.g., **Ꭰ** /a, ʔa/. The onsets /l, hl/, /kw, kʰw/, /ts, tsʰ/, /w, hw/, /j, hj/ are not distinguished in writing. The onsets /k, kʰ/, /n, hn/, /tl, tʰl/ are distinguished before /a/, but not before the other vowels. The onsets /t, tʰ/ are distinguished before /a, e, i/, but not before /u, o, ə̃/. Scancarelli (1992) says that the points of underdifferentiation with respect to the aspirated and unaspirated stops have relatively little role in distinguishing morphemes. She argues that places where Sequoyah did maintain plain–aspirated contrasts are those whose 'frequent appearance simply made them perceptually significant to him'.

Codal /h/ or /ʔ/ is not written, nor is vowel length nor tone. The symbol **Ꮐ** is shown in some versions for /nah/, but Walker (1996) says that it is not used.

To indicate onset clusters or codal consonants not otherwise provided for, the consonant is written with a dummy vowel. For example, /ktʰoːʔa/ 'it is hanging' is written as **ᎬᏙᎠ** <kə̃-to-a>.

13.2 Cree

13.2.1 *Background and history*

In Canada, around 1840, John Evans, a Methodist missionary from England, developed the writing system widely known as *Cree syllabics*. Evans began working on writing systems for Ojibwa when he was in Ontario, using both the Roman alphabet and scripts he devised himself. After moving to Norway House in Rupert's Land (now Manitoba) in 1840, he developed the Cree writing system.

The Cree system spread rapidly. Reports from the late nineteenth century say that virtually every adult Cree speaker was literate; even allowing for some exaggeration, Cree may have had one of the highest literacy rates in the world at the time. At first, the churches opposed the use of Evans' system, as well as the use of Cree itself. The successful spread of Cree writing, without institutional support, however, led the churches eventually to support the Cree script. In 1861, an entire Bible was published in London in Cree writing.

Some small geographic (see the east–west differences in writing codal consonants in table 13.4) and even sectarian variants of the Cree system have arisen. Until the mid-twentieth century, published material tended to be limited to religious material. Since then, however, an increasing amount of secular material has been published using the Cree system, such as schoolbooks, popular magazines, and government publications.

The Cree system has been used for other languages at times, such as the Athapaskan languages Chippeweyan and Carrier; the most successful of these borrowings, however, has been into Inuktitut (§13.3).

Evans was familiar with Sequoyah's writing for Cherokee, with *Devanāgarī* (chapter 11) from India, and also with Pitman shorthand. He apparently drew on shorthand for the shapes of the symbols. Possibly Evans' use of rotation of the consonants to show different vowels was inspired by such models. He might also have been influenced by his knowledge of *Devanāgarī* which treats the consonant as basic and writes vowels as diacritic symbols before, after, above, or under the consonant (depending on the particular vowel).

13.2.2 *Phonology of Cree*

Cree is an Algonquian language, closely related to Ojibwa and Montagnais. It is spoken in central Canada, from northern Québec across northern Ontario into Manitoba. The phonemes of Cree are given in table 13.3.

The phonotactic structure of the Cree syllable is quite simple: (C) V (C). Thus a mora is either a syllable-initial CV sequence or a codal (final) consonant.

13.2.3 *Structure of the Cree writing system*

In the Cree writing system, the symbols represent moræ, i.e., either initial CV sequences (table 13.4) or a codal consonant. With the initial CV symbols, the shape of the symbol determines the consonant, and its orientation determines the vowel. For example, when the symbol points down, the vowel is /e/; when it points to the right, the vowel is /o/; etc. There are also special symbols for codal moræ with different western and eastern versions although <h> is the same in both. The western codal symbols are distinct from the rest of the system; the eastern version of these is a small version of the main symbol (with the /a/ vowel). The first row of table 13.4

Table 13.3 The phonemes of Cree

p	t	tʃ	k	i iː	o oː
m	n			eː	a aː
	s	ʃ			
w	r l	j			

Table 13.4 The symbols of Cree

	e	*i*	*o*	*a*	*Final*	
					West	*East*
Ø	ᐁ	ᐃ	ᐅ	ᐊ		
p	ᐯ	ᐱ	ᐳ	ᐸ	ᑊ	ᑉ
t	ᑌ	ᑎ	ᑐ	ᑕ	ᐟ	ᑦ
c	ᒉ	ᒋ	ᒍ	ᒐ	ᐨ	ᒡ
k	ᑫ	ᑭ	ᑯ	ᑲ	ᐠ	ᒃ
m	ᒣ	ᒥ	ᒧ	ᒪ	ᒼ	ᒻ
n	ᓀ	ᓂ	ᓄ	ᓇ	ᐣ	ᓐ
s	ᓭ	ᓯ	ᓱ	ᓴ	ᐢ	ᔅ
ʃ	ᔐ	ᔑ	ᔓ	ᔕ	ᐡ	ᔥ
w	·ᐁ	·ᐃ	·ᐅ	·ᐊ	ᐤ	
j	ᔦ	ᔨ	ᔪ	ᔭ	ᐩ	ᔾ
l	ᓓ	ᓕ	ᓗ	ᓚ	ᓬ	ᓪ
r	ᕃ	ᕆ	ᕈ	ᕋ	ᕒ	ᕐ
h					ᐦ	

gives the symbols for a null onset; i.e., a vowel with no preceding consonant. An onset /w/ is written as the null onset symbol with a preceding diacritic dot. Vowel length can be indicated by a superscript dot: ᐲ /piː/, ᑳ /kaː/.

Let us now examine the symbol orientation more closely. In all cases, the forms for the vowels /o/ and /a/ are mirror images of each other; i.e., one is formed by flipping the other over (however, the dot for /w/ is always at the left). Beyond this, there are three different orientational patterns. For <Ø p t w r>, the <e> symbols point down; these are rotated 180° to give the <i> series. A further 90° clockwise rotation produces the symbols for <o>.

The symbols for <c k m n s j l>, however, follow a different pattern of orientation. Starting with the symbols for <e>, they are flipped on a vertical axis to give the symbols for <i>. The <i> symbols are then rotated 180° to give the symbols for <o>. The third pattern is used only for <ʃ> which is similar to the second pattern, but the symbol for <ʃe> is rotated 135° clockwise to give <ʃo>.

McCarthy (1995) points out different styles of writing Cree. In more informal writing, vowel length and codal consonants are usually not marked although considerable personal and dialectal variation exists. In formal writing, and in published material, the vowel length and syllable-final consonants are usually indicated.

The classification of the Cree writing system is not completely straightforward. McCarthy (1995) points out that writers of Cree learn the symbols as distinct entities and think of them as equivalent to individual spoken syllables. In discussions about other so-called syllabaries (e.g., Japanese *kana*, Cherokee), we have pointed out that the systems are not really syllabaries, but moraic systems. Thus, we can argue that Cree is a moraic writing system. Note, however, that when we organize *kana* and Cherokee symbols so that the ones with the same consonant are in the same row and those with the same vowel are in the same column, we do not find any recurring graphic pattern in either rows or columns. For Cree, however, the situation is different; the rows and columns each share a certain pattern. The shape of the symbol shows the consonant, and the orientation is a diacritic showing the vowel; the structure of the symbol is transparent, and we can identify the consonant and the vowel components separately. To some degree, then, Cree is like an abugida where the vowels are written as diacritics; however, it is different from a typical abugida in that all vowels are written and there are no consonant clusters. In my view, the Cree writing system is basically moraic with some attributes of an abugida.

Walker (1996) argues that the different orientation patterns used to indicate vowels 'can only have caused great difficulty for the many thousands of people who have struggled to become literate in Cree-Ojibwa syllabics'. Walker's objection seems ill-founded; Cree speakers report instead that the system is remarkably easy to learn. One part of the explanation of Walker's problem is McCarthy's observation, mentioned above, that speakers learn the individual symbols as distinct entities. Although they may be aware cognitively of the orientational pattern of the system, they do not make extensive use of this structure in learning or using the system. Further, coping with three slightly different patterns of orientation seems trivial when compared with the capability of the human mind for dealing with anomalies and irregularities of language and writing.

One drawback to the use of orientation that is occasionally mentioned is that children do not acquire a clear sense of geometric orientation until an age sometime after they have usually started writing. Consider, for example, the confusion that children who use the Roman alphabet often have with the letters <b d> and <p q>. Children thus might find a writing system that depends so crucially on orientation confusing. No hard evidence on this point seems to exist.

The Cree script is an example of the development of a script, as opposed to the invention or borrowing of writing. Clearly, Evans was literate, in fact, familar with several languages and scripts. What is new in the Cree script is the shapes of the symbols, and especially the use of orientation as a diacritic to indicate vowels.

13.3 Inuktitut

13.3.1 Background and history

Inuktitut is spoken across the North American arctic from Greenland to Alaska. In Canada, the terms *Inuit* and *Inuktitut* have come to replace the older word *Eskimo*, a pejorative term from Algonquian, meaning 'meat eater'. The *Inuit* are the people, and *Inuktitut* is the language.

By the mid-nineteenth century, the Anglican missionaries John Horden and E. A. Watkins, working in James Bay with Cree speakers, adapted the Cree writing system for writing Inuktitut. Another missionary, Edmund Peck, who is often incorrectly given credit for creating the Inuktitut script (Harper 1983), was instrumental in spreading the system after 1876, publishing translations of portions of the Bible and other materials. Although the Inuktitut system was sometimes taught in missionary or other schools, it was more often learned from parents or other users. Many first-hand reports describe the system as extremely easy to learn. The Inuktitut script has been widely used by the Inuit in most of Canada except in Labrador. Roman-based systems are used in Alaska and Greenland.

The Inuktitut borrowing showed considerable conservatism until recently, keeping closely to the original Cree model. Many symbols from the Cree system were used for Inuktitut with no difficulty. Although not representing exactly the same phonetic sound, the Cree symbol for <c> was reassigned to Inuktitut /ɡ/ (ᒋ etc.), and the Cree symbol for /r/ was reassigned to Inuktitut /ʁ/ (ᕋ etc.); similarly, the symbols for Cree /o/ were reassigned to Inuktitut /u/ (ᐅ etc.). The resulting system was still **underdifferentiated** by not providing for the Inuktitut sounds /q ŋ v ɬ/. It was also **overdifferentiated** by retaining the Cree four-vowel system, whereas Inuktitut only needed three. Certain dialectal variations in the script had arisen, particularly along sectarian lines; for example, the Anglicans used a superscript dot to indicate vowel length whereas the Roman Catholics repeated the vowel (using the null consonant form). However, despite these small differences, the Cree system was used to write Inuktitut for over a century; in addition, many areas used a variety of Roman-based scripts.

In 1960, the Canadian government appointed Raymond Gagné to establish one writing system for all Canadian Inuit. Gagné came to the conclusion that the moraic (syllabic) system should be abandoned in favour of a Roman-based alphabet. However, as Harper (1983) says, 'Gagné, and through him the Department [of Northern Affairs], seriously misjudged Inuit attachment to syllabic orthography'.

Although the attempt to replace Inuit writing with the Roman alphabet failed, the effort did initiate an orthographic reform of the syllabic writing system. A dual syllabic-Roman orthography was established in 1976 by the Inuit Language Commission. It is shown (based on Nichols 1996) in table 13.5.

13.3.2 The modern Inuktitut script

The symbols of Inuktitut are given in table 13.5.

Since Inuktitut has only three vowels, only three vowel orientations are used <i u a>. Long vowels are shown as a superscript dot: ᐲ <pii>. The sounds /q ŋ/ were provided for by using diacritics: writing /qi/ as ᕿ, /ŋi/ as ᖏ. For /v/ and /ɬ/, new symbols were developed: ᕕ /vi/, ᖤ /ɬa/. The sound /h/ only occurs finally. In the Roman-based script, long vowels are geminated <pii>; /ŋ/ is written as <ng>; /ɬ/ is written either as <ɬ> or as <&>.

Table 13.5 The symbols of Inuktitut. The standard romanization is given with additional phonetic information in square brackets; note that <&> is a symbol for a lateral fricative

	i	*u*	*a*	*Final*
Ø	ᐃ	ᐅ	ᐊ	
p	ᐱ	ᐳ	ᐸ	ᑉ
t	ᑎ	ᑐ	ᑕ	ᑦ
k	ᑭ	ᑯ	ᑲ	ᒃ
g [ɣ]	ᒋ	ᒍ	ᒐ	ᒡ
m	ᒥ	ᒧ	ᒪ	ᒻ
n	ᓂ	ᓄ	ᓇ	ᓐ
s	ᓯ	ᓱ	ᓴ	ᔅ
l	ᓕ	ᓗ	ᓚ	ᓪ
j	ᔨ	ᔪ	ᔭ	ᔾ
v	ᕕ	ᕗ	ᕙ	ᕝ
r [ʁ]	ᕆ	ᕈ	ᕋ	ᕐ
q	ᕿ	ᖁ	ᖃ	ᖅ
ng [ŋ]	ᖏ	ᖑ	ᖓ	ᖕ
ɬ & [ɬ]	ᖠ	ᖢ	ᖤ	ᖦ
h				ll

13.4 Runic

13.4.1 Background and history

The runic alphabet was used to write inscriptions during the Middle Ages in Germanic languages, primarily in Scandinavia and Britain. The Germanic languages are a branch of Indo-European.

The earliest runic writings are found in Denmark and adjacent areas and dated from the first century NEW. Shortly thereafter, Germanic peoples brought the runic writing system to the continent. When the Anglo-Saxons invaded Britain in the fifth century NEW, they took runic writing with them. Because the Norse travelled so widely, runic inscriptions have been found occasionally outside the Germanic area. One inscription is even found in Istanbul on the floor of the Great Mosque (the former Hagia Sophia cathedral). Somewhat surprisingly, Iceland has rather few runic inscriptions, and they are found mainly in churches, all dated after 1200. Greenland has about 40 inscriptions. Claims of runic inscriptions in North America are generally regarded by runologists as unsubstantiated.

The earliest writings are on small portable objects, such as spear-blades, shield bosses, jewellery, combs, buckles, figurines, etc. From rare surviving examples, we know that runic writing was also done on wooden tablets; however, most surviving inscriptions are on stone stelæ. During a twelfth-century winter storm, a group of Vikings became stranded in the Orkneys and took shelter in a tomb where they left about thirty inscriptions on the walls. With the introduction of Christianity, runic writing was gradually replaced by the Roman alphabet. The Christian Church in Scandinavia seems to have tolerated runic writing in view of the many inscriptions with crosses and other Christian symbols. Runic writing never completely died out, although by the late Middle Ages it had become an antiquarian interest. The surviving examples of runic writing are almost all cut or scratched into the writing surface; examples of runic writing on parchment or paper are mostly from late mediæval times. It has been suggested (Haugen 1976), however, that the reason for the small amount of runic writing in Iceland is that the writing was on easily available sheepskin which has since disintegrated.

The origin of the runic alphabet is debated. If the earliest texts date from about the first century NEW, we can reasonably assume that the runic alphabet was developed sometime around the time 0, or shortly before. The Roman, Greek, and northern Italic alphabets have been suggested as possible sources. We must, however, be careful about chronologically appropriate forms. The letters ᚠ ᚱ <f r> (table 13.7) likely come from the Roman alphabet. The letters ᚷ ᛉ <g z> could possibly be related to early Greek chi and psi <Χ Ψ>. The letters ᚲ ᚾ ᛁ ᛊ ᛏ ᛒ ᛖ ᛗ ᛚ ᛟ <k n i s t b e m l o> could (with a bit of imagination) come from either Greek or Latin. North Italic offers parallels for some of the 'distorted ones' <a l u s>. Some of the letters <w ɪ p ŋ> may be original creations.

The mixture of likely sources suggests that stimulus diffusion may have been at work here. We can envision a Norse speaker who travelled in southern Europe and became acquainted with writing from Roman, Greek, or perhaps other sources. This person came home, perhaps not remembering accurately every detail, and created an alphabet with elements drawn from a variety of sources. Moltke (1985) has argued that the actual location of the development of the early runic script was Denmark; this is plausible on the basis of the large number of early Danish inscriptions.

Runic letters are quite angular with no strictly horizontal strokes. The best explanation for this shape is that the runic alphabet was designed to be written on wooden tablets. If the grain of the wood runs horizontally, vertical and diagonal strokes would be clear, but horizontal strokes would be hard to see against the grain.

13.4.2 Proto-Scandinavian phonology

Haugen (1976) reconstructs Proto-Scandinavian phonology, which would be appropriate for early inscriptions from Denmark, as given in table 13.6.

Table 13.6 The phonemes of Proto-Scandinavian

p	t		k	i	u
b	d		g	e	o
f	θ		h		ɑ
m	n		ŋ		
	l	r			
	s	z			
w			j		

13.4.3 *The runic alphabets*

The order of the runic alphabet is known from the many existing abecedaries: <f u þ a r k g w h n i j ɪ p z s t b e m l ŋ d o>; note that /θ/ is normally romanized as <þ> as in Old English. The 24 letters are divided into three groups of eight letters each, known as *ættir* 'families'. We have no idea why the letters are ordered in this way. In modern times, the word *futhark* has been used as a name for the alphabet, 'futhark' being simply the first six letters pronounced as a word.

The individual runes were usually given acrophonic names. The names vary somewhat, but table 13.7 gives common names in their early Germanic reconstructed form. The runic alphabet went through various phases (table 13.7), the best-known being the Germanic (elder) futhark, the Danish (younger) futhark, and the Rök (short-twig) futhark.

The symbol ᚨ is transcribed as /a/ in the Germanic futhark; however, in later versions, it is a nasal vowel usually transcribed as /ą/. The symbol ᛇ in the Germanic futhark is transcribed as /ï/; in the later versions, the corresponding symbol ᛅ in the Danish futhark, and ᛆ in the Rök futhark, represent a non-nasalized vowel and are transcribed as /a/.

The Germanic futhark is the oldest version, probably dating back to the time 0. As you can see, it fits the reconstructed Proto-Scandinavian phonology quite well. The developer of the runic alphabet had worked out a very careful phonemic analysis of the language and developed an alphabet well suited to that analysis.

The Danish futhark, which emerged in the eighth century in Denmark, was a radical revision of the Germanic futhark. The older 24-letter system was reduced to sixteen letters. The language had changed, and the Danish futhark allowed those changes to be represented in the writing system more clearly. But more interestingly from a linguistic viewpoint, the one-to-one relationship between letter and phoneme changed so that one letter represented more than one phoneme. Frequently, we find that over time a language changes, but the writing system does not. A society then sometimes institutes a spelling reform to bring the writing system back into line with the phonology. Many examples of this sort of spelling reform exist. The Danish futhark, however, represents a spelling reform in the opposite direction. Where previously there was a fairly clear one-to-one relationship between phonemes and symbols, now many symbols ambiguously represent two or more phonemes. Why this happened is not clear.

Table 13.7 Three stages of runic symbols (note: an aurochs is the extinct large European ox *Bos primagenius*)

Phoneme	*Germanic*	*Danish*	*Rök*	*Germanic name*
f	ᚠ	ᚠ	ᚠ	*fehu 'cattle, wealth'
u	ᚢ	ᚢ	ᚢ	*ūruz 'aurochs'
θ	ᚦ	ᚦ	ᚦ	*þurisaz 'giant, monster'
a, ą	ᚨ	ᚨ	ᚨ	*ansuz 'god'
r	ᚱ	ᚱ	ᚱ	*raidō 'riding'
k	ᚲ	ᚴ	ᚴ	*kaunaz 'ulcer'
g	ᚷ			*gebō 'gift'
w	ᚹ			*wunjō 'joy'
h	ᚺ	ᚼ	ᚽ	*hagalaz 'hail'
n	ᚾ	ᚾ	ᚿ	*naudiz 'need'
i	ᛁ	ᛁ	ᛁ	*īsa- 'ice'
j	ᛃ			*jēra- 'year'
ï/a	ᛇ	ᛅ	ᛆ	*eihwaz 'yew'
p	ᛈ			*perþ- '?'
z	ᛉ	ᛦ		*algiz '?'
s	ᛊ	ᛋ	ᛌ	*sōwilō 'sun'
t	ᛏ	ᛏ	ᛐ	*teiwas 'god Tiw' (cf. Eng. *Tuesday*)
b	ᛒ	ᛒ	ᛓ	*berkanan 'birch-twig'
e	ᛖ			*ehwaz 'horse'
m	ᛗ	ᛘ	ᛙ	*mannaz 'man'
l	ᛚ	ᛚ	ᛚ	*laguz 'water'
ŋ	ᛜ			*ingwaz 'god Ing'
d	ᛞ			*dagaz 'day'
o	ᛟ			*ōþila 'hereditary land'

In Norway and southern Sweden, a revised alphabet, known as Rök runes, or short-twig runes, was used with symbols of slightly different shape, but with essentially the same structure as the Danish futhark.

The Anglo-Saxons came to Britain in the mid-fifth century NEW, bringing with them the Germanic futhark. Somewhat later, the Norse invaded the northeast part of England, also bringing with them runic writing. Rather than decreasing the number of letters as with the Danish futhark, the Anglo-Saxons increased the number of letters in their futhorc; the British name **futhorc** reflects certain sound changes which had taken place there. Eventually, there were some 31 letters in the Anglo-Saxon futhorc. Runic writing ended in Britain during the tenth century. Most British runic inscriptions are in the Norse language, but about fifty are in Old English.

13.4.4 Mysticism and magic

Sometimes people, usually non-specialists in runology, become fascinated with the supposed magical lore or powers of the runes. The fact that the word *rune* derives from Old English *rūn*, Old Norse *rún* 'secret, mystery', has certainly encouraged this approach. In late mediæval Scandinavia, runes were used for fortune-telling and for writing magical sayings. In recent Nazi times, mystical Aryan powers were attributed to the runes. From a linguistic perspective, any magical properties in runic writing are irrelevant. Runic writing is an ordinary, although interesting, writing system. As Page (1987) says, 'if [the Germanic people] wanted to cut a religious or magical text, if they wished to produce a charm word, they would use runic, the only script they had, for it, just as a modern wizard would be likely to write his magic . . . in Roman characters. But that would not confer upon runes the status of a magical script.' In this context, it is interesting to note that Christianity did not disapprove of runic inscriptions; indeed, many stones with runic writing also have a Christian cross.

13.5 Ogham

13.5.1 Background and history

Ogham inscriptions are Old Irish texts found in Ireland, Britain, and the Isle of Man, dating from the fifth to the seventh centuries NEW (McManus 1991, 1996). The ogham inscriptions are the oldest surviving Irish texts. Manuscript use of the ogham alphabet, known as scholastic ogham, is attested in later texts, notably in *The Scholar's Primer* (*Auraicept na nÉces*).

Inscriptions outside Ireland are located in areas colonized or heavily influenced by the Irish. Ogham inscriptions in Britain, but not in Ireland, are sometimes accompanied by a Latin translation. Some undeciphered inscriptions written in this alphabet, known as Pictish oghams, are found in eastern Scotland. Modern Irish spells the word *oghaṁ*, and Old Irish spelled it *ogam*; both spellings are found in English. The ogham alphabet is also known as *beithe-luis-fern* from the names of the first three letters. The Roman alphabet later replaced ogham for writing Irish.

Irish is a Celtic language, a family itself descended from Indo-European. The ogham script was used only for Old Irish. All the other Celtic languages and later forms of Irish used adaptations of the Roman alphabet.

The ogham alphabet is unusual in its graphic shape (table 13.8). The letters consist of notches and strokes, typically inscribed at the edge of a stone monument. Each letter is formed by 1–5 repetitions of the notches (for vowels) or stroke patterns (for consonants). Notches are on the edge; some stroke patterns are on the left of the edge, some on the right, and some cross the edge. Unfortunately for later generations of readers of ogham, the edge is the part of a monument most likely to be broken off or damaged by weathering. The later manuscript texts are often written horizontally.

In terms of shape, there is no other writing system like ogham. The symbols themselves give us no clue to their origin. One tenuous explanation for the shape is that they developed from the use of the fingers in counting. In structure, however, ogham is a perfectly ordinary alphabet, well suited to the language it was used to write. Ireland was not part of the Roman Empire, but the Irish nevertheless had contact with the Romans, and they were certainly aware of Roman writing. The best guess is that someone devised an original alphabet in Ireland inspired by the Roman alphabet through stimulus diffusion.

13.5.2 The ogham alphabet

The ogham letters are usually arranged in four groups, each group having the same kind of stroke, but differing in the number of strokes. Many letters are associated with various objects, especially trees.

A star-shaped letter was used for /k/ or /e/ in the stone inscriptions, but in later manuscripts this symbol was used for the diphthong /ea/:

k/e (ea) ᚕ *ébad* '?'

In addition, a few other symbols are found only in the later manuscript tradition for the diphthongs which had developed later:

oi	ᚖ	*ór* 'gold'	ui	ᚗ	*uilen* 'elbow'
ia	ᚘ	*pín, iphín* 'pine'	ae	ᚙ	*emancholl* 'double c'

Table 13.8 The ogham alphabet

b	ᚁ	*beithe* 'birtch'	h	ᚆ	*(h)uath* '?'
l	ᚂ	*luis* 'blaze, herb'	d	ᚇ	*dair* 'oak'
f	ᚃ	*fern* 'alder'	t	ᚈ	*tinne* 'metal rod'
s	ᚄ	*sail* 'willow'	k	ᚉ	*coll* 'hazel'
n	ᚅ	*nin* 'fork, loft'	k^w	ᚊ	*cert, queirt* 'bush'
m	ᚋ	*muin* 'neck'	a	ᚐ	*ailm* '?'
g	ᚌ	*gort* 'field'	o	ᚑ	*onn* 'ash'
ŋ	ᚍ	*(n)gétal* 'wounding?'	u	ᚒ	*úr* 'earth'
z	ᚎ	*straif* 'sulphur'	e	ᚓ	*eded* '?'
r	ᚏ	*ruis* 'red(ness)'	i	ᚔ	*idad* '?'

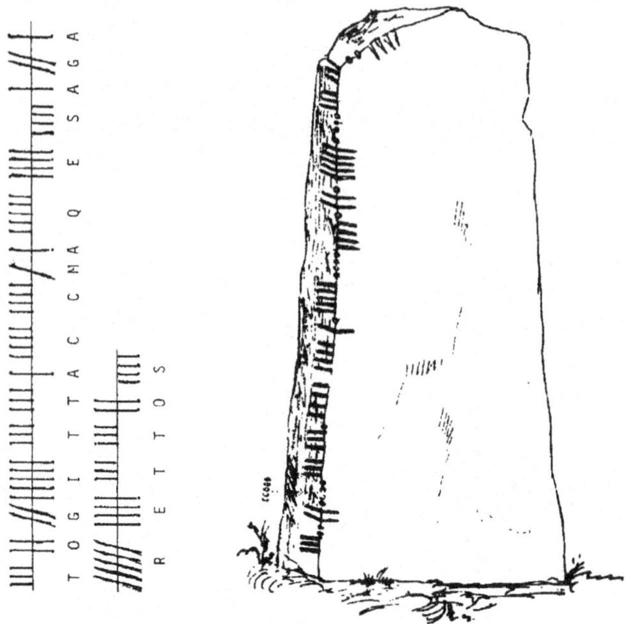

Figure 13.1 An ogham inscription from Kerry, Ireland: 'Of Toictheach son of Sagi Rettos'

13.5.3 Example text

Ogham texts are very short, typically one or two nouns in the genitive case. The stones were likely grave markers or possibly boundary markers.

The text in the inscription in figure 13.1 starts at the lower left corner of the stone and proceeds upwards around the top. Note that the romanization is given in upper-case letters, as is common in ogham studies; also /k/ is transcribed as <C>, and /k^w/ as <Q>.

13.6 Pahawh Hmong

13.6.1 Background and history

We rarely know much about the emergence of a script. With Pahawh Hmong, however, we are fortunate in having a great deal of first-hand knowledge (Smalley et al. 1990). Between 1959 and 1971, Shong Lue Yang developed a script for his language Hmong, spoken on the Laotian–Vietnamese border. Previously illiterate, Shong Lue Yang devised the script and revised it in four versions, each time bringing it closer to an unambiguous phonemic representation of Hmong. With a long familiarity with writing systems in southeast Asia, Smalley felt that the Pahawh Hmong writing system is unique and bears no obvious relationship to any writing system that Shong Lue Yang might possibly have come into contact with.

Table 13.9 The phonemes of Hmong

p	t	ts	tʃ	c	ʈ	k	q	ʔ
p^h	t^h	ts^h	tʃ^h	c^h	ʈ^h	k^h	q^h	
	d							
	d^h							
f		s	ʃ	ç				h
v			ʒ					
m	n				ɲ	ŋ		
^{h}m	^{h}n				^{h}ɲ			
				j				
i	ɨ	u			ai	ua		
e					aɨ	ia		
ɛ		ɔ			au			
		a						

Tones	A	B
	high level	mid rising
	low glottalized	mid level
	low rising	low level
	high falling	falling breathy

The Hmong have a tradition of the sacredness of writing as a gift of God. Shong Lue Yang believed that he was divine and that his script had been divinely inspired. He was known amongst his followers as the 'Mother of Writing'. He taught the script with great success until his assassination in 1971 by the government which feared his growing influence.

Although Shong Lue Yang's fourth and last version of the script appeals to linguists because of its clearer relation to the phonemes of the language and its lack of ambiguity, most Hmong speakers using the script prefer the third revision, shown here. Although the Pahawh Hmong script is highly valued and widely respected amongst the Hmong, a romanization, the Romanized Popular Alphabet, devised by Christian missionaries, is more widely used.

13.6.2 Phonology of Hmong

Hmong is a member of the Miao-Yao language family. Hmong is an isolating language with monosyllabic morphemes. The phonemic system is shown in table 13.9.

There are eight tones. The significance of the column labels A and B will be explained in §13.6.3. Hmong has a large number of onsets, but the only codal consonant is /ŋ/.

13.6.3 Structure of Pahawh Hmong script

Some of the symbols of Pahawh Hmong are shown in table 13.10. The script is written linearly from left to right. The rhyme is written first, followed by the onset.

Table 13.10 Some symbols of the Pahawh Hmong writing system

Some rhymes	A				B			
	hl	lg	lr	hf	mr	ml	ll	fb
/-ɛŋ/	𖬀	𖬀̇	𖬀̇	𖬀̄	𖬁	𖬁̇	𖬁̄	𖬁̈
/-i/	𖬂	𖬂̇	𖬂̇	𖬂̄	𖬃	𖬃̇	𖬃̄	𖬃̈
/-au/	𖬄	𖬄̇	𖬄̇	𖬄̄	𖬅	𖬅̇	𖬅̄	𖬅̈
/-u/	𖬆	𖬆̇	𖬆̇	𖬆̄	𖬇	𖬇̇	𖬇̄	𖬇̈
/-e/	𖬈	𖬈̇	𖬈̇	𖬈̄	𖬉	𖬉̇	𖬉̄	𖬉̈
/-ai/	𖬊	𖬊̇	𖬊̇	𖬊̄	𖬋	𖬋̇	𖬋̄	𖬋̈

Tones				
	hl	high level	mr	mid rising
	lg	low glottalized	ml	mid level
	lr	low rising	ll	low level
	hf	high falling	fb	falling breathy

Some onsets					
/v/	𖬜	/ɳʈ/	𖬜̇	/f/	𖬜̍̄
/ŋk/	𖬢	/nts/	𖬢̇	/ʈʰ/	𖬢̍̄
/s/	𖬮	/ʔ/	𖬮̇	/ɲ/	𖬮̍̄
/ʰl/	𖬥	/ʒ/	𖬥̇	/ntsʰ/	𖬥̍̄
/h/	𖬟	/tʰ/	𖬟̇	/pl/	𖬟̍̄
/m/	𖬦	/tsʰ/	𖬦̇	/q/	𖬦̍̄
/Ø/	𖬭	/ndl/	𖬭̇	/ndʰl/	𖬭̍̄

Numerals									
𖭑	𖭒	𖭓	𖭔	𖭕	𖭖	𖭗	𖭘	𖭙	𖭐
1	2	3	4	5	6	7	8	9	0

The rhyme is written as a combination of the VC-symbol and tone diacritic. The tones are divided into two groups, A and B, as shown in table 13.9. Each rhyme has two symbols: one is used when the tone is from the A-group and the other when the tone is from the B-group. The tones in each group are then indicated by one of four diacritics (including the absence of a diacritic). Three of the four diacritics are the same in the two groups, but one is different. There is no relation in the shapes of the symbols for the same rhyme in the two groups. Many onsets share the same basic symbol with different diacritics; there is no significance to the diacritics other than in distinguishing the different onsets.

As example of the writing of Pahawh Hmong syllables, /vɛŋ-hl/ (where /hl/ indicates a high level tone) is written as ; /vɛŋ-mr/ (mid rising) is written as ; /ŋki-hf/ is written as ; and /ʔau-mr/ is written as 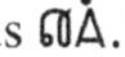.

13.7 Bliss

13.7.1 Charles Bliss and the origin of Bliss symbols

Karl Blitz was born in 1897 in Austria, near the Russian border where several different ethnic groups lived. As a young man, he noted the animosity the different groups showed towards each other and felt this was in large measure due to the fact that they spoke different languages. As a Jew, he was taken prisoner when the Nazis overran Austria in 1938. He managed to escape and fled to England where he changed his name to Charles Bliss. He went to Shanghai to rejoin his wife; there, he was interned by the Japanese in 1943 until the end of the war when he moved to Australia with his wife. In Shanghai, Bliss had become interested in Chinese characters and was fascinated by the fact that all Chinese could communicate in the same written language even if they spoke mutually unintelligible dialects.

In Australia, although Bliss was a chemical engineer, he developed a passionate interest in creating a semantically based writing system which all people in the world could use to communicate with each other. His aim was not to create an artificial language, like Esperanto, but to create a universal writing system that could be 'read in all languages'. In 1949, he published his system as *Semantography* with a second edition in 1965. He then wrote thousands of letters in an effort to find support to publicize his work, but with very little success.

13.7.2 Bliss symbols as an augmentative communication system

In 1971, Shirley McNaughton, a special education teacher at the Ontario Crippled Children's Centre (now the Hugh MacMillan Medical Centre) in Toronto, became aware of Bliss's work. She was looking for a system to help children communicate who had physical difficulties, such as cerebral palsy, which prevented them from speaking, especially younger children who could not yet read. Her previous work had suggested that pictures were helpful, but that by themselves they did not allow the children to express complex thoughts or emotions. With the discovery of Bliss symbols, work at the Centre began on developing a set of the symbols which would be useful for their children's needs. The method was immediately successful, and by 1975 Bliss symbols were being used in a number of centres. Typically a board of about a hundred symbols was used, and a message was created by pointing to the appropriate symbols in turn. Additional symbols could be made available as required. A variety of different devices have been invented to accommodate the needs of people with differing motor difficulties, such as not being able to point precisely with their finger.

Families and professionals alike were extremely pleased with the results. With the aid of Bliss symbols, individuals, both children and adults, who had been largely shut off from many types of interaction with their families, suddenly 'came to life'.

Blissymbolics has been particularly popular in Canada, Scandinavia, and Israel. Committees have been established to create dictionaries and regulate the development of new signs (much the way the national academies of Europe were envisioned). Bliss himself was pleased at the usefulness that his system finally found, but at the same time disappointed that his original goal of better communication for the world had been lost.

The advent of computers has meant that a variety of other techniques and systems have become available for people with speech production difficulties, and the use of Blissymbolics has fallen off in the past years, but it clearly pointed the way in a dramatic fashion.

13.7.3 The structure of Bliss symbols

Let us look now at how the Bliss system works. Most of the work on Bliss has focused on developing symbols for lexical items. We will look at these and return to syntax and other issues later.

Some symbols are pictograms:

⌂ 'house' [car symbol] 'car' ◡ 'container'

Some symbols are abstract pictograms:

♡ 'feeling' ^ 'protection' ~ 'water, liquid'

Some symbols are arbitrary, with no logical connection to their meaning:

□ 'thing' ∩ 'mind' / 'this'

Some arbitrary symbols are borrowed from ordinary writing:

3 'three' + 'addition' ! 'intensity'

Some symbols are semantic compounds:

[cloud symbol]	'cloud'	=	~	'water'	+	— 'sky'
[parent symbol]	'parent'	=	⊥	'person'	+	^ 'protection'
[taxi symbol]	'taxi'	=	[car symbol]	'car'	+	[limited time symbol] 'limited time'

All of this is very much like the way Chinese characters were developed (chapter 3), except that there are no phonetic extensions or semantic-phonetic compounds.

Semantically based diacritics are common:

[room symbol] 'room' [ceiling symbol] 'ceiling' [wall symbol] 'wall'

Symbols called indicators are often used to specify things such as the syntactic category of the term, such as verb tense or number:

'mouth' 'food'

'eat (present)' 'ate, eat (past)' 'eat (future)'

'might have eaten (past conditional)'

'mind' 'minds' 'brain'

'thoughtful' 'think (verb)'

The small cross indicates plural; the small square a thing; the arrowhead pointing down, an adjective; and the arrowhead pointing up, a verb.

A combination of pictograms and compounding is a common way of deriving lexical items:

'say' 'shout' 'discussion' 'argument'

'song' 'opinion' 'nonsense' 'secret'

'knowledge' 'understand' 'explain' 'describe'

The exclamation mark shows intensity. *Discussion* is 'talk going in both directions'. *Song* is 'mouth' + 'a musical note'. *Opinion* is 'mind' + 'mouth'. *Secret* is held in an enclosure. *Knowledge* is 'mind' + 'storehouse'; *understand* is 'knowledge' + 'into' = 'to enter one's store of knowledge'; *explain* is 'say' + 'understand'. *Describe* is 'think' + 'say' + 'be' = 'to say what something is'.

13.7.4 Sentences in Bliss

The materials available to me primarily derive from the attempt to create Bliss symbols in an English-speaking environment. Helfman (1981) has a small section on syntax with directions for forming questions, negative sentences, and commands, as well as suggestions for simplifying statements. The syntax in the more complicated sentences seems more or less to follow English patterns.

The following shows a possible sentence written in Bliss: *I will go with you if you are afraid.*

→ I will go with you if you are afraid.

The first symbol is *I*, written as 'person' + '1' for first person. The second symbol is *go* with the future diacritic. *With* is expressed as a sequence of two plus signs. *You* is like *I*, but with a number 2 for second person. *If* is written as a question mark together with 'either'. The next symbol is *you* again. *Be* is a small version of 'live' (note the absence of verbal inflection). Finally, *afraid* is 'sad' + future + question mark + modifier (sad about the future because of its uncertainties).

To demonstrate the flexibility of Bliss, the next sentence is a famous nonsense sentence in English going back to Noam Chomsky: *Colourless green ideas sleep furiously.*

colourless green ideas sleep furiously

Colourless is written as 'without colour'; 'colour' is 'eye' + 'earth' (what the eye sees from the earth). *Green* is a compound of 'colour' + 'grass'. Bliss defines the colours in terms of common objects. There is an alternative system for naming colours by giving the numbers in the order they appear on a rainbow; green would be 'colour' + '4' in that system. *Idea* is 'mind' + 'down' (a thought issuing from the mind); the plural marker is added here. *Sleep* is 'eye' + 'close' + action indicator. *Furiously* is written here the same as 'angrily' since different symbols for synonyms are avoided: 'much' + 'feeling' + 'opposition' + modifier indicator (having strong feelings against someone or something).

As we will see further in chapter 14, the Bliss system is structurally interesting. All the other writing systems we have studied have large phonological components; however, Bliss is completely semantic. It is unclear to me how personal names are represented in Bliss without the use of some sort of phonetic extension. I suspect that the symbol for a family member named George might well be <G> using the Roman alphabet; however, such usage would be quite limited.

Because Bliss is such an unusual system, we need to ask some basic questions. Is Bliss a writing system? Our definition of writing as the use of graphic marks to represent specific linguistic utterances clearly encompasses Bliss. We have just seen two example sentences that fit this definition. By changing a symbol in Bliss, we systematically change the meaning of the utterance, and a change in the utterance systematically changes the representation in Bliss. A second question is: can anything be written in Bliss? Our own observations that both meaningful and nonsensical sentences can be written in Bliss answer yes to this question; further, the testimony of Bliss users clearly agrees.

Is Bliss independent of language? This was one of Charles Bliss's goals. Here the evidence suggests not. Rather than a writing system completely independent of language, Bliss in fact seems to be like the Roman alphabet; it can be used for any language with a bit of adaptation. Can a sentence written in Bliss by a Hebrew speaker be understood by an English speaker? Obviously, a sentence written in Polish in the Roman alphabet is not understandable by an English speaker; the use of the Roman alphabet might allow the English speaker to make a very rough approximation of the Polish pronunciation, but it would not allow understanding. Bliss, however, by being semantically based, might allow some mutual understanding between different languages to a very limited extent.

Is Bliss a writing system for a distinct language Bliss? Clearly, the Bliss writing system could be used strictly for writing English (or some other language), but in a family situation, it is likely that dialect variations and shortcuts would arise. The resulting language might be English-like, but not exactly English. Note that the person with motor difficulty could use Bliss symbols to express himself or herself, but other family members could reply in spoken English; this situation would tend to keep the Bliss user's language close to English.

Is Bliss semantically based or morphologically based? What linguistic units are represented by the symbols? The answer seems clearly to be that it is semantically based. For example, English has a morpheme *taxi*. This morpheme in English has no possible internal division into smaller meaningful units. The Bliss symbol for 'taxi', however, clearly has internal structure. And indeed, we had many cases of single morphemes written with complex, analysable symbols; e.g., 'cloud', 'parent', and 'song'. The English word 'argument' consists of two morphemes *argu-* and *-ment*, but neither corresponds to any of the parts of the symbol .

Bliss sometimes makes semantic distinctions which do not exist lexically in English: for example, there are six different ways of writing 'I', explicitly set out in the *Blissymbol Reference Guide* (Wood, Storr, and Reich 1992):

'I'	'I'	'I'	'I'	'I'	'I'
(general)	(female)	(male)	(girl)	(boy)	(child)

Clearly, the Bliss symbols correspond to units of meaning, not morphemes, and thus the system is semantically based. In chapter 14, we will examine further how Bliss fits into the general classification of writing systems.

We conclude then that Bliss symbols are semantically based, that anything that can be said in any language can be written down in Bliss symbols, and anything that can be written down in Bliss can be read in any language. Finally, the creation process for symbols used for Bliss uses no devices not otherwise known in creating traditional writing systems.

13.8 Further Reading

Daniels and Bright (1996) have chapters on most of these writing systems. For Cherokee, see also Scancarelli (1992). For Cree and Inuktitut: Burnaby (1985), Harper (1983), McCarthy (1995), W. Walker (1981, 1996). For runic: Antonsen (1989), Haugen (1976), Moltke (1985), and Page (1973, 1987; especially for runes in Britain). For ogham: Lehmann (1989) and McManus (1991). Smalley, Vang, and Yang (1990) is a fascinating story of the development of Pahawh Hmong. For Blissymbolics, see Bliss (1965), Helfman (1981), McDonald (1980), and McNaughton (1985).

13.9 Terms

futhark
overdifferentiated
underdifferentiated

13.10 Exercises

1 Write your own name and city in the scripts of this chapter (except Bliss), paying attention to the sound, not English spelling.
2 What evidence does the Cherokee script provide to show that Sequoyah was illiterate in English?
3 How did the historical development of the Cree and Inuktitut scripts differ from that of Cherokee?
4 How does the Cree script differ from an abjad? from a typical abugida?
5 What internal evidence do the runic and ogham scripts provide that they were the product of stimulus diffusion and not completely original inventions?
6 The Pahawh Hmong system violates a principle that the phonemes of a language and the graphemes of its writing system generally occur in the same order. Could either the onsets or rhymes be considered diacritics of the other?

14 Classification of Writing Systems

Now that we have examined a large number of writing systems in some detail, we can profitably survey them again to see how they can best be classified. The most productive way of organizing writing systems has been to consider what linguistic level is represented by the grapheme. Examining the classification of writing systems will also give us the opportunity to review the crucial structural points of the various writing systems we have surveyed.

14.1 Phonetic, Semantic, and Glottographic Writing

Language is a relationship between sound and meaning, and it contacts the real world at two interfaces: phonetic and semantic. In principle, we can represent an utterance by writing at any of these three levels: phonetic, linguistic, or semantic.

We are familiar with the notion of a **phonetic writing system** which could be used to transcribe the sounds of any utterance in any language in the world; such a system would be similar to the International Phonetic Alphabet (IPA; see Appendix B and International Phonetic Association 1999), which provides an inventory of symbols for a wide variety of phonetic phenomena which occur in human speech with certain rules for using these symbols. The symbols represent pure sound and are not associated with any particular language. That is, the IPA provides symbols sufficient to represent all those phonetic distinctions which are contrastive in some language somewhere. However, as MacMahon (1996) notes: 'Strictly speaking, then, the IPA is not a universal phonetic alphabet in the sense of an alphabet that will provide a notation for every conceivable sound used in a natural language. Rather, it is a selective phonetic alphabet which is constrained by the requirement of phonemic contrastivity.' Even though the IPA may not be a completely phonetic writing system, it is clearly a close approximation.

We can also imagine a semantic writing scheme used to transcribe ideas directly, that is, the meaning of any utterance of any language in the world, although, even in linguistics, such a notion is unusual. Sampson (1985, 1994) argues for the possible existence of a semantic writing system (he uses the term **semasiographic**): 'There would appear in principle to be no reason why a society could not have expanded a semasiographic system, by adding further graphic conventions, until it was as complex and rich in expressive potential as their spoken language' (Sampson 1985,

p. 30). As part of his evidence for a semantic system, Sampson unfortunately used the 'Yukaghir Love Letter' as an example of semantic writing. This document has been frequently described as a message from a Yukaghir woman in Siberia to her boyfriend; it is a rather complicated drawing with no words. In a fascinating bit of academic sleuthing, DeFrancis (1989) showed that the nature of this drawing had been misunderstood. It was not a genuine communication, but rather part of a parlour game played by Yukaghir girls; one girl would make a drawing and the others would take turns guessing at the story behind it.

Sampson also refers to the Cheyenne Indian Letter which we examined in chapter 1 (figure 1.1). Recall that this is a drawing purportedly sent from a father to his son with money and instructions to return home. Sampson considers this as an example of pre-writing on the way to becoming a fully fledged writing system. Apart from these examples, he notes that we occasionally encounter instructions with no words: modern traffic signs, or assembly instructions intended for international use with no words.

DeFrancis (1989) and DeFrancis and Unger (1994) argue strongly that all writing is phonologically based and that semantically based writing is an impossibility. They dismiss not only the Yukaghir letter, but also other types of evidence for semantic writing that Sampson advanced. They state: 'there is no possibility whatsoever that pictographs based on the nonphonetic principle underlying their usage by the Yukaghir and the North American Indians could evolve into a full system of nonphonetic writing'.

The problem with the proposed examples for semantic writing is that either the examples are not concrete or systematic in their meaning or that the system underlying them is not general in its scope. We might be able to draw quite a number of pictures, like the Cheyenne letter, to communicate a considerable range of our activities. However, it would be very difficult to do so in a way that reliably communicated what we intended. In the absence of background information, we might give the Cheyenne letter a wide variety of interpretations: 'Turtle-Following-His-Wife wants Little Man to send $53', 'Little Man wants Turtle-Following-His-Wife to send $53', 'a man who knows Turtle-Following-His-Wife wants Little Man to send his children to him', etc. As DeFrancis points out, it seems impossible to find a systematic basis linking the drawing and its meaning, a system which could be used to interpret other material.

If we turn to signs with no words, such as highway signs, the information provided is, by contrast, quite clear – 'no entry', 'left-turn only', 'yield', but the range of expression is quite limited. No signs exist for 'While you're out, would you mind getting some of that special kind of bread that Marge likes' or 'I dreamt I was a robin last night'. Obviously, we could invent signs for these messages, but there would always be further messages without signs.

Sproat (2000, p. 135) says: 'Nobody has shown the existence of a writing system that is entirely semasiographic, relying on no linguistic basis to communicate ideas, and which allows people to write to one another on any topic they choose. It seems fair to say that the burden of proof is on those who would claim that semasiographic writing is possible to demonstrate the existence of such a system.' If we want to test for a **semantic writing system** (i.e., Sampson's and Sproat's *semasiographic*), we can

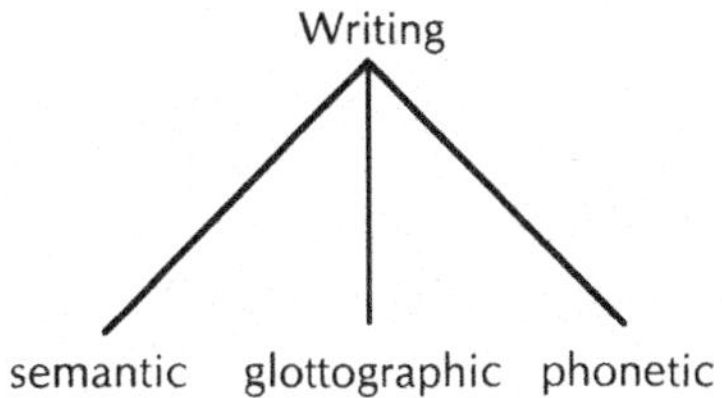

Figure 14.1 Basic classification of writing systems

set two criteria: (a) that it be based entirely on semantically analysable units and not on pronunciation; and (b) that any linguistic utterance be translatable into a corresponding semantic representation and vice versa. Any attempt to describe Chinese writing as semantic fails to satisfy the first criterion since Chinese has a large phonographic component. Both picture writing and the assembly instructions/road signs pictures fail to satisfy the second criterion. However, the Bliss system (chapter 13) is indeed just such a semantic notational system; it meets both these criteria and thus constitutes a semantically based writing system without phonological content. The examples provided in chapter 13 clearly show that any linguistic utterance could be translated into a semantically equivalent text in Bliss and that any Bliss text could be translated into a semantically equivalent linguistic utterance. Undoubtedly, Bliss has faults and deficiencies, but, by and large, it is successful at accomplishing what it sets out to do; in any case, our point here is that such a system is possible.

A basic classification for writing systems (figure 14.1) distinguishes semantic, glottographic, and phonetic writing systems. The semantic branch seems to have only one member, Bliss; the phonetic branch has only the IPA and other similar universal phonetic transcription schemes. The glottographic branch contains all the other ordinary writing systems we have discussed in this book. From this point on, we will set semantic and phonetic writing aside and focus entirely on glottographic writing systems.

The term *ideographic* is commonly found in works on writing with a variety of meanings, often poorly thought out, sometimes referring to morphograms and sometimes to semantic units. Because of the very high chance of confusion, I would strongly urge that this term not be used.

14.2 Glottographic Writing

Glottographic writing systems are the kind of writing systems we have been looking at in this book, except for Bliss and IPA. The intention of such a system is to record the linguistic utterances of a specific language. In the next section, we will discuss the considerable typological variety of glottographic writing systems, but they all have the purpose of giving readers sufficient information that they can construct an appropriate semantic and phonological representation for any written utterance. Many scholars have proposed many different classification schemes for glottographic writing systems. Many of these have a basic structure like figure 14.2.

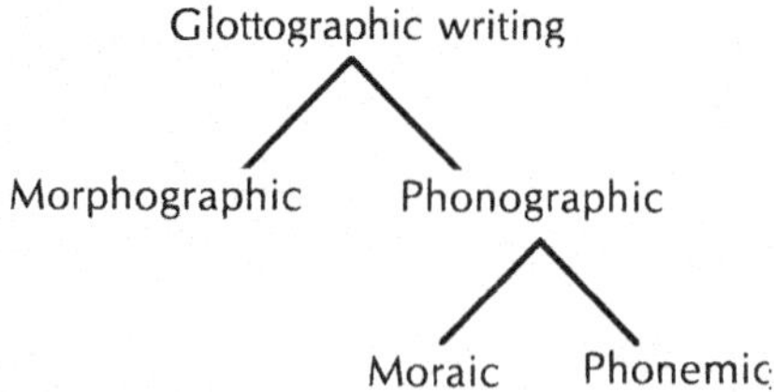

Figure 14.2 Traditional classification scheme of glottographic writing systems

In this scheme, three basic types of writing systems are distinguished. With morphographic systems, the grapheme relates to morphemes: Chinese and Sumerian are usually cited as the best examples of morphographic systems. The phonographic systems relate to phonological units in the language, either moraic or phonemic. With moraic systems, the grapheme represents a mora: Japanese *kana* or Cherokee are good examples of moraic systems (the problems of syllabic vs. moraic are discussed below in §14.5). And with phonemic systems, the grapheme represents a phonological segment, i.e., a consonant or vowel; Finnish and classical Greek are good examples of phonemic writing systems.

This taxonomic scheme has a certain amount of validity to it, but on closer examination, it is problematic. First, writing systems are taxonomically 'messy'. Writing systems are mixtures of some sort or other. Sometimes, the mixture is relatively small and can be set aside. Finnish is often cited for its simple one-to-one relationship between grapheme and segment. We saw in chapter 9 that there are three minor exceptions to this relationship, and also, like most modern writing systems, Finnish uses Arabic numerals, as well as symbols such as <& % = +>, which are clearly morphemically based. If Finnish were our worst case of typological mixture, we probably would not worry a great deal.

Egyptian writing presents a much more serious case of mixture, regularly using both morphographic and phonographic symbols. Writing a word phonographically and then adding a semantic determinative is normal. Many words are always written morphographically; many are always written phonographically. In Maya, the mixture of phonographic and morphographic is similarly thoroughgoing, and variation is so common that it would be difficult to specify a usual or typical way of writing a word in Maya. Japanese writing is the most obviously mixed system of all today, with its use of morphographic *kanji* and the two types of phonographic *kana*. To account for these systems, we need a way to describe mixed systems.

Aside from mixture, a second point has been argued strongly by DeFrancis (1989), who insists that there are no true morphographic writing systems, that all true writing systems are phonographically based. DeFrancis is speaking here of the basic, overriding nature of a system, recognizing that morphographic elements may be present. In particular, he refers to Chinese, where he estimates the phonetic component of characters to be 66 per cent. In his view, the importance of the purely morphographic characters in Chinese has been greatly exaggerated, partly because they are often the characters which are taught first and thus take on a prominence in our mind, and

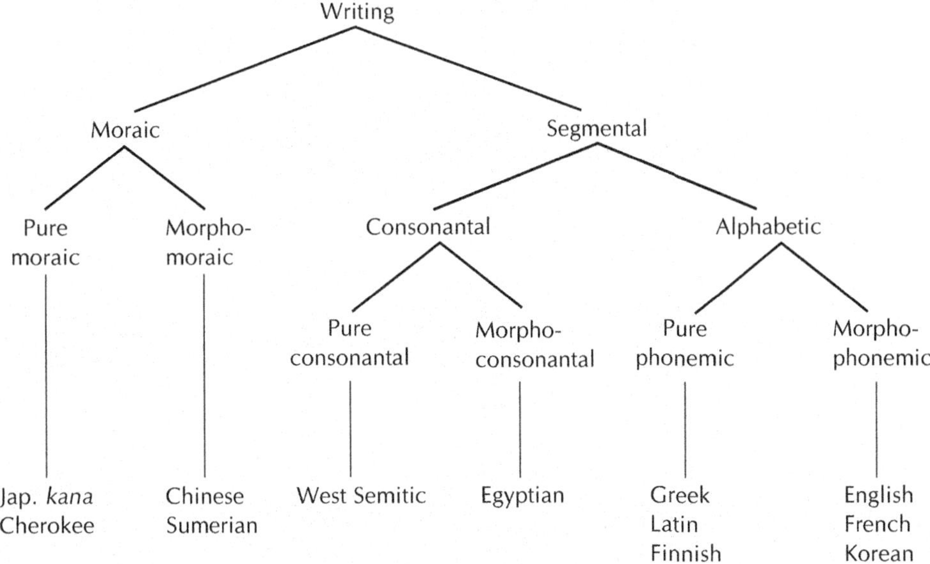

Figure 14.3 DeFrancis' classification of writing systems

partly because the writing system arose from pictographic (and thus morphographic) writing historically. I have argued above that the Bliss system contradicts DeFrancis' general claim about all writing systems, but the somewhat weaker claim that glottographic writing systems are never completely morphographic seems valid.

A third problem arises with writing systems such as English. Basically, English is a phonemic system, but its orthography often contains morphological information. As we saw in chapter 10, it is very common in English spelling to distinguish different homophonous morphemes: e.g., *you*, *yew*, *U*, *ewe*. We still need a way to incorporate this sort of information in the classification scheme.

DeFrancis' (1989) solution is to remove morphographic as a separate category and to add mixed categories: morphomoraic, morphophonemic, etc. A slightly modified version of the chart in DeFrancis (1989) is shown in figure 14.3 (I have substituted *moraic* for his *syllabic*). Note DeFrancis' term *consonantal* for the West Semitic abjads and for Egyptian.

Sproat (2000) argues that DeFrancis erred in equating the difference between *pure consonantal* and *morphoconsonantal* with the difference between *pure phonemic* and *morphophonemic*. Rather, Sproat says, the *morphophonemic* systems differ from the *pure phonemic* systems, not by what is represented by the basic symbols, but rather with respect to the phonological depth of what is represented; it is a mistake 'to equate the lexical orthographic (e.g., the marked spelling of /n/ in *knit*) with the logographic [= our morphographic] components of Chinese writing, an equation that is implicit in DeFrancis's classification'. This distinction is the same as the second and third problems of the traditional classification scheme discussed above (figure 14.2).

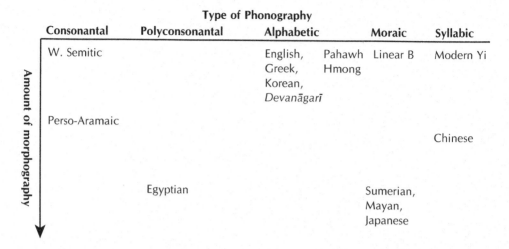

	Type of Phonography					
Amount of morphography ↓	**Consonantal**	**Polyconsonantal**	**Alphabetic**		**Moraic**	**Syllabic**
	W. Semitic		English, Greek, Korean, *Devanāgarī*	Pahawh Hmong	Linear B	Modern Yi
	Perso-Aramaic					
						Chinese
		Egyptian			Sumerian, Mayan, Japanese	

Figure 14.4 Sproat's classification of writing systems (the term *phonemic* has been substituted for his *alphabetic*)

Further, Sproat argues that calling Egyptian consonantal obscures the existence of bi- and triliteral symbols; rather, he views Egyptian as polyconsonantal. Sproat ultimately abandons DeFrancis' hierarchical classification in favour of a two-dimensional analysis (figure 14.4). The dimensions are **type of phonography** and **amount of morphography**. Perso-Aramaic refers to the Middle Persian (§7.3.3) writing with its frequent use of Aramaic morphograms.

I believe that Sproat's distinction of two dimensions, phonography and morphography, is an improvement over earlier classification schemes. Sproat suggests that other dimensions might be added, in particular **orthographic depth** which would distinguish deep (English, Korean, Russian) from shallow (Greek, Finnish, Belorusian). He also mentions the possibility of graphic arrangement as a significant classificatory feature; this would distinguish the very different patterning of *Devanāgarī* and Korean.

In my view, Sproat's dimension of phonography is too unstructured. He presents the various phonographic types simply as a list, going from smallest or simplest unit to the largest or most complex. In particular, lumping a phonemic writing system like Greek with an abugida such as *Devanāgarī* seems odd. Further, I do not see the difference between the consonantal and polyconsonantal systems as an important organizing principle for writing systems in general. The Egyptian use of polyconsonantal graphemes is unique and seems not to occur elsewhere. Sproat's distinction of *consonantal* and *phonemic* is compatible with Daniels' (1996a) distinction of *abjad* and *alphabet*, but I would add *abugida*. I would propose the classification scheme in figure 14.5.

The dimension of orthographic depth is also included: shallow systems are in regular type and deep systems are in upper-case. Finnish, Greek, and Belorusian are examples of shallow phonemic systems, whereas English, Korean, Russian, and

Type of Phonography

Amount of morphography ↓

Abjad	Alphabetic	Abugida	Moraic	Syllabic
W. Semitic	Finnish, Greek, Belorusian; Pahawh Hmong	*Devanāgarī*, BURMESE, TIBETAN	Linear B, CHEROKEE	Modern Yi
	KOREAN, RUSSIAN, SCOTS GAELIC			
Perso-Aramaic	ENGLISH			
				Chinese
Egyptian				
			Mayan, Japanese	Sumerian

Figure 14.5 Revised classification of writing systems (capitals show deep systems; regular type, shallow)

Scots Gaelic are examples of deep phonemic systems. Burmese and Tibetan are deep abugidas in contrast to the shallow Indian abugidas.

14.3 Note: Amount of Morphography and Orthographic Depth

The notions of **amount of morphography** and **orthographic depth** should be carefully distinguished. The amount of morphography is greater if there are symbols which represent morphemes or, in a phonographic system, if the spelling distinguishes different morphemes. Orthographic depth is greater if different allomorphs of the same morpheme are written the same. Thus in English, the use of numerals such as <7 8 9> adds to the amount of morphography, as does the fact that the spelling distinguishes homophonous morphemes such as *by*, *bye*, *buy*. Orthographic depth in English is greater because of the many heterophonous allomorphs which are spelled the same: e.g., *south–south*ern, *child–child*ren, *sign–sign*al.

14.4 Gelb's Unilinear Theory of Development

In 1964, Ignace Gelb, a renowned Semiticist, published an important book on writing systems which influenced much of the subsequent discussion about the typology of writing systems. Gelb argued that writing systems underwent a natural progression from pictographic to syllabic to phonemic; further, he felt that no step in this sequence could be skipped. If we examine the three places where we are sure that writing was invented, we see clear evidence in Mesopotamia and China that writing began with pictographs. With Maya writing, although there is little direct evidence for the early development of writing, an early pictographic stage is quite plausible. (Gelb himself believed that writing had only been created once. He thought that Chinese writing was borrowed from the Middle East, and he wrote before the decipherment of Maya.) Thus, we have no reason to differ with his notion that all writing starts with pictographs. His second point, that writing moves from pictographs to an alphabet via a syllabary, has proved much more contentious.

Gelb claimed that the Semitic script was syllabic (the term *syllabic* has other problems which are discussed in §14.5). His motivation for doing this was influenced by his notion of progression and was rather circular. Although Gelb recognized that the Semitic scripts were quite different from a more typical syllabary such as Japanese *kana*, his view was that each consonantal symbol in the Semitic script actually represented a syllable; for example, a consonant symbol did not represent merely <p>, but <pV> where <V> could be any vowel, i.e., /pi, pe, pa, po, pu/, etc. Most scholars today feel that Gelb was wrong in these claims: first, that there is no invariant drive towards alphabetization; and second, that the Semitic scripts are not syllabaries (Daniels 1990, Justeson and Stephens 1993).

14.5 Syllabic versus Moraic

Writing systems such as Japanese *kana*, Cherokee, Linear B, etc. have traditionally been referred to as syllabic systems. Poser (1992) drew attention to the fact that most of these systems are not in fact syllabic, but moraic. Mora in this sense can be taken as a part of a syllable equal either to the Onset + Nucleus or to the Coda; thus a typical simple mora would have the shape either of (C)V or –C.

In chapter 4, we pointed out that Japanese *kana* represents moræ, not syllables. Most *kana* symbols represent a (C)V sequence, but there are separate symbols for representing the two codal moræ. Thus in *kana*, a syllable such as /kun/ would be represented by two symbols <ku.n>. Cherokee has a very similar system, with CV symbols plus one for codal /s/. If Japanese *kana* and Cherokee were true syllabaries, there would be separate symbols for the closed syllables, and a syllable such as /kun/ would be represented by a single symbol.

Greek Linear B writing (chapter 8) is moraic in a slightly different way. Each Linear B symbol normally represents a mora. To write a word such as /tripos/ 'tripod', Linear B writes <ti-ri-po>. This writing is moraic and not strictly syllabic in two ways. First, a single syllable with an initial consonant cluster /tri/ has to be written with two moraic symbols <ti-ri> (duplicating the vowel) with the convention that the vowel of the first symbol is not pronounced. Second, a codal consonant is simply not written. If Linear B were syllabic, there would be separate symbols for writing syllables with consonant clusters and with codal consonants.

In Sumerian cuneiform writing (chapter 5), aside from the morphographic writing, three types of phonographic symbols exist with the shapes (C)V, VC, and CVC. Long vowels are sometimes written simply as CV (ignoring length) and sometimes by repeating the vowel with a separate symbol CV-V. Closed syllables were sometimes written moraically as CV-VC, but there were also some real syllabic symbols for certain CVC combinations. The phonographic portion of Sumerian writing appears to be basically moraic, with some syllabic writing.

Modern Yi writing has been described as truly syllabic (Poser 1992, Shi 1996, Sproat 2000). Yi (Lolo) is a Tibeto-Burman language spoken in southwestern China. A traditional Yi script exists which appears to have a logographic origin. The Chinese government has proposed a revised script with 819 characters, based solely on phonology. From the information available to me, Yi has 44 onsets, ten vowels, and four tones; as far as I can determine there are no codas. The proposed script has symbols for all occurring phonological possibilities. There are distinct symbols for three of the tones; the fourth tone is written by using the symbols for one of the other tones with a superscript arch diacritic. Without codal consonants, it is difficult to distinguish the difference of a simple CV syllable from a mora. However, the presence of the complex onsets, such as /mb nd tsh ndz tçh/ etc., written with one symbol (as opposed to the moraic way Linear B would have written these onsets), is some indication that the writing may be syllabic, not moraic.

As Sproat (2000) points out, Chinese is a syllabic script in the sense that each syllable has a separate symbol. The Chinese writing system, of course, has a large amount of morphography in that different homophonous morphemes are written with different symbols.

14.6 Korean *Hankul* as a Featural System

Sampson (1985) described Korean *hankul* as **featural**, positing a typological category of featural writing systems. As we saw in §§4.2.4–5, symbols in *hankul* for the different places of articulation share certain shapes, as do the symbols for the different manners. Sampson views these as the graphemes of the writing system. Since they relate to phonological features of the language, he describes the system as featural. The overall *hankul* inventory, however, is sufficiently unsystematic as to the relationship between features and shapes that Sampson's analysis seems forced.

To apply Sampson's analysis (see table 4.24), the letters <m n s g ŋ> would be taken as basic. This is already problematic since they do not share a common manner of articulation. To form the plain stops by Sampson's rules, a line is added, but the labial symbol is exceptional in shape and <g> is already in this category. The aspirated stops are formed by adding a further line or dot; again, the labial shape is exceptional. The tense stops and tense <s> are formed by Sampson by reduplicating the plain symbol; this works well. The liquid <l> would have to be added as an exception.

Some people have argued against the featural analysis on the grounds that Koreans learn the system by memorizing entire syllabic glyphs. Although I reject the featural analysis, this argument is unpersuasive since linguistic systems and human conscious awareness of them are often quite different.

In all, Sampson's analysis seems exaggerated (DeFrancis 1989, Kim-Reynaud 1997, Sproat 2000, Taylor and Taylor 1995; however, see Kim 1997 for a view agreeing with Sampson). The exceptions seem as plentiful as the regularities. Featural characteristics are obviously present. We have already seen that original symbol designs were based on articulatory positions. However, the presence of features does not mean that they form the basic structure of the system. I analyse *hankul* as a segmental writing system, with the individual letters combined into syllable-sized glyphs.

14.7 Conclusion

The importance of writing in our public and private lives is immense. For much of the world today life is almost unimaginable without writing. For 1999, UNESCO reports over 8000 daily newspapers published with a circulation of about 275 million, and over 300,000 books; and vast numbers of unpublished personal notes, letters, and diaries could be considered as well in the total amount of writing. The rate of literacy in a society has become a benchmark for measuring social development.

Surprisingly, writing has been invented very rarely, perhaps as few as three times in the history of the world. The usefulness of writing, however, is such that, once known, it has spread vigorously to other languages. All writing now in use is derived, at least indirectly, from only two writing systems: Semitic and Chinese. Today, there is likely no language which has not been touched by writing to some extent.

Once we humans possess writing, we regularly turn it into a social object. Most often it has been associated with education and the intellectually loftier portions of society. Not infrequently, societies have spoken one dialect or language and written another. Major struggles have resulted for and against changes in the way writing is done in a language.

We have examined many of the historically and linguistically important writing systems of the world. We have seen great variation and intricacy in the way different writing systems work. But much of that variation is related to detail; overall, writing represents language by putting down symbols representing the morphemes and phonemes in the syntactic order of the language involved.

14.8 Further Reading

Daniels (1996a) provides a good general introduction to the field, especially pp. 8–10. Gelb (1963), although outdated and sometimes wrongheaded, is still important reading for this area. Sampson (1985, chapter 2), DeFrancis (1989), and Sproat (2000, chapter 4) present the standard view. The debate in Sampson (1994) and DeFrancis and Unger (1994) is useful, although a bit polemic; Sproat (2000) is particularly good in comparing their views. Coulmas (1989) presents a more semiotic approach. DeFrancis' history of the interpretation of the Yukaghir Love Letter (1989, pp. 24–39) is fascinating.

14.9 Terms

amount of morphography
featural system
glottographic writing system
language
orthographic depth
phonetic writing system
semantic writing system (semasiographic)
type of phonography

Appendix A Some Basic Linguistic Terms

Communication is a very general term for the exchange of information. In this book, we are particularly interested in linguistic communication, that is, communication via the use of language. A **language** is a specific cognitive system which human beings use to communicate with each other. When we speak, we use language to encode our thoughts into sound which can be heard by others; when we listen, we use language to decode sounds produced by others into meaningful messages.

Structurally, **language** can be defined as a complex relationship existing between sound and meaning. Many different languages exist in the world. A major role of **linguistics** is to discover the nature of language in general, and of languages specifically.

Since this is a book on writing, you may wonder where writing fits in. Linguists consider writing to be secondary to sound. All languages are spoken; only some are written. All children learn to speak; some children learn to read and write, but only after they have learned to speak. Learning to speak is a natural, unconscious phenomenon; children learn to speak with no special instruction. Reading and writing, however, require special, conscious training.

We have said that language is a relationship between meaning and sound. Language is normally manifested as sound. If, however, language is manifested instead as graphic marks, then we can call those marks writing (figure A.1).

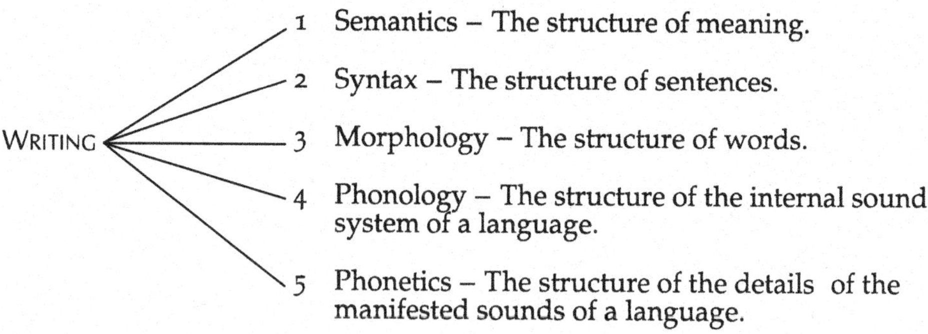

MEANING
WRITING
1 Semantics – The structure of meaning.
2 Syntax – The structure of sentences.
3 Morphology – The structure of words.
4 Phonology – The structure of the internal sound system of a language.
5 Phonetics – The structure of the details of the manifested sounds of a language.
SOUND

Figure A.1 The relationship between writing and language

Linguistics usually divides language into various levels. In Figure A.1, meaning, sound, and writing are considered part of the outside world, not part of language. Language is the cognitive structure linking meaning and sound. We can see from this figure that semantics is the part of language most closely related to meaning, and that phonetics is the part of language most closely related to sound. Writing has a more complicated relationship to language in that units of writing are commonly related to both morphology and phonology, but not generally to semantics, syntax, or phonetics. To illustrate the different levels, we will analyse the sentence *Mary purchased a new bookcase*; this analysis will be followed by other examples for each level.

Semantics

Semantic relations are those of meaning. In our example sentence (*Mary purchased a new bookcase*), *purchase* is the event or action; this event is connected to two semantic units: *Mary* and *bookcase*. In the sentence, *Mary* performs the action and is known as the 'agent'; *bookcase* receives the action and is known as the 'goal'. The time of the event is specified as prior to the expressing of the utterance itself. *A* and *new* give us information about the bookcase.

For other examples, *hot* and *cold* are semantic opposites; a *tulip* is a kind of *flower*, which, in turn, is a kind of *plant*. The sentences *The ball was kicked by Mary* and *Mary kicked the ball* have very similar meanings. In both, *Mary* performs the kicking and is the agent, and the *ball* receives the action and is the goal. The semantic structure of these two sentences is the same, or at least very similar.

Syntax

Syntax describes the structure of the sentence in terms of subjects, verbs, and objects. In English, the normal order of these elements is *subject–verb–object* (SVO). In our example sentence, the agent is realized as the subject and the goal as the object: thus, we get a basic structure of *Mary purchase bookcase* (SVO). The time sequence is realized as past tense. Both the subject and object are noun phrases which have fairly fixed word order in English. Mary is a single word and creates no problem. For the object, the typical word order of a noun phrase is used: *article–adjective–noun.*

In the sentences *The ball was kicked by Mary* and *Mary kicked the ball*, *ball* is the subject of the first sentence, but the direct object in the second sentence. Note that the syntactic structures are quite different, but that the semantic structures are very similar, as noted above.

Morphology

Morphology discusses the structure of words. Several words in our sample sentence have no internal structure: *Mary*, *a*, *new*. We say that each consist of only one morpheme. *Bookcase* obviously consists of two parts, *book* and *case*, which go together to form a compound: each part is a separate morpheme.

The word *foreigners* can be broken into three morphemes: *foreign* 'not native', *-er* 'a person', and *-s* 'plural'. These three parts are minimum meaningful parts in the sense that they are meaningful, but they cannot be further broken down into meaningful units. Minimum meaningful parts form morphemes. *Purchased* also consists of two morphemes: *purchase* and *-ed*, where *-ed* is a suffix indicating the past tense. If we listen carefully to the sound of *purchased*, we notice that the past tense part is pronounced /t/, not /d/ as the writing suggests (this is discussed further below).

Other examples:

1 *basketball – basket + ball*
2 *foolishness – fool + ish + ness*
3 *books – book +* plural
4 *men – man +* plural
   analyzed on the model of *books*
5 *broke – break +* past tense
   analyzed on the model of *purchase*

Morphemes frequently are realized by more than one shape. The different realizations of a morpheme are called **allomorphs.**

We easily divide *lioness* into two morphemes as *lion + ess*, where *-ess* is a feminine suffix. Similarly, we analyze *duchess* as *duke + ess*. Here, the situation is more complicated than with *lioness*. When the morpheme *duke* appears alone, it has the shape *duke*; however, when it occurs before the morpheme *-ess*, it has the form *duch-*. Thus we can say that English has a morpheme *duke* and that the morpheme *duke* has two allomorphs *duke* and *duch-*. *Duch-* also occurs before *-y* 'territory' as in *duchy.*

We say that these allomorphs *duke* and *duch-* are in **complementary distribution** which means that one allomorph occurs in one set of environments (*duke* by itself) and the other occurs in another set of environments (*duch-* before *-ess* or *-y*).

We must be sure to think in terms of sounds, not in terms of writing. In our example above of *purchased*, we saw that the allomorph of the past tense marker is /t/. In a different word, however, such as *rolled*, the allomorph of the past tense marker is /d/. If we were to examine many forms of the past tense in English, we would discover that the choice of /t/ or /d/ is predictable and depends on the last consonant of the verb: thus, after /s/ in *purchase*, we get /t/, but after /l/ in *roll*, we get /d/. The writing system, however, ignores this allomorphic variation and always writes *-ed.* I have enclosed symbols in slant lines here to emphasize that I am talking about sounds.

In another example, with the plural forms *cats* and *dogs*, although the plural morpheme is written *-s*, it is pronounced /s/ in *cats* and /z/ in *dogs*. Thus the plural morpheme has two allomorphs in English: /s/ (after /t/) and /z/ (after /g/). Again, the writing system ignores the allomorphic variation and always writes *-s.*

Phonology

Every language has a basic set of sounds called **phonemes.** Any utterance can be represented in terms of the phonemes of the language. For example, the representation of our example sentence is /ˌmɛɹi ˌpəɹtʃəst ə ˌnu ˈbʊkˌkejs/ (or something similar in other accents of English).

English has the sounds /p t k/. These sounds all **contrast** with each other in the sense that by interchanging them, we create new words: /pɑt, tɑt, kɑt/ *pot*, *tot*, *cot*. (Note that we are talking about sounds here, not letters; thus we always use /k/ to represent the phoneme no matter how it is spelled: *cat*, *queen*, *kick*.) The phonemes of English are given in Appendix C.

Like morphemes, phonemes often have different realizations, known as allophones. For example, in English when /p t k/ come at the beginning of a word, there is a little puff of air afterwards: [p^{h}ɑt, t^{h}ɑp, k^{h}ul] *pot*, *top*, *cool*. The allophones [p^{h} t^{h} k^{h}] have been written in square brackets to emphasize that we are talking about allophones here, not phonemes. Now note that when an /s/ precedes /p t k/ at the beginning of a word, there is no puff of air: [spɑt stɑp skul] *spot*, *stop*, *school*. Thus, we can say that English has the phonemes /p t k/ and each of these has two allophones in complementary distribution: [p p^{h}], [t t^{h}], [k k^{h}].

The term **segment** is used to cover both consonants and vowels. **Syllables** are divided into constituent parts. The vowel is the central part of the syllable, called the **nucleus**. Any consonants preceding the nucleus are known as the **onset**. Consonants following the nucleus are known as the **coda**. The nucleus and the coda taken together form the **rhyme**.

Phonetics

We could describe the phonetic detail of our sample sentence, but this would not be very useful in this book. One example would be the sounds [p^{h} t^{h} k^{h}], which are called aspirated stops; aspirated means that they have a little puff of air, and stop means that while they are being produced the airflow through the mouth is cut off. We could also note that both French and English have the unaspirated stops [p t k], but that only English, and not French, has the aspirated stops [p^{h} t^{h} k^{h}].

This book assumes that the reader has a basic familiarity with phonetic symbols and terminology. Appendix B contains the IPA (International Phonetic Alphabet) chart which explains the symbols. If you are unfamiliar with the descriptions, you might want to review them in the phonetics chapter of an elementary text on linguistics. A more thorough discussion can be found in Rogers (2000).

Bracketing

As we have just seen, a linguistic utterance can be analyzed at many different levels. Linguists use certain notational conventions to help keep the levels straight. Slant lines /tɑp/ are used to indicate a phonemic transcription; square brackets are used to indicate an allophonic or phonetic notation [t^{h}ɑp]. In this book we use italics *top* to write a word generally without focusing on the pronunciation. When we want to draw special attention to the fact that we are talking about an orthographic symbol, we use angled brackets <t>. Thus, we could write: *In English, <c q k> are all used to write the phoneme /k/, as in the word* quick.

Linguistic Level

A linguistic representation may relate to different linguistic levels. It can be described by its position on a continuum between **deep** and **shallow**. A transcription is shallower if it is closer to the phonetic end; a representation is deeper if it gives more morphological information. A **morphophonemic** representation is one related to linguistic units between morphology and phonology. In the examples above of the past tense, the writing system of English regularly represents the past tense morpheme the same way: <-ed>, except for irregular verbs such as *kept*, *sent*, *rode*, *sang* (this simplifies the situation somewhat), even though the past tense morpheme has two different sounding allomorphs /t/ and /d/. In this case, English is using a deep transcription. If English wrote <-t> or <-d> in strict accordance with the sound, it would use a shallow transcription.

Language Change and Dialects

Languages are constantly changing. A simple way of looking at the effect of language change is that if a language is spoken in two areas, and one area undergoes a linguistic change, but the other area does not, the result is that the two areas come to speak different **dialects**. If these dialectal differences accumulate, they may become so great that the dialects are no longer mutually intelligible, and we can then call them different languages. Two languages related in this way are said to form a language family descended from the older language. A well-known example is that Latin changed in various ways in different places, giving rise to several different languages: Portuguese, Spanish, French, Italian, and Romanian.

Variation in language extends beyond dialectal or geographic variation to include also social variations based on variables such as age, social class, education, gender, or sexual orientation.

Appendix B The International Phonetic Alphabet

The International Phonetic Alphabet (IPA) is the standard system for transcribing linguistic utterances. The chart of IPA symbols is given in figure B.1. A detailed description of the system is given in the *Handbook* of the International Phonetic Association (1999).

The IPA was developed in the early twentieth century and became fairly standard in Europe. In North America, several variant symbols arose primarily because of the difficulty of typing the IPA symbols in the days of typewriters. At present, the use of the North American alternatives is very slowly turning towards the use of the standard IPA symbols. The major alternatives are shown in table B.1. Occasionally, scholarly areas (e.g., Assyriology, Egyptology) have certain special uses of their own. The normal transcription of many languages varies from strict IPA usage – *pīnyīn*, for example, in Chinese.

Table B.1 Common North American alternatives to IPA usage

IPA	*North American*
ʃ	š
ʒ	ž
tʃ	č
dʒ	ǰ
j	y
y	ü

THE INTERNATIONAL PHONETIC ALPHABET (revised to 1993, updated 1996)

CONSONANTS (PULMONIC)

© 1996 IPA

	Bilabial	Labiodental	Dental	Alveolar	Postalveolar	Retroflex	Palatal	Velar	Uvular	Pharyngeal	Glottal
Plosive	p b			t d		ʈ ɖ	c ɟ	k ɡ	q ɢ		ʔ
Nasal	m	ɱ		n		ɳ	ɲ	ŋ	ɴ		
Trill	ʙ			r					ʀ		
Tap or Flap				ɾ		ɽ					
Fricative	ɸ β	f v	θ ð	s z	ʃ ʒ	ʂ ʐ	ç ʝ	x ɣ	χ ʁ	ħ ʕ	h ɦ
Lateral fricative				ɬ ɮ							
Approximant		ʋ		ɹ		ɻ	j	ɰ			
Lateral approximant				l		ɭ	ʎ	ʟ			

Where symbols appear in pairs, the one to the right represents a voiced consonant. Shaded areas denote articulations judged impossible.

CONSONANTS (NON-PULMONIC)

Clicks		Voiced implosives		Ejectives	
ʘ	Bilabial	ɓ	Bilabial	ʼ	Examples:
ǀ	Dental	ɗ	Dental/alveolar	pʼ	Bilabial
!	(Post)alveolar	ʄ	Palatal	tʼ	Dental/alveolar
ǂ	Palatoalveolar	ɠ	Velar	kʼ	Velar
ǁ	Alveolar lateral	ʛ	Uvular	sʼ	Alveolar fricative

VOWELS

Front — Central — Back

Close: i • y —— ɨ • ʉ —— ɯ • u

ɪ ʏ ʊ

Close-mid: e • ø —— ɘ • ɵ —— ɤ • o

ə

Open-mid: ɛ • œ —— ɜ • ɞ —— ʌ • ɔ

æ ɐ

Open: a • ɶ —— ɑ • ɒ

Where symbols appear in pairs, the one to the right represents a rounded vowel.

OTHER SYMBOLS

ʍ Voiceless labial-velar fricative

w Voiced labial-velar approximant

ɥ Voiced labial-palatal approximant

ʜ Voiceless epiglottal fricative

ʢ Voiced epiglottal fricative

ʡ Epiglottal plosive

ɕ ʑ Alveolo-palatal fricatives

ɺ Voiced alveolar lateral flap

ɧ Simultaneous ʃ and x

Affricates and double articulations can be represented by two symbols joined by a tie bar if necessary. k͡p t͜s

SUPRASEGMENTALS

ˈ Primary stress

ˌ Secondary stress

ˌfoʊnəˈtɪʃən

ː Long eː

ˑ Half-long eˑ

̆ Extra-short ĕ

| Minor (foot) group

‖ Major (intonation) group

. Syllable break ɹi.ækt

‿ Linking (absence of a break)

DIACRITICS Diacritics may be placed above a symbol with a descender, e.g. ŋ̊

̥ Voiceless	n̥ d̥	̤ Breathy voiced	b̤ a̤	̪ Dental	t̪ d̪
̬ Voiced	s̬ t̬	̰ Creaky voiced	b̰ a̰	̺ Apical	t̺ d̺
ʰ Aspirated	tʰ dʰ	̼ Linguolabial	t̼ d̼	̻ Laminal	t̻ d̻
̹ More rounded	ɔ̹	ʷ Labialized	tʷ dʷ	̃ Nasalized	ẽ
̜ Less rounded	ɔ̜	ʲ Palatalized	tʲ dʲ	ⁿ Nasal release	dⁿ
̟ Advanced	u̟	ˠ Velarized	tˠ dˠ	ˡ Lateral release	dˡ
̠ Retracted	e̠	ˤ Pharyngealized	tˤ dˤ	̚ No audible release	d̚
̈ Centralized	ë	̴ Velarized or pharyngealized	ɫ		
̽ Mid-centralized	e̽	̝ Raised	e̝ (ɹ̝ = voiced alveolar fricative)		
̩ Syllabic	n̩	̞ Lowered	e̞ (β̞ = voiced bilabial approximant)		
̯ Non-syllabic	e̯	̘ Advanced Tongue Root	e̘		
˞ Rhoticity	ɚ a˞	̙ Retracted Tongue Root	e̙		

TONES AND WORD ACCENTS

LEVEL		CONTOUR	
e̋ or ˥	Extra high	ě or ˩˥	Rising
é ˦	High	ê ˥˩	Falling
ē ˧	Mid	e᷄ ˧˥	High rising
è ˨	Low	e᷅ ˩˧	Low rising
ȅ ˩	Extra low	e᷈ ˧˦˧	Rising-falling
↓	Downstep	↗	Global rise
↑	Upstep	↘	Global fall

Figure B.1 The IPA chart (from International Phonetic Association. © 1993 by the International Phonetic Association. Reproduced with permission. http://www.arts.gla.ac.uk/IPA/ipa.html)

Appendix C English Transcription

English examples are occasionally given in this book in transcription, and the Glossary gives the pronunciation of many less familiar terms. The usage followed in these transcriptions is given below.

Table C.1 Key to English transcription

Consonants:					
/p/	*pot*		/b/	*beat*	
/t/	*tot*		/d/	*dot*	
/tʃ/	*chin*		/dʒ/	*gin*	
/k/	*cot*		/g/	*got*	
/f/	*fought*		/v/	*vote*	
/θ/	*thin*		/ð/	*then*	
/s/	*seal*		/z/	*zeal*	
/ʃ/	*shot*		/ʒ/	*pleasure*	
/h/	*hot*		/m/	*meat*	
/n/	*not*		/ŋ/	*hang*	
/l/	*lot*		/ɹ/	*rot*	
/w/	*wit*		/j/	*yacht*	
Vowels:					
/i/	*beat*			/u/	*boot*
/ɪ/	*pit*			/ʊ/	*put*
/ej/	*hate*	/ə/	*sofa, purr*	/ow/	*boat*
/ɛ/	*pet*	/ʌ/	*but*	/ɔ/	*door*
/æ/	*pat*			/ɑ/	*pot, paw*
/aj/	*ride*				
/aw/	*loud*				
/ɔj/	*choice*				
Stress (marked at beginning of syllable):					
	Primary	/ˈ/	/ˈsʌpəɹ/	*supper*	
	Secondary	/ˌ/	/ˈdɔɹˌnɑb/	*doorknob*	
	Unstressed	unmarked	/əˈpiɹ/	*appear*	

The pronunciation given especially for borrowed words is intended to represent a standard English pronunciation, not necessarily what a native speaker of the language would say. In many cases, alternative pronunciations are to be heard.

The accent of the transcriptions is that of Toronto, where the author lives. Speakers of other accents will probably be able to adjust the pronunciation to fit their own accent. (For further information on this, see Rogers (2000), especially chapter 6.)

Note that in this dialect, the vowels of *caught* and *cot* are merged as /ɑ/; both words are pronounced /kɑt/. The vowel /ɔ/ only occurs before /ɹ/ as in *door* /ˈdɔɹ/. The vowel /ə/ occurs stressed before /ɹ/; otherwise it occurs only in unstressed syllables (including before /ɹ/ in unstressed syllables): *purr* /ˈpəɹ/, *upper* /ˈʌpəɹ/, *sofa* /ˈsowfə/. The words *merry*, *mary*, *Mary* are all pronounced as /ˈmɛri/.

Appendix D Glossary

abecedary /ˌejbiˈsidəɹi/. A text showing the letters of an alphabet in their standard order.
abjad /ˈæbˌdʒæd/. A phonographic writing system in which symbols correspond to consonants in the language, but vowels are not typically written: e.g., many Semitic systems.
abstract pictogram. A pictogram which represents an abstract object by a conventional drawing; e.g., a single line which represents the number *one*.
abugida /ˌɑbuˈgidə/. A phonographic writing system in which vowels are typically written as diacritics on consonants and one vowel is not written: e.g., scripts of India, Ethiopic.
Achæmenid /əˈkimɛnɪd/. The Persian Empire during the period 553–330 OLD.
acrophony /əˈkɹɑfəni/. The principle by which a pictographic symbol takes a phonographic value from the first sound of the name of the object it represents: e.g., a picture of a tulip could be used to represent the sound /t/ in English since /t/ is the first sound of /ˈtjulɪp/. Adj. **acrophonic** /ˌækɹəˈfɑnɪk/.
acute accent. A diacritic [´] of the Greek and Roman alphabets.
Akkadian /əˈkejdiən/. An ancient Semitic language of Mesopotamia, particularly around the ancient city of Akkad /ˌæˈkæd/. See **Assyrian** and **Babylonian.**
akṣara /ˈɑkʃɑɹɑ/. In Indian scripts, an orthographic syllable. An *akṣara* is an open syllable with maximal onset, consisting of a vowel and the entire preceding consonant cluster: e.g., <hi-ndi>, where the hyphen divides the *akṣaras.*
allograph /ˈæləˌgɹæf/. A non-contrastive unit in a writing system; a member of a grapheme. In the Greek alphabet, <σ> and <ς> are allographs of the same grapheme *sigma.* **Classes of allographs** – allographs which are defined by a feature such as upper case, lower case, roman, italic, bold.
allomorph /ˈæləˌmɔɹf/. A non-contrastive meaningful unit in a language; a member of a morpheme. In English /djuk/ and /dʌtʃ-/ are allomorphs of the same morpheme *duke.*
allophone /ˈæləˌfown/. A non-contrastive unit of sound in a language; a member of a phoneme. In English, [t] and [tʰ] are allophones of the same phoneme /t/.
alphabet. A type of writing system in which each symbol typically corresponds to a segment (consonant or vowel) in the language: e.g., the Roman, Greek, and Cyrillic alphabets.
amount of morphography. A dimension in the taxonomy of writing systems arranging writing systems by how much morphographic information is encoded in the writing system.
Anglo-Saxon. An alternative name for Old English.
Arabic. An important version of the Semitic abjad, derived from the Aramaic abjad. The Arabic language is the most widely spoken Semitic language today and is the liturgical language of Islam.
Aramaic /ˌɛɹəˈmejɪk/. An important version of the Semitic abjad, giving rise to many other versions. The Aramaic language is an historically important Semitic language, originally spoken in Syria and later widely used as a chancery language and lingua franca in the

Middle East. **Aramæan** /ˌɛɹə'miən/. A speaker of Aramaic, from Aram /ə'ɹæm/, the Biblical name for Syria.

Armenian. An alphabet derived from Greek in the fifth century NEW for the Armenian language.

Assyrian /ə'siɹiən/. An ancient Semitic language of Mesopotamia, particularly of the north. See **Akkadian** and **Babylonian.**

ateji /ˌɑ'tejdʒi/. In Japanese, words of more than one character with the characters chosen by phonetic extension.

aybuben. The name of the Armenian alphabet.

Babel /'bejbəl/. Biblical name for Babylon, best known for its ziggurat in the phrase 'tower of Babel'.

Babylonian /ˌbæbɪ'lowniən/. An ancient Semitic language of Mesopotamia, particularly around Babylon (= Babel /'bejbəl/).

Babylonian Captivity. The captivity of the Israelites in Babylon (586–538 OLD).

báihuà /'bajˌhwɑ/. 'Plain speech'; a tradition of writing in colloquial Chinese, coexisting with Classical Chinese. *Báihuà* formed the basis of Modern Standard Chinese.

Bible. The name for the scriptures used by Jews and Christians. Christians commonly refer to the Hebrew scriptures as the Old Testament and to the specifically Christian scriptures as the New Testament, and use the term 'Bible' to include both.

biconsonantal grapheme. A grapheme representing two consonants, as in Egyptian.

bold. In typography, letterforms with heavier weight: e.g., **<a>** as opposed to <a>.

borrowing of a writing system. The adaptation of a writing system originally used for one language for a different language; e.g., the borrowing of the Semitic abjad to write Greek. Cf. **creation of a writing system** and **invention of writing.**

bound grapheme. A grapheme which occurs only in combination with other graphemes, often a diacritic. See **free grapheme.**

boustrophedon /ˌbustɹə'fidən/. Writing that alternates direction from right to left and left to right in alternating lines. Greek βουστροφηδόν 'as an ox ploughs'. Adj. **boustrophedal** /ˌbustɹə'fidəl/.

breathings. Diacritic marks in Greek to indicate the presence or absence of /h/. The presence of /h/ is shown by a **rough breathing** above a vowel <ἡ ἁ>; its absence is shown by a **smooth breathing** <ἠ ἀ>.

calendar round. In the Maya calendar, a repeating cycle of 52 years, consisting of a ***tz'olkin*** and a ***haab.***

calligraphy /kə'lɪgɹəfi/. Beautiful writing; writing as an art form. Adj. **calligraphic** /ˌkælɪ'gɹæfɪk/.

Cantonese /'kæntəˌniz/. A southern dialect of Chinese spoken in Guangdong (Canton) and Hong Kong; also known as Yuè.

cartouche /ˌkɑɹ'tuʃ/. An oval drawn around portions of an Egyptian king's name in hieroglyphic writing.

Champollion, Jean-François (1790–1832) /ʃãpɔʎɔ̃/. The French decipherer of Egyptian hieroglyphics.

chancery language. The language or dialect used for administrative purposes by government officials.

chữnôm /'tʃuˌnɑm/. (Viet. 'southern script'). A type of early Vietnamese writing involving invented characters modelled on Chinese.

circumflex accent. A diacritic <ˆ> of the Greek and Roman alphabet; in Greek, sometimes appearing as <˜>.

Classical Chinese. The dialect of Chinese used for writing before 1900 NEW.

Classical Greek. Ancient Greek of the period 600–300 OLD.

clay tablet. The normal writing surface of cuneiform writing.

coda. In a syllable, any consonants following the nucleus.
communication. A general term for the transmission of messages. **Language** is one form of communication.
complementary distribution. A distribution of objects, such that none occurs in the environment of the other, e.g., *duke* and *duch-*, or [t] and [tʰ], as discussed in Appendix A. See **contrastive distribution.**
complex numeral. In Chinese, a complex form of a number grapheme, used to avoid fraud.
complex symbol. A combination of a free grapheme (or basic symbol) and a diacritic: e.g., <ñ>, where <n> is the free grapheme (or basic symbol) and <˜> is the diacritic.
contrast (verb). To form two distinct units. Two units contrast if they occur in the same environment with different meanings.
contrastive distribution. A distribution such that two objects occur in the same environment, e.g., /s/ and /z/ as discussed in Appendix A. See **complementary distribution.**
Coptic /ˈkɑptɪk/. 1. The name used for Egyptian language since the third century NEW. (The people are **Copts** /kɑpts/.) 2. The Greek-based writing system used for the Coptic language.
cranberry grapheme. A grapheme occurring in only one environment; e.g., in English, <q> typically occurs only before <u>.
cranberry morpheme. A morpheme occurring in only one environment; e.g., the morpheme *cran-* only occurs before *berry*.
creation of a writing system. The creation of a new writing system by stimulus diffusion; the creator is aware of the existence of writing: e.g., Cree, Cherokee. Cf. **borrowing of a writing system** and **invention of writing.**
creative spelling. A non-standard spelling, intended to be amusing or eye-catching.
cuneiform /ˌkjuˈniəˌfɔɹm/. An ancient type of Middle Eastern writing made with a wedge-shaped stylus pressed into clay.
cursive writing. Writing done with minimal lifting of the writing tool; writing done quickly.
Cypriot /ˈsɪpɹiət/. Writing of early Cyprus: Cypro-Minoan (1500–1200 OLD, undeciphered) and Cypriot (800–200 OLD, Greek).
Cyrillic /sɪˈɹɪlɪk/. An alphabet, possibly created by St. Cyril, commonly used in Slavic language where the religion has been mainly Eastern Orthodox.
Dead Sea scroll. Hebrew and Aramaic manuscripts found near the Dead Sea in Israel, containing many of the oldest manuscripts of the Jewish scriptures.
decipherment. The successful process of reading and understanding a previously unreadable text.
deep. A deep writing system is more closely related to morphophonemic units in language, as opposed to phonemic units. A deeper writing system will have more cases of different allomorphs written the same. See **shallow** and **orthographic depth.**
demotic /dəˈmɑtɪk/. The most cursive form of Egyptian writing. See **hieroglyphic** and **hieratic.**
demotike /dimotiˈki/. A more informal form of the modern Greek language. See ***katharevousa.***
Devanāgarī /ˌdevəˈnɑgəɹi/. An important modern script of India, used for Hindi and other languages.
diacritic /ˌdajəˈkɹɪtɪk/. A bound grapheme which modifies the value of the basic symbol to which it is attached; e.g., in <é>, <´> is a diacritic, and <e> is the basic symbol.
dialect. A variety of a language, particularly a regional one.
dialect character. In Chinese, a non-standard character used to represent a morpheme, found in a certain dialect, but not in Modern Standard Chinese.
differentiation. A method of creating a symbol: an ambiguous symbol used for two different things is disambiguated by altering its shape in one of the uses. For example, if in a language, the symbol X is ambiguously used to represent two different morphemes, differentiation might use X to represent one morpheme and X̥ to represent the other.

diglossia /ˌdaj'glɑsiə/. A sociolinguistic situation in which two very different varieties of a language are both used, one for writing and the other for speech. **Bilingual diglossia** – a type of diglossia in which one language is used for writing and another for speech. Adj. **diglossic** /ˌdaj'glɑsɪk/.

digraph /'dajˌgɹæf/. A sequence of two graphemes which represents a linguistic unit normally represented by one grapheme: e.g., in English, the grapheme sequence <sh> represents the phoneme /ʃ/ which is normally represented by a single grapheme.

distance number. In Maya writing, a time period which is to be added to or subtracted from a date in the text to give a new date.

Dravidian /dɹə'vɪdijən/. The major language family of southern India.

emblem glyph. A Maya glyph showing the name of a city.

-emic /'imɪk/. A level of more abstract, contrastive units.

-etic /'ɛtɪk/. A level of more concrete, non-contrastive units.

Etruscan /ə'tɹʌskən/. 1. A language formerly spoken in Italy to the north of Rome. 2. An alphabet used for Etruscan borrowed from Greek and borrowed in turn by the Latin-speaking Romans.

featural system. A taxonomic term, used by Sampson (1985) to categorize Korean *hankul*; the use of diacritic features in *hankul* is made a crucial taxonomic point. Generally rejected by other scholars.

final. In Chinese, the part of the syllable except any initial consonant or the tone.

free grapheme. A grapheme which occurs independently. See **bound grapheme.**

full-figure variant. In Maya writing, a large allograph, usually occupying two writing spaces.

furigana /'fuɹigɑnə/. Small *hiragana* placed near a character to show its pronunciation.

futhark /'fuˌθɑɹk/. The name of the runic alphabet; its Anglo-Saxon form is known as *futhorc.*

Ge'ez /'giˌɛz/. A Semitic language, of the South Arabian group; the traditional language of learning and liturgy of Ethiopia.

Georgian. An alphabet derived from Greek by the fifth century NEW for Georgian, a Caucasian language.

Glagolitic /ˌglɑgə'lɪtɪk/. An early alphabet used for Slavic languages, possibly derived from cursive Greek.

glottographic writing system /ˌglɑtə'gɹæfɪk/. A writing system used to transcribe the linguistic units (e.g., morphemes or phonemes) of a certain language; e.g., most of the writing systems discussed in this book.

glyph. A unit of organization in Maya writing.

Gothic. An alphabet used for the Gothic language, derived from Greek in the fourth century NEW.

graffito /gɹə'fitow/ (pl. **graffiti** /gɹə'fiti/). An informal writing, as on a wall or other public surface.

grapheme /'gɹæˌfim/. A contrastive unit in a writing system; a class of allographs. The English alphabet has 26 graphemes; each character in Chinese is a grapheme.

grave accent. A diacritic <`> of the Greek and Roman alphabets.

Great English Vowel Shift. A major set of sound changes in English which took place around 1450 NEW, affecting the long vowels of English.

gunu /'guˌnu/. In cuneiform writing, a diacritic used to differentiate one symbol from another.

haab. In the Maya calendar, a repeating cycle of 365 days.

hamzah /'hɑmzɑ/. An Arabic symbol ء for the glottal stop /ʔ/.

hanca /'hɑndʒɑ/. The Korean name for Chinese characters (= Ch. *hànzì*).

hankul /'hɑŋgəl/. In Korean, the alphabet normally used for writing today.

hànzì /'hɑndzə/. The Chinese name for characters.

head variant. In Maya writing, an allograph, particularly of a numeral, which incorporates a human head.

Hebrew. An important Semitic language. After dying out as a spoken language, Hebrew was revived and is spoken in Israel today; it is the liturgical language of Judaism. **Old Hebrew abjad.** Writing system used for Hebrew before the Babylonian Captivity, derived from the Phœnician abjad. **New Hebrew abjad.** Writing system used for Hebrew since the Babylonian Captivity, derived from the Aramaic abjad; also used for Yiddish, Ladino, and other languages spoken by Jews.

heterography /ˌhɛtəˈɹɑɡɹəfi/. A situation in which two different linguistic units are written differently, e.g., *blue–blew*, *cat–dog*. Adj. **heterographic** /ˌhɛtəɹəˈɡɹæfɪk/.

heterophony /ˌhɛtəˈɹɑfəni/. A situation in which two different linguistic units sound different, e.g., *cat–dog*, *bow* 'bend over'/'bow and arrow'. Adj. **heterophonic** /ˌhɛtəɹəˈfɑnɪk/.

hieratic /ˌhajəˈɹætɪk/. A form of Egyptian writing, more cursive than hieroglyphic, and more formal than demotic.

hieroglyphic /ˌhajɹəˌɡlɪfɪk/. The earliest pictographic form of Egyptian writing.

hiragana. See ***kana.***

homography /həˈmɑɡɹəfi/. A situation in which two different linguistic units are written the same, e.g. *bow* 'bend over'/'bow and arrow', *well* 'hole for water'/'not sick'. Adj. **homographic** /ˌhɑməˈɡɹæfɪk/.

homophones /ˌhɑməˈfown/. Two different words in a language with the same pronunciation.

homophony /həˈmɑfəni/. A situation in which two different linguistic units sound the same, e.g., *well* 'hole for water'/'not sick', *blue–blew*. Adj. **homophonic** /ˌhɑməˈfɑnɪk/.

hyangchal /ˈhjɑŋtʃɑl/. In Korean, an historic type of writing of poetry using phonetic extension of characters.

ideogram. A term found in some literature on writing systems with a variety of meanings, best avoided.

Indian grammarians. Scholars of the fourth century OLD who developed a sophisticated analysis of certain aspects of Sanskrit grammar.

Indo-Aryan /ˌɪndowˈɛɹijən/. A branch of Indo-European; the major language family of northern India, Pakistan, Nepal, and Bangladesh.

Indus Valley /ˈɪndəs/. In Pakistan, an early society with an undeciphered script.

initial. In Chinese, the first consonant of a syllable.

initial series. In Maya writing, a date at the beginning of the text, often written with special doubly wide glyphs.

internal structure of writing. Rules of the writing system independent of the language being written; e.g., the Roman alphabet is always written left to right, no matter what the language.

invention of writing. The invention of writing, with no previous knowledge of writing at all; e.g., cuneiform, Chinese, Maya. See **borrowing of a writing system** and **creation of a writing system.**

italic. In typography, a slanted style of letterforms.

itwu /ˈidu/. In Korean, an historic type of character-based writing, used until 1900.

Johnson, Samuel (1709–84). An important English lexicographer, author of *Dictionary of the English Language.*

jukujikun /ˌdzuˈkudʒiˌkun/. In Japanese, words of more than one character with the characters chosen for their semantic value.

kana /ˈkɑnə/. Either of two moraic systems used in Japanese writing: ***hiragana*** /ˈhiɹəˌɡɑnə/, a cursive form used especially for writing affixes, and ***katakana*** /ˈkɑtəˌkɑnə/, an angular form used especially for writing borrowed words and other special uses. See also ***furigana*** and ***kanji.***

kanbun /ˈkɑnˌbun/. The writing of Classical Chinese in Japan (= Ch. *wényán*).

kanji /ˈkɑndʒi/. The Japanese name for Chinese characters (= Ch. *hànzì*).

katakana. See ***kana.***

katharevousa /ˌkɑθɑˈɹɛvuˌsɑ/. A more formal form of the modern Greek language. See ***demotike.***

kokuji /ˈkowkuˌdʒi/. In Japanese, characters invented in Japan and not existing in Chinese.

kun*-reading** /kun/. A reading of a character in Japanese using a native Japanese pronunciation. A **semantic *kun uses the pronunciation of a native Japanese word; a **phonetic *kun*** extends the *kun*-reading of a native Japanese word to other Japanese words having the same pronunciation. See ***on*-reading.**

kwukyel /ˈkugjəl/. In Korean, an historic type of writing, especially used for Buddhist texts, employing phonetic extension for writing affixes.

Landa's alphabet. A portion of a sixteenth-century NEW document written by Bishop Diego de Landa giving information about the Maya writing system.

language. A complex system residing in the human brain, relating meaning and sound; a form of **communication.**

language academy. An institution, found in certain countries, usually charged with the responsibility of establishing standards with respect to language.

Latin. The language of ancient Rome and a language of learning for western Europe for centuries; the Romance languages are descended from Latin. See **Roman alphabet.**

lenition /ləˈnɪʃən/. A phonological process of weakening, in which a stop typically becomes a fricative, and a fricative becomes /h/ or disappears. A phenomenon in Scots Gaelic and other Celtic languages, affecting the writing system.

letter. A single grapheme of an alphabet.

Levant /ləˈvænt/. The land of the eastern Mediterranean: Syria, Lebanon, Israel, Palestine, Jordan. Adj. **Levantine** /ˈlɛvənˌtajn -ˌtin/.

ligature /ˈlɪgəˌtjuɹ/. Two graphemes which are joined and written as one unit; e.g., <æ> for <ae>. **Structural ligature** – a ligature which functions as a separate grapheme in the writing system. **Non-structural ligature** – a ligature which functions as a sequence of two graphemes in the writing system. **Quasi-ligature** – a sequence of two symbols which functions as a single grapheme in the writing system; i.e., as though it were a structural ligature.

Linear A. An undeciphered script of ancient Crete.

Linear B. A mixed morphographic and moraic script of Mycenæan Greek.

linear organization. The way in which symbols in a writing system follow each other; e.g., in the Roman alphabet, writing goes in horizontal lines from left to right with the next line vertically below the last. **Non-linear elements** – elements of a writing system which occur outside its overall linear organization: e.g., accents in the Roman alphabet generally go above the letter they are associated with.

lingua franca /ˌlɪŋgwəˈfɹæŋkə/. A language adopted as a common language by speakers of different native languages.

linguistic. Relating to language.

linguistics. The scientific study of language.

literacy. The ability to read and write.

long count. In Maya writing, a count giving a precise date with reference to an arbitrary point in time.

main symbol. The more prominent symbol to which diacritics are added; a main symbol is often free and can stand alone.

Mandarin /ˈmændəɹɪn/. 1. The dialect of Chinese historically used by civil servants. 2. Northern and western dialects of Chinese. 3. Equivalent to Modern Standard Chinese.

Masoretic text /ˌmæsəˈɹɛtɪk/. The standard text of the Hebrew scriptures, edited by the **Masoretes** /ˈmæsəˌɹits/ in the seventh century NEW at Tiberias (in modern-day Israel).

mater lectionis /ˌmɑtɛɹ ˌlɛktiˈownɪs/ (Lat. literally 'mother of reading'; pl. ***matres lectionis*** /ˈmɑtɹejs/). In Semitic abjad writing, the use of a consonant symbol to represent a vowel.

Maya /'majə/. One of the sure cases of invention of writing; a people of Meso-America. *Maya* is used as the general adjective form; *Mayan* is used in referring to language.

Mesopotamia /ˌmɛsowpə'tejmijə/. The land between the Tigris and Euphrates rivers; modern-day Iraq.

Middle English. English between 1100 and 1500 NEW.

Modern English. English after 1500 NEW.

Modern Standard Chinese. The standard written dialect of Chinese today, very similar to the spoken Chinese of Beijing; also known as *pǔtōnghuà*.

monoconsonantal grapheme. A grapheme representing a single consonant; common in alphabets, abjads, and abugidas, but in Egyptian distinct from bi- and triconsonantal graphemes.

mora /'mɔɹə/ (pl. **moræ** /'mɔɹi/). A phonological unit larger than a segment and smaller than a syllable, typically of the shape CV.

moraic system /ˌmɔ'ɹejɪk/. A writing system in which the graphemes typically represent moræ.

morpheme /'mɔɹˌfim/. A contrastive meaningful unit in a language; a class of allographs. In English, *book* and *table* are different morphemes; *blueness* consists of two morphemes – *blue* and *-ness*.

morphogram /'mɔɹfəˌgɹæmɪ/. A single grapheme of a morphographic writing system. A grapheme which represents a morpheme of the language.

morphographic writing system /ˌmɔɹfə'gɹæfɪk/. A writing system in which the graphemes typically represent morphemes.

morphophonemic /ˌmɔɹfəfə'nimɪk/. Having to do with linguistic units between the phonological and morphological levels of language.

mxedruli. The name of the Georgian alphabet.

Mycenæan /ˌmajsə'niən/. An early Greek culture centered in Mycenæ /ˌmaj'sini/.

Nabatæan /ˌnæbə'tiən/. A version of the Aramaic abjad which developed in the Sinai and northern Arabia; the Nabatæan abjad developed into the Arabic abjad.

nucleus. The vowel of a syllable.

numeric value. The use of a letter to represent a number.

obverse. The front side of an inscription. See **reverse**.

Old English. English before 1100 NEW.

Old Persian. The language of the Persian cuneiform inscriptions, from the sixth to fourth centuries OLD.

on*-reading.** A reading of a character in Japanese using a borrowed Chinese pronunciation. A **semantic *on uses the pronunciation of a borrowed Chinese word; a **phonetic *on*** extends the *on*-reading of a Chinese word to other Japanese words having the same pronunciation. See ***kun*-reading.**

onset. In a syllable, any consonants preceding the vowel.

oracle-bone writing. The earliest form of Chinese writing, found on bones and shells.

orthographic depth. The relationship of language and writing, considered from the point of abstractness of the linguistic units involved. See **deep** and **shallow**.

orthographic dialect variation. Two recognized ways of writing the same language or certain words of the same language. In English, there is a significant, although small, amount of dialect variation between spellings used in the United States and the rest of the English-speaking world.

overdifferentiated. Describing a relationship between writing and language in which some orthographic distinctions do not correspond to any phonological contrasts. See **underdifferentiated.**

palatalization. A phonetic process by which sounds come to be produced with the tongue closer to the hard palate: e.g., /t/ → /tʃ/.

papyrus /pə'pajɹəs/. 1. A paper-like writing surface made from the papyrus plant *Cyperus payrus*. 2. A text written on papyrus (pl. **papyri**).

Persian. An Indo-European language belonging to the Indo-Iranian family.

Phaistos disk /'fajˌstows/. A clay disk from Crete with undeciphered writing.

Phœnician /fə'niʃən/. Early writing and people of the northern Levant.

phoneme /'fowˌnim/. A contrastive unit of sound in a language; a class of allophones. In English, /t/ and /d/ are different phonemes.

phonemic /fə'nimɪk/. Having to do with the sound system of a language, especially with regard to contrastive units.

phonetic. 1. adj. Having to do with the sound system of a language, especially without regard to contrast; allophonic. 2. n. In Chinese, the phonetic component of a semantic-phonetic compound, especially used in traditional systems of ordering characters in a dictionary; see **radical.**

phonetic extension. A method of creating a symbol by extending the use of a symbol to other instances of the same sound; e.g., if, in a certain language, the symbol # represents the word /kɑ/ in a certain morpheme, phonetic extension would lead to its use to represent the phonological sequence /kɑ/ in any situation.

phonetic writing system. A writing system intended to be useful in transcribing the sounds of any language, e.g., the International Phonetic Alphabet.

phonogram. A single grapheme of a phonographic writing system, representing a phonological element of the language: i.e., a syllable, mora, or phoneme.

phonographic writing. Writing whose graphemes relate to phonological units (phonemes, moræ, syllables) of a language.

phonological complement. A grapheme which repeats phonological information already given by another grapheme, as in Egyptian and Maya.

phonological extension. A method of creating a symbol: the use of a symbol is extended to other words having the same sound; e.g., in English, the extension of the use of a pictogram of a *bee* to refer to the morpheme *be*.

pictogram. A grapheme created by pictography; a morphogram which graphically portrays the object it represents; e.g., a picture of a flower to represent the morpheme *flower*.

pictography. A method of creating a symbol: a (stylized) picture is used as a morphogram for the object pictured.

picture writing. Pictures which tell a story, but which are not related to specific linguistic utterances; not considered real writing although having some elements of graphic communication.

pīnyīn /ˌpin'yin/. The current standard romanization for Mandarin Chinese.

pointing. The use of diacritics to indicate vowels in a Hebrew text; sometimes also used for Arabic texts. Such a text is called a **pointed text.**

polygraph /'pɑlɪˌɡɹæf/. A sequence of graphemes which represents a linguistic unit normally represented by one grapheme: e.g., the grapheme sequence <sch> is used in German to represent the phoneme /ʃ/, although a phoneme is usually written with one grapheme.

polyphone /'pɑlɪˌfown/. A single grapheme which represents two or more phonological units of a language: e.g., <x> in English for /ks/.

Prakrit /'pɹɑkɹɪt/. A later form of Sanskrit.

PRC. People's Republic of China.

Proto-Canaanite /'pɹowtow-'kejnəˌnajt/. Early writing of the southern Levant, developed from Egyptian and leading to the Semitic abjad.

Punic /'pjunɪk/. Referring to the African colonies of the Phœnicians, particularly Carthage.

pǔtōnghuà /putoŋ'hwɑ/. Modern Standard Chinese.

quốcngữ. The adaptation of the Roman alphabet for writing Vietnamese.

Qur'ān. The sacred text of Islam. (The most common English pronunciations are /kə'ɹæn/ or /ˌkɔ'ɹæn/, but /kə'ɹɑn/ is occasionally heard. A common alternative spelling is *Koran*.)

radical. In Chinese, the semantic component of a semantic-phonetic compound, especially used in referring to traditional systems of ordering characters in a dictionary. See **phonetic.**

reading pronunciation. See **spelling pronunciation.**

rebus writing. See **phonetic extension.**

relationship of language and writing. This relationship describes the level of linguistic unit (e.g., morpheme, phoneme) represented in the writing system of that language.

reverse. The back side of an inscription. See **obverse.**

rhyme. In a syllable, the nucleus and rhyme taken together.

Roman. 1. Pertaining to Rome. 2. (lower-case) In typography, the ordinary form of letterforms, not italic or bold.

Roman alphabet. The alphabet borrowed from Etruscan and Greek to write Latin. The Roman alphabet was borrowed for writing languages in western Europe and then to many languages throughout the world.

Sanskrit /'sænskɹɪt/. The earliest attested form of Indo-Aryan.

schwa /ʃwɑ/ (in Hebrew often /ʃə'wɑ/). 1. A diacritic in Hebrew to indicate the vowel /ə/ or to show the absence of a vowel. 2. In linguistics, a phonetic symbol [ə] for a mid central vowel.

script. A general term for a writing system without regard for its structural nature.

seal. An engraved object used to make an impression on clay, wax, or paper.

segment. A consonant or a vowel, but not the tone.

semantic complement. A grapheme which gives additional semantic information, as in Egyptian.

semantic extension. A method of creating a symbol: the use of a symbol is extended to other morphemes having the same or similar meaning; e.g., a pictogram of a leg used to refer to the morpheme *leg*; semantic extension might further extend the use of this pictogram to represent semantically related morphemes such as *walk*, *run*, *go*.

semantic-phonetic compound. A grapheme consisting of two parts, one semantic and one phonetic; for example, in Chinese, the grapheme for /mā/ 'mother' consists of two parts, one meaning 'woman' and the other representing the sound /ma/.

semantic-semantic compound. A grapheme consisting of two parts, both semantic; for example, in Chinese, the character for 'home' is said to consist of a pig under a roof.

semantic writing system. A writing system intended to be useful in transcribing any utterance in any language in terms of its meaning, e.g., the Bliss system.

semasiographic writing. An alternative name for a semantic writing system.

Semitic /sə'mɪtɪk/. A branch of the Afro-Asiatic language family; an important language family for writing including Arabic, Hebrew, Aramaic, Akkadian, and Ethiopian.

shallow. A shallow writing system is related to phonemic units in language, as opposed to morphophonemic units. A shallower writing system will have more cases of different allomorphs written differently. See **deep** and **orthographic depth.**

simplified character. In Chinese, a simplified form of certain **traditional characters** introduced in the PRC in the mid-twentieth century.

spelling pronunciation. A pronunciation which agrees with typical spelling conventions, but which goes against the traditional pronunciation. For example, the pronunciation of *boatswain* as /'bowtˌswejn/, instead of the traditional /'bowsən/. Also **reading** pronunciation.

spelling reform. A proposal for revising the spelling system of a language, often with a view to making the system easier to learn.

Standard Arabic. The variety of Arabic used in writing and in formal speech.

stele (Greek /'stili/, pl. **stele** /'stili/). An upright slab of stone or other hard substance used for writing or art (e.g., a tombstone). Sometimes the Latin form *stella* is used (/'stɛlə/, pl. *stellæ* /stɛli/).

stimulus diffusion. The borrowing of an idea without necessarily borrowing all the details.

stroke order. The order in which the strokes of a symbol are written, especially in Chinese. In European contexts, the equivalent term is *ductus*.
stylus /ˈstajləs/. A pointed tool used for writing, as on clay or wax.
subscript. Written below the normal level of writing, as the <2> in <H_2O> or the diacritic in <ḫ>.
Sumerian /ˌsuˈmɛɹijən/. Ancient language of Mesopotamia; the first language to be written.
superscript. Written above the normal level of writing, as the <2> in <x^2> or the diacritic in <é>.
syllabic. Refers to a writing system in which the graphemes typically represent syllables.
syllable. A phonological unit generally uttered without a break; typically syllables have a vowel and may have consonants before or after the vowel.
symbol. A general term for a graphic mark without regard to its graphemic status.
tablet. A piece of clay or wax used for writing.
tanwīn /ˌtɑnˈwin/. In Arabic, three special symbols to indicate the indefinite article:

/man/ تً, /min/ تٍ, /mun/ تٌ.

Tiberian /ˌtajˈbiɹijən/. The dialect of Hebrew used in the Bible, from the Israeli town Tiberias. See **Masoretic.**
token. In the Middle East, small clay objects used for record-keeping.
tone. Contrastive pitch patterns in a language. In Chinese, each word has a specific tone which may distinguish it from other words with the same consonants and vowels.
traditional character. In Chinese, the traditional form of certain characters which was replaced by a **simplified character** in the PRC in the mid-twentieth century.
transcription. A representation of the pronunciation of a text.
transliteration. A representation of a text in which each grapheme is given in a romanized form.
triconsonantal grapheme. A grapheme representing three consonants, as in Egyptian.
tughra /ˈtuɣrɑ/. Ornate signature of senior official in the Ottoman empire.
type of phonography. A dimension in the taxonomy of writing systems distinguishing the ways in which phonological information is portrayed in a writing system.
tz'olkin /ˈtsolkɪn/. In the Maya calendar, a repeating cycle of 260 days.
Ugaritic /ˌjugəˈɹɪtɪk/. A cuneiform abjad used for the Semitic language Ugaritic; found at Ugarit /ˈjugəɹɪt/ (Ras Shamra /ˌɹɑʃ ˈʃɑmrɑ/).
umlaut /ˈumˌlawt/. A diacritic used with the Roman alphabet, consisting of two superscript dots <¨>.
underdifferentiated. Describing a relationship between writing and language in which some phonological contrasts are not indicated in the writing of that language. See **overdifferentiated.**
unit discrepancy. A difference in the number of units in a specific linguistic–graphemic relationship.
Uruk /ˈuˌruk/. An ancient Mesopotamian site of very early cuneiform writing.
vague year. In the Maya calendar, the ***haab***.
Ventris, Michael (1922–56) /ˈvɛntɹɪs/. The British architect who deciphered Linear B.
virāma /vɪˈɹɑmə/. In Indian scripts, a diacritic used to indicate the absence of a following vowel.
vowel pointing. See **pointing.**
vulgar Latin. The dialect of the common people in ancient Rome, as opposed to the formal dialect used by the upper classes, particularly in literature. The Romance languages are generally derived from vulgar Latin, not formal Latin.

Wade–Giles romanization. The most commonly used romanization for Chinese until replaced by *pīnyīn* in the mid-twentieth century.

Webster, Noah (1758–1843). An important American lexicographer, author of the *American Dictionary of the English Language.*

wényán /ˈwɛnˌjɑn/. Classical Chinese.

writing. The use of graphic marks to represent specific linguistic utterances.

writing brush. In Chinese writing, the normal writing tool.

writing group. In Arabic, a group of letters which are connected to each other. Most letters in a word are connected to each other, but certain Arabic letters cannot be connected to a following letter; thus, the next letter starts a new writing group. Every new word starts a new writing group.

writing system. A system for graphically representing the utterances of a language.

Yiddish /ˈjɪdɪʃ/. A Germanic language commonly spoken until recently by Jews in eastern Europe, written with the Hebrew abjad.

Bibliography

Abbott, Nabia. 1939. *The Rise of the North Arabic Script and its Kur'anic Development.* Chicago: University of Chicago Press.

Ahn, Pyonh-Hi. 1997. 'The principles underlying the invention of the Korean alphabet', in Kim-Reynaud, 89–105.

Albright, W. F. 1966. *The Proto-Sinaitic Inscriptions and Their Decipherment.* Harvard Theological Studies, 22. Cambridge, MA: Harvard University Press.

Allen, James P. 2000. *Middle Egyptian: An Introduction to the Language and Culture of Hieroglyphs.* Cambridge: Cambridge University Press.

Antonsen, E. H. 1989. 'The runes: The earliest Germanic writing system', in Senner, 139–58.

Atkinson, B. F. C. 1933. *The Greek Language.* New York: Faber & Faber.

Bauer, Thomas. 1996. 'Arabic writing', in Daniels and Bright, 559–64.

Baxter, William H. 1992. A *Handbook of Old Chinese Phonology.* Berlin: Mouton de Gruyter.

Bellamy, James A. 1989. 'The Arabic alphabet', in Senner, 91–102.

Bender, M. L., Sidney W. Head and Roger Cowley. 1976. 'The Ethiopian writing system', in M. L. Bender, J. Bowen, R. L. Cooper and C. A. Ferguson, eds., *Languages in Ethiopia,* 120–9. London: Oxford University Press.

Bennett, Emmett L. 1996. 'Aegean scripts', in Daniels and Bright, 125–33.

Bermant, C. and M. Weitzman. 1979. *Ebla: An Archæological Enigma.* London: Weidenfeld & Nicolson.

Best, Jan and Fred Woudhuizen, eds. 1988. *Ancient Scripts from Crete and Cyprus.* Leiden: E. J. Brill.

Best, Jan and Fred Woudhuizen, eds. 1989. *Lost Languages from the Mediterranean.* Leiden: E. J. Brill.

Bliss, Charles. 1965. *Semantography.* Sydney: Semantography Publications.

Bolozky, Shmuel. 1997. 'Israeli Hebrew phonology', in Kaye, 287–311.

Boltz, William. 1994. *The Origin and Early Development of the Chinese Writing System.* New Haven, CT: American Oriental Society.

Boltz, William. 1996. 'Early Chinese writing', in Daniels and Bright, 191–9.

Bonfante, Giuliano and Larissa Bonfante. 1983. *The Etruscan Language: An Introduction.* Manchester: Manchester University Press (new edn. 2002).

Bonfante, Larissa. 1990. *Etruscan.* London and Berkeley: British Museum and University of California Press.

Bonfante, Larissa. 1996. 'The scripts of Italy', in Daniels and Bright, 297–311.

Bottéro, Jean. 1992. *Mesopotamia: Writing, Reasoning, and the Gods.* Chicago: University of Chicago Press.

Bright, William. 1990a. 'How not to decipher the Indus Valley inscriptions', in Bright 1990c, 118–23.

Bright, William. 1990b. 'Written and spoken language in South Asia', in Bright 1990c, 130–46.
Bright, William. 1990c. *Language Variation in South Asia*. Oxford: Oxford University Press.
Bright, William. 1996. 'The Devanagari Script', in Daniels and Bright, 384–90.
Bright, William. 1999. 'A matter of typology: Alphasyllabaries and abugidas'. *Written Language and Literacy* 2.45–56.
Brustad, Kristen, Mahmoud Al-Batal and Abbas Al-Tousi. 1995. *Alif Baa: Introduction to Arabic Letters and Sounds*. Washington: Georgetown University Press.
Burnaby, Barbara, ed. 1985. *Promoting Native Writing Systems in Canada*. Toronto: OISE Press.
Carney, Edward. 1994. A *Survey of English Spelling*. New York: Routledge.
Chadwick, John. 1967. *The Decipherment of Linear B*. 2nd edn. Cambridge: Cambridge University Press.
Chadwick, John. 1987. *Linear B and Related Scripts*. Berkeley and London: University of California Press and British Museum.
Chadwick, John, et al. 1986–98. *Corpus of Mycenæan Inscriptions from Knossos*. Cambridge: Cambridge University Press.
Chao Lin. 1968. *A Survey of Chinese (Han) Characters*. Hong Kong: Universal Book Co.
Chen Ping. 1999. *Modern Chinese: History and Sociolinguistics*. Cambridge: Cambridge University Press.
Chiera, Edward. 1966. *They Wrote in Clay*. Chicago: University of Chicago Press.
Coe, Michael D. 1992. *Breaking the Maya Code*. London: Thames & Hudson.
Coe, Michael D. 1999. *The Maya*. London: Thames & Hudson.
Coe, Michael D. and Mark Van Stone. 2001. *Reading the Maya Glyphs*. London: Thames & Hudson.
Collon, Dominique. 1990. *Near Eastern Seals*. Berkeley and London: University of California Press and British Museum.
Comrie, Bernard, ed. 1987. *The World's Major Languages*. Oxford: Oxford University Press.
Comrie, Bernard. 1996a. 'Adaptations of the Cyrillic alphabet', in Daniels and Bright, 700–26.
Comrie, Bernard. 1996b. 'Languages of Eastern and Southern Europe', in Daniels and Bright, 663–89.
Cooper, Jerrold S. 1996. 'Mesopotamian cuneiform: Sumerian and Akkadian', in Daniels and Bright, 37–57.
Coulmas, Florian. 1989. *The Writing Systems of the World*. Oxford: Blackwell.
Coulmas, Florian. 1996. *The Blackwell Encyclopedia of Writing Systems*. Oxford: Blackwell.
Cross, Frank Moore. 1989. 'The invention and development of the alphabet', in Senner, 77–90.
Cruz-Urube, Eugene. 2001. 'Scripts: An overview', in Donald B. Redford, ed., *The Oxford Encyclopedia of Ancient Egypt*, vol. 3, 192–8. New York: Oxford University Press.
Cubberley, Paul. 1993. 'Alphabets and transliteration', in Bernard Comrie and Greville G. Corbett, eds., *The Slavonic Languages*, 20–59. London: Routledge.
Cubberley, Paul. 1996. 'The Slavic alphabets', in Daniels and Bright, 346–55.
Cunningham, Alexander. 1877 (reprint 1961). *Inscriptions of Asoka*. Varanasi: Indological Book House.
Curtis, A. 1985. *Ugarit (Ras Shamra)*. Cambridge: Cambridge University Press.
Dani, Ahmad Hasan. 1963. *Indian Palaeography*. Oxford: Oxford University Press.
Daniels, Peter T. 1990. 'Fundamentals of grammatology'. *Journal of the American Oriental Society* 110.727–31.
Daniels, Peter T. 1991. 'Is a structural graphemics possible?' *LACUS Forum* 18.528–37.

Daniels, Peter T. 1994. 'Reply to Herrick'. *LACUS Forum* 21.425–31.
Daniels, Peter T. 1996a. 'The study of writing systems', in Daniels and Bright, 3–17.
Daniels, Peter T. 1996b. 'Aramaic scripts for Aramaic languages', in Daniels and Bright, 499–514.
Daniels, Peter T. 1999. 'Some Semitic phonological considerations on the sibilants of the Greek alphabet'. *Written Language and Literacy* 2.57–61.
Daniels, Peter T. and William Bright. 1996. *The World's Writing Systems.* Oxford: Oxford University Press.
Davies, W. V. 1990. 'Egyptian hieroglyphics', in J. T. Hooker, ed., *Reading the Past: Ancient Writing from Cuneiform to the Alphabet.* London: British Museum.
DeFrancis, John. 1984. *The Chinese Language: Fact and Fantasy.* Honolulu: University of Hawai'i Press.
DeFrancis, John. 1989. *Visible Speech: The Diverse Oneness of Writing Systems.* Honolulu: University of Hawai'i Press.
DeFrancis, John and J. Marshall Unger. 1994. 'Rejoinder to Geoffrey Sampson: "Chinese script and the diversity of writing systems"'. *Linguistics* 32.549–54.
Deighton, Lee C. 1972. *A Comparative Study of Spellings in Four Major Collegiate Dictionaries.* Pleasantville, NY: Hardscrabble.
Diringer, David. 1962. *Writing.* London: Thames & Hudson.
Driver, Sir Godfrey. 1976. *Semitic Writing: From Pictograph to Alphabet.* Oxford: Oxford University Press.
Drogin, Marc. 1980. *Medieval Calligraphy: Its History and Technique.* New York: Dover.
Earnshaw, C. J. 1988. *Sho: Japanese Calligraphy, An In-depth Introduction to the Art of Writing Characters.* Rutland, VT: Charles E. Tuttle.
Ebbinghaus, Ernst. 1996. 'The Gothic alphabet', in Daniels and Bright, 290–3.
Edgerton, William F. 1940. 'Egyptian phonetic writing'. *Journal of the Oriental Society* 60.473–506.
Elliott, Ralph W. V. 1996. 'The runic script', in Daniels and Bright, 333–9.
Emmison, F. G. 1967. *How to Read Local Archives 1550–1700.* London: The Historical Association.
Faber, Alice. 1981. 'Phonetic reconstruction'. *Glossa* 15.233–62.
Faber, Alice. 1997. 'Genetic subgrouping of the Semitic languages', in Robert Hetzron, ed., *The Semitic Languages*, 3–15. London: Routledge.
Falk, Harry. 1993. *Schrift im alten Indien: Ein Forschungsbericht mit Anmerkungen.* Tübingen: Gunter Narr Verlag.
Fang-yü, W. 1958. *Introduction to Chinese Cursive Script.* New Haven, CT: Far Eastern Publications, Yale University.
Faulkner, Raymond O. 1988. *A Concise Dictionary of Middle Egyptian.* Oxford: Griffith Institute.
Feuerherm, Karljürgen G. 1998. *Introduction to Akkadian through Codex Hammurapi.* Photocopied notes. University of Toronto.
Fischer, Steven Roger. 2001. *A History of Writing.* London: Reaktion Books.
Fisher, J. H. 1977. 'Chancery and the emergence of standard written English in the fifteenth century'. *Speculum* 52.870–99.
Gamkrelidze, Thomas. 1984. *Alphabetic Writing and the Old Georgian Script.* New York: Caravan Books.
Gardiner, A. 1973. *Egyptian Grammar.* 3rd rev. edn. Oxford: Griffith Institute.
Gardiner, Alan H. 1916. 'The Egyptian origin of the Semitic alphabet'. *Journal of Egyptian Archæology* 3.1–16.
Gaur, Albertine. 1979. *Writing Materials of the East.* London: British Library.

Gaur, Albertine. 1984. *A History of Writing*. New York: Charles Scribner's Sons.
Gaur, Albertine. 1994. *A History of Calligraphy*. New York: Cross River.
Gelb, Ignace. 1963. *A Study of Writing*. Chicago: Chicago University Press.
Gibson, M. and R. D. Biggs, eds. 1977. *Seals and Sealing in the Ancient Near East*. Malibu: Undena.
Glaister, Geoffrey Ashall. 1996. *Encyclopedia of the Book*. Newcastle, DE and London: Oak Knoll Press and British Museum.
Goerwitz, Richard L. 1996. 'The Jewish scripts', in Daniels and Bright, 487–98.
Gragg, Gene B. 1996. 'Mesopotamian cuneiform: Other languages', in Daniels and Bright, 58–70.
Graham, A. J. 1982. 'The colonial expansion of Greece', in John Boardman and N. G. L. Hammond, eds., *The Cambridge Ancient History* (2nd edn., vol. III, Part 2), 83–162.
Grant, Bruce K. 1982. *A Guide to Korean Characters*. Elizabeth, NJ: Hollym.
Green, M. W. 1981. 'The construction and implementation of the cuneiform writing system'. *Visible Language* 15.345–72.
Green, M. W. 1989. 'Early cuneiform', in Senner, 43–58.
Greenspan, J. S. 1981. *Hebrew Calligraphy: A Step-by-Step Guide*. New York: Schocken.
Grimme, Hubert. 1935. 'A propos de quelques graffites du temple de Ramen'. *Revue Biblique* 64.90–5.
Gruendler, Beatrice. 1993. *The Development of the Arabic Scripts*. Atlanta, GA: Scholars Press.
Gurney, O. R. 1981. *The Hittites*. London: Penguin.
Haarmann, Harald. 1991. *Universalgeschichte der Schrift*. Frankfurt: Campus.
Haile, Gatatchew. 1996. 'Ethiopic writing', in Daniels and Bright, 569–76.
Haley, Allan. 1990. *ABC's of Type*. New York: Watson-Guptill.
Hannas, William C. 1997. *Asia's Orthographic Dilemma*. Honolulu: University of Hawai'i Press.
Harbaugh, Rick. 1998. *Chinese Characters and Culture: A Genealogy and Dictionary*. New Haven, CT: Yale Far Eastern Publications.
Harper, Kenn. 1983. 'Writing in Inuktitut'. *Inuktitut* (Part I) 53.1–35 and (Part II) 53.35–83.
Harris, John F. and Stephen K. Stearns. 1992. *Understanding Maya Inscriptions*. Philadelphia: University Museum of Archæology and Anthropology, University of Pennsylvania.
Harris, William V. 1989. *Ancient Literacy*. Cambridge, MA: Harvard University Press.
Hary, Benjamin. 1996. 'Adaptations of Hebrew script', in Daniels and Bright, 727–42.
Haugen, E. 1976. *The Scandinavian Languages: An Introduction to Their History*. London: Faber & Faber.
Hawkins, David. 1986. 'Writing in Anatolia: Imported and indigenous systems'. *World Archæology* 17.363–75.
Hayes, John H. 1990. *A Manual of Sumerian Grammar and Texts*. Malibu: Undena.
Healey, John F. 1990. *The Early Alphabet*. London: British Museum.
Helfman, Elizabeth S. 1981. *Blissymbolics: Speaking without Speech*. New York: Elsevier/Nelson.
Herrick, Earl M. 1994a. 'Of course a structural graphemics is possible'. *LACUS Forum* 21.413–24.
Herrick, Earl M. 1994b. 'Reply to Daniels' reply'. *LACUS Forum* 21.432–40.
Hetzron, Robert. 1987. 'Semitic languages', in Comrie, 654–63.
Hinz, W. 1972. *The Lost World of Elam*. London: Sidgwick & Jackson.
Hoch, James. 1996. *Middle Egyptian Grammar*. Society for the Study of Egyptian Antiquities, Pub. 19. Mississauga, ON: Benben Publications.
Holisky, Dee Ann. 1996. 'The Georgian alphabet', in Daniels and Bright, 364–9.

Hooker, J. T., ed. 1990. *Reading the Past: Ancient Writing from Cuneiform to the Alphabet*. London and Berkeley: British Museum and University of California Press.

Houston, S. D. 1989. *Maya Glyphs*. Berkeley and London: University of California Press and British Museum.

Hsu, James C. H. 1996. *The Written Word in Ancient China*, 2 vols. Toronto: Tan Hock Seng.

Huehnergard, John. 1997. *A Grammar of Akkadian*. Atlanta, GA: Scholars Press.

Hwa, Khoo Seow and Nancy L. Penrose. 1993. *Behind the Brushstrokes: Appreciating Chinese Calligraphy*. Hong Kong: Asia 2000.

Inouye, Kyoko. 1987. 'Japanese: A story of language and people', in Timothy Shopen, ed., *Languages and Their Speakers*, 241–300. Philadelphia: University of Pennsylvania Press.

International Phonetic Association. 1999. *Handbook of the International Phonetic Association: A Guide to the Use of the International Phonetic Association*. Cambridge: Cambridge University Press.

Jackson, Donald. 1987. *The Story of Writing*. New York: Holt, Rinehart and Winston.

Jasim, Sabah Abboud and Joan Oates. 1986. 'Early tokens and tablets in Mesopotamia: New information from Tell Abada and Tell Brak'. *World Archæology* 17.348–62.

Jeffrey, L. H. 1961. *The Local Scripts of Ancient Greece*. Oxford: Oxford University Press.

Jensen, Hans. 1970. *Sign, Symbol, and Script*. London: George Allen & Unwin.

Justeson, John S. and Terrence Kaufman. 1993. 'A decipherment of Epi-Olmec hieroglyphic writing'. *Science* 259.1703–11.

Justeson, John S. and Laurence D. Stephens. 1993. 'The evolution of syllabaries from alphabets: Transmission, language contrast, and script typology'. *Die Sprache* 35.2–46.

Kaye, Alan S. 1996. 'Adaptations of Arabic script', in Daniels and Bright, 743–62.

Kaye, Alan S., ed. 1997. *Phonologies of Asia and Africa*. Winona Lake, IN: Eisenbrauns.

Keightley, David N. 1989. 'The origins of writing in China: Scripts and cultural contexts', in Senner, 171–202.

Kent, R. G. 1953. *Old Persian: Grammar, Texts, Lexicon*. New Haven, CT: American Oriental Society.

Khan, Geoffrey. 1997. 'Tiberian Hebrew phonology', in Kaye, 85–102.

Killingley, Siew-Yue. 1998. *Learning to Read Pinyin Romanization and its Equivalent in Wade-Giles: A Practical Course for Students of Chinese*. Munich: Lingcom Europa.

Kim, Chin W. 1997. 'The structure of phonological units in Han'gŭl', in Kim-Reynaud, 145–60.

Kim, S. 1981. *Inversions: A Catalog of Calligraphic Cartwheels*. Peterborough, NH: Byte.

Kim-Reynaud, Young-Key, ed. 1997. *The Korean Alphabet: Its History and Structure*. Honolulu: University of Hawai'i Press.

King, Ross. 1996. 'Korean writing', in Daniels and Bright, 218–27.

Knorosov, Yuri V. 1952. 'Drevniaia pis'mennost' Tseltral'noi Ameriki'. *Sovietskaya Etnografiya* 3.100–18.

Kober, Alice E. 1945. 'Evidence of inflection in the "Chariot" tablets from Knossos'. *American Journal of Archæology* 49.143–51.

Kramer, S. N. 1963. *The Sumerians*. Chicago: University of Chicago Press.

Kratochvil, Paul. 1968. *The Chinese Language Today*. London: Hutchinson University Library.

Lambert, Hester M. 1953. *Introduction to the Devanagari Script*. London: Oxford University Press.

Larsen, M. T. 1989. 'What they wrote on clay', in K. Schousboe and M. T. Larsen, eds., *Literacy and Society*, 121–48. Copenhagen: Academisk Forlag.

Lass, Roger. 1987. *The Shape of English: Structure and History*. London: Dent.

Lauf, D. I. 1976. *Tibetan Sacred Art: The Heritage of the Tantra*. London.

Ledyard, Gari. 1997. 'The international linguistic background of the correct sounds for the instruction of the people', in Kim-Reynaud, 31–87.

Lehmann, Ruth P. M. 1989. 'Ogham: The ancient script of the Celts', in Senner, 159–70.

Li, David C. S. 2000. 'Phonetic borrowing: Key to the vitality of written Cantonese in Hong Kong'. *Written Language and Literacy* 2.199–233.

Li, Gertraude Roth. 2000. *Manchu: A Textbook for Reading Documents.* Honolulu: University of Hawai'i Press.

Lieberman, Stephen J. 1980. 'Of clay pebbles, hollow clay balls, and writing: A Sumerian view'. *American Journal of Archæology* 84.339–58.

Loprieno, Anthony. 1995. *Ancient Egyptian: A Linguistic Introduction.* Cambridge: Cambridge University Press.

Lounsbury, Floyd. 1989. 'The ancient writing of Middle America', in Senner, 203–37.

MacMahon, Michael K. C. 1996. 'Phonetic notation', in Daniels and Bright, 821–46.

Macri, Martha J. 1996. 'Maya and other Mesoamerican scripts', in Daniels and Bright, 172–82.

Mair, Victor H. 1996. 'Modern Chinese writing', in Daniels and Bright, 200–8.

Mallery, Garrick. 1893. *Picture Writing of the American Indians.* Washington: Government Printing Office. Repr. 1972, New York: Dover.

Martin, Samuel E. 1997. 'Commentary', in Kim-Reynaud, 263–77.

Masica, Colin P. 1991. *The Indo-Aryan Languages.* Cambridge: Cambridge University Press.

Mathews, Peter. 1996. *Notebook for the Inaugural Maya Hieroglyph Workshop at Calgary.* Calgary: Department of Archæology, University of Calgary.

McCarthy, Suzanne. 1995. 'The Cree syllabary and the writing system riddle: A paradigm in crisis', in Taylor and Olson, 59–75.

McDonald, Eugene T. 1980. *Teaching and Using Blissymbolics.* Toronto: The Blissymbolics Communication Institute.

McManus, Damian. 1991. *A Guide to Ogam.* Maynooth: An Sagart.

McManus, Damian. 1996. 'Ogham', in Daniels and Bright, 340–5.

McManus, Damian and Eric P. Hamp. 1996. 'Celtic languages', in Daniels and Bright, 655–63.

McNaughton, Shirley. 1985. *Communicating with Blissymbolics.* Toronto: The Blissymbolics Communication Institute.

Michalowski, Piotr. 1996. 'Mesopotamian cuneiform: Origin', in Daniels and Bright, 33–6.

Miller, Roy Andrew. 1956. *The Tibetan System of Writing.* Washington: American Council of Learned Societies.

Miller, Roy Andrew. 1967. *The Japanese Language.* Chicago: University of Chicago Press.

Miller, Roy Andrew. 1986. *Nihongo.* London: Athlone.

Millward, C. M. 1988. *A Biography of the English Language.* Fort Worth, TX: Holt, Rinehart & Winston.

Mistry, P. J. 1996. 'Gujarati writing', in Daniels and Bright, 391–4.

Mitchell, T. F. 1954. *Writing Arabic: A Practical Introduction to the Ruq'ah Script.* Oxford: Oxford University Press.

Moltke, E. 1985. *Runes and Their Origin: Denmark and Elsewhere.* Copenhagen: National Museum of Denmark.

Montgomery, John. 2002. *How to Read Maya Hieroglyphs.* New York: Hippocrene.

Moore, Oliver. 2000. *Chinese.* London: British Museum Press.

Mountford, John. 1990. 'Language and writing-systems', in N. E. Collinge, ed., *An Encyclopædia of Language*, 701–39. London: Routledge.

Müller-Yokota, Wolfram. 1989. 'Scrift und Schriftgeschichte', in Bruno Lewin, ed., *Sprache und Schrift Japans*, 185–221. Leiden: E. J. Brill.

Naveh, J. 1970. *The Development of the Aramaic Script*. Jerusalem: Israel Academy of Sciences and Humanities.

Naveh, J. 1982. *Early History of the Alphabet: An Introduction to West Semitic Epigraphy and Palæography*. Jerusalem and Leiden: Magnes and E. J. Brill.

Naveh, J. 1988. 'The origin of the Greek alphabet', in Derrick de Kerckhove and Charles J. Lumsden, eds., *The Alphabet and the Brain: The Lateralization of Writing*, 84–91. Berlin: Springer Verlag.

Nguyễn Độnh-Hoà. 1959. 'Chữ Nôm: The demotic system of writing in Vietnam'. *Journal of the American Oriental Society* 79.270–4.

Nguyễn Độnh-Hoà. 1996. 'Vietnamese', in Daniels and Bright, 691–5.

Nichols, John D. 1996. 'The Cree syllabary', in Daniels and Bright, 599–611.

Nissen, Hans J. 1986. 'The archaic texts from Uruk'. *World Archæology* 17.317–34.

Nissen, Hans J. 1988. *The Early History of the Ancient Near East 9000–2000 B.C.* Chicago: University of Chicago Press.

Nissen, Hans J., Peter Damerow, and Robert K. Englund. 1993. *Archaic Bookkeeping: Early Writing and Techniques of Economic Administration in the Ancient Near East*. Chicago: University of Chicago Press.

Norman, Jerry. 1988. *Chinese*. Cambridge: Cambridge University Press.

O'Connor, M. 1996a. 'The alphabet as technology', in Daniels and Bright, 787–94.

O'Connor, M. 1996b. 'Epigraphic Semitic scripts', in Daniels and Bright, 88–107.

O'Neill, P. G. 1973. *Essential Kanji*. New York: Weatherhill.

Ormond, L. 1981. *Writing: The Arts and Living*. London: Her Majesty's Stationery Office.

Page, R. I. 1973. *Introduction to the English Runes*. London: Methuen.

Page, R. I. 1987. *Runes*. London and Berkeley: British Museum and University of California Press.

Palmer, L. 1980. *The Greek Language*. Atlantic City, NJ: Humanities Press.

Paradis, Michel, Hiriko Hagiwara, and Nancy Hildebrandt. 1985. *Neurolinguistic Aspects of the Japanese Writing System*. New York: Academic Press.

Parkes, M. B. 1993. *Pause and Effect: An Introduction to the History of Punctuation in the West*. Berkeley: University of California Press.

Parkinson, Richard. 1999. *Cracking Codes: The Rosetta Stone*. Berkeley: University of California Press.

Parpola, Asko. 1994. *Deciphering the Indus Script*. Cambridge: Cambridge University Press.

Parpola, Asko. 1996. 'The Indus Script', in Daniels and Bright, 165–71.

Pettinato, G. 1981. *The Archives of Ebla: An Empire Inscribed in Clay*. Garden City, NY: Doubleday.

Picchioni, S. A. 1985. 'The direction of cuneiform writing: Theory and evidence'. *Studi Orientali e Linguistici* 2.11–26.

Poppe, Nicholas. 1968. *Mongolian Language Handbook*. Washington: Center for Applied Linguistics.

Poser, William. 1992. 'The structural typology of phonological writing'. Presentation to the Linguistic Society of America, Philadelphia, PA.

Possehl, Gregory L. 1996. *Indus Age: The Writing System*. Philadelphia: University of Pennsylvania Press.

Postgate, J. N. 1992. *Early Mesopotamia*. London: Routledge.

Powell, Barry B. 1991. *Homer and the Origin of the Greek Alphabet*. Cambridge: Cambridge University Press.

Powell, Marvin A. 1981. 'Three problems in the history of cuneiform writing: Origins, direction of script, literacy'. *Visible Language* 15.419–40.

Pratt, Terry K. 1993. 'The hobgoblin of Canadian English spelling', in Sandra Clarke, ed., *Focus on Canada*. Amsterdam: John Benjamins.

Proskouriakoff, Tatiana. 1960. 'Historical implications of a pattern of dates at Piedras Negras, Guatemala'. *American Antiquity* 25.454–75.

Pu Yi. 1964. *From Emperor to Citizen*. Trans. by W. J. F. Jenner. Beijing: Peking Foreign Language Press.

Quibell, J. E. 1898. 'Slate palette from Hiraconopolis'. *Zeitschrift für Ägyptische Sprache und Altherthumskunde* 36.81–4.

Quirke, Stephen and Carol Andrews. 1988. *The Rosetta Stone: Facsimile Drawing with Introduction and Translations*. New York: Harry N. Abrams.

Ramsey, S. Robert. 1987. *The Languages of China*. Princeton: Princeton University Press.

Ratliff, Martha. 1996. 'The Pahawh Hmong script', in Daniels and Bright, 619–24.

Reiner, Erica. 1973. 'How we read cuneiform texts'. *Journal of Cuneiform Studies* 25.3–58.

Ritner, Robert K. 1996. 'The Coptic alphabet', in Daniels and Bright, 287–90.

Roaf, M. 1990. *Cultural Atlas of Mesopotamia and the Ancient Near East*. Oxford: Oxford University Press.

Robertson, Merle Greene. 1991. *The Sculpture of Palenque*. Vol. IV. Princeton: Princeton University Press.

Rogers, Henry. 1972. 'The initial mutations in modern Scots Gaelic'. *Studia Celtica* 7.63–85.

Rogers, Henry. 1995. 'Optimal orthographies', in Taylor and Olson, 19–31.

Rogers, Henry. 2000. *The Sounds of Language: An Introduction to Phonetics*. Harlow: Pearson Education Ltd.

Roop, D. Haigh. 1972. *An Introduction to the Burmese Writing System*. New Haven, CT: Yale University Press.

Sack, Ronald H. 1981. 'The temple scribe in Chaldean Uruk'. *Visible Language* 15.409–18.

Salomon, Richard. 1996. 'Brahmi and Kharoshthi', in Daniels and Bright, 373–83.

Salomon, Richard. 1998. *Indian Epigraphy: A Guide to the Study of Inscriptions in Sanskrit, Prakrit, and the Other Indo-Aryan Languages*. Oxford: Oxford University Press.

Sampson, Geoffrey. 1985. *Writing Systems: A Linguistic Introduction*. Stanford: Stanford University Press.

Sampson, Geoffrey. 1994. 'Chinese script and the diversity of writing systems'. *Linguistics* 32.117–32.

Sanfaçon, Roland. 1997. *Chinese–English–French Dictionary*. Sainte-Foy, Québec: Les Presses de l'Université Laval.

Sanjian, Avedis K. 1996. 'The Armenian alphabet', in Daniels and Bright, 356–63.

Sass, Benjamin. 1992. *Studia Alphabetica: On the Origin and Early History of the Northwest Semitic, South Semitic, and Greek Alphabets*. Göttingen: Universitätsverlag Schweiz.

Scancarelli, Janine. 1992. 'Aspiration and Cherokee orthographies', in Pamela Downing, Susan D. Lima, and Michael Noonan, eds., *Linguistics of Literacy*, 135–52. Amsterdam: John Benjamins.

Scancarelli, Janine. 1996. 'Cherokee writing', in Daniels and Bright, 587–92.

Schele, Linda and David Freidel. 1990. *A Forest of Kings*. New York: William Morrow.

Schele, Linda and Peter Mathews. 1998. *The Code of Kings: The Language of Seven Sacred Maya Temples and Tombs*. New York: Scribner.

Schele, Linda and Mary Ellen Miller. 1986. *The Blood of Kings*. New York: George Braziler.

Schendge, Malati J. 1983. 'The use of seals and the invention of writing'. *Journal of the Economic and Social History of the Orient* 26.113–36.

Schenker, Alexander. 1995. *The Dawn of Slavic: An Introduction to Slavic Philology*. New Haven, CT: Yale University Press.

Schmandt-Besserat, Denise. 1989. 'Two precursors of writing: Plain and complex tokens', in Senner, 27–42.

Schmandt-Besserat, Denise. 1992. *Before Writing*. 2 vols. Austin: Texas University Press.

Scragg, D. G. 1974. *A History of English Spelling*. Manchester: Manchester University Press.

Seeley, Christopher. 1991. *A History of Writing in Japan*. Leiden: E. J. Brill.

Segert, Stanislav. 1984. *A Basic Grammar of the Ugaritic Language*. Berkeley: University of California Press.

Senner, Wayne M., ed. 1989. *The Origins of Writing*. Lincoln, NE: University of Nebraska.

Senner, Wayne M. 1996. 'Germanic languages', in Daniels and Bright, 642–51.

Sharer, Robert J. 1994. *The Ancient Maya*. Stanford: Stanford University Press.

Shi, Dingxu. 1996. 'The Yi script', in Daniels and Bright, 239–43.

Shibatani, Masayoshi. 1987. 'Japanese', in Comrie, 855–80.

Shibatani, Masayoshi. 1990. *The Languages of Japan*. Cambridge: Cambridge University Press.

Simon, W. 1959. *How to Study and Write Chinese Characters*. London: Percy Lund Humphries.

Sircar, Dinesh Chandra. 1971. 'Introduction to Indian epigraphy and palaeography'. *Journal of Ancient Indian History* 4.72–136.

Skjærvø, P. Oktor. 1996. 'Aramaic scripts for Iranian languages', in Daniels and Bright, 515–35.

Smalley, William A., Chia Koua Vang, and Gnia Yee Yang. 1990. *Mother of Writing: The Origin and Development of a Hmong Messianic Script*. Chicago: University of Chicago Press.

Smith, Janet S. (Shibamoto). 1996. 'Japanese writing', in Daniels and Bright, 209–17.

Smith, Janet S. and David L. Schmidt. 1996. 'Variability in written Japanese: Towards a sociolinguistics of script choice'. *Visible Language* 30:46–71.

Smith, Vincent A. 1909. *Asoka: The Buddhist Emperor of India*. Oxford: Oxford University Press.

Sohm, Ho-Min. 1997. 'Orthographic divergence in South and North Korea: Toward a unified spelling system', in Kim-Reynaud, 193–218.

Soothill, William Edward. 1889. *Student's 4000 Chinese Characters and Pocket Dictionary*. London: Kegan Paul.

Soudavar, A. 1992. *Art of the Persian Courts*. New York: Rizzoli.

Sproat, Richard. 2000. *A Computational Theory of Writing Systems*. Cambridge: Cambridge University Press.

Stevens, John. 1995. *Sacred Calligraphy of the East*. Boston: Sambhala.

Stevens, John. 1996. 'Asian calligraphy', in Daniels and Bright, 244–51.

Stimson, Hugh. 1975. *Introduction to Chinese Pronunciation and the Pīnyīn Romanization*. New Haven, CT: Yale University, Far Eastern Publications.

Stroud, Ronald S. 1989. 'The art of writing in ancient Greece', in Senner, 103–19.

Sussmann, Ayala and Ruth Peled. 1993. *Scrolls from the Dead Sea*. Washington: Library of Congress.

Swiggers, Pierre. 1996. 'Transmission of the Phœnician script to the West', in Daniels and Bright, 261–70.

Taylor, Insup and David R. Olson, eds. 1995. *Scripts and Literacy: Reading and Learning to Read Alphabets, Syllabaries and Characters*. Dordrecht: Kluwer.

Taylor, Insup and M. Martin Taylor. 1995. *Writing and Literacy in Chinese, Korean and Japanese*. Amsterdam: John Benjamins.

Testen, David D. 1996. 'Old Persian cuneiform', in Daniels and Bright, 134–7.

Thompson, Edward Maunde. 1893. *Handbook of Greek and Latin Palæography*. London: Kegan Paul.

Thompson, J. Eric S. 1950. *Maya Hieroglyphic Writing: An Introduction.* Washington: Carnegie Institution.
Threate, Leslie. 1996. 'The Greek alphabet', in Daniels and Bright, 271–80.
Tiu^{n} Hak-khiam. 1998. 'Writing in two scripts: A case study of digraphia in Taiwanese'. *Written Language and Literacy* 1.225–48.
Tozzer, Alfred M. 1941. 'Landa's Relación de las Cosas de Yucatán'. *Papers of the Peabody Museum of Archæology and Ethnology*, 18. Cambridge, MA: Harvard University Press.
Tuttle, Edward. 1996. 'Romance languages', in Daniels and Bright, 633–42.
Ullman, B. L. 1980. *Ancient Writing and Its Influence.* Toronto: University of Toronto Press and Medieval Academy of America.
Unger, J. Marshall. 1996. *Literacy and Script Reform in Occupation Japan.* Oxford: Oxford University Press.
Vail, Gabrielle and Martha J. Macri. 2000. 'Introduction to special issue: Language and dialect in the Maya hieroglyphic script'. *Written Language and Literacy* 3.1–11.
Vallat, François. 1986. 'The most ancient scripts of Iran: The current situation'. *World Archæology* 17.335–47.
Vallins, G. H. 1954. *Spelling.* London: André Deutsch.
van der Kuijp, Leonard W. J. 1996. 'The Tibetan script and derivatives', in Daniels and Bright, 431–41.
Vanstiphout, H. 1979. 'How did they learn cuneiform?' *Cuneiform Studies* 31.118–26.
Venezky, Richard L. 1970. *The Structure of English Orthography.* The Hague: Mouton.
Venezky, Richard L. 1999. *The American Way of Spelling: The Structure and Origins of American English Orthography.* New York: Guilford.
Versteegh, Kees. 1997. *The Arabic Language.* Edinburgh: Edinburgh University Press.
Voegelin, C. F. and F. M. Voegelin. 1964. *Languages of the World.* Anthropological Linguistics. Sino-Tibetan Fascicle 1, vol. 6, no. 3, p. 28. Bloomington, IN: Archives of Languages of the World.
Wakelin, Martyn. 1988. *The Archæology of English.* London: Batsford.
Walker, C. B. F. 1987. *Cuneiform.* Berkeley and London: University of California Press and British Museum.
Walker, Willard B. 1981. 'Native American writing systems', in Charles A. Ferguson and Shirley Brice Heath, eds., *Language in the USA*, 145–74. Cambridge: Cambridge University Press.
Walker, Willard B. 1996. 'Native writing systems', in Ives Goddard, ed., *Handbook of North American Indians*, vol. 17: *Languages*, 158–84. Washington: Smithsonian Institution.
Wallace, Rex. 1989. 'The origins and development of the Latin alphabet', in Senner, 121–35.
Weninger, Stefan. 1993. *Ge'ez.* Munich: Lincom Europa.
Wheatley, Julian K. 1996. 'Burmese writing', in Daniels and Bright, 450–6.
Wilson, Hilary. 1993. *Understanding Hieroglyphs.* London: Michael O'Mara Books.
Wood, Claudia, Jinny Storr, and Peter A. Reich, eds. 1992. *Blissymbol Reference Guide.* Toronto: Blissymbolics Communication International.
Woodard, Roger D. 1997. *Greek Writing from Knossos to Homer: A Linguistic Interpretation of the Origin of the Greek Alphabet and the Continuity of Ancient Greek Literacy.* New York: Oxford University Press.
Woodhead, A. G. 1981. *The Study of Greek Inscriptions.* Cambridge: Cambridge University Press.
Woudhuizen, Fred. 1993. *The Language of the Sea Peoples.* Amsterdam: Najade.
Xuéxí Hànyǐng Cídiǎn. 1998. *Learner's Chinese–English Dictionary.* Shanghai: Nanyang Siang Pau.
Yǐn Bīnyōng and John S. Rohsenow. 1994. *Modern Chinese Characters.* Beijing: Sinolingua.

Index

Note: Page numbers in *italics* refer to illustrations.

CPSIA information can be obtained
at www.ICGtesting.com
Printed in the USA
BVOW04s1725301217
504047BV00006B/14/P